CARTER GLASS:
A Biography

By RIXEY SMITH and NORMAN BEASLEY

Price $3.00

HERE, with a wealth of information drawn from Senator Glass himself and from his papers, is the story of one of the most brilliant, independent, and courageous leaders the South has ever produced. Few contemporary Americans have had a more remarkable career. Beginning as radical free-silverite, a follower in 1896 of Bryan and Senator Daniels, Carter Glass developed into a convinced Wilsonian Democrat, and has followed in that faith ever since. By far the largest part of the book deals with the administrations of Woodrow Wilson and Franklin D. Roosevelt; and these two sections offer a striking contrast, for Glass wholeheartedly admired and supported Wilson, while he has vehemently distrusted and opposed Roosevelt. Since he emerged from his silverite phase, Glass has built his public service upon a set of consistently maintained and vigorously urged principles. He is a liberal, not a radical, and his devotion to Jeffersonian individualism has tinctured and restrained his faith in social legislation; he is willing to go as far as Wilson went but not much further. He insists upon sound finance as a cornerstone of the state; takes a broad view of America's international obligations; detests group-pres-legislation for special interests; and abominates a leadership that yields to expediency. This book tells how effectively he helped Wilson build the Federal Reserve system and finance American and Allied effort during the World War. It rises to a new climax in its account of his unremitting antagonism to the monetary and economic measures of the New Deal, and particularly to the abandonment of gold, the heavy spending, and the N.R.A. While the volume is loosely and unsystematically put together, and written in hasty journalistic style, it is interesting throughout and contains new facts that illuminate many important events of the last twenty years. Good use is made of letters and diary-jottings by the Senator. Incidentally, the biography gives a pleasing portrait of a high-minded, generous-hearted Virginia gentleman who has never once yielded his sense of right. Some day Glass will have a much fuller biography; meanwhile, this fills a distinct need, and fills it well.

ALLAN NEVINS

CARTER GLASS

A Biography

Photo © Bachrach

CARTER GLASS TODAY

CARTER GLASS

A Biography

BY

RIXEY SMITH

and

NORMAN BEASLEY

WITH AN INTRODUCTION BY

SENATOR HARRY FLOOD BYRD

AND A PREFACE BY

DOUGLAS SOUTHALL FREEMAN

LONGMANS, GREEN AND CO.

NEW YORK · TORONTO

1939

CARTER GLASS

FIRST EDITION

PRINTED IN THE UNITED STATES OF AMERICA

AN APPRECIATIVE INTRODUCTION

By the Junior Senator from Virginia

Samuel Butler said a long time ago that "Every man's work is always a picture of himself."

This book is a story of Carter Glass at work for seventy years. It is a fascinating and inspiring story, alive with varied incident, touched with sentiment, tense with vital decisions and dramatic in the recital of political contests and spirited debates.

From the beginning Glass was a fighter, brave, fearless and capable. The little boy, who was called "Pluck" seventy years ago, still maintains his title, the day this is written, in a committee debate on the national currency.

Glass never chose the easier way. From the day when General Lee surrendered and Glass, a boy of seven, refused to give the road to the first Yankee cavalrymen he had ever seen, he began to realize that freedom is a challenge. He accepted the challenge and worked his way from compositor to reporter, from reporter to editor and from editor to owner and publisher of prosperous newspapers.

Busy as he was he found time to read Plato, Burke and Shakespeare and to absorb the political philosophy of Thomas Jefferson. All the while he was enlarging his vocabulary – writing down for study every word he did not understand – until he came to public life equipped with a versatile forensic style. He never talks unless he knows what he is talking about, but, when he does, he presents his case with a picturesqueness and persuasiveness that compel attention.

Someone has said that it takes a strong man to pass successfully from one era to another. Glass had the strength to survive the poverty and oppression of Reconstruction and to understand the problems of a new age, increasingly industrialized and mechanized. He has done this because he possesses in rare degree character, capacity, courage and indomitable energy.

From Clerk of the Common Council of Lynchburg he went to the Virginia Senate and in 1901 he found an opportunity for the sort of service he could best give his state in the convention that framed a new Constitution for Virginia. In that convention skilled lawyers admitted the strength of Glass, not himself a lawyer, in debate ; and his fellow-townsman, Senator John W. Daniel, said that without Glass a new Constitution might well have failed to emerge from the long months of contest and controversy.

New and vivid strokes were painted in the developing picture of Glass by his brilliant work in the Constitutional Convention and soon we find him in the United States House of Representatives. Appointed to the Banking and Currency Committee in 1904, the supreme opportunity soon came to him to be the chief architect of the Federal Reserve System. He became the great post-war Secretary of the Treasury and won Woodrow Wilson's intimacy, trust and praise. He came to the Senate and is the outstanding Senator Virginia has ever contributed to the nation's chief deliberative council.

The picture of Carter Glass is here, in this book, almost complete. Let us survey it with pride. Here is a character composed of truth, sincerity and courage. He hates deceit and detests a lie. He is the soul of honor, but he possesses a rarer integrity which we call intellectual integrity. He has convictions, does this Jeffersonian Democrat, and he will not compromise those convictions for political preferment or for any other reason. He is a strong and straight thinker, a brave and decisive actor, who knows how to make clear the reasons for his decisions and the justification for his actions. His colleagues in the Senate know this and hence, Glass compels the respect and the affectionate admiration of all of them.

I feel for Senator Glass a great admiration that is not exceeded even by my warm affection for him. I am very glad, therefore, that his remarkable work should here be recounted by understanding and sympathetic pens for the observation of that work reveals the picture of a great man.

"Every man's work is always a picture of himself."

Harry Flood Byrd

March 3, 1939

IN THE VIRGINIA TRADITION

To see Carter Glass in the company of his colleagues is to observe one of the chief ills of representative government and the prime remedy for that ill. More than affection for the man and respect for his years is exhibited in the attitude of his fellow-senators. The strong members recognize in him the inflexibility of character. Weaklings regard him wistfully as the possessor of the quality they need to hold their self-respect and to vitalize the public service. Many a Congressman, after seeing the Virginian in committee or on the floor has said to himself, "I wish I had the courage of Carter Glass."

He always has had that courage and the intellectual honesty which makes courage more than physical daring or mental bravado. There never was anything pliant about him. His knees were not hinged to authority. When he entered public life, there was not in Virginia a more persistent champion of unpopular causes or a more determined rebel against the mis-styled democracy that makes unfathered decisions in the smoke of a hotel room at midnight. Forty years' observation of his career does not offer a single instance where he advanced himself otherwise than by his intelligence, his study, his character and his courage.

If this was his own inheritance, it was no less the tradition of his State. Virginia has sent feeble men to Congress, of course, but she rarely has kept them there. In the few cases where timeservers have held their seats by political cunning, they have had the contempt of those whose good opinion is most to be desired. Those Virginians who have remained longest in public life have not been the cleverest politicians but the most courageous leaders.

To define this leadership and the public respect for it, one must go back to the Virginia House of Burgesses, which antedates the Congress of the United States by 170 years. With rare consistency, the voters of colonial Virginia named their natural leaders as their Burgesses. Politics was the avocation of gentlemen in Virginia ; office was not their reward but their responsibility. One may follow for generations the same family names on the roster of the House of Burgesses, not because the men who bore those names were the richest of the patricians but because they were the men who had the intelligence to form considered opinion and the courage to voice it without thought of personal gain or loss.

The abolition of entails in Virginia, with the consequent division of the baronial estates after the American revolution, was followed by the great migration. Many families did not survive the economic strain of the "critical period of American history." New names appeared on the roll of the General Assembly, but the old tradition remained. When the hour for weighty decisions came, the natural leaders did not fail the State nor the State the leaders. Patrick Henry declined to be Secretary of State under Washington or to accept the office of Chief Justice of the Supreme Court, but at a time when he was too feeble to stand long on his feet, he returned to the House of Delegates of Virginia to oppose what he considered a destructive trend. That was typical.

As the new Federal government grew in prestige, it naturally attracted many of the men who previously had served the Old Dominion. They were chosen in party elections and they were disputed often on the hustings, but they were conceded the right of individual decision without which there can be no representation of the nation's best. The exercise of that right was contested and was established even in the sensitive matter of States rights. Because the Jeffersonian legislators regarded Virginia as a sovereign State, they reasoned that they could instruct the United States Senators, Virginia's ambassadors to the council of the nation precisely as the General Assembly in the era of the Federation had instructed the delegates to Congress. In 1811, during the wrathful debate over the recharter of the Bank of the United States, the Senators from Virginia were instructed to vote against recharter. One of them was of that mind. The other, William B. Giles, spoke in opposition but voted under protest in accordance with his instructions. A little more than twenty years later, in successive tests, William C. Rives and John Tyler resigned their seats rather than follow instructions that ran counter to their convictions. Benjamin Watkins Leight neither heeded instructions nor resigned. He had defended prior to that time the right of a State to instruct Senators, but he had excepted those instances in which a Senator felt that adherence to instructions was a violation of the Constitution or an act of moral turpitude. He considered that the vote he was called upon to cast fell within these reservations and he put his judgment against that of the General Assembly. He paid for his conviction with his office, but he fixed the tradition that a Senator should be free, in the exercise of his best judgment, to vote as he saw fit and not as other politicians desired.

The tradition thus established a century ago has been maintained. Carter Glass has exemplified it and has honored it. He has scorned to hold office by dispensing patronage, by avoiding issues, or by accepting the counsel of self-seekers. It may be permitted one who has stood at the listening post of a daily newspaper in Virginia for thirty years to record that he never has heard of a single bill concerning which Senator Glass sought the advice of a politician in the State. He will listen to argument. Evidence he will analyze with sound judgment, but look at the political weather-vanes or consult the barometer of his own political fortune – never!

This is as Virginia desires. For almost seventy years, save for one brief period of political insurgency in the 1880's and the anti-Smith vote of 1928, Virginia has been Democratic. This has not resulted in atrophy of political thought but rather in the transfer to the primaries of the interest that usually attaches to the general election. Factional rivals are as vigilant as sharpshooters of the opposing army would be. Senator Glass has faced this fire many times in the past but he defied it even before his great labors for the Federal Reserve system and his service as Secretary of the Treasury lifted him, in the estimation of his constituents, to the rank of statesman. Today he is no more independent, no more outspoken, than he was in the days when as a representative from the Lynchburg district he was subject to challenge at the polls every two years by those he never sought to conciliate. That Virginia approves his independence, admires his courageous character and accepts his decisions even when some of the voters disagree with him, is more than a tribute to him or to his State. It should be a lesson to politicians that intelligent courage pays. For that is the moral of the Virginia tradition.

DOUGLAS SOUTHALL FREEMAN

CONTENTS

LIST OF ILLUSTRATIONS

CARTER GLASS

CHAPTER ONE

A boy, a baseball bat, and "a gang from across the river."

The heavy clay dust in the wagon tracks was still cool. It felt good squirming up between the toes of his brown, bare feet as, with the sun at his back, the seven-year-old boy walked along a timbered road in Virginia. It was early summer. The year was 1865.

For nearly a mile the road led uphill, through clumps of white oak, tulip poplars and plume-topped pine. The boy did not mind the climb, for he had tagged along with his brothers on woodland jaunts all over Campbell County, to the swimming holes in the James River, and through tracts of hemlock and beech to where the white sycamores stood guard along Backwater and Beaver Creeks.

But the sun was making itself felt now, and perspiration stood out among the freckles big sister Nannie so often teased him about. Why all this walking in the growing heat, he thought – and, he didn't know; he was just walking, for "a boy's will is the wind's will. . ." He took off his cap and wiped his thin, moist face. His hair was very curly and slightly red.

At the hillcrest he stopped, looking back at the town. Lynchburg, scattered over its seven hills, was below him – the white frame houses and neat brick buildings, the new railroad tracks, and the broad spread of the James River, where packet boats used to ply down-river to Richmond and back; on the opposite bank rose the tree-dotted hills of Amherst Heights.

From where he stood the boy could see the Fair Grounds, where so short a time ago men in gray were forever marching up and down. He could just barely remember – there had been the local volunteers, recruited from among the seven thousand whites who lived in Lynchburg. Twelve full companies had drilled there and marched away. The Rifle Grays, the Lynchburg Rifles, the Beauregard Rifles and the Second Virginia Cavalry had gone to places like Bull Run, Manassas and the Wilderness. Some had come back with an arm or a leg missing. Many would never come back.

And now the talk was all of approaching Yankee armies, for the war was ended these past several weeks.

He walked on, trying to figure it all out. Nannie said the Yankees were big, blue-coated devils who burned houses and cut off little boys' ears. Mothers warned their young not to go beyond Floyd Street where, a year before, trenches had been bravely dug. As for the boy, he still had only the haziest notion of what war was, but he did know it kept a fellow from having any fun. In fact, it was still that way. He gritted his teeth and began kicking up the thick dust in the wagon tracks.

He was more than two miles from home, where the road wound through thick woods, when he heard hoofbeats – and, then, they cantered into view. His eyes went wide with wonder. Their uniforms were blue. It was a troop of Yankee cavalry.

He thought in flashes. What would the other fellows do if they were there? Take to the woods, perhaps, and climb a tree. Nannie would scream, and old Sarah, his colored nurse, would spread her voluminous skirts for a hiding place. But the immediate impulse was to pick up a rock and heave it.

With a stubbornness born of inward defiance he refused to step off the road as the troop of horsemen came toward him. He didn't know which made him the madder, these Yankees, or the fact that he hadn't heaved the rock, and run, while still there was time.

"Hi, sonny !" laughed a voice.

Lip curling in scorn the boy stared at the man. The next thing he knew the officer was reaching down and was hoisting him, arms flailing and feet kicking, up to the pommel of the saddle.

The boy never forgot that ride, but it was all too rough and bouncing and breathless to remember clearly in detail. The officer seemed jovial and high-spirited, and he might have liked him, only – "damn Yankee !" And the questions, one question in particular : What was he going to be when he grew up ? "A major, like my father, and shoot Yankees." The men laughed uproariously, and it made him still madder.

The officer set him down as they rode into the city, and in another moment the soldiers were gone, galloping down the narrow streets. Only a pall of dust lingered to prove it hadn't been a dream.

He stood staring after them. Then he turned and started toward his home. His pace quickened as he realized what had happened. The freckle-faced boy broke into a run.

Young Carter Glass had a story to tell. . .

Union troops who hadn't been able to penetrate Lynchburg during four years of war were now in the city.

Born in Lynchburg on January 4, 1858, Carter Glass came into a heritage of freedom. Thomas Glass, the immigrant, came to Virginia in 1648, patented land in New Kent County (the part now Hanover) in 1670, it being located on Totopotomoys branch, near the present village of Studley. The Glasses were among the first of the pioneers who pushed on into the interior. About one hundred years after Thomas Glass landed, his grandson, Robert Glass, was among the residents of Goochland County.

Forty years later, Thomas W. Glass, the grandfather of Carter Glass, was born in Goochland County, where he lived until he was about fifteen years old. Later he went to the adjoining county of Fluvanna where, apparently, he worked in the tavern of Robert Cawthorne, whose daughter, Lucinda, he married about 1818.

At this time there was much talk going on in Virginia over the feasibility of a canal from the seaboard to the Ohio, hence soon after he was married, Thomas W. Glass moved, along with the Cawthornes and hundreds of others, to Amherst County, where the Blue Ridge Canal was to pass through the mountains. The people envisaged a great period of prosperity ahead, and hurried to take up the timber lands and the water rights.

From 1820 to 1835, Thomas W. Glass engaged in farming and, probably, had some part in the construction of the Canal. During the latter year he became Superintendent of Locks on the upper section of the mountain division, but he resigned in 1837 to resume farming. He died in Amherst County in 1847, and was buried on the right-of-way of the old canal, about half way between Snowden and Balcony Falls.

Carter Glass' mother was Elizabeth Christian, great granddaughter of Henry Christian, a captain in the Revolutionary War ; also, the forebears of his father, Robert Henry Glass, had fought in Washington's armies. His mother died when he was two years old, leaving sister Nannie to preside over the quiet and comfortable home overlooking the James River. There he lived with his brothers, Robert Henry, Jr., Edward Christian and Paulus Powell. His father was publisher of the *Lynchburg Daily Republican*, as well as Postmaster.

Plain speaking, twenty-four-year-old Robert Henry Glass had come to Lynchburg in 1842 to take over the editorship of the *Republican,* after having served as a practical printer in the shop of his uncle, Robert Cawthorne, publisher of the *Fincastle Democrat.* More than a century before his hardy frugal Scotch-Irish ancestors had settled in Virginia, so that to him had come naturally a knowledge of its people. Through his books, and from his newspaper desk, Robert Henry Glass saw the world, and grew acquainted with it – in books there were Plato and Shakespeare, the letters of Junius, the writings of Jefferson, the political philosophy of Edmund Burke ; across his desk there came news dispatches from Washington, New York and Boston, from London, Paris and Berlin.

This was a day when a forthright journalist often had to drop his pen and grab a pistol. The nation, rapidly dividing into hostile camps, rocked with a warfare of words over States' Rights and slavery, while President Buchanan dallied with the greatest crisis since 1776. Editorial tilts between the *Lynchburg Virginian* and the *Republican* flared to white heat ; and one of Lynchburg's loveliest spots is still known as "Point of Honor" – the old duelling ground.

All Virginia had come to know Robert Henry Glass as a fearless and articulate champion of Jeffersonian democracy when, on being appointed Postmaster in 1853, he disposed of his interest in the paper. But five years was as long as he could ignore the call of the press ; shortly after Carter was born he repurchased the *Republican.* His trenchant, unsparing pen soon made it the dominant Democratic organ in southwestern Virginia.

In the summer of 1860 rival editor Joseph Button of the *Virginian* publicly accused Editor Glass of influencing Postmaster Glass into purposely delaying that paper's delivery. Glass being in Charleston at the time, his associate publisher, George W. Hardwicke, printed a scathing rebuttal. The inevitable duel brought two Hardwicke brothers face to face with several Button men. Pistols cracked. Joseph Button lay dead on the grass. Another was wounded. The Hardwickes were acquitted.

Robert Henry Glass was a rather spare man of medium height, perhaps five feet, ten inches, with reddish brown hair, bright, penetrating brown eyes, prominent nose and, as described by his friends, "a Virginia gentleman of the old school, amiable and gracious to a degree. He never passed a woman on the street, whether he knew her or not, that he did not lift his hat"; and, as Carter Glass remembers, "however much he might be absorbed in reading a newspaper or a book, he invariably put them aside whenever one of his children came into his room."

Elizabeth Christian Glass was a high-spirited, gallant little lady of notable piety who governed her own home, her children and her husband. As evidence of her determination there was the time, early in their married lives, when Robert Henry Glass was challenged to a duel by a rival editor. The challenge was accepted, and the terms of the meetings were being arranged, when, in some mysterious way, Elizabeth Christian Glass received an intimation of the situation.

An understanding woman, she did not say anything to her husband ; a practical Christian woman who abhorred the taking, or threatening, of life, she went before the local judge and swore out a warrant for both men, had them arrested and bound over in heavy penalty to keep the peace.

Naturally, this greatly mortified her husband ; but there was nothing he could do about it. The duel was not fought, although tempers remained uncooled. The two men settled their differences, on the street – with canes.

Carter Glass scarcely remembered, although he was to learn, that his father had been among the first to offer his services to Virginia, just as he was to learn Virginians had written, in May,

1776, "all men are by nature equally free and independent." By these famous words, they had declared not only their own political freedom, but their intentions toward slavery.

From the north, when Carter Glass was born, insurrection was being stirred . . . in Southampton a Negro preacher had led a rising that killed fifty-seven white people . . . mobs were rescuing fugitive slaves from Federal officers . . . Garrison and Phillips were denouncing the Union, the Constitution and the South for giving shelter to the traffic. And, as a state, Virginia had fallen to second rank in the Union. Deserted farms and emigrating population all spoke of the state's decline.

This, then, was the heritage – "all men are by nature equally free and independent" – to which Carter Glass was a direct heir, because his forebears, on both sides, had fought for it for themselves, and for all whites and colored alike.

This, too, was the turmoil into which he was born.

His father was a delegate to the fateful Democratic convention in Charleston in 1860. At the announcement of Lincoln's election South Carolina seceded. The other cotton states followed. True to their traditions, Virginians invited states of the North and South to meet with Virginia commissioners in Washington on February 4, 1861, to adjust the controversy. In his newspaper Robert Henry Glass backed up the declaration of the Virginia Assembly which insisted that the Union having been formed by consent of the states, the Government had no right to maintain it by force and "we will resist the same by all means in our power."

Accepting Virginia's invitation, twenty states met in Washington. Their deliberations were unavailing. In the meantime Virginia had declared for the Union, and in Lynchburg Editor Glass was espousing the same cause, having, some two or three years before, exchanged letters of comment and mutual encouragement with Stephen A. Douglas, then tilting in brilliant oratory with the lank Illinois lawyer, Abraham Lincoln.

For almost two months after his inaugural Lincoln's policy was undefined and through those two months the Virginia delegates were under constant pressure from North and South. And of each evening, at dusk, in Lynchburg – as in Richmond, Charlottesville, Danville and scores of other Virginia towns and cities – men and women converged on the Courthouse Square.

Almost it seemed prearranged, although there was no prearrangement to it. They soon learned if there was any late news from Washington, talking with each other, clustering under the blazing torches, listening and applauding speakers who denounced the North, or speakers who sided with the cause of unity. Among the former were young fire-eaters who wanted war ; among the latter were men such as Robert Henry Glass who pleaded for peace.

With the shots at Sumter Lincoln gave the answer – he called for 75,000 soldiers, and Virginia was requested to send her quota – against the South.

The news came to Lynchburg, as it came to a thousand other American towns, North and South. That evening, in Courthouse Square, there was only one voice.

To coercion Virginia had but a single answer.

Robert E. Lee refused the chief command of the Union armies, and gravely offered his sword to his native state. . .

Holding tightly to the hand of his sister Nannie, three-year-old Carter Glass watched his father ride away to serve as a major on the staff of General Floyd. In the little group stood Nannie, who was twelve years old ; Robert Henry, Jr., who was ten ; Edward Christian, who was eight ; Paulus Powell, who was five. Their aunt, Fannie Christian, and the old colored nurse, Sarah, were left at home to care for them.

Poverty years followed. Food was scarce and what there

was was shared with the soldiers who stood guard continuously over the munitions works that was located a few blocks from the Glass home. The job of postmaster was no more. The newspaper from which the little family had drawn most of its income was being published, but under great difficulties. Yet their plight was no different from that of the other townspeople.

Early in his boyhood Carter Glass began to understand that freedom is a challenge. He came to be proud of his people; proud of the uniforms; proud, too, of the Stars and Bars that fluttered from so many windows, housetops and flagpoles. Like his brothers, his sister, and all the other children of the South, he was older than his years – for war does that to children. So it was that though he was but five years old, he stood solemnly with the townspeople who crowded the banks of the James on a May day in 1863.

At their backs Lynchburg was darkened with black bunting while in the canal below them was the old packet boat, *John Marshall.* In a flag draped coffin on its deck lay Stonewall Jackson, the warrior of Manassas, Chancellorsville and the Valley campaigns. The funeral cortege made a memorable impression . . . there, the name of John Marshall, patriot of the Revolution and the great Chief Justice in the early growth of the Republic; and there, the body of Jackson, who had led Southern patriots in another revolution.

And those other days, when the squat-legged sawhorse in back of the woodshed was a foaming steed on which, a hell-for-leather cavalryman, he carried secret dispatches to General Lee. Yankee riders were always at his heels but with the fleetness of his fancy he never failed to leave them far behind while into the firelit camp of General Floyd he sped, leaped to a fresher steed, saluted smartly as his father proudly watched, and spurred on into the perilous night.

Or, as in fancy, the scene changed, and he and his father rode abreast, two gallant majors, leading a fierce onslaught against the enemy fortress where Nannie, a prisoner, leaned from a turret window imploring rescue. Bang ! Bang ! and the gate is theirs. Bang ! Bang ! – but blue-coated hordes swarm out from the garrison to surround them. Back to back he and his father stand with slashing swords, fighting their way into the fort – and then, back they come, with Nannie in front of him on his saddle, to thunder furiously away to safety.

But, no, that is Nannie calling. The day dream ends. The furious charger is only a sawhorse now. Nannie is doing her youthful best to take his mother's place in the home ; in their father's absence, Ed, Bob, Paul and Carter resolutely try to fill his shoes. They accepted the responsibility and often went hungry in quiet pride.

These were days when, as his hoe turned the rich Virginia soil, the freckled boy's eyes were sharp for earthworms. They went into the bait can, for angling had taken on an added zest. A good catch of fish was more than sport ; it brought priceless addition to their frequently scant supper. About him as he dropped his line into the James on these days hung an air of dead earnestness.

. . . Then there were days goldenly mellow. Walking home with his string of fish, the way led through rolling fields and pastureland. Perched atop a farm gate he often paused to gaze back on the rustic panorama, colored now with the copper light of evening, and as great mounded clouds passed slowly over, the sighing wind wrote brief inscriptions on fields of waving grass.

As a child he was not aware of the ambiguities called Beauty and Art ; but in years yet to be unrolled from the tireless spindle of the sun, the man was to return to these same acres that he might regain strength and earthy perspective for battles to be fought beyond the horizon of Piedmont Hills.

But hovering over the years of early childhood, the dark giant of war seemed to lurk in every shadow, behind every bush, beyond each hill. When boulders of thunder rolled across the sky the hungry youngster thought he heard the roar of enemy cannon, and he was not always wrong.

In June, 1864, General Hunter and his Union army had fought their way to "Sandusky," just out of town a half-mile west of Quaker Church. Darkness halted the musket fire, although cannon roared through the night. In the morning, after repeated attacks, Hunter retreated. The following Sunday, as on every other Sunday, the boy, with Nannie and his brothers, went off to the Court Street Methodist Church where he heard the minister praying for peace – and, childlike, he wondered what it would be like when Peace came, how much longer there would be tears in Nannie's eyes, why the few men folks sat so stiff and tight-faced. . .

On April 1, 1865, Grant at last broke Lee's thin line, and marching out of Petersburg, the gray-coated soldiers saw the red glow of burning Richmond reflected in the sky.

The war had been fought.

In his mother's family, Carter Glass had lost eighteen relatives. In his *Reminiscences of the Civil War* General John O. Gordon tells the story :

"I recall nothing in history or even in romance which equals in uniqueness and pathos the fate that befell them. The decrees of that fate were uniform and inexorable. One by one, these kinsmen fell in succeeding engagements. In every fight in which the regiment was engaged one of this brave family was numbered among the dead. As battle succeeded battle, and each, with appalling regularity, claimed its victim, there ran through company and regiment the unvarying question,

'Which one of the Christians was killed today, and which one will go next?'

"Yet among the survivors there was no wavering, no effort to escape the doom which seemed surely awaiting each in his turn. With a consecration truly sublime, each took his place in line, ready for the sacrifice which duty demanded. For seventeen successive engagements the gruesome record of death had not varied. Then came Cedar Creek. Only one of the gallant eighteen was left. His record for courage was unsurpassed. A number of times he had been wounded, and in the deadly hand-to-hand struggle at Cold Harbor he had been pierced by a bayonet. Faithful to every duty, he had never missed a fight.

"When the orders were issued for the night march and the assault at dawn upon Sheridan's army, a deep fraternal concern for this last survivor of the Christians was manifested by all of his comrades. He was privately importuned to stay out of the fight; or, if unwilling to remain in camp while his comrades fought, he was urged to go home. Whether he yielded to these warnings and entreaties will probably never be known. He was seen by his comrades no more after that night march to Cedar Creek. Many believe that he was loyal 'even unto death,' and that he lies with the heroic and 'unknown dead' who fell upon that eventful field."

In Lynchburg, even after General Lee surrendered to Grant at Appomattox, thirty miles away, the Stars and Bars flew defiantly at full staff. It was flying over the office of the *Lynchburg Daily Republican* when Lee surrendered. Without comment, Major Robert Henry Glass, who had been invalided out of the Confederate army nearly two years before, quietly pulled it down. A few days later and on his desk was a letter postmarked Washington. It was from Lincoln, offering to reappoint him postmaster. Politely, but firmly, he declined the office.

Then – an assassin's bullet, and the reins fell loose from Lincoln's dead hands. Andrew Johnson became President. Soon, Virginia was no longer a state. On the maps it was Military District No. 1. The Fair Grounds was crowded with Union troops. As told, Carter Glass, at seven, was first to see them come.

Under protection of the soldiers a locust swarm of carpet-baggers descended upon Virginia . . . and through the Negro voters radicals were in complete control.

Practically all Virginians of any experience were disfranchised, and disqualified from holding public office. It was not long before Negro radicals were surpassing even their white leaders in exorbitant demands . . . a short while longer and Negroes were drawing the color line themselves.

A constitutional convention was called, and after nearly five months of debate the exasperated military governor ended the session by refusing to pay any more expenses – but not before out of the convention had come a constitution that disqualified practically every white man in the state, by the "test oath" of no aid given to the Confederacy, and gave all Negroes suffrage without qualification.

Now Virginians banded together and out of the darkness flamed into light the figures of men and women – Robert Henry Glass among them with his clear words. An appeal was made to Washington. On the eve of his inauguration to the Presidency, General Grant decreed that the disfranchising oath and the constitution be voted upon separately.

That turned the tide. The constitution was ratified, the oath rejected. The carpet-baggers were out of office. A new congress of conservative Republicans turned deaf ears to the cries that went up from radicals within their own party.

In his *Lynchburg Daily Republican* Robert Henry Glass hailed the victory; and in the house overlooking the James

River the Glass family was growing up. In 1863, Miss Meta Sandford, of Fayetteville, N.C., had become the second wife of Robert Henry Glass; and, in her, Carter Glass had found a mother to take the place of the one he had scarcely known.

As for schooling, it was haphazard. During the war school buildings had served as hospitals. Reconstruction brought the Union troops, who used them as barracks. Behind, they left broken and scattered equipment, the disheartening residue of plunder.

Typical was the school presided over by Henry L. Davies, a Confederate veteran who had lost a leg in the fighting. It was housed in an old building and blackboards stretched across the front walls. In the forward corner, opposite the one where laggard scholars were made to stand wearing the dunce cap, was a faded globe on which the teacher traced the boundaries of the world. On the rear walls hung yellowed maps, and gilt-framed lithographs of Washington, Jefferson and Lee. Dominating the room stood the teacher's desk, and in front of the half-dozen rows of screwed-down school desks, were rows of hard benches for recitation periods.

For Davies, in the rural tradition, taught all grades. The result was that Carter Glass mastered not only his own lessons but, like a sponge, absorbed the literature, history and grammar from classes two or three years further advanced. Nor did the crippled pedagogue have any need for the proverbial hickory stick; when a pupil began to flounder his fumbling mind was prodded by the formidable swings and pokes of a home-made crutch.

But the curriculum of education, that synthesis of observation and understanding, was not then – just as it has never been – confined to the classroom. The boy heard the drawling talk of the oldsters in corner store and livery stable, holding forth staunch opinions ranging from where Cain could have got his wife to the doom that was certain to engulf the South as a result of national policies of trade and tariff.

He heard, too, the impassioned arguments against proposals by Dr. William Henry Ruffner for a progressive and centralized school system. Boylike, he sided with his elders; only the boy's suspicions had a more personal touch. Like many a boy before him, and many a boy since, he saw little sense in going to school. He found more use for the crotch of a willow branch, because he could make a slingshot out of it, than he did for the crutch of Teacher Davies; and he knew there was one thing that had taught him a more convincing lesson against swearing than had his Sunday School teacher.

It happened this way. Having spent impressionistic years among soldiers, he had gathered a vocabulary that was a source of entertainment to the philosophers of the livery stable, a source of surprise to his father, and not at all a source of comfort to his sister Nannie, or to his stepmother.

There came a day when he wanted to go along with the older boys on a fishing expedition, and for the third time they had chased him down the road. They stopped, and he stopped to give them a tongue lashing. In emphasis, but still keeping his eyes on the other boys, he reached down to paw around for a handy stone.

Instead of a stone, his groping fingers fastened upon a blacksnake. That ended his swearing. "It scared," as he said long afterwards, "fifty years of cuss words right out of my mouth." "Dad bum!" became the height of explosiveness through the rest of his life.

Small for his age, nevertheless the boys of the neighborhood thought twice about the busy, hard little fists before riling him. It was legendary that the boys from "across the river" were tough, and no one labored harder than they to keep that legend alive. Two hefty bullies, Cinders and Big Dan, lorded it over the crew, and when word came that an undersized red head didn't think they were so tough, they laid plans to spike that heresy once and for all.

"How 'bout a marble game?" an accomplice of theirs asked young Glass on this particular day.

"What'cha got, just commies?"

"Taws – good ones, too." And from his pockets he drew a glittering wealth of agates and glassies.

"All right, we'll pitch to the line."

"Aw, let's don't pitch here, Carter. Come on up the alley a ways where the ground's smooth."

But when they got up the alley the other boy proceeded to forget all about marbles.

"Now," he announced, "you're in for a lickin'."

"Huh! Who's goin' to give it?"

"Cinders and Big Dan."

Carter jeered. "Who says so?"

Two new voices broke in, and two shaggy heads popped up over the alley fence – Cinders and Big Dan. For an instant there was an empty whirling feeling in the pit of the intended victim's stomach . . . but only for an instant. Just as Cinders dropped from the fence he was met with such a fury of fists that he was knocked sprawling. With Big Dan closing in, Carter Glass began to run.

He was a nimble sprinter, and the heavier boy, pounding after him, was soon winded. When Carter heard his pursuer panting and gasping for breath, he suddenly turned. The strategy of the unexpected carried the day. It was weeks before Big Dan ventured over the river again.

When he did he brought his gang with him, and they challenged the town boys to a ball game. The town boys were the better players, but with Big Dan as umpire the score was soon one-sided. Along about the fifth inning Carter cracked out a two-base hit along the third base line that scored two runners. Smirkingly, Big Dan called it a foul. There was a hot chorus of protests, and the gang from across the river started what they were looking for – a free-for-all.

This time instead of charging in with his fists, Carter grabbed up the one baseball bat that served both teams. Sputtering defiance of the whole "dad-bummed bunch," he raced toward them. The invaders scattered in sudden remembrance that the river was the quickest way home.

"Gee !" exclaimed one of Carter's teammates, "it took pluck to do that !"

The young gladiator had acquired a nickname. Even now he occasionally gets a letter that begins "Dear Pluck."

CHAPTER TWO

Ink-stained fingers reach for a pencil.

At thirteen the boy was taken out of school. Times were hard. Carter Glass had to go to work. Nor did he greatly mind.

He much preferred the smell of printer's ink to the classroom recitations of the crippled Confederate soldier. Besides, what could old Davies teach him that his father didn't already know ten times as well? He enjoyed his walks with the Major . . . literature, war, reconstruction, problems of politics and government, farming – his father elucidated them in terms of self-taught common sense. Here was a teacher who made of learning a fascinating pursuit.

He was not alone in his respect for his father's innate wisdom. On street corners, in stores, at the depot, or evenings on the front verandah when the Lynchburg editor rocked in his easy chair, the boy sat, chin in hand, listening as friends and neighbors gathered to discuss and argue the topics of the times, and to listen to the Major's well-considered opinions. Often his father talked his editorials before he wrote them, and about his speech there hung the same informative and challenging air that distinguished the paragraphs he published. Some of these conversations went far beyond the boy's depth, but he remembered and hoarded what puzzled him as ammunition for further questioning and speculation.

He went to work as a carrier for the newspaper. No shop, front door, sidewalk, alley or foot path in that city of hills was unfamiliar ground to this slender stripling and his load of *Lynchburg Republicans*. Here, too, he listened to the native wit of the Negroes, and the natural philosophy of the hill farmers . . . what he heard, and saw, he stored away. At fourteen, he became a printer's devil, that he might learn the mysteries of type.

Silently, and with finality, the gate had swung shut on his boy's playland. Long since the squat-legged sawhorse had lost its romance in the chore of sawing wood. Robbing melon patches was no longer in the curriculum of boyish enterprise. The swimming holes in the James River saw him seldom. Rather, his mind was on more serious matters.

He now peered anxiously into the mirror to watch and to gauge the progress of the down on his cheeks and his upper lip. He wished there was something that would make it grow faster. Perhaps lard would do it; but it didn't. He tried his father's razor in the theory of stimulating growth by elimination, but stopped the operation on reaching a point near his chin, looked anxiously for cuts, found none, and kept on, touching lightly with the sharp open blade through to the end – to become panicky when the down didn't show up again for many days.

Occasional evenings still found him playing baseball, but it was a man's sport – cockfighting – that attracted him most. It was a diversion popular in Virginia; and the boy trained his own birds.

He had some red-breasted games, also some blue games. One day a neighbor, whose birds had been worsted in several battles, borrowed a rooster from a professional cockfighter. The result was disastrous for the young apprentice's birds. Not to be outdone, however, he wrote General McGill, a Confederate officer who lived in Pulaski, and asked him to send "one of his best game birds." The bird came. It cost the boy twenty-five dollars. Calling it "Dusty Miller" in recognition of its breed, Carter installed him in the back yard, and waited. It wasn't long.

The next morning the interloper came swashbuckling onto the Glass property. There came a flap of wings, a flurry of feathers, and a thrust of sharp spurs. The invader was dead.

Outraged, the professional cockfighter demanded payment. Just as hotly the victorious cock's owner pointed out that the dead rooster was a trespasser. The incident passed, but a week later Dusty Miller was missing.

High and low the boy hunted. Negro friends assured him the bird was held prisoner in no Lynchburg chicken coop. The search was widened. Wherever there was a cockfight, there was Carter Glass looking over the entries. Finally, at Sandy Hook, he spotted Dusty Miller.

"Who owns this bird?" he demanded.

"I reckon as I do," replied a man.

"I reckon you don't," snapped the boy. "He's my bird – where did you get him?"

The stranger said he had bought him from a friend.

"What's your friend's name?"

The man gave him the name of the Lynchburg professional cockfighter.

"You'll swear to that?"

"Well – well – I don't want to get anyone in trouble, but – maybe you'll sell this bird?"

"H'm," mused Carter. "How much?"

The man hesitated, then slowly offered: "I can't go any higher'n fifty dollars."

The boy struggled to keep a straight face, to seem very casual. He pondered for several minutes, wondered if he could get more, but finally made the sale.

With the money in his pocket, he returned to Lynchburg. He had accomplished three things. He had found his bird, learned the name of the thief, although he intended doing nothing about it, and had made a good profit.

He continued to enjoy cockfighting, but by now he was seventeen and beginning to dream of becoming a reporter and then an editor ; beginning, too, to shape the key to fit the door wherein he might enter and know the man he wanted to be, for it is in adolescence the emerging mind begins to flex and feel its muscle.

There remained the long talks with his father, just as there remained tedious hours of exacting toil in setting to type his father's editorials, the happenings of the town and country correspondence. But if day demanded the labor of his hands, so did night give pasturage to his dreams.

Many, many nights his kerosene lamp burned late, lighting the pages of Plato, Burke and Shakespeare. One can see the young man as he gets up from his chair and goes to where a huge dictionary – an inexhaustible arsenal for men whose weapons are words – lay open. He finds his word, jots down its meaning. Then remembering, he finds in his pockets scraps of paper with random words scribbled on them. He looks them all up, jots down their meanings, and returns to his book.

Presently he leans back in his chair to stare at the wainscoting above the shelves in his father's library, looming indistinct in the semi-darkness beyond the lamp's circle. His growing mind is gymnastic in the age-old exercise of speculation, logic and reason that is philosophy.

This night it is Shakespeare. Had he, as the old pedants affirmed, come from the humble village of Stratford, a youth untutored and untraveled, to put imperishable plays upon the stages of the world ? Or, was it not more likely that in the secluded study of Sir Francis Bacon, a cultured, worldly aristocrat, this poetry was born ; a roistering young actor in the Mermaid Tavern hired to hide the true authorship with his signature ? Already, Carter Glass had delved deep into the old controversy – for the controversy had intrigued him, just as it was to intrigue him more in later years and he was to come to believe that Bacon was the dramatist.

But, whichever it was, in the Virginia night a ghost walked again to whisper as ink-stained fingers slowly reached for a pencil to underline "the time is out of joint" ; and the youth reads on, blinking, until the pages blur and their meaning escapes him. Often the stars have paled and pastel blue is at the windowpane challenging the lamp before his eyes are closed.

Even more than his father, he found in Nannie a receptacle for his dreams. Now, at twenty-six, she was more than a sister to the youth ; she was his counselor, just as she was to remain as sister and counselor to him all through her life. His brothers were young men now. Robert Henry, Jr., was working as a bookkeeper. Edward Christian was a school teacher and afterward for fifty-two years school superintendent. Paulus Powell was a printer. To the family had come seven more children. Maggie, Marion, John, Douglas, Lula, Cora and Meta.

Carter was still in the shop setting type when he wanted to be a reporter, meeting people, writing about them. But times were still hard. The paper could afford but one reporter ; and that job was filled. It was discouraging and, boylike, he often said to himself : "Some of these days unless the Major gives me a reporter's job I'm going to start looking for something else." More and more, of evenings, he found himself at the railroad station watching as inverted funnel stacks poured out hot smoke, as pistons jammed forth clouds of steam, and as the brakemen swung mightily on brake wheels, bringing trains to squawling stops. He grew to know the trainmen and he liked to listen as they made casual mention of such far places as Washington, New York, Savannah and New Orleans.

CARTER GLASS — AGE 14
The notation was made by Glass many years later

He thought he'd like to be a railroad man. This thought he expressed to Nannie.

"Now don't be foolish, Carter," she admonished him. "What would you be doing working for a railroad? You're cut out to be a newspaper man. Quit fussing and fretting. Just as soon as the paper can afford it, you'll be a reporter. You just stop this silly talk about going to work for the railroad."

Worried, Nannie told her father, but the Major only smiled and ridiculed her fears. The boy would stick where he was – or, if not, would come back to the newspaper "because it's in his blood and he can't get rid of it."

His father was right. Accepting Nannie's advice, the youth did put aside thoughts of leaving. Though but seventeen, he was becoming deeply interested in government – not politics, but government. By having lived impressionable years in the Reconstruction period, he knew the lengths to which political oppression could go. By observation, he knew there were men who would capitalize on emotion for their own greed.

Plato, with his super-logical concept of an ideal state, was stirring him, furnishing his mind with stimulus to rout out those who seek, and keep, political office at the expense of conscience. Through the influence of Burke he saw the legislature of Virginia as a deliberative body with one interest – that of the state; and the Congress a deliberative body in which each state is represented and having but one interest – that of the nation. He saw that, and he was beginning to understand the real meaning of Burke's words: "Factions in republics have been, and are, fully capable . . . of the most cruel oppression and injustice to all men of whatever state or persuasion, religious or political."

In one of his father's books he marked these words from Jefferson's first inaugural speech :

> Economy in public expense, that labor may be lightly burdened ;
> The payment of our debts and sacred preservation of the public faith ;
> I am for a government rigorously frugal and simple, applying all the possible savings of the public revenue to the discharge of the national debt ; and not the multiplication of officers and salaries merely to make partisans, and for increasing, by every device, the public debt, on the principle of its being a public blessing.

More than sixty years afterwards he was to remind his party, and his President, of this fundamental tenet in the political faith of the founder of the Democratic party.

Now, however, he could only support it with his thinking.

In 1876, Major Glass moved his family to Petersburg, where he had accepted the editorship of *The Petersburg News*. Carter went along to work as a printer, but in the hope that the one newspaper job he wanted most – being a reporter – would develop. He remained with the newspaper until he was nineteen ; and, as is the way of youth, he became more and more discouraged. Through a friend he heard that a job as clerk in the Lynchburg auditor's office of the Atlantic, Mississippi & Ohio Railway (afterwards the Norfolk & Western) was open. He applied for it, and got it. Then he told Nannie and his father. Nannie scolded him, but his father only smiled. "I think the experience will do you good, son. It will make a better newspaper man out of you."

He would miss Nannie. He knew that. He would miss his father's editorials, and their talks together. He knew that, too. Also, he would miss his stepmother, whom he had grown to love, as he might have loved his own mother, had she lived. "But," he told himself, just as he repeated it to Nannie, "I'm almost a grown man now. I'm nineteen. It's time for me to start making my own way, if I'm ever going to be independent." He was determined – he would make his own way.

Back to Lynchburg he went, and the familiar scenes recompensed him, so he argued, for what he had lost. As things turned out, they more than recompensed him.

It was while employed by the railroad company an incident occurred that was to be vividly recalled many years later.

As is the way of youth, each year found him growing less and less oblivious to the attractions of femininity. He had not kept pace with the other lads of his age in this matter ; his job and his studious evenings had interfered. But now such functions as church socials, picnics and hayrides began to take on added lustre. He acquired an eye, and a quick one.

One Sunday morning in Lynchburg, that eye brightened and quickened. He was standing on a corner, waiting for a horse-drawn trolley to take him to church, when a young lady, accompanied by her mother, also stopped. Enchanted, the son of Major Robert Henry Glass stared – and he stared so hard that the young lady could not ignore it completely. As the car stopped, the shapely head beneath its lace bonnet rose in imperious disdain. One withering look as she stepped into the car and the young Romeo so forgot himself that he lacked the courage to follow. He walked to church.

Also, as is the way of youth, the pretty face receded in his mind. There were other girls and, too, there were bills of lading and invoices that, long since, had lost whatever fascination they had held. He was again thinking seriously of leaving the railroad office and some way, somehow, getting back into newspaper work – only, he would not go back as a printer. He thought of all the places the trains that went by his window would take him ; and he was sure in one of those places there was a newspaper that could, and would, give him a job, or make room for a cub reporter.

It was while he was speculating this way that his brother,

Robert Henry, Jr., came from Petersburg to visit him. During the evening, and after all his eager questions regarding his father, Nannie, his stepmother and his sisters and brothers had been answered, Bob began reviewing the political situation in Petersburg and the fight their father was putting up, in the columns of his paper, to rid the community of an exceedingly objectionable politician.

"You don't mean to tell me the Major's not going to win that fight?" questioned Carter banteringly.

"I don't know – he couldn't keep the man from getting the nomination," replied his brother.

"What? You mean to tell me that fellow got the nomination?"

"Yep."

"Well, I'll be . . . listen, do you suppose the Major'd print it if I wrote a broadside? I know that creature – I'll disembowel him, if the Major will only print it!"

"Why don't you take a whack at it, and I'll take it back with me."

With pencil and paper the youth went to work. With each finished page he shoved it across the table for his brother to read. When he finished, he threw the pencil on the desk, rubbed the ache out of his back, and grinned:

"I'd like to see the Major's face when he reads that, but more than even that, I'd like to see the recipient's face when he reads it, if the Major prints it."

Major Glass printed it in *The Petersburg News* just as his son had written it.

The party nominee was beaten, the independent candidate elected.

With his pen, Carter Glass had begun to dig his way into the soil and soul of his native state.

Soon afterward there came to him in the railroad office a friend, J. P. Bell.

"Carter," said Bell, "Albert Waddill, Editor of the *Lynchburg News*, has asked me to recommend a young man for the job of reporter on the paper. The one he had has quit – got a better job, I guess – and Waddill needs someone to take his place. Know of anyone who would like the job?"

Suspecting Bell was hoaxing him, Carter laughed: "If you're serious, you don't need to look any further, and if you're just fooling, I can give you a lot of names."

"I'm not fooling. Thought maybe you'd like the job so dropped around to see you."

At twenty-two this was work he had long dreamed of doing, and it was with more than a little pride he saw his personals and miscellaneous local items in print. Although the paper was rather primitive, with comparatively small circulation, printed on a hand-turned press, which had been used in Richmond to print Confederate money, Glass would not have traded jobs with any metropolitan reporter. After the dreary hours hunched over the compositor's rack, and the confinement of the freight office, he welcomed the freedom of ranging Lynchburg in search of news.

Commonplace news, most of it, but it brought him into close contact with all manner of people. He sought out and questioned the white and the black, the well-to-do and the poor. He listened to the problems of tradesmen, lawyers, planters, clerks, farmhands – the people of Piedmont Virginia. But with the urge to reap headlines that is typical of all young reporters, he yearned for the Big Assignment. He had not long to wait. One morning telegraph keys chattered reports of a coal-mine disaster at Pocahontas, in Southwest Virginia.

He covered the disaster with consummate thoroughness –

interviewed survivors, talked with grieving mothers and wives, questioned the mine owners; and he was disheveled and breathless when he rushed into the single telegraph station in the town.

"You'll have to wait," the operator told him in answer to his hurried question, "this gentleman has the wire, and it's the only one we've got."

"This gentleman" was a reporter from a rival newspaper.

"How long will it be?" questioned Glass.

"This is my wire, Glass," answered the reporter. "I've got it, and I'm going to keep it, if I have to stay here all day and rattle off words to this operator."

Dashing into the street, the red-headed cub reporter raced to the nearest livery stable, hired the fastest horse, and set out at a furious pace for the nearest town, five miles away.

He filed the longest story the *Lynchburg News* had ever received by wire. It was a story that surpassed the account in the rival newspaper. It contained more detail, more color, more accurate information – all the things that go to make up a real story. In writing it, and getting it to his paper, young Glass gained a reputation and a new nickname, for when he returned from Pocahontas, Wyatt Johnson, the Negro porter, was first to greet him with a hearty "How do, Poke!" That nickname stuck to him for years.

At the age of twenty-three, a modest appointment marked his entry into a public career. He became clerk of the Lynchburg City Council. The salary was $300 a year and little was expected of him beyond the traditional routine. He was not content. Things needed doing. The city was growing; and the council must help it grow. With this in mind he negotiated, in 1886, an agreement with the Richmond & Alleghany Railroad for a one-track right-of-way through the city, in return for which the city was paid $5000.

In the meantime he had gone to live in the home of John Archer Caldwell. He had left behind in Petersburg a girl to whom, in a boyish sense, he was engaged. But in the Caldwell home there was a daughter, lovely, dark-eyed, young. A native of Lynchburg, Aurelia McDearman Caldwell had received her diploma at seventeen, and was now teaching in the public schools. The girl in Petersburg was forgotten – and in his twenty-eighth year, two memorable events occurred.

His diligent work as a reporter was rewarded with promotion to the editorship of the newspaper ; and his no less diligent courtship of the charming schoolmistress was rewarded with her consent. His bank account was meagre ($60) but his confidence in the future knew no bounds.

On January 12, 1886, Carter Glass and Aurelia McDearman Caldwell were married, the ceremony taking place in the Westminster Presbyterian Church which then stood on the site of what is now Lynchburg's City Hall.

Spirited editorials on a host of topics now began coming in a stream from the young editor's untiring pen. Letters of commendation and abuse came from his readers. He examined them impartially, and the circulation grew.

One day, two years later, Waddill sat down beside Glass' desk, picked up a copy of *The News*, glanced at it, put it down and told his young editor that he wanted to retire and suggested that Glass buy the newspaper.

Glass shook his head.

"Question of money ?" asked Waddill.

"Yes."

Waddill proposed that Glass borrow the money from friends.

Glass hesitated, and again shook his head, saying, "I couldn't bring myself to go to them."

Waddill smiled. The conversation ended. A few days

later R. H. T. Adams, a relative through his mother's side of the family, approached Glass and offered to lend him the money. Waddill had gone to Adams, explained his desire to retire, and added that he had become so attached to Glass personally that he wanted him to have the paper. The purchase was made. The price was $13,000. Four thousand dollars was paid down. Glass was given four years in which to meet the deferred payments.

On Sunday morning, April 8, 1888, Albert Waddill made the following statement in what was formerly his newspaper:

"I hereby announce to the friends and patrons of the *Lynchburg News,* and to the public, that I have sold the paper with its appurtenances and goodwill to Mr. Carter Glass.

"But in thus absolving myself of all business and pecuniary connection with *The News* it is impossible to divest myself of an earnest solicitude in its future welfare. I am therefore much gratified that the ownership of the paper has fallen to one who, while as yet a very young man, has achieved an enviable name for character, capacity, and indomitable energy. Eight years since his connection with the paper commenced as local editor, his influence, felt from the first as a positive force, increased with experience and ripened powers until, a year ago, the responsible office of editor-in-chief was committed to Mr. Glass. The ability with which he has discharged the exacting duties of this position affords a certain assurance of a continued and increasingly successful career for the paper."

In reply, Glass wrote:

"As will be seen from the above announcement, I have purchased the *Lynchburg News* . . . As the views then expressed have undergone no change [this was in reference to a statement made when he assumed the editorship] it is not necessary for me now to enlarge upon them further than to reaffirm my unswerving attachment to the principles and policies of the Democratic party. . . It will be ever uppermost in the wishes of the present proprietor and editor to promote the prosperity of this city and the contiguous section, and to uphold to the utmost of his ability the honor and welfare of the State."

CHAPTER THREE

The Lion Tamer's Done For

Now that he was launched upon a publishing career Glass found himself confronted with manifold responsibilities.

Several thousand readers relied upon his editorial acumen to interpret for them the social and political significance of trends and events. More extensive reading and deeper study of regional problems were required of him, and he had less time for it. He had to train himself to think accurately and fast, to strip off nonessentials and strike at the core of things in order to salvage time for the duties constantly demanding his attention.

It was excellent training, destined to prove its value in crowded years to come.

Constantly arising and on his desk were questions concerning purchases of supplies, reportorial assignments, policies toward other papers, attitudes of city and state officials, advertising rates, printers, pressmen, even the deportment of delivery boys. He had risen from printer's devil to publisher, and the vigor and tang of his personality made itself felt all the way back along the line, with the human element entering into every phase.

He was grieved one day to learn that Wyatt Johnson, trusted employee of more than forty years, had been stealing white print paper and selling it to a storekeeper. First, he was tempted to overlook this transgression but the more he thought about it, the more he was determined that honesty in the personnel should be maintained. He called the old Negro on the carpet and dismissed him.

In the shop the following morning he found Wyatt on the

job as usual. The young publisher was inwardly pleased, but he strove to make his voice sound stern :

"Look here, you old rascal, I thought I fired you yesterday !"

"You cain't fiah me, Poke," Johnson grinned. "Why, I was aworkin' fo' yo' daddy 'fo' you was born."

Wyatt was right. Glass could not fire him.

Within two years the outstanding notes were paid off – the newspaper was his. One year more and *The Virginian*, rival morning paper, came on the market. It was the second oldest daily paper in Virginia, and had been edited by several of the most notable and brilliant editorial writers in Virginia. The owner of it had acquired and merged with it the old *Lynchburg Republican*, founded by Robert Cawthorne, Glass' uncle ; and, too, it had been owned and edited by Robert Henry Glass. Without delay, Carter Glass purchased it, and merged it with *The News*.

Now there were only two newspapers in Lynchburg, *The News* in the morning, and in the afternoon, *The Advance*, which was edited by Robert Henry Glass, who, a few years before, had returned from Petersburg.

But, if anyone expected the two papers to echo one another in sentiment and opinion, he miscalculated the characters of these two men. They saw alike on major political issues ; but there were other questions. Democrats, as everyone knows, have been known to disagree, and it was the nature of neither of these to ask nor give quarter. Soon Lynchburg citizens were enjoying, hugely, the brisk editorial tilts between father and son.

After one of these friendly but spirited controversies had filled their journalistic arena for several days, Carter Glass landed a telling punch. The ink was scarcely dry on that edition of *The News* when the door of his office burst open.

Storming in, his father slammed a copy of the newspaper down on the littered desk, and pointing a quivering finger at the offensive paragraph, shouted:

"Where did you get that?"

"I keep a scrapbook," calmly replied the younger man. "You wrote that about three years ago."

The Major blinked in anguished recollection, then turned and stamped out of the office, snorting as he went: "I have no respect for a person who keeps a scrapbook."

There was that other day, too, when a crowd gathered in front of the newspaper plant. A few old men who had seen blood on the grass at "Point of Honor" wagged dubious heads, although, for the most part, a holiday humor prevailed. Presently all grew silent and made way for a dour-looking woman who, with fire in her eyes and an old horse pistol sticking out of her muff, strode through the throng, and into the building.

She was the wife of "The Lion Tamer," a strapping fanatical evangelist who had come to Lynchburg to dethrone the Devil for his seats of local eminence. In a sheet called *The Earth*, the fanatic had made the town's outstanding people the targets for his abuse. Discreetly, however, he had skirted any open affront to Glass, but haplessly made a particularly scurrilous attack on the Reverend Dr. George W. Carter. This was the clergyman after whom Carter Glass was named. A blistering editorial lashed forth, one that closed by saying "though the creature might remain in the community, hereafter he would walk the street with the brand of a malicious liar upon his forehead."

The "Lion Tamer's" bluff was called, but his was the valor of which the better part is discretion. From his boarding-house room he had sent forth his wife to battle, and soon she was striding into Glass' office, flourishing the horse pistol and demanding to know if the man sitting quietly behind the desk was "responsible" for the editorial.

"Certainly I'm responsible," came the instant reply. "I wrote it."

This brought forth a stream of invective, punctuated by many threatening motions with the pistol. Glass was amused. "In Virginia, ma'am," he said, "no gentleman can fight a lady. However, if there is any male member of your establishment who will demand satisfaction he will get it without delay."

"My husband, sir, is out of town," she retorted, and opened up her verbal artillery once more.

Glass continued to listen, grew weary of the tirade, and told her: "You've had your say, so please go. If you don't, I'll have to call a policeman."

She went. The crowd dispersed. In *The Earth* the Lion Tamer, devoid now of influence, but not entirely of humor, wrote the postscript:

"The Lion Tamer's done for, and he didn't die game,
He sold all the lions he had intended to tame."

About this time, too, *The Advance*, the only afternoon paper published in the city, was offered for sale. Glass promptly purchased it – and the merry editorial tilts with his father took on even greater zest. But the young publisher's mental horizon was broadening; the boundaries of his interest in public affairs were widening beyond city and county limits to encompass state and nation. Steadily his editorials increased in perspective and depth.

Through twenty harassed years the state had staggered under debt. In 1866 the last legislature of the old regime pledged full payment of principal and accumulated interest for borrowings before and during the war between the states; and against formidable odds ever since conscionable legislators had fought to keep the name of Virginia unblemished by the stain of repudiation. They were smeared for their honesty by such serviceable political epithets as "Bourbons" and "Tories," for the demagogues had swarmed to the arena over the fallen fences of the old constitution, which was supplanted by the Underwood document during the Reconstructionist shambles of 1868.

Carpetbaggers, scalawags and radical Republicans, driven from state control in 1868, still fired from ambush in the shadow of the polls. Illiterate Negroes, comprising one-third of the population, warned that the conservatives conspired to bring them under the bondage of slavery again and, dazzled with promises of Federal patronage, were herded into evangelical rallies. Reluctant to relinquish the Old Dominion from their hold on a solid Republican South, politicians in Washington contributed funds. Out of these were paid the poll tax for the Negro, and he inscribed his "x" as instructed.

The scrupulous white element stood by its standard – the Funding Act of 1871. But out of the crippled financial condition of the people the radicals encouraged confusion and despair, then capitalized with slogans of short-cuts past the heavy fiscal milestones. And out of this came spurious leadership built upon a spoils system holding unblushing tenure in gerrymandered districts. They called themselves Readjusters, and their leader, General William Mahone, styled himself "the champion of the people."

In 1879, drawing power from regimented state officials, county judges, asylum directors and school appointees, Mahone narrowly missed being elected governor. Two years later he smilingly took his seat in the United States Senate.

The debt was readjusted in a way satisfactory to the bondholders, whereupon, as Mahone resorted to other maneuvers for power over the purse strings, the people began to recognize the real danger in "Mahoneism." His bloody-shirted agitation precipitated the Danville race riot on November 3, 1883. A youthful red-haired reporter covered the Democratic convention in Lynchburg that condemned Mahone in 1883 and the November elections that made the condemnation stick. Now, in 1888, his Senate career ended, Mahone returned to his home at Petersburg, Virginia, and to some supervision of the paper he controlled, *The Richmond Whig*. Once more, publicly and dangerously, he was dreaming of the governorship.

Carter Glass went to work with an astringent pen. He, too, could ease his mind of epithets. Mahone was "the wily leader of the mongrel party" . . . "a nervous, active, industrious and even a bold manipulator of political forces," and his domination was "a daring but none the less talkable scheme of political adventures."

The fusillade continued. When Mahone yearned piously for that time "when the ballot shall go unhindered and election returns shall honestly express the free will of the people," it was too much for the young publisher to stomach.

"If this man," he wrote, "is not the very personification of audacity and unmitigated impudence, we give it up. If we do not see here an unabashed miscreant stealing the livery of Heaven to serve the devil in, the like will never be known on this earth.

"The first and only serious disgrace that ever attached to the 'managerial policy' of the Democratic party in Virginia, or any portion of it, is ascribed to the ballot thefts and the thuggism inaugurated by William Mahone as chairman of the Fourth District Congressional Committee. The tissue ballot was never heard of outside of the districts under Mahone's malign influence, and it was he who devised the system of fraud, and it was under his personal supervision that the swindles were practically consummated."

Public-spirited partisans sprang in behind Glass. In the elections of 1889 their nominee, Phil McKinney, for governor was swept into office, along with the greatest majority of conservative Democrats since the War.

Virginia had come through a bitterly fought quarter century with her fiscal integrity still upright. The Readjusters, and their General Mahone, were down for the count.

His forthright castigation of the corrupt Mahone machine won Glass many friends, and enemies, but the circle of his readers continued to grow. Literature, politics, theology, agriculture, foreign affairs — these are but a few of the fields invaded by his editorials.

In 1888, analyzing the Boulanger Affair in Paris, and averring that the objections cooked up by the French against their would-be leader "were as numerous as huckleberries in summer" . . . and on the occasion of the death of the English writer, Matthew Arnold, penning a two-column interpretation of Arnold's essay on American civilization, "In the ideal society of the future 'elevation and beauty are not everything, but they are much, and they are indispensable.' "

Championing England's statesman Gladstone, in his religious controversy with Ingersoll. Returning to a current article by the former in the *North American Review,* writing:

"The variety, breadth and accuracy of the great Englishman's learning is a matter of continued surprise. He moves gracefully with his theological armor upon him, and in this paper has undeniably dealt a strong blow to vulgar infidelity.

"As regards the damaging influence of the Darwinian hypothesis, which is still a problem and not a conquest of science, it is shown that the admission of its truth does not necessarily impugn the Christian evidences, the theory that moral ideas involve no responsibility is torn into tatters, and the climax is capped by palpable instances in which it has been ruthlessly trampled underfoot by its advocate. Thus England's Christian statesman has rebuked America's blustering infidel.

". . . The mighty champion of eloquent sophism and graceful, fascinating blasphemy will answer it as a matter of course. Even John Jasper can reply indefinitely and with imperial scorn to all the arguments leveled against his astronomical dogma 'the sun do move.' "

Again in theological tenor, in the following year writing of a recent archeological find:

"A few years ago all Christendom was interested in the discovery and publication of a little book entitled *The Teachings of the Apostles*. . . Last year, Dr. Carl Schmidt, a German archeologist, announced the most important find yet made. It was a tattered book entitled *The Acts of Paul*. This book was known by the fathers of the early Church. It was usually regarded as apocryphal, but was sometimes accepted as Canonical. A few extracts from this book have been known to the Christian world, but the book itself has been lost for ages. . .

"Our Canonical book, *The Acts of the Apostles,* leaves Paul in Prison at Rome. It appears from the lately recovered book that Paul was acquitted and went to Spain, after which he returned to Rome, was arrested, condemned and executed. This is a confirmation of the commonly accepted belief among Christians."

Although only thirty, the assimilation of data pointing to Bacon as the true Shakespeare was already a deeply intrenched and absorbing literary hobby. In 1888, Ignatius Donnelly was calling the scholastic world's attention to an allegedly pro-Shakespeare cryptogram; and the red-headed editor was battling happily for his firm belief:

"Be there never so great an impostor on the earth as Ignatius Donnelly with his great cryptogram, the argument that Lord Bacon wrote Shakespeare's plays, if it is worth anything at all, is unshaken by that circumstance." And he quotes a noted Shakespearean scholar, Thomas Davidson, as saying that the fact of the cipher's being a failure, if it was, "does not in any way settle the question of the authorship of the plays or touch the Baconian theory."

And so considering his stand against Mahoneism, and his fluent pen, it was not surprising that party leaders in Virginia, seeking an able and active exponent for their views, should select and elect the young publisher to be a delegate to the Democratic National Convention of 1892.

It was a serious and subdued delegate of thirty-four who boarded the train that night for Chicago. Here, he felt, modest as it might be, was a mission of much broader aspect than any newspaper assignment. Though but one of many, nevertheless his was to be a voice in the choosing of a nation's leader. The experience awakened something within. He returned to Lynchburg dimly glimpsing a future in whose frays his voice might be heard.

In the summer of 1894 a number of friends tried to induce him to stand for Mayor of Lynchburg. For a time the idea appealed to him. Finally, he decided against it; and on July 28, expressed his convictions in a letter to Nathaniel C. Manson:

Dear Nat:

As you were the first friend with whom I advised about running for the office of Mayor, so you are the first to whom I shall communicate my decision not to be a candidate. After the fullest deliberation, I have cheerfully concluded that I was not cut out for a politician in any particular, and that if I possess any genius at all, it is that sort which finds its best expression in newspaper work. Until I conceived the notion of standing for Mayor, I never dreamed of what a miserable business running for office has come to be ; and since my determination not to bother with the thing, I have experienced a relief of mind which convinces me that my decision is right, even though I have good reason to believe that I could get the place without great effort. Thanking you for your kind offer to aid me, I am

Your grateful friend,
(signed) Carter Glass.

On May 7, 1896, Carter Glass suffered one of his greatest losses for on that day, his father, Robert Henry Glass, died.

Shortly afterwards came the now historic Democratic convention of 1896 ; and again the young publisher went as a delegate.

CHAPTER FOUR

"The infamy of the document needs no exposition by me."

The chief conflict between the parties, aside from the perennial tariff debates, was the question of currency.

Silver was demonetized in the Republican "crime of 1873," an act condemned by the Democrats as favoring the "idle holders of idle capital" over the debt-paying classes.

Cleveland, in his second term, deserted his radical supporters and went over to the enemy – the gold standard. Business was bad, and the old theory that more money meant more wealth was revived by people whose proposed panacea was "the free and unlimited coinage of silver" in the ratio of 16 to 1. Free-silver politicians massed in a growing chorus.

The old-minded Republicans had met in St. Louis and nominated William McKinley. The East wanted gold, the West wanted silver and the South had made no decision when Carter Glass left Lynchburg for Chicago.

When he arrived the city was in its shirtsleeves, for that July 1st in 1896 was a scorching day. In the Coliseum on South Wabash Avenue, Texas Longhorns, Kansas Jayhawks, Hoosiers, down east Yankees and Southern planters sat beneath their lettered standards and mopped wet faces as they drowsed under the drone of routine monotony voiced from the flag-draped platform. Richard P. Bland, the free-silver Congressman from Missouri, seemed the most likely choice to oppose McKinley.

South Carolina's Senator Tillman spoke bitterly in behalf of silver. Senator Hill, of New York, denied the efficaciousness of the moonbeam metal and held for gold. Vilas, of Wisconsin, and Russell, of Massachusetts, spoke in turn, their voices droning in concert with the flies that streamed in and out through the open windows.

Then, as Russell finished speaking, Glass saw a darkly handsome man in a deacon's coat and carrying a broad black Stetson rise from the Nebraska delegation and walk quickly to the stage.

The previous day William Jennings Bryan had been denied the rights of an accredited delegate by the National Committee, of which Josephus Daniels was a member, but he was unperturbed. He knew men on the credentials committee – and here he was. Now as he began to speak in a ringing baritone the sweltering crowd stirred to attention.

From a high western window a patch of late afternoon sunlight fell upon the platform, casting a golden aura about the man who spoke for silver. No master showman could have staged the thing better – the Byronic collar and black bow tie, the commanding assurance of the well-rehearsed lines, the auspicious moment, the young Lochinvar crusading from the West. The convention was swept from its lethargy on a tide of eloquence that soared into Biblical rhythm to raise into a resounding challenge the needs and aspirations of the common man.

"We have petitioned and our petitions have been disregarded; we have entreated and our entreaties have been scorned. We beg no more, we petition no longer – we now defy!"

The delegates were on their feet, torn between desires to listen and to yell. Glass was one of hundreds suddenly aware that before them stood one of the greatest orators since Patrick Henry.

"Thou shalt not press down upon the brow of labor this crown of thorns.

"Thou shalt not crucify mankind upon a cross of gold!"

Men stood on chairs, flailing one another with their coats and with newspapers, sailing their Sunday hats into the air in ecstatic abandon. Bryan was heaved aloft on the shoulders of the milling crowd, and through the pandemonium there began an impromptu parade of state banners to the Nebraskan's standard. "South Carolina will cast her sixteen votes," Senator Tillman was shouting, "for that matchless knight of the West, the emancipator of white slaves, William Jennings Bryan!"

What would Virginia do? Its delegates were still bitterly divided on the currency question. Carter Glass fought his way to the Virginia standard.

Another young man, dark and slight of stature, had already seized it. Glass grabbed and there was a lusty tug-of-war until they discovered they were both trying to tug in the same direction. In triumph together they bore Virginia's banner, stacked it with all the others now surrounding Nebraska's, and shook hands. His new friend's name was Walter Addison.

Delirium passes, friendship remains. Glass recovered quickly from the intoxication of the Commoner's eloquence, but he and Walter Addison were to remain close friends from that day. Addison was an idealist, high-minded, sincere, and he also was a newspaperman. A little later he came to Lynchburg as editor of Glass' morning paper.

There he proved to be more than an able lieutenant. Until his death he served as a good right arm in the career of the developing statesman.

But years before the convention that nominated Bryan, Glass found one of the great inspirations for his own later public career. It was the reply by Senator Lucius Q. C. Lamarr to resolutions adopted by the Mississippi legislature.

On April 14, 1878, Lamarr, on the floor of the Senate, was addressing the Chair.

"Mr. President," he said, "having already expressed my deliberate opinions at some length upon this very important measure * now under consideration, I shall not trespass upon the attention of the Senate further. I have, however, one other duty to perform ; a very painful one, I admit, but one which is none the less clear. I hold in my hand certain resolutions of the Legislature of Mississippi, which I ask to have read."

Upon the order of the Vice President, the chief clerk read :

Whereas in the judgment of the Legislature of the State of Mississippi and the people whom we represent, the act now pending before the Congress of the United States remonetizing silver will restore public confidence and relieve the existing public distress, and will not violate the faith of the general government, nor impair the national credit ; therefore,

(1) Be it resolved by the Senate of the State of Mississippi (the House of Representatives concurring) That our Senators be instructed, and our Representatives requested, to vote for the act remonetizing silver, and to use their efforts to secure its passage.

(2) Be it further resolved, That the Secretary of State transmit immediately a copy of that resolution to our members of Congress.

As the clerk sat down, Lamarr, still on his feet, continued :

"Between these resolutions and my convictions there is a great gulf. I cannot pass it. Of my love to the State of Mississippi I will not speak ; my life alone can tell it. My gratitude for all the honor her people have done me words cannot express. I am best proving it by doing today what I think their true interests and their character require me to do. During my life in that State it has been my privilege to assist in the education of more than one generation of her youth, to have given the impulse to wave after wave of the young manhood that has passed into the troubled seas of social and political life. Upon them I have always endeavored to impress the belief that truth was better than falsehood, honesty better

* Bland Bill

than policy, courage better than cowardice. Today my lessons confront me. Today I must be true or false, honest or cunning, faithful or unfaithful to my people. Even in this hour of their legislative displeasure and disapprobation I cannot vote as these resolutions direct. I cannot and will not shirk the responsibility which my position imposes. My duty, as I see it, I will do ; and I will vote against this bill.

"When that is done my responsibility is ended. My reasons for my vote shall be given to my people. Then it will be for them to determine if adherence to my honest convictions has disqualified me from representing them ; whether a difference of opinion upon a difficult and complicated subject to which I have given patient, long-continued, conscientious study, to which I have brought entire honesty and singleness of purpose, and upon which I have spent whatever ability God has given me, is now to separate us ; whether this difference is to over-ride that complete union of thought, sympathy, and hope which on all other and, as I believe, more important subjects, binds us together. Before them I must stand or fall ; but be their present decision what it may, I know that the time is not far distant when they will recognize my action as wise and just, and, armed with honest convictions of my duty, I shall calmly await results, believing in the utterances of a great American who never trusted his country in vain, that 'truth is omnipotent, and public justice certain.' "

When news of Lamarr's stand came into his newspaper office, Glass was so impressed that he sent to Washington for a full copy of the oration. He read it, and reread it, translating it into his own work as an editor ; and using it as one of the foundation stones of his own future.

In 1897, he was called upon to make the principal speech in behalf of J. Hoge Tyler for governor. Slight of build, and only five feet, four inches tall, he was no impressive platform figure, but words, slipping sharp and incisive from the left side of his mouth, cut into the emotions of his audience. Tyler was nominated ; Glass himself was launched upon a political career.

But before he was forty, the driving energy he instinctively devoted to his work was too much for the frail physique. His digestion was almost ruined, the result of eating his meals irregularly, and that let down the bars for a host of other bodily ills. Friends feared he was going to die – and he was sure of it. But his most difficult ordeal, when there was so much that needed doing, was to obey his doctor ; for the doctor said "rest."

Some men select their professions, or draw them fortuitously from the grab bag of opportunity ; others have careers thrust upon them. Carter Glass chose journalism ; but the public of Virginia called him into public life. It was inevitable, and in accord with his credo that the office should seek the man. After nearly half a century the office still seeks the man.

Remembering the Hoge Tyler speech, Virginians insisted that Glass represent Lynchburg and Campbell County in the State Senate. Opposed to him was Don Halsey, a nephew of Senator John W. Daniel. Glass took no part in the campaign, he could not even vote because he was ill. His vote was not needed.

His method was first to master the detail of law-making. Quietly he devoted himself to painstaking committee work and the unassuming but arduous study of legislative processes. He was assigned to the Committees for Country and Town Organization, Fish and Game, Examination of Second Auditor's office and – a portent of the future – the Committee of Finance.

Precarious health again put him in bed in the Watkins Glen hospital when, in 1901, he was elected over Randolph Harrison as a delegate from his district to the Constitutional Convention called to write a new organic law for Virginia.

For years the Old Dominion had been struggling to rehabilitate itself from the ravages of the war between the states, but every move was blocked by the old Underwood Constitution, ignoble legacy of carpetbaggers and radicals. The true Virginian's innate genius for self-government was frustrated by its blind documentary restraint. Suffrage laws were obnoxious, almost unbearable ; irresponsible and illiterate voters, both black and white, were prostituted to the baser purposes of machine politics which Glass had often castigated in his newspapers. There were no provisions for regulation of railroads and corporations. These, in cahoots with the local political machines, were running the state. Legislation was crooked as a cow path. Glass convinced his physician his recovery was complete ; and entrained for Richmond without delay.

The Convention opened and immediately struck a snag. Glass and his colleagues were asked to take the oath of allegiance – to the Underwood Constitution. Merely a matter of form, the proponents said, but the man just risen from a sick bed refused to swear allegiance to a document he had been elected to replace.

Technical hairsplitters hemmed and hawed, argued the old constitution was in force until a new one should be adopted, that there would be a taint on the legality of the new if the old were not properly administered. Railroad attorneys – obstructionists scheming for dissension and delay – pulled desperately at the delegates, but political morality was not absent. The majority rallied to Glass' support.

In the midst of the Convention Glass was forced to go home to Lynchburg and to bed.

Meanwhile it was around the suffrage provision, the very heart of the new constitution, that the real battle raged. Glass' fellow townsman, Major John W. Daniel, senior United States Senator serving as Chairman of the Suffrage Committee, was stalemated by two bitterly irreconcilable factions. Majority and minority reports were repeatedly at variance. Daniel hastened to the Lynchburg bedside and appealed to the sick man to come back to the Convention and write a compromise.

Glass came, bearing no olive branch. Though necessarily taking something from each side, the document he wrote was mainly his own ideas of what a suffrage provision should be. Unwittingly this gave the obstructionists the opening they were looking for.

Before the document was more than half written questions were posed : Should the new constitution be submitted to the voters under the elective franchise of the old constitution, should it be submitted to only the new electorate or simply be promulgated by the Convention ?

The old electorate was the regimented grandstand to which the railroad and corporation lawyers were playing ; since the new constitution proposed to disfranchise a goodly portion of them, they knew full well it would be defeated. Glass wanted to submit to the new electorate, knowing it would be approved.

On September 5, 1901, the Lynchburg State Senator addressed the Convention.

"I want to declare that no Constitution can be framed by this Convention which could be so obnoxious to my sense of right that I would desire to wield as a cudgel against its existence the votes of 146,000 misguided Negroes ; and it does not seem to me that, if I am not willing to use these poor people as an instrument to subvert the work of this Convention, which may not suit me, no other member of this body should be willing to appeal to that depraved suffrage to defeat any part of the work of the Convention which may not suit him."

After referring to the preceding three months of indecision and delay, he added: "It is my belief that if this Convention would today declare that it will not entertain the idea of submitting the work of its hands to the sanction of these people whom it shall pronounce unfit to exercise the right of suffrage, the brake will be broken from the wheel and we shall be enabled readily, but deliberately, bravely but conservatively, to proceed to a determination of matters which have been committed to our charge.

"Thinking in this wise, I stand here to defend my position against those who have so fiercely assailed it and to vindicate the truth and right of the declaration that the dominant political party in Virginia did not and never intended to pledge its faith to the enemies of constitutional revision that the temple should be destroyed as soon as it should have been constructed!"

For nearly two hours he continued his argument, going deep into the annals of Virginia history to give validity to his points. When one delegate asserted that the people in his county had changed their notions regarding the Convention's authority to declare the new constitution, Glass said: "I hope that this is another case of Galileo, who, when he was hauled up by the Council and required at the peril of his life to recant his theory that the earth did move, met the exigency of the occasion and recanted; but, impressed by the eternal truth, gritted his teeth and said under his breath, 'Nevertheless, it moves!'"

He recalled to them the years of his youth, spent under the yoke of the carpetbaggers. "The Constitutional Convention which put upon us the present system of popular suffrage consisted of 24 manumitted slaves, 14 native white Virginians, 13

New Yorkers, 1 Pennsylvanian, 1 member from Ohio, 1 from Maine, 1 from Vermont, 1 from Connecticut, 1 from South Carolina, 1 from Maryland, 2 from England, 1 from Scotland, 1 from Nova Scotia, and 1 from Canada. A native of New York, detested by Virginians, was made president of the body. . .

"The doorkeepers were Negroes and the chaplain was from Illinois. All the pages except one were Negroes or sons of Northern men. General Schofield, of Military District No. 1, was the arbiter of questions of supremest importance. Around them camped as guardian angels were the soldiers of the Federal Army, and in their midst as counsellor and friend was that knightly spirit, General Benjamin F. Butler, of Massachusetts!

"The infamy of the document they drafted needs no exposition by me. The calamities, the wasting of expenditures, are a part of the saddest history of this State. The privileges of franchise which it inaugurated have for thirty years held in subjection the commercial, the material and the intellectual progress of a race of men whose forebears fashioned this nation.

"Overwhelmed, worn out by means of defense, were we not at the mercy of a despot worse than any tyrant king? Did Underwood and Hunnicutt, Kelsoe and Hine, and all the others of their type put this right of suffrage upon us by our willing consent? Did they not thrust it upon us in passion and in bitterness and verily at the point of the bayonet? Did they not, six years after the ratification of the Constitution, resist by the force of Federal arms the inevitable attempt of the white Virginians of the Black Belt to nullify its awful consequences?"

He made no protestations, he said, as to his feeling for the Virginia Negro, avowing that in matters most nearly related to his material and civil welfare the white race of the Commonwealth was his very best friend.

"I find little fault and pass no censure upon him for his misguided course in the politics of the State. His conduct in this regard is as much referable to those who misguided him as it is an evidence of his own incapacity to exercise the right of franchise. But I confess my amazement that it should have been proclaimed upon this floor the other day that the white people of Virginia are the beneficiaries of Negro toleration, and that but for this characteristic of the Negro, exercised in our behalf at the period of reconstruction, we would not be permitted today to sit in this hall for the purpose of passing upon his right of suffrage.

"There were twenty-four Negroes in the Underwood Convention, and when Hine moved that, in addition to those who had already been disfranchised, all persons who had held any position in the army ranking above first lieutenant should be excluded from the right of voting, twenty-two of the twenty-four Negroes joined with ten Northern men in voting for the proposition.

"When again the same Mr. Hine proposed to disfranchise all original secessionists, the same twenty-two Negroes voted for that infamous proposition. When the disfranchising clause proposed separately was submitted to a vote of the people, 84,410 Negro votes were cast for it. When the ironclad oath was, by direction of General Grant, submitted separately to the people, 83,458 Negro votes were cast for it."

Although a majority of his colleagues did not concur in his recommendation of submitting to the white electorate, he had annihilated the scheme of the obstructionist bloc. Ultimately the Convention took the bit in its own teeth and proclaimed the constitution outright without submitting it to anybody. It is still in effect.

Some weeks later Major Daniel, speaking before the Virginia Bar Association at Hot Springs, omitted to accord Glass the credit his friends considered his due. Some of them complained, whereupon the Major wrote promptly to Glass reiterating an opinion of earlier date, that "I consider you the most important man to Virginia in the State Constitutional Convention," and stating "but for Glass there would perhaps have been no new Constitution, nor any acceptable and timeworthy suffrage reform."

For eight years Glass was a member of the Board of Visitors of the University of Virginia, appointed first by Governor Tyler and continued by his successor in the gubernatorial chair. He had not served long on this board before he reached the conclusion that the institution could not progress under the faculty management which had prevailed since the founding of the university by Thomas Jefferson. This conviction was shared by other members who, with him, had witnessed demonstrations of jealousy and dissension among the faculty.

Therefore it was proposed to change the then existing management by appointing a President of the University. It was found that the best legal construction of the Virginia Code affirmed that it made no provision for such an officer. Uninfluenced, however, by talk about "putting an autocrat over the faculty" and "renouncing Mr. Jefferson's plan of government," the board devised a scheme for selecting a member of the faculty with merely nominal professorial functions and large executive powers, nearly akin to those of a presidency. The provision was carefully worded ; this professor was supposed to lecture on "political philosophy," a subject said to have been given sparse attention theretofore. Further, he was to be designated as Chairman of the Faculty.

This device was intended to flank the apparent prohibition of the state statute ; and the Board informally, without dissent, authorized a committee of three members – Miles, Hunton and Harmon – to tender the appointment to Woodrow Wilson who, born at Staunton, Virginia, and an alumnus of the University, was then a professor at Princeton.

Insistent correspondence on the subject followed. It was reported that Wilson indicated a willingness to accept, but was deterred on learning the attitude of the faculty against a presidency. Several years later, however, Wilson explicitly denied ever having done more than to give the offer "serious consideration." He was aware of the hostility of the faculty, but had every reason to know that its members were in no degree opposed to him personally. Moreover, the protests against his leaving Princeton could not be resisted.

This failure so disappointed Glass that he resigned from the Board ; but certain prominent citizens, including members of the Board and faculty, induced Governor Tyler to persuade him to continue.

The incident is recalled as important chiefly because it very likely changed subsequent American history. Had Wilson gone to the University of Virginia he would never have been elected Governor of New Jersey, nor thereafter President of the United States. With fervent expression of satisfaction Glass has frequently mentioned the failure of this project as truly providential.

The Board of Visitors was not shaken in its determination to change the managerial policy of the University. Three years later it was again resolved to attempt the "political economy" project. Colonel George W. Miles, a Board member, was prominently considered for the post, but violent antagonism caused him to decline to permit the use of his name in connection with the place.

A little later an effort was made to embody in the new Virginia Constitution of 1901–2 a prohibition of a presidency for the school. Glass, ranking member after the Chairman of the Convention Committee of Education, was joined by his colleagues in resistance. An appeal to the General Assembly to alter the apparent prohibition in the State Code, approved by the faculty itself and warmly urged by the press, was favored and an amendment enacted affirmatively requiring the Board to appoint such an executive head.

Immediately there were various eager candidates for the position, but before there could ensue an unseemly scramble for the place, the Board, again informally, appointed a committee composed of Carter Glass, Eppa Hunton and G. W. Miles to ascertain if Dr. J. J. McBryde, then President of the Virginia Polytechnic Institute, would accept the presidency of the University. Dr. McBryde found it impossible to accept the honor.

Under authority of the amended statute, the Board then elected Dr. Edwin A. Alderman the first President of the University of Virginia. Previously he was President of Tulane University. Glass, who became an intimate friend of Dr. Alderman, is now the last surviving member of the Board of Visitors that elected him.

CHAPTER FIVE

"How many newspapers has this man Glass?"

At the turn of the century the great telephone monopoly ruled the communications of the nation. Fat millions were spent on hired counsel and outright bribery, purchasing the shrewd talents of men who knew just what legislative ropes to pull. And these expenditures were modest compared with the many more millions that were being taken from the pockets of the public in rates and in stock schemes.

Because there were many smiling gentlemen with no scruples about serving two masters, this monopoly – along with the railroads and public-service corporations of all sorts – was plying its trade boldly and unabashed to gain control of state legislatures, and their committees. To the citizens of Virginia the efforts of the Virginia Telephone Company to obtain a state charter seemed a praiseworthy local enterprise; but it was the disguised subsidiary of the huge corporation – and the proposed charter reeked with concessions and special privilege.

Here again, high-lighting a brief career in the Virginia state senate, we find a redhead grabbing up a bat and wading single-handed into a corrupt gang from "over the river."

One summer morning Glass was on the train between Lynchburg and Washington, on his way again to the hospital at Watkins Glen. Senator Daniel was seated directly in front of him, reading the morning *Richmond Times-Dispatch.* Dozing in his seat, Glass was aroused by an excited voice:

"Look here, Carter," Daniel exclaimed, "the Senate has passed the telephone bill!"

"What?" asked Glass, and grabbed the newspaper Daniel was holding out to him.

Visions of Watkins Glen fled from his brain like fog before a hurricane. Completely forgetting self, he got off the train at Washington, and within the hour he was on his way back to Richmond.

There he found a most astonishing situation. Only two of the eleven committee members charged with consideration of the bill had any knowledge of any committee action on it, and these two were in the employ of the telephone company!

Glass sought out the lieutenant-governor, and other officials of the Senate. None could remember the bill ever coming up. It did not take long for him to get to the bottom of things. Apparently a journal clerk had "co-operated" with the two members of the Senate, and a powerful lobby outside the Senate. So far as the state senate was concerned, the bill was on the statute books.

The fight was on!

Going directly to Governor Tyler, Glass found no help. Governor Tyler was in a position which, in those days, was considered embarrassing – his own son was in the employ of the telephone people. Glass turned to his friends in the Senate and House, only to find them wavering under the pressure of all the county bosses and local bosses who could be hauled into Richmond. Undeterred, he took the floor in the Senate.

Under the old capitol dome, in the great chamber beneath the aging chandeliers, men elected to obtain justice for their constituents tried their marksmanship on the spittoons, gazed abstractedly at one another, licked and examined their cheroots with singular intentness, or stared at the blackened ceiling – anything to avoid the brown eyes of the man who stood before them, naming names, arguing, reasoning, pleading, threatening.

He had appeared before the House Committee and explained how the bill had been eased through the Senate. He had rallied the Senate membership and had it pass on his resolution calling for the return of the bill to the Senate. Now he was tearing the mask from the lobby, ripping its pretense to shreds. With corrosive words and logic that was caustic in its bite he explained how the bill left the citizens of Virginia at the mercy of an uncontrolled monopoly.

Up in the gallery, in the shadow of a massive pillar, the chief lobbyist turned and asked his first lieutenant :

"How many newspapers has this man Glass ?"

"Two."

"Only two !" he almost yelled. "I thought he had a hundred ! Every man I talk to says, 'I'm afraid of what Glass will say in his papers.' "

When the roll call came Glass won. Later, when a decent charter bill was arrived at in committee, the telephone company refused it in high disgust. It gained nothing by its refusal, and later came to accept, gratefully.

Years afterward, in discussing that fight, Glass recalled :

"That was the goldarnedest row I think I was ever in. They had the most unconscionable lobby ever gathered together in Richmond. They brought up the judges, the clerks, the treasurers and anybody else they could corral to work on the delegates. You couldn't tell which way a man was going to jump, nor how long he would stay put. There was a member from Halifax, and I will never forget him, nor the courage he displayed.

"Some people afterward affected to wonder why I should be so fond of such a thoroughgoing politician as Billy Barksdale. But, I was ; and largely because he gave me his word he would vote against the charter bill, and kept it, in the teeth of the fact that his own father-in-law, the county judge, with whom he made his home, and every official and friend of his of any importance in Halifax County, was in Richmond to get him to vote for the bill.

"And," Glass continued, "Barksdale was always my friend, although at one time, after I had been in Congress several terms, he toyed with the idea of running against me. A mutual friend interposed and told him I was a sick man, and he ought not to run against me because it might kill me. 'The devil you say,' said Barksdale, 'he'll be in Congress long after you and I are both dead and buried and in hell.'" Here Glass added, "Poor fellows. I am still in Congress and they are both dead and buried but, I sincerely trust, not in hell."

As early as 1899, long before the enactment of the 17th Amendment, Glass believed implicitly in the immunity of a United States Senator from state instruction. The influence of Senator Lamarr, of Mississippi, was present in this belief. In an editorial more pertinent to his own future than he could have dreamed, he wrote :

"It has long been a disputed question whether State legislatures have the right to instruct their United States Senators. The usual form of legislative resolution is, 'we instruct our Senators and request our Representatives.' Sometimes the Senator obeys the instructions and votes contrary to his own judgment. Sometimes the Senator evades compliance by tendering his resignation. Sometimes the Senator defies the legislature and votes according to the dictates of his own judgment.

"In that case, the legislature can do nothing but ask for his resignation. If the Senator does not choose to resign, the legislature has no power to enforce the demand. The legislature can make a Senator but it cannot unmake one. This fact seems to indicate that after a Senator is once elected he has the right to follow his own judgment and advocate any measures that he thinks will promote the welfare of the country and oppose what he believes is a bad policy.

"If the legislature has the right to demand the resignation of a Senator, no man could be sure of holding his seat for the full term of six years. He might be elected by a Republican legislature. The next legislature might be Democratic and demand his resignation for the reason that he no longer represented the political views of the body which elects Senators. The framers of the Constitution never intended to clothe the legislature with the power to unmake Senators.

"Therefore, the conclusion is justified that a United States Senator has the right to refuse obedience to instructions and act independently of the legislature."

In embyro, a statesman was taking his characteristic stand.

One December day in 1902 Carter Glass boarded a train at the Lynchburg station and waved from a window to the friends on the platform who had come to see him off.

It was by no means the first time he had traveled this route, but this time he was not bound to Watkins Glen, although his doctor thought it would be better if he were. This was a trip he would remember all his life. The shops, sheds and the trim green and white homes of his native city slid rearward past his window, giving way to the rolling open country . . . he was on his way to represent this land he loved, its planters, merchants, printers, blacksmiths and barbers – his neighbors and his friends – in the national Congress.

A new gate was swinging open. In the years that stretched ahead stood milestones that were to be quietly raised into monuments. In the beginning four candidates had been arrayed against him, one withdrew and Glass received more votes than the remaining candidates combined ; and was elected overwhelmingly over his Republican competitor.

Mentally he smiled as he recalled his moment of consternation, during one of his first campaign speeches, at Halifax, when an old gentleman with a long beard rose suddenly in the audience and pointing a shaking finger, quavered : "Young man, I indict you for first-degree murder !"

CARTER GLASS
About the time he first went to Washington

There was a great hubbub and confusion, and cries of "Throw him out!" But Glass had held up his hand for silence. "This is a Democratic gathering," he said. "Let him have his say." A grin appeared on his lips as he thought of his own relief, and the relief on the faces of his friends, as the old man concluded his statement:

"You have just killed your rival candidate!"

But his own natural restraint checked any vaulting ambitions to set the Capital afire with a resounding entry into national politics. For the Democratic Party the time was decidedly out of joint. They were much in the minority, and divided among themselves between the mirages of Bryanism and the conservatism of their Hills and Parkers. Ten years were to elapse before a Princeton professor was to lead them to political dominance. At the moment Theodore Roosevelt, riding high, wide and handsome from San Juan Hill, was swaggering his way through both parties – and history – with Congress clinging to his coattails.

The railroad journey proved exhausting. At his Washington hotel he retired early but slept badly.

When Glass was a Lynchburg reporter one of the most famous of Virginia lawyers, John S. Wise, was running for a Congressman-at-large. Repeatedly he had tried to induce his opponent to join him in platform debate, without success. Glass covered a rally one evening which Wise opened by reading what purported to be a subpoena he had sent his adversary. While he was intoning the legalistic phrases a donkey in a neighboring lot emitted a stentorian bray. Wise raised his eyebrows.

"Can that be he now?" he asked.

Now that Glass had been elected to Congress it was the same Wise who was employed by the political group representing the colored voters to go to Washington and challenge his right to a seat in the House of Representatives. Wise based his arguments on the suffrage provision Glass had written into the Virginia Constitution, disfranchising illiterates, both black and white, and requiring a poll tax to be paid six months prior to an election in order to prohibit the purchase of votes.

When the House refused to grant his petition, Wise went to see the President. Theodore Roosevelt refused to intervene. The Wise wit again came to the fore.

"Mr. President," he said, "I was out West recently, and I heard your name and Washington's on everyone's lips."

As Roosevelt's face began to light up with pleasure, Wise concluded : "I mean, of course, Booker T. Washington." He was referring to the fact that the eminent Negro, it was said, had recently been entertained in The White House.

Whatever remaining chance Wise might have had of influencing Roosevelt into listening further to protests against seating Glass ended right there. The following day the publisher took his seat in the second session of the 57th Congress.

Most newly elected Congressmen look forward, eagerly, to the customary opportunity to rise before their colleagues and make a "maiden speech." Glass resisted this time-honored temptation. Already he had a definite conception and well considered philosophy of the duties of his office ; in them he saw little need to gravitate toward the spotlight. He ridiculed "the perennial and ubiquitous demagogy of a certain class of politicians," smiled at "their amusing rhetorical exhibitions in behalf of the people," and sensed the danger of "losing direction in an oral fog." He made no speech until his third term, when he had been in the House of Representatives five years and twenty-four days ; then he spoke briefly in memory of John F. Rixey, his friend and Representative from the Eighth Virginia District :

". . . Sprung from a good ancestry and reared in an atmosphere of refinement, nobody better understood, and no life has more surely conformed to, that philosophy which teaches that well-being of the soul depends only on what we are and that nobleness of character is nothing else but the love of good and the scorn of evil. . ."

Rarely, too, does a first-term Representative receive a choice committee assignment. In this respect Glass was singularly fortunate. But not immediately. He would have much preferred Foreign Affairs, but he found himself a member of the Committee on Public Lands. Quietly and painstakingly he began to study Public Lands, but all the time keeping his interest in the history of the world. His look-ahead made him realize that the United States was a continually growing world power . . . and there was his increasing friendship with John Sharpe Williams, the minority leader of the House.

He cast his vote as a Congressman for Williams as Speaker. Vain hope. When the ballots were counted Williams had 167 ; Joseph G. Cannon, of Illinois, had 198.

But under Williams' shrewd and formidable eyebrows was an uncanny nose for ability and brains. Detecting material beyond the run of the mine, he kept watching Glass and finally decided to give him his chance.

Early in March, 1904, he sought out the Virginian to inquire :

"Are you satisfied with that committee you're on ?"

"Well, I – I . . ."

"What committee do you want ?" interrupted Williams.

"Foreign Affairs," promptly answered the young Congressman.

"H'm," mused Williams, "I had something else in my mind, but I'll see what I can do."

A day or so later he again saw Glass. "I can't wangle that appointment for you, Carter," he said, and went on to explain that a fellow Mississippian wanted the post. "But how would it be if I got you a place on Banking and Currency? That's what I was thinking about, in the first place."

"I don't know anything about it," hesitated Glass, and added: "but I guess I can learn."

"If you go at it the same way you've gone at Public Lands there won't be any doubt about it," complimented Williams. "Besides, with all this agitation about money, I think it a better appointment than Foreign Affairs. Just watch your knitting, Carter, and you'll have a great opportunity to distinguish yourself."

In those days prior to 1911, the Speaker of the House had all appointive powers in committees. To "Uncle Joe" Cannon went Williams.

Cannon's eyebrows went up. "That's a pretty important committee for a young member," he remarked; and after a pause, asked: "What does he know about banking and currency?"

"Says he doesn't know anything," answered Williams. "But down there in the Virginia Senate he was a member of the Committee on Finance. I think he knows more about it than he's letting on, and just pulling my leg when he says he knows nothing about it."

"Well, I don't know," demurred Cannon. "It ain't customary to name freshmen Congressmen on such important . . ."

"I know," interrupted Williams. "But he's a good man; and I want him."

"All right, if you say so, John," acquiesced Cannon. And so, on April 1, 1904, the Speaker of the House announced that Representative Carter Glass, of Virginia, had resigned from the Committee on Public Lands, and was placed on the Committee on Banking and Currency.

Glass had told Williams the truth. He did not know a great deal about the subject. He also told Williams the truth when he told him he "guessed he could learn."

It was during this time that Glass had one of his first experiences with automobiles. He was speaking in Rocky Mount and had been detained longer than he anticipated. There was an engagement in Lynchburg that evening – and it was imperative that he keep it.

There was no train from Rocky Mount, but there was one leaving from Roanoke, thirty miles away – and it was due to leave in less than two hours. Searching the town for transportation, he finally found it in the form of a White Steamer owned by the blacksmith. Hurrying into the shop, he informed the proprietor:

"I've got to get to Roanoke."

"Yup."

"Got less than two hours to do it in – you can earn yourself twenty dollars if you'll crank up that machine you've got standing outside, and catch that train for me."

Without a word, the blacksmith divested himself of his apron, and began pouring water into the coils of his "horseless carriage." Pretty soon he had steam up, and motioned for Glass to throw his bags into the rear seat, and get in with them.

Then began a wild, careening ride, through winding roads with enormous clouds of dust settling on the fields and barns and houses behind them – splashing and skidding through shallow creeks, twisting around tortuous turns, missing trees by the side of the road but not missing boulders in it until, finally, they rounded one curve to narrowly miss plunging off and into a deep ravine.

Gasping for breath, Glass leaned forward and shouted in the blacksmith's ear:

"Take your time, mister, it isn't going to do you any good to make that train and find me dead in the back seat."

With never a turn of his head, the blacksmith broke his silence, to bellow :

"Contract didn't say anything about alive."

They made the train. Glass was so weak from exhaustion that the blacksmith had to carry his bags for him.

The detailed days of committee work and long evenings of study lengthened into years. The elections of 1904 came and went, with great hue and cry for the "full dinner pail," and the political career of Carter Glass continued exceptionally free from opposition at the polls.

The celebrated Virginia criminal lawyer, Jack Lee, at one time announced himself for Congress in opposition. Glass had refused to support a friend of Lee's for the local superintendency of county schools, thereby causing a rift in their friendly relations. A mutual friend went to Glass and urged him to withdraw.

"You know, Carter," he said, "you told me, some time ago, that you had made up your mind not to run again."

"Yes, I said that," returned Glass. "I am tired of public life."

"And I told Jack Lee. That is why he has announced himself."

"You forget I told you, in confidence, that I did not expect to run, but I did not authorize you to go and tell Jack Lee." After a pause Glass went on, "If Jack Lee will say the reason he announced himself is because of what I confided in you, I will promptly withdraw."

Two weeks passed before there was any word from Lee. Then suddenly he telephoned.

"Carter," he said, "I've canvassed the district thoroughly. Should I spend ten thousand dollars – and I can't afford to spend it — I think I might be able to lick you. Might be, I said — and I would like to lick you because of the stubborn stand you've taken about that superintendent of schools business. I want you to know one thing else, too — I did not announce myself because of anything our mutual friend told me, so I'm going to withdraw."

The reason Glass had considered withdrawing was the same reason that had determined him not to stand for mayor of Lynchburg a number of years previously. He felt himself better equipped to spend his life in newspaper work. He begrudged the time spent away from his papers, and separated from his family in which there were now four children, Powell, Carter Jr., Augusta and Mary Archer.

He despised the vote-swapping methods prevalent in Congress, took little or no part in Washington social life, and found his amusement in occasional attendance at boxing bouts or baseball games. His favorite team then, as later, was the Philadelphia Athletics, and his favorite manager, Connie Mack. In the House of Representatives he was scarcely known, and the few who did know him called him "the taciturn gentleman from Virginia," and it was not until March 4, 1907, that "the taciturn gentleman," provoked beyond his patience, projected himself and his opinions into legislative debate.

The question concerned the tariff on paper and wood pulp. Mr. Hitchcock was making a vigorous assault on the high prices superinduced by the rates in the Dingley law. Mr. Payne, Republican leader, was defending them. He pointed to the rise in wages resulting from the tariff, and maintained that the price of paper had not advanced in proportion. As a matter of his own knowledge, he stated, some publishers had paid less than $2 a hundred pounds for their paper in the past year. Here was something the member from Lynchburg knew something about.

"May I suggest to my colleague, before he gets further away from the question of wages," he said, "that the amount of wages paid out by all the newspapers of the United States is forty times as much as wages paid out by the paper manufacturers of the United States?"

As to the other matter involved:

"May I further suggest to my colleague, in response to the chairman of the Committee on Ways and Means, the gentleman from New York, that he would find it very difficult to produce testimony here that any of the smaller newspapers of this country during the year 1907 obtained their paper at less than $2? I know that I am paying $2.35 and am threatened with an exaction of $2.75 for my supply next year."

CHAPTER SIX

Campaigning for an office he could not win.

In January 1911, two or three Lynchburg friends dropped into the Raleigh Hotel to see Glass. John W. Daniel, also of Lynchburg, and senior Senator from Virginia, was dead. Without delay, Governor William Hodges Mann had appointed his predecessor in office, Ex-Governor and Ex-Congressman Claude A. Swanson to fill the temporary vacancy. Glass' visitors, while not politicians, were citizens who were concerned with Virginia politics. They were in Washington to make an appeal. They wanted Glass, and not Swanson, to represent them in the Senate of the United States.

The Congressman listened, and when they concluded their plea, said to them:

"You know, of course, you are asking me to start a fight I can't win."

"No, we don't know that. We think you can."

"You think that because you don't know anything about politics," returned Glass, bluntly. "However, I feel that it is important for the future of the Democratic Party in Virginia to expose the reprehensible excesses of a political machine that is as unfair as any organization ever put together. I agree somebody has got to smash it.

"But, I do not want to deceive you; and you must not deceive yourselves. The candidate who bucks this machine can't win. Through twenty years, and more, this organization has been intrenching itself so deep that dynamite won't blast it out, but" – and Glass paused – "perhaps if we can flush it into the open we can punch a few holes in it."

"Then you will make the run?" eagerly inquired his visitors.

"I have already reached that decision. After Senator Daniel's death I proffered my support to Harry St. George Tucker, if he desired it. I preferred to fight for him unhampered by any personal interest. That situation has changed. Against personal inclination and at the sacrifice of individual ease and peace, I have determined to make this race."

"We're with you, Carter," they chorused.

"Thank you, but there is more to the proposition than I have told you. I am not in this thing alone. There is another Congressman from Virginia who is independent of this machine. He is William A. Jones, of the First District. Jones and I have been talking things over. As the situation stands, our two Senators will both have to ask for the voters' favor this year. Jones thinks there is a chance for him to win, but I know there isn't for me. But Jones has insisted that I abandon my advocacy of Tucker, and run myself. So, Jones is going to run against Martin, and I am going to run against Swanson. Perhaps, together, we can wake up the Virginia electorate so that by the time elections come again a political machine will be minus some of its cylinders. However, keep this information to yourselves – the announcements will be made in due course, and we want to make them ourselves."

On January 23, Glass and Jones made their announcements. The machine countered by issuing a statement in which it was implied that Glass was "a Republican," because of the position he had taken on the Payne-Aldrich tariff measure.

Eastern manufacturers, who dominated the Ways and Means Committee, wanted to put lumber, largely a Southern and Western product, on the free list. Glass, with four other Virginia Congressmen, voted against the proposition and were roundly criticized as "incidental protectionists." Even at the time, Glass did not sit supinely under the accusation. In fact, he did not even wait until he got to the House floor.

From his home in Lynchburg, on April 22, 1909, he had issued a blistering retort. Declaring himself "a tariff for revenue Democrat," but recognizing the apparent fact that "the country at the last election overwhelmingly rejected the Democratic method of dealing with the tariff question, and charged the Republican party in Congress with the duty of revision on distinctly protection lines," he struck out at his critics:

"Anybody who pleases to think that, under the circumstances, it was the duty of a Southern Democrat to sit in the House, and, merely to exploit a theory he was powerless to make effective, see the industries of his own State and section sacrificed to the rapacity and utter selfishness of another section, is quite welcome to that opinion. I am not that much of a doctrinaire, or that sort of a dreamer."

In answering the charge, Glass referred to this statement of two years previously, and added: "The late Senator John W. Daniel thought so much of my point of view that he had it inserted in the Congressional Record." In addition, he pointed out:

"Senator Thomas Staples Martin voted as I did on this Payne-Aldrich Bill," then went on to ask: "Does the 'Governor's temporary appointee' condemn my vote on the lumber schedule of the Payne-Aldrich Bill?"

Swanson remained silent. An influential newspaper printed an "exposé" of Glass' record in the House. To this Glass sent an answer, and when the newspaper refused him its columns, he tried to buy advertising space in which to publish his reply. It refused this, too. That gave him a second opportunity. He blazoned the facts in his own newspapers, drawing from the editor of the other newspaper a letter of personal apology and an explanation – "with ownership of the paper resting where it is, I can do nothing."

But these two skirmishes were but the prelude for the attack that was to come. All sorts of manufactured stories were circulated over Virginia. Glass was threatened with "an opposition newspaper in Lynchburg," and when he defied the machine to do it, pressure was brought to bear on his advertisers to cancel their contracts; and on his readers to cancel their subscriptions. A good bit of advertising was canceled; and some circulation was lost. The opposition invaded his working organization, trying to coax reporters and printers to other Virginia cities with promises of "better pay." In this it was not successful.

Openly, it was declared: "Failing to wait and become the organization candidate for Governor, Glass is to be punished for his presumption in avowing himself a candidate for the Senate," and to that, the Congressman retorted: "In the first place, no one can, or could, convince me that I should be an 'organization' candidate for governor – I never want to be, and I never would be, that kind of a governor – and, in the second place, this war against me has risen to the dignity of disrepute, if it has not sunk to the level of contempt."

To efforts at building backfires in his own Congressional district, he replied:

"In my district, alone of all the districts in the United States, I am to be, and I am being, harassed by avowed candidates for Congress two years before my present term expires – if the people of my district want any one of them more than they want me, let them have him. I shall pay no attention to such puerile efforts."

Up and down the state went Glass; and up and down the state went Jones, each campaigning for an office neither could win; and Glass knowing it. Into Rockbridge, Bedford, Campbell, Newport News, Williamsburg, Charlottesville, Fredericksburg, Norfolk and every other Virginia town and community they went to leave behind a battered, if not broken, political organization.

And, finally, into Richmond, the machine stronghold and the state capital, went Glass.

"You had better stay away from that hall tonight," counseled a friend.

"Why?"

"Because it is going to be 'packed' by your enemies and, likely as not, some rocks will be thrown your way."

Glass grinned in delight. "Looks like we've got our adversaries scared."

"Looks like you're the one that had better be scared," growled his friend.

"You'll be there, won't you?" asked Glass.

"Sure, and so will other friends of yours; but that ain't so many, considering. . ."

"Oh, I wasn't thinking about that – I was just thinking you oughtn't to miss the fun. I'm going to throw some rocks on my own account."

Barring the whoops of his friends it was a sullen and a silent audience that crowded the hall. Wasting little time with amenities, the Congressman plunged in:

"I cannot say that I am here tonight in response to any widespread demand by the people of Virginia that I be a candidate to succeed the late Major Daniel in the United States Senate. No, far from that. I regret to believe that the people of Virginia at this time entertain too little concern about that and kindred questions of a political nature. Hence it may be more accurately said that I am here because of a definite and personal conviction that 'there is something rotten in the State of Denmark.'"

Informing his audience it was his belief that "the high office of Senator in the Congress of the United States belongs to the people of Virginia, and not to a cabal of public men," Glass stated it as his view that those who aspire to such position should make their appeal to the electorate, and not to politicians. He went on to point out that it had never entered his mind to be a candidate for the Senate.

"But," he added, "when it appeared that the office had been negotiated for six months before Major Daniel was even taken ill – dickered for, not even as a reward of party service, but as an incentive to pernicious factional activity – and that the pursuit of it scarcely waited upon the stroke of paralysis that months afterwards caused Daniel's death ; that so feverishly and eager was the purpose to set in motion the enginery of factional control that it was even sought to hold in session the General Assembly to await the ebbing tide of the Lame Lion's life, I resolved that the people of Virginia should be given an opportunity to repudiate or confirm that species of politics.

". . . There is no machine in Virginia ! If so, then why this outcry – and why may I not aspire to a seat in the United States Senate which has not yet been filled by the people to whom it belongs ? What is the so vastly superior title of the governor's temporary appointee as to render my candidacy presumptuous ? I am a Democrat, and always have been . . . as far as I know, nobody, in or out of Congress, has ever suspected me of serving any interest but that of the American people. Nobody has ever sought, by intimation or open charge, to identify me with any irregularity of any description whatsoever. Mine is not a brilliant record, but it is an honest one. It is presented with the utmost diffidence, yet with a confidence that is willing to have it contrasted with the record of the governor's temporary appointee. . .

"For twenty years there has been no issue as to men or measures raised in the politics of Virginia upon which I have not taken a stand that no man could misapprehend. In State matters I stand first and foremost for clean politics. I stand for honest elections, whether the result may mean success for one faction or another, or of one party or the other. It was for this reason I fought for a Constitutional Convention – fought for it in the General Assembly, fought for it on the hustings, fought for it in party convention. It was upon this principle that in the convention I advocated the bipartisan system of election boards and election officers. I think any man who cheats at elections should be mercilessly pursued and landed in the State's prison, and I think any set of men who practice, connive at, or countenance fraud, should be indignantly driven from power.

". . . More than ten years ago I resigned from the State Democratic Executive Committee because it would not repudiate the corrupt fusion in Norfolk county and the frauds which prevailed in consequence thereof, and I went in person to Norfolk and denounced the thieves who were prostituting the elections and parceling out the spoils. From that day to this I have maintained my attitude of hostility to that sort of practice and to that sort of knaves. I do not want their votes. I would feel humiliated to receive them. . .

"Perhaps you will expect me to charge that machine politics and machine politicians are entirely responsible for this state of affairs. I shall do nothing of the kind. They are the moving causes, and the actual instruments of this defiance of the popular will; but the responsibility for it rests largely upon the people in Virginia who detest dishonesty, but so lightly regard their own sovereign rights that they tamely submit to such shameless misgovernment. My appeal is not to the men who sanction or perpetuate such irregularities; not to the politicians who profit by them; not to the official combination that thrives by the cohesive power of pecuniary reward;

but my appeal is to the patriotic masses of Virginians who have an inherited right to value their liberties and a traditional incentive to assert them.

"I do not exculpate the party organization from its responsibilities for prevailing conditions. It has possessed the power to correct these evils, and has not only failed, but has refused to do it; and yet, nearly ten years after the Constitution of Virginia was proclaimed imposing upon the Legislature and executive a solemn obligation to safeguard elections, the people are left defenseless against the intrigues and ill practices of election knaves. . . These election officers at the behest and in the behalf of any interested persons, can literally fill their books with the very class of voters the Constitutional Convention intended to exclude and there is no statutory method of redress. What is the explanation of this condition? Why has there been no legislation? Isn't it because there are men who want to pay other men's poll taxes for corrupt purposes, and isn't it because there are men who want to put on the registration books other men for corrupt purposes? If it isn't this, then it has been culpable ignorance and wanton indifference to the public welfare.

"If there has been or is office brokerage in Virginia, I am against it. And what I mean by office brokerage is that system of politics which gives the public places to men, not upon merit, nor even upon their party service, but purely because of their servility to one branch of the Democratic party. I shall not seriously argue whether or not such a combination exists in Virginia. The fact that it dispenses 90 per cent of the official patronage to its devotees is a mathematical certainty of its existence.

"I believe in trusting the people as the real source of power. I believe it is right and expedient that they shall elect directly most of their important public servants. I would favor the election of United States Senators by direct vote of the people. Frankly I once had doubts, fearing that the Corporations might intervene and secure men partial to their own interests ; but experience and observation have made me penitent and cheerfully willing to take the risk with the people. I would make the law so stringent that any railroad or public corporation would rue the day that it devoted the money of its stockholders to political purposes, and I would severely restrict their pernicious activity in the politics of the State and nation."

Having dealt with the corruption and the corruptors of the Virginia machine, Glass then turned his verbal guns squarely on his rival candidate. Excepting for the yells of encouragement from his friends, his audience had listened in hostile silence.

"It has been suggested and predicted that I would tonight assail the record of my competitor as a member of Congress and as Governor of Virginia. I regard his public record as properly subject to public criticism, and I shall not, during this senatorial campaign, hesitate to identify him with the political machine whose excesses and delinquencies I have described, nor to hold him to strict accountability for anything he has done which he should not have done and for everything he has left undone which he should have done, but when I make this criticism I want to do it in his presence and not in his absence. I want to do it face to face before the people of Virginia with full opportunity to give and take and to let the people decide. . . There is one aspect of the subject, however, to which I feel justified in alluding, because it has been widely discussed in the newspapers of the State and because I have been, in a way, involved in the criticism.

"I refer to the fact that the administration of my competitor as governor of the Commonwealth was characterized by extravagance and terminated in utter depletion of the Treasury.

I make reference to this incident because my competitor has had ample opportunity to consider and make answer to this charge projected by reputable public journals and substantiated by ample proofs. The discussion is pertinent because at the very outset of this senatorial contest the partisans of the governor's appointee have sought to make it appear that he should not be molested in his ambition to be Senator because the people of the State owe him a debt of gratitude for his brilliant and business-like administration. The real facts seem to be that Governor Montague turned over to his successor in office a genuine surplus of more than a half-million dollars, unappropriated and unexpended; that during his administration my competitor had the advantage of additional revenue raised under the operation of tax reforms provided by the Constitutional Convention amounting to $4,650,000, which gave him a total amount of available money of $5,000,000 more than was available for public purposes under the administration of Governor Montague.

"Yet, with this tremendous excess, the State, under his administration, had to ask for favors of the railroad corporations and had to borrow a quarter of a million dollars from the banks and, at the end of four years, was left in a state of financial prostration. Brilliant and Business-like!

". . . They have the audacity to say that my competitor left a surplus of $787,449.10 in the treasury. But they studiously fail to say that against that apparent balance there was that day due and paid $518,526 to the school fund and that one month later, on the first day of March, 1910, the apparent balance in the treasury was only $51,081, made up of the fixed credits to the Bureau of Insurance, the commissioner of agriculture, and the military fund which, if paid, would have left an actual deficit at the end of his administration of about $30,000.

"Driven into a corner on this proposition the machine organs frantically demanded to know what appropriations should have been curtailed . . . and by this sort of questioning they seek to frighten all critics off the trail. I stand here to answer for myself that the governor of Virginia, sworn to safeguard the public interest, should have cut off any, or every, appropriation rather than have bankrupted the public treasury. What is a man's nerve for if it is not to be exercised in emergencies?

". . . I shall not pursue the subject in all its details here tonight; but, if it please him, I shall be willing to go with this and all the other issues that may be projected before the people of Virginia and discuss them with my competitor."

Swanson declined the challenge, preferring to conduct a Fabian campaign to the risk of standing beside his challenger and before the people of Virginia. As for Glass, his speech brought him forcibly to the attention of Virginia. He had turned a hostile, silent audience, paid to disagree with him, into an audience that got to its feet and cheered as he left the platform. He walked down the aisle and the crowd separated into a lane; and hands that would put their marks against him on the ballot reached out to slap his shoulders in encouragement.

The speech was the highspot of his campaign, although by no means the end of the fight, or his last visit to the state capital.

A few nights later he received a telephone call from Candidate Jones. "I've got a friend up in New Jersey," said Jones; "and I've invited him to come down into Virginia and make a speech in behalf of clean government."

"You don't mean Woodrow Wilson!" exclaimed Glass.

"None other."

"When is he coming?"

"That's what I wanted to talk to you about. Governor

Wilson said he could come almost any time it was convenient for us."

"Dad bum!" exploded Glass. "Get him here right away. But, wait a minute – you just can't invite the Governor of New Jersey to come into Virginia to make a speech . . . that would be interference, and the people of Virginia would resent it, even if Mr. Wilson was born here."

"I'm not inviting him, personally," chuckled Jones. "I'm thinking about having the State Legislature invite him. . ."

Over the telephone the two men discussed that idea, worked it out and, in due time, a formal invitation was issued by the Virginia Legislature to the Governor of New Jersey.

Glass met Wilson in Washington as the New Jersey Governor was on his way to Richmond. "I was anxious to meet him," he later recalled. "From a distance he looked to me like Presidential timber. The minute I saw him, and listened to him, I was confident I was seeing, and hearing the next President of the United States." That day a friendship began between two men.

Accompanied by Glass, and a group of Virginia legislators, Wilson went on to Richmond from Washington. His speech, in combination with the efforts of Glass and Jones, impaired the power of the state political machine. Henry Stuart was elected Governor without opposition. Since 1911, there has been no effective political machine in Virginia.

With defeat at the polls still fresh, Glass received a package through the mails. It was a small package, neatly wrapped, and as he broke it open a gold medal fell into his hand. Accompanying the trophy was a card on which was written:

Dear Dad:

There is one member, at least, of the Glass family who can run a race, and win.

Carter, Jr.

More than a little amused, as well as pleased, Glass sent the medal to a jeweler and had it made into a watch fob. As a member of Washington and Lee University track team, his son, a few days after the elections, had won a 440-yard race at a track and field meet in Baltimore.

Also, there was an aftermath of the campaign that, for a time, threatened tragedy. Some years previously Glass had been asked by a group of business men to put into writing their estimate of Senator Martin. Although intending to vote for Martin, he had declined to write the article saying he did not agree with some of the things he knew they wanted him to write. Particularly certain references to Governor Montague. They persuaded him, telling him that all they sought was the expression of their own ideas in simple English. Reluctantly and confidentially Glass prepared the appraisal, which was never used but was stored away in the files of a mutual friend.

In some way, and in the absence of the mutual friend, the appraisal, accredited to Glass as his own estimate of Senator Martin, reached the desk of Alfred B. Williams, a brilliant editorial writer on a Roanoke newspaper. Williams made good use or, rather, as Glass thought, misuse, of the confederate material.

In return, Glass wrote a reply that fairly blistered. Instead of holding the Representative responsible, Williams promptly challenged Walter Addison, the editor of the paper owned by Glass, to a duel.

Addison was just as prompt in accepting. He boarded the next train for Roanoke. Walking into Williams' office, he said : "Well, Alfred, I am here to answer your challenge and I am ready to proceed at any time."

Looking up from his desk, Williams inquired as to Addison's seconds.

"I have none," responded Glass' editor. "I have no friends

that I would care to have involved in a duel. It is against Virginia law to engage in dueling, and while I do not mind, under the circumstances, breaking that law myself, I have no intention of asking my friends to break it." Addison suggested that the two go out to a designated place in Montgomery County and proceed with the proposed duel on an agreed signal.

Frowning, but in no wise mollified, Williams objected that Addison's point was very irregular, and he would have to consult his friends. The upshot of the matter was that the duel was called off, provided both newspapers should publish an innocent looking little paragraph saying that neither side meant any offense.

At this juncture of affairs Addison was compelled to disclose the whole matter to Glass, and the Representative promptly put down both feet, one on the duel and the other on the method of settlement. He told Addison that under no circumstances would he permit anyone to fight a duel for him, nor would he print anything in his newspaper that would seem to detract "a jot or tittle from the editorial I have written about the affair in question."

Addison made a second trip to Roanoke, explaining the situation to Williams, and to the friends of the editorial writer. The matter was dropped.

CHAPTER SEVEN

The President finds a man to lead the fight.

When the tinder box of Central Europe flared in July, 1914, a money panic in the United States became imminent in a few hours. Gold began flowing in a great river to England, as the British urgently demanded immediate payment of all debts due in American commerce. The telephone on the desk of Secretary of the Treasury McAdoo rang incessantly and insistently – "Wall Street calling." His advice was to close the Stock Exchange, while he rushed to Congress for an emergency measure whereby he could issue currency to stem the catastrophe.

On Sunday evening, August 2, with Germany's ultimatum to Belgium making spread of the disaster certain, McAdoo met New York financiers in the Pennsylvania railroad station, strove to reassure them. Later that night he exclaimed to his wife, "Hang it all, Ellen, if we just had time to get the Federal Reserve System in operation, we would be equipped to deal with this situation !"

With a frantic speed-up born of increased need they did get the Federal Reserve Act, passed the previous December, in operation, and through a perilous time it withstood the enormous strain.

Some years later Carter Glass wrote : "If there was a trace of exaggeration in the estimate of that seasoned English economist who declared the Federal Reserve System 'worth to the commerce of America more than three Panama canals,' nevertheless, it must be conceded that, in the crucial test of the World War, it was found to be more indispensable to civilization than three times three Panama Canals. This merely means that I agree with the considered judgment of those eminent bankers of this and other lands who have said that the World War could not have been financed but for the Federal Reserve Act. And if not financed, of course, it could not, except at infinitely greater sacrifice, have been won by the United States and associated nations. Thus, in a final analysis, the real value of this one achievement of Wilson's administration might be fairly appraised by simply leaving to the human contemplation what further slaughter and destruction would have ensued or what would be our situation today had we lost the war with the Central European powers!"

That observation appeared in 1927 in Glass' book, *An Adventure in Constructive Finance.* The story of that adventure took root in the wayward events of several preceding years, came to flower in a twenty-two months' struggle by an unswerving few against massed opposition, and bore fruit in a governmental achievement without parallel in modern times.

1907 was a year of panic. Fortunes fled down the rat holes of bottom-dropping credit, a scurried currency. Widow's mite and miser's hoard alike were puffed away by the chilling winds of – what? Nobody knew exactly what, but never had the antiquated currency system of the nation appeared to worse advantage. Glass had been a member of the House Banking and Currency Committee nearly four years. He was assiduously studying the problem, as he had promised John Sharpe Williams he would, when a dazed Republican leadership, with recent assurances of a "full dinner pail" still rattling emptily in their ears, and a new Presidential election staring them in the face, grew desperately aware that "something had to be done!"

What they did was to create and deviously coax through a bewildered Congress the precarious Vreeland-Aldrich Currency Law, confessedly an emergency measure, early in 1908. Its short life was not a merry one; until amended by a Democratic Congress, not one dollar of emergency currency was ever issued under its provisions. Glass opposed it from its ambiguous inception. His colleagues on the Currency Committee selected him to write the dissenting report. Militantly he led the opposition and, on May 27, 1908, made the only speech against it which was quoted in his party's campaign book in the next general elections. It was his first speech before the House of Representatives.

With his now famous habit of speaking from the left corner of his mouth the Roman-nosed legislator's words were verbal rapiers, slicing the measure loose from its scientific pretense and leaving its unlovely bones rattling to the full gaze of the multitude.

"The only emergency," he said, "is the necessity which party leaders imagine confronts them to 'do something' even though it be the wrong thing." And referring to the majority report: "This report, Mr. Speaker, enjoys the unique distinction of having been signed by all the Republican conferees of Senate and House, but not approved by a single one. There is scarcely a feature in this composite bill which has not been soundly condemned by the Republican leaders of Congress. Those features which appeal to members of the House have been mercilessly criticized in the other chamber, and those which suit the Republican managers of the Senate have been severely denounced here. Thus, upon high Republican authority, the conference report embodies a measure which is fifty per cent House infamy and fifty per cent Senate infamy, thereby making the whole thing utterly bad.

"Once I heard John J. Ingalls describe *Paradise Lost* as 'that matchless epic which everybody praises and nobody reads.' And so we have here a bill for which every member on that side will vote, but in the provisions of which not one of them believes. The bill is utterly wrong in principle, as any bill must be which merely provides an emergency currency. What the country needs is not a makeshift legislative deformity, designed to help out a desperate situation, but a wise and careful revision of the entire banking and currency system of the United States, whereby panics may be prevented or their violence diminished."

Finally, after categorically enumerating the dangers and deficiencies of the bill, he summed up :

"It is sufficient to point to the exhaustive hearings before the House Committee on Banking and Currency to show that this bill, both as to its Vreeland features and its Aldrich features, has been condemned by the wisest bankers, the ablest merchants, the best financial experts, the most eminent textbook writers in America and abroad. The bill, should it pass and receive executive sanction, will do infinite harm. It will, as Secretary Gage declared, prove a deception, or, precisely to quote him, 'a narcotic to woo the country into false repose' from which we will 'awaken at last in trouble and real agony.' "

Then with a last riposte he concluded :

"The only, or I should say the best, defense to the bill is the belief of the Rhode Island Senator that the Vreeland 'iniquities' will never be invoked, and the equally confident prediction of the gentleman from New York (Vreeland) that the Aldrich 'infamies' are merely surface manifestation."

It was old King Caucus, abetted by gag-rule, that catalyzed the Vreeland-Aldrich document into a nation's law. By caucus action the committee was discharged before the bill could be printed and put in its possession ; and the bill, not yet dry from the printing press, did not reach the House until debate had proceeded for an hour. Five hours later, under a rule which prohibited the offering of a single amendment, it was passed. Not ten members actually knew what it contained.

Frequent claims have been made that the measure saved

the situation at the outbreak of war in 1914, but it was quite a different statute that temporarily averted financial upheaval then. In 1913 it had been radically amended by the framers of the Federal Reserve Act and its life prolonged until the reserve system could be set up. On the plea of frantic bankers, in 1914, it had to be hastily and radically altered a second time before it could be made operative in the emergency. The $368,000,000 of notes issued under the Act were retired as quickly as possible after the Federal Reserve banks opened for business. Before Congress, on September 7, 1916, Glass pointed out, among other significant things, that two banks in New York City alone which took out $41,000,000 of the emergency notes in 1914 could not have got one dollar under the terms of the unamended Vreeland-Aldrich Act. And of the $2,977,066 collected by the Treasury as tax on emergency notes, only $11,559 represented collection at a tax equal to the minimum rate of the original Vreeland-Aldrich Bill.

Singularly enough, one feature of the new currency law proved more monumental to fruitlessness and futility than the statute itself. As if recognizing the transience of the structure they were presumably setting up, the authors accepted and incorporated a provision creating the National Monetary Commission. At an expense of $102,357.37 the members ransacked the four corners of the globe to compile a pretentious library of finance. A praiseworthy enterprise – were it not for the fact that virtually all this data was already in the Congressional Library. They climaxed their achievement with a voluminous report, and this together with the accompanying paraphernalia was at last interred to gather cobwebs in the basement of the Library of Congress. The matter is worth mentioning merely because of a persistent fable that this commission's work and report were the basis, in some remote degree, of the Federal Reserve Act.

Having elected Taft in 1908, and with the 1912 elections imminent, the Monetary Commission, headed by Senator Nelson W. Aldrich, bestirred itself from its four years of meditation, and laid in the lap of Congress its proposed cure for currency evils – the "Aldrich plan."

It provided for a central bank to be owned and managed by the stockholding banks, authorized to do business with banks only. As Glass later described it, "the central bank was given important privileges and accorded certain governmental exemptions. It was likewise invested with unusual powers for a privately owned enterprise. The mechanism was quite involved; but it was so arranged that the larger banks of the country must inevitably become predominant and the control of credits continue to be exercized by a few powerful institutions in the large financial centers. Its distinguishing feature was centralization as against mobilization of the credits of the nation. . ."

The bill was referred to the committee, which divided itself to war on two fronts. The first section, under Chairman Pujo, went after the "Money Trust." This investigation, employing Samuel Untermeyer, a New York lawyer, as special counsel, made sensational headlines and achieved certain reforms. The sub-committee, with Carter Glass named chairman on April 30, 1912, was committed to the quieter, more tedious and more laborious task of devising a reserve banking plan.

So pleased were the tamers of the "Money Devil" with what they had done that they thought it would be a very advantageous coup if they were to supersede the other sub-committee and handle the currency question, but the country-editor-chairman and his associates were of a different mind. They refused to tolerate interference. Glass had availed himself of the brilliant assistance of an expert adviser, Dr. H. Parker Willis, skilled economist and financial journalist. It was principally these two who, with infinite patience, tackled the almost incredible amount of detail involved in their preliminary work.

That June at Baltimore the Democratic National Convention rejected the Aldrich plan and the idea of a central bank. That November Woodrow Wilson was elected President of the United States. That winter Wall Street's "prophets of woe" began to grumble of impending panic and doom.

"What does this college professor Wilson know about banking?" they indignantly asked one another; and entrenched themselves behind their money bags to await the worst.

And, on November 7, Carter Glass wrote the President-elect as follows:

Lynchburg, Va., November 7, 1912.

Hon. Woodrow Wilson,
Princeton, N.J.
Dear Governor Wilson: —

Accept, if you please, my very earnest congratulations on your remarkable victory at the polls last Tuesday. It betokens the re-establishment of real representative government at Washington; and many people are praying that the wholesome influence of your election may reach Virginia and aid in its redemption.

I am writing especially to inquire when you think I may have a brief interview with you concerning the matter of revising our currency system. I am chairman of the House Committee to which has been referred the bill and report of the Monetary Commission and which is charged with the consideration of the entire subject of a reorganization of the banking and currency system. While we did not think it would be prudent to complicate the Presidential contest by taking any definite action at the last session of Congress, the committee has not been idle. With the assistance of Prof. H. Parker Willis, formerly of Washington & Lee University, we have gone into much work of detail and have, indeed, formulated, tentatively, a substitute for what is known as the Aldrich bill. I think the committee would not like to proceed without some suggestions from you as to the nature of the work already done and as to what you think should be done. The probability is that we shall not be able to pass a bill in the 62nd Congress, but that you will have to approve or disapprove currency legislation by the 63rd Congress. For this and other obvious reasons it seems to me that it is essentially important that the matter should be brought to your attention as early as possible by Dr. Willis and myself.

I know that you are now overwhelmed with correspondence; but I would like to hear from you at your convenience.

With cordial regards,
Sincerely yours
(signed) Carter Glass.

On December 19, Glass received this telegram:

Hon Carter Glass,
H of R Washn DC
Would like very much to meet you and the other gentleman Thursday afternoon December twenty sixth at two thirty o'clock.
Woodrow Wilson.

And, on the evening of December 25, a second telegram:

Hon. Carter Glass
House Representatives Washington DC.
Confined by attack of cold. Would you be kind enough to come to Princeton.
Woodrow Wilson.

Horse-drawn snow plows had cleared the right of way for the train that steamed into the station at Princeton, New Jersey, on the raw, blustering afternoon of December 26, 1912. A few newspaper reporters, with hands in pockets and coat collars up, were pacing the platform, stamping numbed feet against the cold. From among the newly arrived passengers they singled out two overcoated, mufflered, middle-aged men, briefly questioned the shorter of the two and went into the telegraph office to file routine dispatches that would make no front page headlines – for it would have required abnormal prescience for any one to have written:

"This is an historic day in America, and the world. Within

two hours a great federal reserve system, under which the entire economic life of a nation will soon be permanently organized, will here be born."

Red though his nose, the old Irish coachman who awaited at the platform's end was glad it was winter. Otherwise, he would have had to don linen duster, goggles and visored cap and driven the infernal automobile which the state had provided for its Chief Executive just that year. Now the contraption, useless save in summer, was standing on jacks in the stable – or garage, as some were beginning to call it. His grin of greeting was a wide one as Carter Glass and the committee expert, Dr. Willis, entered the carriage. He cracked his whip and the wheels creaked merrily over the packed snow.

Icicles adorned the "little house on Cleveland Lane" to which they drove. It was an attractive three-story dwelling, half-timbered outside in the English manner, with big bay windows. Through one of the frosted windows an aged Negro butler saw the carriage approach. He went to the bed in the large studio room where a gaunt, square-jawed, gray-eyed man lay abed, propped the pillows high beneath his head, and hurried to answer the doorbell. When Glass learned that Governor Wilson was suffering a severe cold, and had canceled every other engagement for the day, he suggested that they come at another time. But the President-elect, intent upon a speedy and sweeping currency reform, insisted on proceeding at once with the business at hand.

A fire blazed cheerily in the huge fireplace. Christmas decorations were still up ; stacked here and there were packages opened and unopened, and hundreds of holiday cards were piled on tables and mantel. Glass, fresh from his own Christmas Day celebration with his family at Lynchburg, was here by express invitation. Woodrow Wilson, himself an avid student of currency since 1897, was thoroughly familiar with the Virginian's record on the House Banking and Currency Committee, knew that for a decade he had been advocating a new currency system of district or regional banks. Such a system the former Princeton President had come to regard as the most fundamental and far-reaching aspect of his whole program of "The New Freedom."

Also Governor Wilson knew that this slight, sandy-haired visitor, just turning fifty-four and beginning to gray, was a sincere and devoted student of banking matters, that he was of a sufficiently detached and liberal nature to have been the leader of an anti-machine movement in Virginia not altogether dissimilar from his own in New Jersey.

As for Carter Glass, he had heartily approved when Mr. Wilson had written : "America is never going to submit to guardianship. America is not going to choose thraldom instead of freedom." . . . "Are we going to settle the currency question so long as the government listens only to the counsel of those who command the banking situation ?" . . . "There is a sense in which a democratic country forces statesmanship upon every man of initiative, every man capable of leading anybody ; and this I believe to be the particular period when statesmanship is forced upon bankers and upon all those who have to do with the application and use of the vast accumulated wealth of this country."

Although those were views identical with his own, the chairman of the congressional sub-committee later confessed a feeling of distinct humility in the presence of their author.

The bedside interview lasted two hours, during which Wilson asked innumerable questions, and Glass made innumerable answers. Finally, as the sick man balanced his spectacles on his thumb and thoughtfully rubbed his eyes, the Lynchburg Congressman drew from his pocket a few sheets covered with his own fine handwriting, and from this memorandum he explained and enlarged his views. As these took form Governor Wilson's interest grew keen; the dull gray eyes began to glow. "In my judgment," he presently announced, "you are far on the right track." And he made a few suggestions, the most noteworthy being that which resulted in an altruistic Federal Reserve Board supervising the system instead of the Comptroller of the Currency, already endowed with dictatorial banking powers.

Before those two hours ended the President-elect knew he had found a man to lead the fight for currency reform. Here from his own native Virginia was a man who knew banking, but was no banker . . . a man who knew the credit needs of commerce as distinguished from stock gambling and financial manipulation, and yet a man who had never invested a dollar in the market himself . . . a man from a constituency primarily agrarian, yet free from any small-town or back-country prejudices against business, big or little.

In the words of Mr. Wilson: "I was simply amazed at the array of knowledge and understanding of the whole field of currency reform shown by Representative Glass."

And in the words of Representative Glass as written by him in a letter to Mr. Wilson on December 29:

I have been thinking much about the subject of our interview at Princeton on Thursday and am trying in my mind to reduce the suggestions there made to something tangible in order that the hearings before my sub-committee, beginning January 7th, may be directed to a definite, even though tentative, plan of currency reform. I am a little afraid that the embarrassment of being between the fire of two learned professors was somewhat confusing on Thursday; but I have some very distinct notions about the lines we should pursue and especially about the situation that will confront us at Washington. On this latter point there is some illumination in a letter I have just received from one of the great New York bankers invited to the hearings of my sub-committee. There is this paragraph:

"The American Bankers Association, as a body, at its meeting in New Orleans a year ago, endorsed the Aldrich bill. It would seem, therefore, impossible for us as members of the Currency Commission of the American Bankers' Association, to take any other position or do anything else before your committee than to endorse that bill, if we were to appear before you officially."

I felt certain before receiving this letter that we would encounter this difficulty. The bankers intend to fight for the Aldrich plan as it is drafted in order to get the same thing in a different form. They do not intend that the $350,000 expended by the Monetary Commission and the additional $300,000 expended by the Citizens League in "educational work" shall be wasted. I much apprehend that "educational work" with some of these gentlemen means ability to organize influences and to bring pressure to bear to drive schemes through Congress merely because they want them and not entirely because they should have them. Might it not be well to draft a bill on the Regional Reserve Bank lines, taking care of all the details discussed last Thursday and put on the advocates of the Aldrich bill the burden of showing that a central superstructure should be imposed, requiring them to suggest a superstructure that should not possess the evils of bank monopoly and the dangers of centralized power? We may ourselves have in readiness such a "capstone" as I understood you to suggest having the wholesome powers of a central supervisory control.

If I might have a further brief talk with you some day at your convenience before we begin the hearings, I think matters would be decidedly facilitated. I know how busy you are and I dislike to take up any part of your time; but I likewise know what a powerful factor you must be in the solution of this problem if we are to have any currency legislation at all.

But both men were heartened there that day in Princeton, Governor Wilson to go on to Trenton and clean up his desk against the momentous March 4; Glass to return to Washington and the long-contemplated battle he was ready, at last, to begin.

CHAPTER EIGHT

"The ghost of Andrew Jackson haunted my couch."

For half a century the United States endured what bankers and economists called the most barbarous currency system on earth, and which Carter Glass declared "a positive indictment of the statesmanship of the nation."

From its beginnings the American financial policy was mixed and makeshift. A few faltering steps in the right direction, yes, but nothing to assure national security. In 1863 every bank had its own plates, printed its own money. Seven thousand different kinds of bank notes were in circulation, and of these 1700 were issues of the spurious "wildcat banks"; and, beyond these, more than 3000 kinds of counterfeit notes.

In 1863, as in 1913, a new President was working for a solution.

"I know of no way," said Abraham Lincoln, in speaking of the proposed banking act, "which promises so certain results, and is at the same time so unobjectionable as the organization of banking associations under a general Act of Congress, well guarded by its provisions. To such associations the Government might furnish circulating notes, on the security of the United States bonds deposited in the Treasury. These notes . . . being uniform in appearance and security, and convertible always into coin, would at once protect labor against the coils of a vicious currency, and facilitate commerce."

And so, on April 11, 1864, Representative Hooper, of Massachusetts, introduced into the 38th Congress a bill somewhat lengthily titled, "An Act to provide a national currency secured by a pledge of United States bonds, and to provide for the circulation and redemption thereof."

The bill, known then as now, as the National Bank Act, was passed and signed by President Lincoln on Friday, June 3, 1864.

For nearly fifty years thereafter practically nothing was done to strengthen the banking structure. In the meantime, the nation had grown from an agrarian country into an industrial one ; and from a population of 32,000,000 to a population of nearly 100,000,000.

And, for nearly fifty years, indifference, the false security of ignorance and the political obstruction of privilege stood stolidly as barriers on the road to reform, despite the fact that in the midst of great prosperity illogical catastrophes had overtaken the country five times in the thirty years immediately preceding 1913. Paradoxically, prosperity seemed actually to produce disaster.

"The Siamese twins of disorder," Glass has written,* "were an inelastic currency and a fictitious reserve system. . . The sum total of the idle bank funds of the nation was congested at the money centers for purely speculative purposes. Nobody seemed to discern the absolute necessity of subduing at exactly the same time the twin evils of inelasticity in the currency and of pyramiding reserves by book balance. Little could be accomplished by correcting one fault and leaving the other to persist.

"The national currency was inelastic because it was based on the bonded indebtedness of the United States. The ability of the banks to meet the currency needs of commerce and industry was largely measured by the volume of bonds available. And the total was constantly being diminished by reductions in the national debt. For half a century we banked on the absurd theory that the country always needed a volume of currency equal to the nation's bonded indebtedness and at no

* *An Adventure in Constructive Finance*, 1927

time ever required less, whereas we frequently did not need as much as was outstanding and quite as often required more than it was possible to obtain. So, when more was needed than could be gotten, stringencies resulting in panics would be precipitated, to cure which, for the moment, clearing-house certificates would unlawfully be resorted to as a substitute for bank notes. When currency was redundant, when the volume was more than required for actual commercial transactions, instead of taking it through the expensive process of retirement, it was sent by interior banks to the great money centers to be loaned on call for stock and commodity gambling."

The plan Glass presented at Princeton proposed to make several reserve pyramids, stronger because smaller, out of the ever-toppling big one. Credits would be decentralized by reserve balances as then impounded being compulsorily withdrawn and transferred to a certain number of regional banks. These banks would issue federal reserve notes based on a gold and liquid paper cover . . . a flexible currency founded on commercial assets, the intrinsic wealth of the nation, rather than on bonded debt.

Money panics would be averted, and banks would be made the instruments, not the masters, of business. Thus oversimplified, the system strikes the layman today as little more than common sense, but a quarter of a century ago it was revolutionary, and the myriad technical details, the countless legal snarls and ramifications, and the implicit denials of special privilege to the manipulators of finance, all combined to create for the Virginian and his colleagues an almost superhuman task.

A majority of the bankers of the nation quietly united to oppose any real currency reform. A well-manned and richly financed group organized to "educate the country" into accepting its central bank plan sponsored by the Monetary Commission, and shrewd propaganda everywhere was doing its devious work. But as yet the Glass sub-committee was not suspect, was not taken seriously, and this proved fortunate. While the range-finders for the big guns of the monied interests scanned the legislative horizon for more impressive battlements to bombard, saving their salvos for big game at the exigent moment, the Lynchburg Congressman was left unmolested to raise his fortifications in preparation for the fight to come.

Exhaustive hearings which were to last six weeks began in January, and in accord with the President-elect's suggestion these were directed to the plan outlined in Princeton. It was desired to test its feasibility before the unsparing criticisms of practical bankers, and at the same time disclose the nature and extent of the banking opposition.

There was a vigorous protest when at the very outset Glass announced that the committee felt precluded from considering the "Aldrich Plan" or any other central banking measure, since Wilson and the new Congress had been elected on a party platform that rejected them. Repeatedly it was objected that party platform declarations should not control currency legislation, over-looking the fact that party government was, and still is, an inevitable process.

But the bankers would not desist in their demands for the Aldrich plan, or some kind of central bank to be owned and operated for bankers. There were some notable exceptions, however ; some, when confronted with the regional scheme as a secondary proposition, consented to go along with the committee. "I have never refused half a loaf merely because I couldn't get it all," was the laconic remark of George M. Reynolds, Chicago banker. Among others who joined with Reynolds in doing helpful educational work were Paul M.

Warburg of Kuhn, Loeb & Co. and Henry P. Davison of J. P. Morgan & Co.

The hearings, extensive and illuminating, strengthened the determination of those in charge to proceed with the regional measure. And under the most intense pressure from powerful financiers whose co-operation he would need in crucial days to come, Glass firmly refused to repudiate his party's platform, which promised:

> We oppose the so-called Aldrich Monetary Bill, or the establishlishment of a Central Bank, and we believe the people of this country will be largely freed from panics and consequent unemployment and business depression by such a systematic revision of our banking laws as will render temporary relief in localities where such relief is needed, with protection from control or domination by what is known as the "money trust."
>
> Banks exist for the accommodation of the public and not for the control of business. All legislation on the subject of banking and currency should have for its purpose the securing of these accommodations on terms of absolute security to the public and of complete protection from the misuse of the power that wealth gives to those who possess it.
>
> We condemn the present method of depositing Government funds in a few favored banks, largely situated in or controlled by Wall Street, in return for political favors, and we pledge our party to provide by law for their deposit by competitive bidding by the banking institutions of the country, national and state, without discrimination as to locality, upon approved securities and subject to call by the government.

There were rumors of a concerted effort to sidetrack currency legislation, or failing that, to set aside the rule of seniority and select a chairman of the House Banking and Currency Committee for the 63rd Congress who would be "less hostile to the Aldrich Bill than Glass." The committee expert, Dr. Willis, was greatly disturbed when a powerful New York banker observed: "You know, Willis, there *is* such a thing as getting a committee chairman who will accept our plan."

Willis repeated that remark to Glass – as the banker expected he would – and on January 27, 1913, the Virginian wrote a letter to Governor Wilson expressing anxiety for immediate action, and venturing the opinion that it was going to be a little "difficult" to enact legislation even with the full power of the administration behind any bill agreed upon. This elicited immediate response. Wilson replied, summoning Glass to a further conference on the suggested bill.

In the executive offices in Trenton, on January 30, Glass presented what he termed "the first draft of the Federal Reserve Act, made by the committee expert at my direction."

It embodied the suggestions previously made by Wilson, and two vitally important provisions of which the President-elect had not yet been apprised. One, suggested by Dr. Willis, was for open market transactions by regional banks, with the double purpose of enabling them to utilize idle funds in dull seasons in order to earn expenses and acquire surpluses, and of compelling compliance with the reserve-bank rediscount rate. The other, suggested by Glass, proposed an abolition of exchange charges and the establishment of par collections. Both new provisions were heartily approved by Wilson ; later both were bitterly opposed by the banking interests. But they stayed in. This draft of the currency bill, though tentative still, contained nearly every fundamental provision subsequently enacted into law.

Unlike the man at the sick-bed interview five weeks earlier, here was an enthusiastic President-elect grooming himself intellectually and spiritually for the arduous days that lay ahead. Although he jokingly claimed himself "woefully ignorant of banking affairs," he exhibited a clear comprehension of the issues involved and displayed a real zest for discussing details.

Two things were settled at this Trenton conference. Wilson explicitly committed himself to the regional-bank system ;

and Glass was assured he would succeed to the chairmanship of the House Banking and Currency Committee in the ensuing Congress. Told of the New York banker's observation "there is such a thing as getting a committee chairman who will accept our plans" ; and reminded that on March 4, the tenure of the 62nd Congress expired, and with it the existence of the Glass sub-committee charged with currency reform, Wilson tugged at his long chin as, slowly, a grin of anticipated pleasure spread over his lips and crinkled up into his eyes.

He outlined some swift thoughts ; and Glass chuckled with him. Wilson might be a novice in politics, as some said, but he was no novice in strategy.

Because tariff legislation was first on the Administration's calendar, Wilson, immediately after his inauguration, had the House of Representatives appoint only a Committee on Ways and Means ; and it heartened the opposition to the regional banking bill when the House allowed three months to elapse before naming a Banking and Currency Committee. It gave the banking opposition three months of unexpected delay to strengthen their lines. Likewise – and this they did not know – it gave to the prospective chairman of a committee not yet existent freedom from any distracting obligation to confer with former committeemen, bankers, politicians or meddlers in general.

There is much material for rumination in the events of these crowded days. The Federal Reserve fight was drawing him from comparative obscurity. The countless comments ; letters from friends, heartening . . . letters from critics, hostile . . . a few of them so bad the authors were ashamed to sign their names ; others, the writers so bad they were not ashamed to sign . . . a heartening letter from Richard Evelyn Byrd, who was Wilson's campaign manager in Virginia . . . but heartening comments few, hostile comments many.

Discouragement frequent . . . why the urge to drive his flesh against the nights of study and examination, the days of committee meetings and legislative travail? Wherein the gain of advancing against the barrage of propaganda inspired by certain bankers . . . certain bankers who were now aware that, in Congress, was a legislator not subject to their blandishments, not impressed by their names, not in awe of their fortunes. . .

Their maneuverings; their malignings . . . Wall Street pulling wires to prevent Glass from being made chairman of the committee . . . nevertheless, with Willis, pushing the work forward – saying little, accomplishing much – sharpening weapons for the final fight . . . that Woodrow Wilson's Administration might have credit for this legislation.

The currency measure was closely guarded because every other currency bill had been battered to bits before it could even get a start. Wilson, Glass and Willis feared their federal reserve bank bill would be subjected to the same attacks should its revolutionary provisions be prematurely disclosed. Already special groups were desperately trying to learn what the bill contained and were endeavoring to have Glass accept parts or all of their production. By remaining in New York much of the time, Dr. Willis was able to keep in touch with the banking community. It was at this time Dr. Willis wrote Glass:

> While I was a good deal encouraged a few days ago at the fact that the bankers were swinging around into support of something like what we have been working on, I think it is essential to bear in mind that they are doing all this in full expectation of getting us to adopt such a "strong" plan as to come close to the Aldrich plan. This raises the question whether it is expedient to put this plan in the hands of any person to pass around among themselves until we ascertain the prospects in Congress. I shall by the end of the week have the bill in as good shape as I can get it. I do not wish to go ahead with new features without getting instructions

from you, so I am endeavoring simply to improve it strictly on lines that you and I have talked of.

Meanwhile speculation and activity were rife around White House and Capitol. Congress sat up and blinked when Woodrow Wilson delivered his opening message in person ; no President had done that for 113 years. (Next day a newspaper cartoon depicted Theodore Roosevelt moaning "Why didn't I think of that?") And many a Congressman reluctantly dropped his sporting catalogue and put away his fishing tackle when the President immediately issued a proclamation for an extra session in April. Presumably, this was just to handle the tariff ; but newspapers, legislators and lobbyists began to wonder whether the Chief Executive would also bring up the currency question. Glass knew he would, but this knowledge he did not divulge.

He and his technical expert were by no means the only ones quietly at work. While the tariff debate held the spotlight, behind closed doors many an aspirant for a rôle in banking legislation was writing and rehearsing his screed. In this connection the following extracts from the diary of Colonel E. M. House are singularly illuminating :

> March 13, 1913 : Vanderlip and I had an interesting discussion regarding currency reform.
>
> March 27, 1913 : Mr. J. P. Morgan, Jr., and Mr. Denny of his firm, came promptly at five. McAdoo came about ten minutes afterwards. Morgan had a currency plan already formulated and printed. We discussed it at some length. I suggested that he should have it typewritten and sent to us today.

It was unfortunate that Morgan had already incurred the expense of having his plan printed. Whether he went to the additional trouble of having his plan typed is not a matter of general knowledge. It was never heard of again.

In April, Wilson asked Glass to have prepared for him a brief digest of the federal reserve bill, as then drafted. This was done. Colonel House obtained it in some way and without delay sent it on to Paul M. Warburg, New York banker, who was genuinely interested in currency reform. Later Colonel House turned in to Secretary of the Treasury McAdoo an unsigned and unidentified criticism of the digest. It called for radical alterations which were not made, and advocated a number of things which were never done. Afterward, the criticism was traced to Warburg.

Writing in 1926, Glass, in referring to this criticism, pointed out: "Of course, no censure is attached to Mr. Warburg, for whom I have the highest respect and warmest personal regard. He simply was unalterably hostile to certain fundamental provisions of the federal reserve bill, and in plain terms persistently said so. This he had said at the committee hearings in January, which made it quite futile to have him repeat it in April as a contribution in writing from Colonel House to the great cause of monetary reform."

Despite their differences of opinion, Glass liked Warburg for his courage; admired him for his frankness. Some he did not like; some he did not admire.

Shortly after the selection of the House Banking and Currency Committee on June 3, with Glass as chairman, there began to unfold in Washington a plot to wreck the measure.

The Secretary of the Treasury, who had seemed to favor the bill, invited Glass to a Washington club for a discussion. There it soon became obvious that McAdoo had been listening to some of his New York friends. The committee chairman was astonished when the Secretary suggested that, unless drastic changes were made, the measure would prove repugnant to radicals on the one hand and bankers on the other. How could a bill be drawn, Glass wondered, to please two strictly adversary groups?

Returning to his hotel the Congressman found a letter from George M. Reynolds. Vaguely it seemed to convey a warning . . . certain men in high places were disposed to disagree on the currency question. "I am very sorry I missed you last evening . . . I would have *said* some things to you which I do not feel I can consistently *write*. I sincerely hope President Wilson is much more in sympathy with your bill than some others I have seen and heard of. . ."

What did he mean? Glass' cloud of perplexity was soon dissipated. His telephone rang . . . the Treasury calling. "Would Mr. Glass come right over? An important matter." Glass went, and McAdoo handed him the outline of a currency bill providing for a Treasury bureau control. The scheme had all the elements of a central bank. There would be an enormous issue of treasury notes to supersede the outstanding greenbacks and gold certificates, and it seemed to contemplate a seizure of the gold in trust behind the certificates. He looked up from his reading:

"Are you serious about this?"

"Hell, yes!" exclaimed McAdoo.

Still Glass was not convinced. "You can't be," he said. "Why, such a bill as this would never pass Congress!"

"It has the endorsement of bankers. . ."

"What bankers?" interrupted Glass.

"George M. Reynolds, of Chicago, for one. . ."

"What?"

"It has the endorsement of Senator Owen. . ."

"Having heard some of Owen's theories, I can believe that – but . . . Reynolds!" Glass shook his head, but McAdoo assured him it was true.

Glass' consternation is revealed in this passage from his book: "Needless to say, I left the Treasury building astounded.

It seemed an end of currency reform for the time – a nullification of fourteen months of hard work and inconceivable nervous strain. I was never more certain of anything in my life than this proposal, if seriously attempted, would cause both a political upheaval in the country and a revulsion in financial circles. It did not require many minutes for me to make the wires hot."

Soon Glass was armed with a responsive flood of protests from leading bankers, business men and economists – among them E. D. Hulbert, James A. Forgan, A. Barton Hepburn, Sol Wexler, Festus J. Wade, and – George M. Reynolds. The latter wired he had been misunderstood, then wrote :

"If the people in the Treasury Department interpreted their interview with me to mean that I approve their Bill, then I must confess that we may expect a reasonable amount of trouble in dislodging them from their present position, for I have no hesitation in saying to you that I told them frankly I regarded the matter as entirely unsound, un-American, contrary to proper policy, and that I could not agree with them in the matter at all."

As these communications, all of like tone, were beginning to litter his desk, a telephone call came from The White House. Unaware that the new House committee chairman was already informed of the proposed substitute for his measure, Wilson stated that he had a paper from Samuel Untermeyer in advocacy of a new currency scheme. He wanted Glass to examine it. Later in the day the document arrived by messenger, accompanied by a note written in the President's spencerian hand :

> This is Mr. Untermeyer's paper to which I referred. When you have read it, will you let Mr. McAdoo have it ? I have only this copy.
>
> Woodrow Wilson.

At last the cat was out of its little bag – for though he had heard talk in certain quarters, this was the first Glass knew of the origin of the extraordinary plan.

The New York lawyer, as told, had tried to get the Money Trust investigation away from the House Banking and Currency Committee and into the hands of Congressman Robert L. Henry, of Texas, Chairman of the Rules Committee. Glass had opposed his appointment, preferring the services of William A. Glasgow, of Philadelphia. But after Glasgow had declined the position, Glass had acquiesced to the Untermeyer appointment on the openly avowed theory that "a person who has been a skillful practitioner of certain pursuits, the evil nature of which it was desired to expose and correct, might prove more adept in effecting the exposure than a man who had never engaged in such practices."

Untermeyer more than fulfilled expectations. His exploits during the investigation created a nation-wide sensation. Next, as also previously stated, he set himself to the task of getting the problem of currency reform shifted to the Money Trust Committee. Failing here, he retired to his residence, palatial Graystone, on the banks of the Hudson River, from which he finally emerged with his masterpiece.

But the White House latch-string was scarcely his to pull. However, there was Colonel House; and two weeks earlier the Colonel had written Woodrow Wilson:

May 20, 1913.
145 East 35th St.,
New York City.

The President,
The White House,
Washington, D.C.,
Dear Mr. President:

Supplementing our telephone conversation of last night I want to add that I believe that a sound currency bill can be worked out along the lines suggested by Mr. Untermeyer and one which Primus (Bryan) and Senator Owen will probably accept.

His plan is not different from the one we have in mind excepting that it is his purpose to have the government issue all currency and to be responsible for its payment.

After talking to you I explained it over the 'phone, much more fully, to Pythias (McAdoo) and he also thought that something might be worked out that would be satisfactory.

Untermeyer tells me that some of the bankers here would approve such a measure.

The difficulty is that Untermeyer wants too large a share in the making of the measure, but I think this can be overcome by bringing about a general agreement between Primus, Pythias, Owen and Glass, after first getting Untermeyer committed to it.

I understand the objections to having him in conference; at the same time, an hour with you would do wonders toward bringing about the desired result.

Everyone goes with him and at the lunch that he gave Mr. Bryan the other day there met at his home people of all creeds and conditions. There was a strange mingling of the interests and the reformers and I do not believe that a conference with him would do any harm.

Pythias or Owen could get him to Washington and when he was there you could arrange to see him for an hour in the evening and it is quite possible that no one would know.

Yours very faithfully,
(Signed) E. M. House.

To such a clandestine conference, with Mr. Untermeyer being furtively slipped into the White House at night, President Wilson declined to accede. Instead, on the evening of June 5, the President summoned Glass for a discussion of the new development.

The President sat in silence while Glass dissected the Untermeyer scheme. "I tried," Glass later said, "to make it a vivisection." Quietly, when he had concluded his objections, Wilson admonished him: "I am surprised, Glass, at your vehemence. Mac tells me the scheme has the approval of many bankers."

This was an observation for which Glass was prepared. "Who are the bankers, may I ask?"

"George Reynolds, of Chicago, for one – and he is one of twelve men controlling the credits of the nation."

From his pocket Glass drew the Reynolds letter, and read it aloud. There was a moment of silence. Then, the President reached for a pen, made a note on a pad.

"I fear Mac is deceived," he said slowly, and added: "But, fortunately, the thing has not gone so far it cannot be stopped."

With those words immense relief surged through the slight, taut frame of the harassed Virginian, as he felt the wildly rocking boat of federal reserve legislation gliding back to smoother waters. Of the finale of this fiasco, he has written:

"The President had given his decision against the scheme, and McAdoo met the situation like a prince. Not for an instant did he exhibit a sign of resentment or even disappointment. He felt he had been misled. . . From that moment he never wavered . . . his zest in behalf of currency reform . . . proved a powerful incentive to success. . . But, heaven help us, what a narrow escape that was from wrecking currency reform and precipitating another government bank upheaval! The ghost of Andrew Jackson stalked before my face in the daytime and haunted my couch for nights."

CHAPTER NINE

"Damn it! Don't resign! Outvote them!"

On March 18, 1913, for the first time in the history of the United States Senate, a Committee on Banking and Currency was named. Senator Robert D. Owen, of Oklahoma, was selected chairman.

The first draft of the Federal Reserve Act, strictly tentative and designed to be hammered over and over again, had never seen the light of day; but by Glass' direction the second draft was submitted to Senator Owen on May 21, by the House committee expert. The Senator's co-operation was earnestly requested and Dr. Willis spent the entire day explaining the bill and listening to Owen's criticisms. At the close of the interview, according to Dr. Willis, Senator Owen said: "I think well of the bill. It is a carefully framed measure. It can be passed."

At this interview Senator Owen disclosed that he also had prepared a currency bill, and a week later, in a "strictly confidential note," he sent it to Dr. Willis for analysis. On June 6, the same day the President was denying the Treasury Bureau scheme, the House expert forwarded his analysis of the Owen bill to Glass. "I will submit it to the President at the earliest opportunity," Glass notified Willis. "Meanwhile, I shall give Owen a copy of the Glass bill revised to date."

The bill prepared by Senator Owen was never introduced to either branch of the Congress. Quite possibly it is true that great minds pursue the same course; many of the Owen provisions, as pointed out by Dr. Willis in his *The Federal Reserve System* resembled provisions contained in the Glass bill explained so carefully to the Senator just two weeks previously. Some of Owen's own provisions were pronounced unwise by the expert, others declared unworkable. As a basis for the legislation President Wilson refused to have anything to do with it.

Then Secretary McAdoo and Senator Owen fell into step with Glass and his confreres and the President signaled full speed ahead on currency reform. The tariff tableau was in its final phase, soon the stage would be cleared for the currency bill, and it was imperative that it be fully rehearsed and ready to make its bow before Congress as an administrative measure. And yet, with curtain time so tensely imminent, the cast was still in controversy concerning several doubtful features of the program.

Should the bankers be permitted to select members from their own ranks, to sit on the Federal Reserve Board? Glass, foreseeing inevitable charges of exposing the banking business of the country to political control, and fearful of the whole plan being sabotaged if bankers were excluded, was for giving them minority representation. He had so drafted the bill; not to do so was to him "essential injustice and political inexpediency."

At a White House conference on the topic Senator Owen sided with Secretary of State Bryan in opposition to banker representation. McAdoo agreed with Glass, but later in the evening suggested a compromise. It was up to Wilson to decide. The House Chairman argued his case. But the President's mind was already made up. He decided against banking representation.

Glass was not complaisant in this decision. Back at his hotel he pondered the matter far into the night. He discussed it with one of his committee members, Bulkley, of Ohio, and was heartened by his vigorous protest against this "real weakness of the bill." Next morning he sent a note to the President:

"At the risk of being regarded pertinacious I am going to ask if you will not consider the advisability of modifying somewhat your view of bank representation on the proposed Federal Reserve Board. The matter has given me much concern, and more than ever I am convinced that it will be a grave mistake to alter so radically the feature of the bill indicated. . .

"You will note that the bill requires the three members selected by the banks to sever all bank connections before qualifying. Might it not be well at least to take Mr. McAdoo's suggestion and have the President select these men from a list approved by the banks?"

Wilson was adamant. Glass was exasperated. But if there was a rift in the hitherto close understanding between these two men, it was a brief one; for the so-called "intractable Glass" later said: "I was soon to revive the conviction that Mr. Wilson knew more about these matters than I did."

But, at the time, it was with inward satisfaction he could scarcely suppress that he headed a delegation from the Currency Commission of the American Bankers Association, including Forgan and Wade, Sol Wexler and Perrin, Howe and others, to The White House to convince the President how wrong he was.

Adjoining the Cabinet room in the large, comfortable Executive office lined with rows of leather-bound volumes, Woodrow Wilson sat behind his desk, courteous and contained. Before him in a semi-circle, frowning and gripping chair arms in their tense concern, were leading bankers of the nation, arbiters for years of the country's credits. Carter Glass sat outside the circle; this time he was not there to plead nor argue, but to listen.

Forgan and Wade, used to having their own way, spoke bluntly, bitterly. Peremptorily and arbitrarily they protested and condemned. They were not awed and they did not mince matters. In marked contrast Perrin and Wexler were sauve, conciliatory. As these notables drove home point after point with which Glass was in agreement, he "actually experienced a sense of regret that I had a part in subjecting Mr. Wilson to such an ordeal."

Finally the arguments ended and there was a strained, expectant pause. The President's jaw was set, and he turned cold, gray eyes in the direction of Forgan and Wade, before he asked, very quietly: "Will one of you gentlemen tell me in what civilized country on the earth there are important government boards of control on which private interests are represented?"

There was a painful silence for what seemed an interminable minute, as the President's eyes fell on first one man, then another.

"Which of you gentlemen," Wilson further inquired, "thinks the railroads should select members of the Interstate Commerce Commission?"

Still there was silence. Tamed for the moment, the lions of finance could think of no convincing reply to either question. The subject was dropped, and other questions of currency began to creep in. In the end, and as compensation for denial of banker representation, the President requested Glass to devise a Federal Advisory Council of Bankers, authorized to sit in at stated times with the Federal Reserve Board but only, as said, in an advisory capacity. With that they had to be satisfied, and the interview ended.

The primary purpose of the proposed act being to rid the country of bond-secured national bank notes, this provision was the very heart of the bill, the *sine qua non* of currency reform. And now, to Glass' consternation, he learned that the provision had been eliminated. Bryan had insisted upon it;

Owen was in agreement ; and at that very moment McAdoo was sanctioning it. Word came to him that Wilson was also swinging to this point of view.

Glass hurried to the White House, spoke his mind, and immediately issued a public statement of his determination to have the feature restored, if possible, in committee or in the House. In that move Wilson silently supported him.

While the bill's future was thus hanging in precarious balance, Glass began working in still closer relationship with representatives of the American Bankers Association. Acting for their committee, Wexler and Reynolds got him to agree to do all in his power to retain the feature to rid the country of the bond-secured national bank notes ; and also to revise the bank-reserve provision so as to permit a percentage of credit balances kept with correspondent banks to count as reserves. For their part, providing these changes were made, the two bankers pledged their support of the bill, and indicated they would ally with it the full force of the Currency Commission of the Bankers Association.

But strangely enough that organization quickly proved to be fickle. Glass had with difficulty battered down committee and Presidential reluctance ; Wilson had thought the reserve modification too high a price to pay for banker support. Then, within a few days, the House Chairman received an unexpected jolt through the mail. Wexler, with Reynolds' approval, renounced the agreement and withdrew their support.

On July 3, Glass sent the following note to Wexler :

"I do not imagine you will be surprised to have me express astonishment at the contents of your letter. Each and every one of the modifications suggested by your committee in my room at the Raleigh Hotel was drafted by me and submitted to you ; and, as I distinctly understood, was approved. It was upon the assurances of yourself and Mr. Reynolds that, with these alterations, you would get behind the bill, that I prevailed upon my colleagues to agree. In view of these facts I was amazed to receive your letter saying you would not support the bill after having agreed to do so. If we are to have your hostility in addition to that of the radical element, we will bring out a bill not half as good as this one, and you gentlemen will be responsible."

Wexler made epistolary rebuttal. After berating the administration for not wanting to "do anything that is economically sound," he went on to say, "Neither Mr. Reynolds nor I have stated we will oppose the bill, notwithstanding it has not been rewritten according to the suggestions we made. We certainly shall use every effort to have the bill amended along sound banking lines, as we cannot conceive any reason for the extreme obstinacy of the framers of the bill."

Glass again reminded them that not only had the changes they proposed been embodied, but their very form had received their positive sanction. Still they argued for further amendment until, in disgust, the chairman expunged the concessions from the bill. Then began a fight for their restoration. Three days before the bill became law, on December 20, Reynolds telegraphed that it was "imperative to the success of the new system that the currency bill be so modified as to allow at least one-fourth of the reserve and country banks and ordinary reserve city banks to consist permanently of balances due from correspondents in reserve and central reserve cities."

Glass had offered them what probably would have amounted to more than one-fourth ; they had accepted and promised support. After renouncing the arrangement, and severely criticizing the proponents of the bill . . . well, this last-minute appeal found no response. In Glass' opinion it was fruitless to renew a fight for ground once won, and then relinquished, what with his confreres and the President feeling about it as they did. They got nothing.

Meanwhile, the intramural mêlée over the note-issue provision was fast getting out of hand. Growing impatient, Bryan was beginning to kick up the dust of discord ; and right behind him was Senator Owen, kicking up more dust. Because the Secretary of State's large Congressional following, once united with the Republican opposition, could certainly defeat the bill, certain administration stalwarts over-confidently undertook to "manage" Bryan. Futile task. For twenty years Bryan had publicly advocated government issues. He was sticking to his guns, ready to stake his political existence on his stand.

Unscientific, unsound though it might be, Bryan's was ever a soul wherein visionary utopianism transcended all practical knowledge. He sent word to the President, and to Glass, that he would support no bill that did not provide for "a government note."

Wilson's worry eventually came to be shared by Glass. On May 15, he wrote the President :

"Mr. Bryan has twice indicated his desire to discuss currency matters with me ; but, if I may venture to say so, I think his talk should first be with you. I find he is opposed to bank issues and disposed to government issues. It is my notion that this would get us into all sorts of trouble."

But it seemed the President did not want to talk with Bryan either. He had little patience with whims and yet, reluctant by harshness to wound the Nebraskan's sensibilities, he relied on others to win him over. When decision could no longer be deferred Wilson summoned Glass to the White House and declared he "wanted federal reserve notes to be obligations of the United States."

Glass was dumbfounded. With all the earnestness of his being he reminded the President of what was behind the Federal Reserve note :

"The liability of the individual member bank, with the double liability of its stockholders ; the considerable gold cover with the 100 per cent commercial secondary reserve ; the liability of the regional banks, individually and jointly, as well as the double liability of the member banks ; the banking instinct behind every discount and every rediscount transaction ; the right of the regional bank to reject business and, finally, the power of the Federal Reserve Board to withhold notes.

"There is not, in truth, any government obligation here, Mr. President !" Glass declared. "It would be a pretense on its face. Was there ever a government note based primarily on the property of banking institutions ? Was there ever a government issue not one dollar of which could be put out except by demand of a bank ? The suggested government obligation is so remote it could never be discerned."

The House Chairman paused for breath. The twitching of the President's left eye, always a barometer of tension, betokened his earnestness as he replied :

"Exactly so, Glass. Every word you say is true ; the government liability *is* a mere thought. And so, if we can hold to the substance of the thing and give the other fellow the shadow, why not do it, if thereby we save *our* bill ?"

Glass saw the point. He didn't like it – but, he saw it. With a wry face, the President expressed his distaste for such tactics and, in referring to the impending, or likely, coalition in the Congress in opposition, inquired "what else can we do ?" Glass agreed there was nothing else they could do and agreed to go along under cover of this innocuous camouflage.

Bryan and his Senatorial friend were placated by this wraith of a concession, and their allegiance to the measure secured.

In the midst of all this debate, Glass received a message from Lynchburg.

In his employ was William Elliott, a colored man, who had been his butler ever since he was old enough to serve. As he grew older, Elliott fell victim to a certain fault – and, according to the Glass family, his only fault. That fault was a spasmodic addiction to certain spirituous fluids. However, at the time, Glass did not know of this weakness.

In the Congressman's possession, in Lynchburg, was a new automobile. Eyeing this method of transportation on one ebullient afternoon, William invited four friends to go for a ride. Somehow, the automobile got mixed up with a post, and one of its occupants was fatally injured.

The state police apprehended William, deserted by three companions who had fled into a nearby woods. Commandeering the damaged car, the police took William and the injured man to the hospital. While the others were indoors, Elliott started for the Glass home, leaving word he was sorry, but he had to get back to serve dinner. On the way he ran into another car parked on the side of the street. Again he was arrested, this time by the city police.

In Washington the following day Glass searched his copy of the *Lynchburg News* for an account of the accident. It wasn't there. He was displeased, thinking he would be charged with censoring legitimate news on the ground that it was inimical to his own household. He wrote a stern letter.

Promptly, and with spirit, his nephew Robert Glass explained. The Congressman had seen only the first edition, from which the item had been omitted to make space for more significant last-minute state and telegraph news. But it had been prominently displayed on page 3 of all subsequent editions.

Elliott had to stand trial for reckless and drunken driving in the city ; and for manslaughter in the county. There was consternation in the Glass household. Glass refused to do anything about it. He maintained that William ought to go to the penitentiary for the rest of his life, and expressed the hope that the authorities would so decide.

William got off fairly easy in the city trial, but when the manslaughter charge came up, things looked pretty bad. Mrs. Glass induced one of the boys, Powell, to appear as a character witness, but when the evidence was in, William's future place of abode seemed certain. It was at the moment when the defendant's lawyer – hired by the Glasses – was to begin his plea that the door to the courtroom opened and in walked the Congressman.

Glass took the witness stand, swore William was the best Negro that ever lived in the United States, that he had never known him to take a drink before in his life, and he pleaded so earnestly he rescued his butler from imprisonment. However, a fine of $200 was levied. The Congressman reached into his pocket, brought out a roll of bills, and paid it.

With that trouble off his mind, Glass hurried back to Washington.

The third draft of the banking bill was now ready, and on June 19, Glass sent it to each member of his committee with the following overture :

"I have this evening received from the public printer a limited number of printed copies of the tentative draft of a currency bill made at the suggestion of my colleagues who served with me on the sub-committee of Banking and Currency which held exhaustive hearings last winter on the subject of currency reform. I am sending members of the Banking and Currency Committee the copy of this tentative draft for such consideration as they may care to give it.

"There is, of course, no obligation whatsoever upon any member of the committee to agree to any provision of this bill. In its present form it simply represents the result of many months of hard work, based upon the hearings referred to and upon repeated conferences invited by the President and the Secretary of the Treasury upon the assumption that, as ranking member, I was to be made chairman of the Banking and Currency Committee. . . Feeling assured that I shall have your cordial co-operation in the effort to secure a satisfactory measure that will solve this long-standing problem in the interest of the country, I am . . ."

This was the bill, and no other, that was made the basis of the Federal Reserve Act. It was approved by the President, with four changes, and agreed to by McAdoo and Owen. It was favorably reviewed by W. T. Thompson, Solicitor of the Treasury; and by George E. Roberts, Director of the Mint. Introduced as H.R. 7837, it was referred to committee.

Weeks were to pass before it could be reported out and during those weeks there was more than a little sniping from the rear. Like Proteus of old, a new champion was rising out of the restive sea of opposition, hopeful of gaining a foothold in the land and leading the flocks of Bryan's followers into an agrarian revolt. This was Congressman Henry of Texas.

The room of the House Banking and Currency Committee was directly below the room of the House Committee on Rules, of which Henry was chairman. Little groups of agrarians began to drift into the offices of the Banking and Currency Committee. Making obstruction their weapon, they kept worrying at Glass and his associates. As fast as one group would be placated, another would appear; then another, and another . . . with the Chairman of the Rules Committee always finding new schemes for presentation by his myrmidons.

In vain Glass protested to Henry until, at last, after a particularly senseless and flagrant effort at obstruction, he went to the President and offered to resign. It was the only time Glass ever heard Wilson swear :

"Damn it !" the President barked, "don't resign, old fellow. Outvote them !"

Glass accepted the advice. The bill emerged triumphantly from committee without a single amendment of its essential provisions.

The long, stultifying tedium of shadow-boxing was out of the way. The climax came in what will rank as one of the most memorable caucuses ever held in either branch of the national legislature.

Congressman Henry told newspaper reporters that Bryan was backing the insurrection, ready to loose "his legions and measure strength with the Wilson element." The Texas Congressman claimed control ; and did have a formidable bloc of votes. "The Texan was an engaging talker," recalled Glass, "and an exceedingly likable fellow ; but he knew as much about banking and currency questions as a child about astronomy. He was not a vicious demagogue ; but a very insinuating one." Henry confidently relied on rallying the members from the agricultural districts by conjuring with the still-magic name of Bryan for the defeat of "this Wall Street Currency Bill," and the substitution of his own.

"The currency scheme evolved by this passionate band of economic guerillas was 'fearfully and wonderfully made.' " Among its extraordinary provisions was one calling for three new kinds of currency, totaling nearly a billion, to be classified as "Agricultural Currency," "Commercial Currency," and "Industrial Currency." These funds were to be parcelled out with lavish hand to subsidize agriculture, commerce and industry. And the Federal Reserve Board was to be made up of farmers, laborers, bankers and ex-Presidents of the United States !

Henry maligned the committee and assailed the President, in terms that constituted a challenge to Wilson's leadership of the party. He invoked Bryan, allegedly his backer, quoting a speech from the Commoner, made years before, against "executive aggression." Andrew Jackson was disinterred and his United States bank fight twisted into a specious analogy to his side of the controversy . . . and he made a great clatter about the "big money interests" behind the Glass bill.

Entirely extemporaneously, Glass spoke in reply. It is unfortunate that his speech, because of the secrecy that controls a party caucus, is lost to record. It is said he started out rather lamely, but as he gradually warmed to his subject his followers began to yell in approval :

"Give 'em hell, Carter !"

"Why use dynamite," dryly interjected Glass, "when insect powder will do the work ?"

Exposing its absurdities, he took the Henry measure apart and showed it did not tick. Referring to its penalties against those who refused to exchange their wares for the depreciated currency proposed, he ventured to ask "if it was proposed to dangle the hangman's noose before the tradesmen of America when they should turn from Henry's currency as they would the drippings from a pest-house ?" He wasted little time on this abortive bill, but moved on to an explanation and defense of the committee measure.

This he made in a measured, repressed tone, but when it came to Henry's assault on Wilson, anger crept into his voice : "because Woodrow Wilson, in the exercise of his constitutional privilege, pleased to confer with members of the Banking and Currency committee concerning provisions of this bill, he is arraigned in a Democratic caucus as a political martinet.

I take leave, as a Democrat associated with this Administration in a great work for the country, to express the belief that no man ever lived whose course of conduct in public affairs was prompted by a higher degree of patriotism than the conduct of President Wilson in his effort to reform the banking and currency system of the nation."

And when it came to the opposition's trump card, the much exploited implication that Bryan was in tune with Henry, Glass topped it in a manner that hit their ears like a thunder-clap.

"I have here a letter. It is dated today – August 22, 1913. I should like to read one paragraph from it – a paragraph which is pertinent to this caucus :

My dear Mr. Glass :

. . . The papers have reported members of Congress as presenting views which were alleged to be mine. I do not know to what extent these reports may exaggerate what has been said and done ; but you are authorized to speak for me and say that I appreciate so profoundly the service rendered by the President to the people in the stand he has taken on the fundamental principles involved in currency reform, that I am with him in all the details. If my opinion has influence with anyone called upon to act on this measure, I am willing to assume full responsibility for what I do when I advise him to stand by the President and assist in securing the passage of the bill at the earliest possible moment. . .

Very truly yours,
W. J. Bryan.

Frustrated, Henry vainly tried to answer while the caucus roared with hoots of derision, and the unrestrained yell of victory. Against the din, the Henry group raged in all but drowned-out counterpoint, except for one despairing yip : "Bryan doesn't know a damn thing about this bill !"

Glass heard him. "How prodigal," he smiled, "would have been the praise of the wisdom and patriotism of Mr. Bryan had he taken part with those who condemn, rather than with those who applaud, the effort of the Administration to rescue the country from the continuing peril of a dangerous banking and currency system" . . . and proceeded, in the intervals between tumults, to flay the last bit of life out of the Henry proposals.

It wasn't a victory ; it was a rout.

The vote of the caucus was 168 to 9.

CHAPTER TEN

"The whole country appreciates the work you have done."
— Woodrow Wilson.

With the approval of party caucus, Glass did not have much difficulty piloting the bill through formal consideration by the House Banking and Currency Committee, and reporting it favorably to the House of Representatives. True, Republican committeemen had been called into consultation for the first time ; they did little more than propose minor amendments.

In the House antagonism brought forth dissidents who deplored "political control" in the powers designated to the Federal Reserve Board, the compulsion of national bank membership and the transfer of bank reserves from the money centers to the proposed regional banks. They hammered at the "confiscatory" nature of one federal reserve bank being compelled to rediscount the discounted paper of another. This operation was defended and retained. Time proved its worth. In the critical post-war period it transferred $250,000,000 from stronger to weaker regions, cured many situations in credit extensions, averted a toppling of innumerable commercial houses, and saved at least one federal reserve bank from being wrecked.

Before the vote Glass was faced with the necessity, and the opportunity, of making his first major speech on the floor of the House. This utterance* fills nine and one-half pages of the *Congressional Record* of September 10, 1913.

Unlike his caucus speech, this was no impromptu flare of extemporaneousness. Back of his lengthy and exhaustive analysis of the currency situation and the bill proposed to correct it were ten years of silence and preparation. Not only was the

* For full speech see appendix.

wine ripe and properly aged, but the vine itself from which the grapes were plucked had taproots, reaching far back to the hills of youth and home and suffering no savor of the earth to escape.

The House passed the bill, 287 to 85. Only 3 Democrats voted in opposition; 48 Republicans voted for it, 82 against. It was an overwhelming victory, and Glass was cascaded with congratulatory telegrams and letters from every state in the Union. Said the President: "Glass, using only one side of his mouth, talked that Bill through Congress. I wonder what he could do if he were to use both sides." McAdoo paid his tribute:

THE SECRETARY OF THE TREASURY

Washington,
September 20, 1913.

My dear Glass:

I want to congratulate you sincerely upon your really great achievement in the passage by the House of Representatives of the Glass Bill to reform the currency system of the country. It is a measure upon which you have done so much tedious, intelligent, and effective work that I can well understand your gratification now that the worst of your labors is over.

You are, more than any other single man, entitled to the credit for this real victory in the name of the people of this country, and your name will always be linked with the first constructive financial measure passed by Congress since the enactment of the National Banking Act. You have led the fight with singular ability and with a high order of statesmanship. I am only too glad to have the opportunity of paying this just tribute and of telling you, as well, of the great pleasure and satisfaction it has given me to be your earnest, although not always effective, co-laborer and coadjutor in this needed measure of vital reform.

Always, with warm regards, I am
Sincerely yours,
W. G. McAdoo.

Hon. Carter Glass,
Lynchburg, Va.

And, indicative of the reaction even in circles of high finance was this communication :

St. Louis, September 23, 1913.

Hon. Carter Glass,
Washington, D.C.

Hearty congratulations on passing your bill, even though I do not approve all its provisions. I want to thank you cordially for your devotion to the cause of banking and currency reform. One becomes a better citizen by coming in contact with men entrusted with regulating the affairs of the nation and there finding such untiring energy, unfaltering integrity and indomitable spirit.

Festus J. Wade.

As for Glass, he did not omit his expressions of gratitude to those who stood by him. One of the first to receive recognition was the Nebraskan who, with power to do infinite mischief, had remained loyal to the Administration :

Washington, D.C.
September 25, 1913.

My dear Mr. Bryan :

Looking back over the remarkable campaign for currency reform just ended in the House, one thing stands out, conspicuous in the retrospect, and that is that we are immensely indebted to you for effective aid in critical periods of the contest in committee and in caucus. I desire to thank you for your great assistance to me and to the cause, and also to express my personal gratification at the manner in which you have disappointed your enemies and pleased your friends by standing firmly with the President for sound legislation in behalf of the American people. The country and your party are greatly obliged to you for the skill and discernment with which you have helped along the fight, and I am particularly grateful.

Sincerely yours,
Carter Glass.

Hon Wm. J. Bryan,
Secretary of State,
Washington, D.C.

The scene of battle shifted now to the Senate and to the Banking and Currency Committee of that body, where old enemies assumed many shapes and vestments at once. They plead for delay. As Glass described it, "halted now in their expectations, they still imagined they could defer action until their lines could be reformed." The Senate was weary of the extra session. "Adjournment and respite would enable it to return in the early winter with fresh minds to wrestle with such a complicated problem;" so they said, and so their journals and their spokesmen iterated and reiterated. The President refused to yield, and kept the Senate in session well into the Christmas holiday season.

Unable to obtain delay, the bombardment began anew. While the hearings dragged ponderously for weeks, the same old witnesses and the same old objections drearily hammering over the same old brass, the big guns of the big bankers were brought into place for a real barrage. Not only did the American Bankers Association meet in Boston and mightily condemn the Glass Bill, but the larger Clearing House Associations and the United States Chamber of Commerce, with hundreds of its subsidiaries, were prevailed upon to join in the attack.

"At one point of the compass," says Glass, "an eminent banker would reveal 'alarming inflationary features' and, at the same moment, in another financial center, the business community would be warned that the shift in reserve funds would 'precipitate a disastrous constriction of commercial credits amounting to $1,800,000,000!' It made no difference to these adversaries that both things could not happen at the same time. They kept repeating their nonsense."

Culminating the attack, they brought into action "the big Bertha of the Eastern banking community" and pointed it squarely at The White House. This was a studiously prepared central bank plan, with all the "compulsion, confiscation and political control" which they were denouncing in the Administration Bill, and a good deal more besides. None other than their able Frank A. Vanderlip of the National City Bank, of New York, rushed to Washington to intercept a few influential Senators; as for the President, he refused to accord Vanderlip an interview.

Propaganda was becoming savage; persuasion to the point of coercion was in motion for the central bank scheme. Wilson issued a statement leaving no doubt as to where he stood, then called upon his lieutenants to take the field. He asked Glass to defend the pending measure before the Chicago Association of Commerce and the Economic Club of New York City.

The New York affair brought him into joint debate with Vanderlip. The scholarly financier was to have been aided by Sol Wexler, New Orleans banker, but the latter was unable to attend and Professor Joseph French Johnson, of New York University, took the stage in his stead. It was confidently expected in the East that the Administration would be utterly routed, its bank bill demolished.

For such a saturnalia the ballroom of the Hotel Astor was a-glitter with fashion and beauty, the horseshoe boxes of the mezzanine packed with guests of high degree, with the diamond tiaras of the ladies seeming to wink in delighted anticipation under the refulgence of the great electroliers. Below, eleven hundred bankers and business men in evening dress waited expectantly.

In Vanderlip they were not disappointed. His was an admirable address. Urbane, eloquent, forceful in its presentation of the case for a central bank – and a masterpiece of special pleading – it captivated the assemblage, and the air was whitened again and again by a thousand waving napkins.

What he said sounded like a million dollars, and the million-dollar crowd thundered its delight.

There were a few, a very few, in that throng who pitied the graying Virginian when he rose to make rebuttal. Twenty minutes later, like Icarus, his adversary's triumph had fallen to the earth. Vanderlip was astounded to see the same gentlemen and the same ladies and the same napkins beating the air in even more vociferous tribute to Glass.

To the hostile criticism of the note-issue provision, the "unscientific blot" against which he himself had protested to Wilson, Glass said with complete candor :

"To those who advocate government issue, it may be said we have it here in terms, with discretion in the Reserve Board to issue currency on application or to withhold. To those who contend for bank issues, as I do, we may say that, in the practical operation of the system, you have it here ; because only upon application of a bank can the government issue. To those who affect solicitude for the government's credit, it may be pointed out, as a practical fact, that the security behind the note is many times more than sufficient to protect the government before the note holder can reach the Treasury counter. Thus we have yielded to the sentiment for a government issue, but retained the substance of a bank issue. The section constitutes a compromise ; it provides a composite note. But no man here can put his finger on a solitary element of unsoundness in it."

As for his speech, its significance was appraised by Dr. Lyman Abbott, of the *Outlook*, in which he wrote :

"Those who think that discussions of the currency bill are always dry and technical should have been at the dinner of the Economic Club of New York City held at the Astor Hotel. It was the occasion of a remarkable debate upon the merits of the bill now before Congress – a debate in which Professor

Joseph French Johnson, of the chair of Political Economy of New York University, and Mr. Frank A. Vanderlip, President of the National City Bank of New York City, opposed the bill, while Senator Owen, of Oklahoma and Representative Carter Glass, of Virginia, defended it.

". . . Aside from the value of this debate as a contribution to public knowledge regarding the creation and construction and provisions of the Bill, it was a notable illustration of the power of the orator to influence his audience by sheer force of character and intelligence. We suppose Mr. Glass would be the last man to regard himself as an orator – indeed, he apologized for what he feared was the ineffectiveness of his address on the ground that as a journalist he was a better writer than speaker. But his apology was unnecessary. . .

"Mr. Glass accomplished perhaps more than he himself realized in removing misconceptions, misunderstandings, and prejudices regarding the bill, which unfortunately have prevailed to too large an extent in the financial metropolis of the country.

"The entire country knows that the almost unanimous objection of the bankers to the bill has been based upon the features of government control, so it was pointed out that the sole question here was whether the people would fare better under government control than under exclusive banker control of the country's reserve funds. The bankers protest that under the Glass bill the National Banks are 'compelled' to come into the system by law, whereas the Aldrich bill made their coming in a 'voluntary' matter. Mr. Glass demolished this objection by pointing out, amid the laughter and approval of his hearers, that the Glass bill 'compels the bankers to come in, while the Aldrich bill made it impossible for them to stay out,' and pertinently asked what practical difference a banker could find in the two provisions. . .

"The most singular fact which was brought out at this dinner was the absolute right-about-face which the bankers of the country have made on the question of government control. Six months ago, having protested that the Glass bill provided too much government control, the bankers now protest, if Mr. Vanderlip may be accepted as expressing the best sentiment of American bankers, that the bill does not insure sufficient government control and power!

". . . To understand what a radical change this means in the attitude of the bankers one has but to read the resolutions of the American Bankers Association, passed only a few weeks ago, denouncing presidential appointments to the Federal Reserve Board as a dangerous injection of politics into American finance. . ."

This was indeed the beginning of the end. The Federal Reserve Bill emerged from a battle-torn Senate banking and currency committee without the blessing of a favorable report; and it withstood the unexpected onslaught of such able men and strategists as Senator Hitchcock and Elihu Root. On December 19, it passed the Senate, and went to conference.

We do not need to examine the work of the conferees. The testimony in the Senate itself is explicit that Glass and his House associate won out on every important point of difference, and that the bill, as signed by the President, was substantially the Glass Bill as originally reported and passed by the House of Representatives.

Perhaps one of the most noteworthy features of the conflict was that, in an atmosphere bristling with epithets and odored with intrigue, the House Chairman had refrained from conducting his fight along partisan lines. The battle had been furious; nothing in Andrew Jackson's war against the United States Bank charter had exceeded the intensity of it. Personal and party asperities had abounded; much mud had been thrown. But when Glass made his final presentation to the House of Representatives, he concluded with these words:

"We have not desired to approach or consider the question from the standpoint of party politics. It is too universal a problem for that. It is not a matter for party advantage. I have kept in constant contact and pleasant intercourse with the ranking minority member of the committee, giving him every successive reprint of the bill, affording all the information that he might desire, and inviting in good faith such suggestions as he might care to make.

"And now, Mr. Chairman, sure of our ground, yet conscious of human limitations, we submit this bill to the judgment of the House, challenging a fair consideration of its provisions and devoutly invoking the patriotic cooperation of our colleagues in what should be a great service to the country and a memorable achievement of the Sixty-third Congress."

Exactly one year had passed since Glass had gone through snow and cold to visit Woodrow Wilson at Princeton, New Jersey, his pocket bulging with hand-written memoranda having to do with regional banks, stock issues, government deposits, refunding bonds, boards and reserves. Now, with little in his inside pocket besides a letter just received, he went again through snow and cold, by invitation, to visit the same man — this time in the white pillared mansion in Washington.

The letter which was warming his pocket was from the President. It said:

THE WHITE HOUSE
WASHINGTON

December 23, 1913.

My dear Mr. Glass:

May I now express my admiration for the way in which you have carried the fight for the currency bill to an extraordinarily successful issue. I hope and believe that the whole country appreciates the work you have done at something like its real value and I rejoice that you have so established yourself in its confidence.

With sincere admiration,
Cordially yours,
Woodrow Wilson.

Hon. Carter Glass,
House of Representatives.

The President was in a happy frame of mind. As twilight descended upon The White House, a considerable miscellany of guests assembled in the Executive offices – Vice-President Marshall, Secretary Bryan, Secretary McAdoo, Senator Owen, Speaker Champ Clark, Treasury officials, the First Lady, Congressmen of both parties, White House attachés and the gentlemen of the press. A brief but interesting ceremony was about to begin, and high spirits attended it. It was as though Christmas had come two days early.

The clock hands stood vertical at the hour of six. Smiling, Woodrow Wilson strode to his desk, started to sit down, then hesitated. He gazed around the room – where was Glass? Obscured in modesty, the Virginian had taken an inconspicuous position behind the crowd at the back of the room. He was promptly pushed forward to a place beside the desk, and the President clasped his hand.

"I must do the deed first," said the President, as he sat down, "and perhaps I will have something to say afterward."

Then using four gold pens, he signed the Federal Reserve Act. With the first he wrote "Approved, 23 Dec. 1913," and presented the pen to Glass. With the second he wrote "Wood," handed the pen to Owen. The third pen wrote "row" and went to McAdoo. The fourth wrote "Wilson" and was reserved for Senator Chilton, of West Virginia, who had sent it to The White House with a request that it be used.

"The deed" having been accomplished, the President arose

with "something to say." His speech was brief and hurried:

"I need not tell you that I feel a very deep gratification at being able to sign this bill, and I feel that I ought to express very heartily the admiration I have for the men who have made it possible for me to sign it.

"There have been currents and counter currents, but the stream has moved forward. I think that we owe special admiration to the patience and the leadership and the skill and the force of the chairmen of the two committees, and behind them have stood the committees themselves exercising a degree of scrutiny and of careful thought in this matter which undoubtedly has redounded to the benefit of the bill itself. . ."

He expressed gratification for the considerable number of Republican votes cast for the measure, stated his surprise at its "sudden acceptance" by public opinion. Business men, he said, had opened their eyes to find in this supposedly hostile measure a serviceable friend. He concluded by rejoicing that he was able to bestow this Christmas gift upon American business.

An informal reception followed.

Since then it has been universally conceded that the Federal Reserve System has proved the most feasible and effective scheme of national reserve banking ever devised in this country. Created for the requirements of peace, it nevertheless buttressed and mobilized the nation's wealth for its role in the World War. It has saved billions in commerce, prevented panics, preserved the country again and again from disaster, and more than any other single achievement of government has served to raise the United States from a provincial position to the status of a world power.

Broaden the picture, search rhetoric for metaphor to fix it in the context of the American saga . . . or listen to the long-drawn tick-tock of the clock of factual occurrence, day by day, then and now . . . still the dispassionately revolving disc that is called History perpetuates here a mortal achievement adjusting the world to its time.

CHAPTER ELEVEN

The Treasury post is offered, and accepted.

To his Lynchburg home on March 10, 1915 came a letter from McAdoo which began, "My dear Glass: Please accept my hearty congratulations on your election to the Chairmanship of the Committee investigating the rural credit situation. . ." Outcome of the Glass committee's deliberations was the enactment of this country's first Farm Credit Act.

This was timely, for with half the world at war it was devolving upon the other half to feed it. American agriculture was faced with the responsibility, and must needs expand to the opportunity, of raising from the earth more foodstuffs than ever before in history. Those who in later years periodically charged Glass with lack of feeling for the farmer apparently omitted to remember that he had been a pioneer in perceiving their problems and legislating for their credit needs.

But other needs than agriculture's that year were demanding the vigilant scrutiny of Wilson and, in his lesser station, Congressman Glass. Talk of preparedness vied with pleas of pacifism in an apprehensive nation, and the voice of the latter contingent was being submerged under the wave of horror swept to these shores by the *Lusitania* tragedy. Young men began planning to leave their labor and enter training camps, among them the Glass boys, Powell and Carter Jr.

Teutonic periscopes rose from the Atlantic in menace to the American export trade, and what Glass branded "the undersea Sneak" imperilled the lives of American travellers abroad. In condemnation of Wilson's stern stand against German maritime aggression, critics of the Administration accused him of risking war to assert the abstract right of "some fool Americans to joy-ride on the seas."

By March 1916, this pacifist-political bloc, in a mood of legislative rebuke, sought to usurp the diplomatic prerogatives of the Executive with the McLemore resolution to warn American citizens against traveling on armed merchantmen of the belligerent powers, except at their own risk. In a notable speech before the House, Glass sprang to Wilson's defense :

"With a caution that provoked the taunts of the truculent ; with a courage that excited the apprehensions of the timid ; with an undeviating frankness and firmness that commanded the respect of foreign nations, as they confirmed the faith of millions of his own countrymen, the President has for eighteen months applied himself to the task of preserving the peace without impairing the honor of the Republic."

Wilson, he maintained, had stood on his constitutional rights and unhesitatingly avowed his position to all the nations of the earth. Nor had he been a suppliant before Congress for an empty vote of confidence.

"He has declined to be a party to any such petty travesty. Nothing of a nature so obsequious as that is presented here. Members of Congress challenged the purposes and authority of the President and we are now counterchallenged to maintain the supremacy of law over the practices of piracy ; to assert the cherished rights of civilization against the incursions of oceanic barbarism ; to execute, if we dare, the threatened capitulation of Congress to the atrocious idea that international honor is a fantasy and moral obligation a dream !"

Was it true, he demanded, that the Congress stood ready to withdraw the protection of the Government to its citizens who might choose to exercise the rights which international law, for the whole period of this country's existence, had assured them ? Was Congress so restless to make this cowardly and humiliating surrender that it would resort to the amazing experiment of trying "by legislative furor" to nullify the diplomatic achievements of the President in maintaining the conceded rights of neutral nations against the unscrupulous aggressions of belligerent powers? That, he insisted, was the undodgeable gravamen of the issue.

"I know, as every other Member of the House must know," he bluntly stated, "that the plain parliamentary intent of laying a proposition on the table is to kill it – to bury it without ceremony or tears. That is why I shall vote to table the McLemore resolution.

"I want the people of Virginia to know that I oppose any surrender, actually or implicitly, of any vital American right merely to propitiate a war-mad foreign nation, which already has strewn the seas with the dead bodies of helpless American victims. I want them to know that I have no absolution for such a crime; that I stand for full reparation and ample security, and am utterly opposed to the suggested interference of Congress with the diplomatic functions of the President.

"I want them to know that I should despise myself for a vote cast here to warn American citizens that they must travel the free waters of the globe in merchant ships at their own peril, without their country's protection. I want them to know that I would tear to tatters my commission as a Member of the House of Representatives could I imagine that the people of Virginia would have me do a thing so repugnant to my sense of national honor and so at variance with my conception of national self-respect."

Referring to stout warnings to the Imperial German Government by Wilson and Secretary Lansing against any repetition of the *Lusitania* atrocity, he said: "Yet, with phrases like these ringing in our ears, resonant with fine sentiment and high resolve, we are asked abjectly to disavow the admonition which they convey and, lost to shame, decry the memory of our *Lusitania* dead! Shall this House today proclaim to the world what Dumba * is said to have been told in a corner, that the Government of the United States did not exactly mean what it said ?"

As he saw it, the Congress proposed to forbid the people to exercise their rights for fear it might be called upon to vindicate them. Some gentlemen, he realized, favored merely "a simple warning," unaccompanied by any surrender of technical rights. He pointed to the emptiness of such a farce, and foresaw the face-losing repercussions of any such act in other lands. "Any sort of warning would convey the idea of concession, would be tantamount to yielding, would cover us with odium and excite against us the just indignation of the American people. God save us from the degradation and from the universal execration involved in it !"

Into his summation he threw all the fervid eloquence which he at the moment could muster.

"Every one of us in authority here is for peace. The whole Congress is for peace. The President of the United States for many months, by night and day, has kept a vigil for peace. With enduring patience, with amazing skill, oblivious to all things else, he has passionately sought, by every conceivable means to keep this country out of the maelstrom of war. Neither taunt nor threat has shaken his purpose or diverted him from his course. But there are some things better than life, as there are other things worse than death. This human body, bereft of the soul which reveals the image of God, is but a whited sepulcher ; and so a nation with its righteous spirit quenched is as a tossing derelict of the sea.

"We are asked to do a thing today that would waste, indeed with palsy, every worthy aspiration of our national existence and shame us through the remaining years. Warn American citizens from the seas ! Of course the President will not do it.

* Austrian diplomat in U.S., 1913–15

'Twere to abandon, as he so finely said, the 'very essence of the things which have made America a sovereign nation'; yes, and to celebrate approvingly the never-to-be-forgotten day when a thousand innocent human beings, victims of maritime stealth and atrocity, were suddenly plunged into the cold embrace of the fathomless deep. Why, sir, their very spirits would ride upon the waves to mock our battle craft from the oceans. Their outraged memory in some fateful form would cling to our ships avengingly and cast derision in the faces of our sailors in every port of the civilized earth."

And finally he lashed out at the propaganda of the pacifists:

"Like unto the proposal to discredit the Nation is the pathetic, perfervid talk about desolating American homes and distressing American mothers by sacrificing their sons to the god of war. The nearest approach to war which this country has recently made was when Members of Congress sought to impede the President's plans for maintaining an honorable peace. The surest prelude to intolerable affront from one direction is the manifestation of a cowardly submission from the other; and unless it be conceived that no injury, however great, no insult, however grievous, could provoke this Nation to resentment, the course proposed by meddling resolutions is most certain to invite aggression and ultimately to precipitate war.

"And there are some things worse than war. Virginia has homes which might be desolated and mothers who might be distressed and sons who might be sacrificed. But I pray God that the mothers and sons of Virginia who live appreciate their heritage from those who, 'being dead, yet speaketh.' Two of Virginia's boys are my own – stalwart, manly fellows, for either of whom I would die a thousand times – and I would have them hear me say, without a tremor, in the spirit which I hope animates their hearts, that I would rather be pursued through time and eternity by the pitiful apparition of their shattered forms than to see my country dishonored and its flag hauled down in disgrace!

"I shall vote to lay this resolution on the table."

And on the table it was laid. Some days afterward Glass was the recipient of a note:

My dear Glass:

Thank you with all my heart for your speech on American rights on the seas.

Cordially and faithfully yours,
(signed) Woodrow Wilson.

Three months later, when Glass was in St. Louis, a delegate to the Democratic National Convention, he found in his hotel box another communication from The White House. Wilson had wired:

Am suggesting your selection as Secretary National Committee I earnestly beg that you will not decline we will see that you are relieved of all detail of work I greatly need your moral influence and your guidance which I perfectly trust

Glass' reply is typical:

I gravely doubt the wisdom of your suggestion but I will not withhold any service which it is thought I may render you or the party

In this secretarial post he labored assiduously for his political chief, in the drafting of the Democratic platform, as well as in the ensuing campaign which resulted in the defeat of Charles Evans Hughes, who had emerged, much to the Virginian's disapproval, from the non-partisan robes of a Supreme Court Justice to enter the political arena.

It was a crucially close contest, fought to a finish. In 1912, the country had been predominantly Republican, and only the party split precipitated by Theodore Roosevelt's bolt from the ranks had enabled Wilson to win. Now a reunited opposition strove to wrest the reins of government, and for many anxious hours after the casting of the final ballot no one knew the outcome. It was late in the day after election that the California returns tardily tipped the balance to a Democratic triumph.

During the campaign, aside from lauding the President for having kept the nation out of war, his party spokesman pointed with justifiable pride to the passage of the Federal Reserve Act during his Administration. The Republicans, much to the amazement of the truly informed, countered with the trite claim that it was a mere outgrowth and modification of the old Aldrich plan.

On the floor of the House on September 7, Glass ripped the vitals out of this absurd contention. To accomplish such disembowelment he had but to lard his scathing sarcasm with a sprinkling of pregnant facts – that before the Academy of Political Science Aldrich himself had savagely assailed the Federal Reserve bill, and that in both branches of the Congress the Republican minority had voted heavily against it.

Motivated not only by gratitude for the Congressman's loyalty and service, but by confidence in his ability as well, the President felt impelled to reward him with a promotion of distinction. One day he mentioned that McAdoo might soon resign as Secretary of the Treasury, and ventured the suggestion that Glass would be just the man to take his place. Glass made no response to the remark, indicated no eagerness for the Cabinet post, and nothing further was said on the subject.

A full year later the ubiquitous Colonel House drew Glass aside to tell him McAdoo was planning to resign, and that he would use his influence with the President to get Glass appointed as his successor. The Virginian smiled and said nothing.

The first fateful week of April, 1917, found America in a state of extreme tension. War with Germany, most people realized, was decidedly imminent. Organized civilians under military instruction were drilling in public parks with wooden guns. New barracks were being built for the thousands of young men enrolled in training camps. Both the Glass boys held commissions in the Reserve Corps. And public-minded men of high financial station, cognizant of the fact that war was costing Britain $35,000,000 a day, were forming committees and instituting drives to mobilize the nation's money. They wanted war on a cash basis, a pay-as-you-enter war.

On April 2 the armed American ship *Aztec* went down, the victim of a mine or torpedo. Herbert Hoover was in London, directing relief for the Belgians. Suffragettes, mindful of the fact that war had brought suffrage to English and Russian women, were militantly picketing The White House. At 8:30 that evening Woodrow Wilson called for half a million volunteers and asked Congress to declare war. Representative Flood and Senator Martin, both of Virginia, introduced resolutions to that effect.

Next day U. S. Steel boosted wages, and promised steel to the Government at half price. England and France were applauding the President's decision, Germany was fencing for delay. The pacifist minority was giving up hope, but Senator Robert M. La Follette was filibustering to block the resolutions. His opposition was overridden and on April 4, the Senate voted 82 to 6 for war. The House adjourned until ten o'clock the following morning.

Next day Glass sat through a stormy seventeen-hour session, which concluded at 3:12 A. M. April 6 with a vote of 373 to 50.

America was at war!

Hoover was speedily summoned home to supervise conservation of food supplies. Theodore Roosevelt beseeched the President for an army commission which would authorize him to organize a division for service overseas, but upon the advice of Secretary of War Newton D. Baker, Wilson declined to grant it. From Tallahassee, Florida, former Secretary of State Bryan made the front pages with a telegram asking Wilson to enroll him as a private.

No newspaper, however, was privy to Glass' personal appeal to the President to raise the army age limit that he might enlist. Then fifty-nine, he offered his services in any capacity for which Wilson might deem him fit. He felt, he said, that inasmuch as he had voted to send American youth to war, he could never live in peace with himself again unless he shared the same hardships of war and the same privilege of serving his country. He saw the President and in unqualified terms stated his desire – then insisted.

"It will do you no good to insist," said Wilson. "I will see to it personally that they don't accept you."

Then, from the depths of his disappointment, he heard the President add : "Glass, I need you here, with me. You can serve your country far better where you are."

Still determined, Glass wrote Wilson. In answer there came a letter in which the President expressed appreciation for "the fine spirit behind your desire to go to France with our armed forces" and again denied him the privilege.

But he did serve, striving constantly to unify the factions frequently threatening disruption to the Presidential leadership so vitally imperative in time of war. Militantly he sprang into action when, on January 19, 1918, Senator Chamberlain of Oregon, Chairman of the Committee on Military Affairs, stood before an association called the National Security League in New York and made this remarkable declaration :

"The Military Establishment of America has fallen down. There is no use to be optimistic about a thing that does not exist. It has almost stopped functioning, my friends. Why? Because of inefficiency in every bureau and in every department of the Government of the United States."

In direct answer Glass addressed Congress:

"The country was aghast at that terrific impeachment of the Government of the United States. It was a passionate, a comprehensive arraignment; it startled the nervous system of the Nation as the clanging of a fire bell in the night. Instantly public opinion became tense. Immediately it was realized that the Oregon Senator had done what Edmund Burke said he could not do; he had drawn an indictment of a whole people. I say that because this is a representative Government, equally free from the impedimenta of heredity and the constraints of autocratic power. And if it truthfully may be said that the American people have erected a Government that fails to function in the face of imminent peril, what more accursed accusation could be written in the book of fate?

"If, with good reason, it may be charged that the people of the United States, with their constitutional freedom of speech and of the press, have been so indifferent to their liberties and so insensible of their own security as to commit every bureau and department of Government to incompetent hands, would we not better welcome, rather than resist, the invasion of Teutonic kultur? If what Senator Chamberlain said at New York is true, it denotes the irretrievable breakdown of democracy at a time when only the triumph of democracy in arms may compensate for the glorious oblation of men who have died and men who yet shall perish that heaven may be kind to those who hereafter will inhabit the earth."

During the interrupting wave of applause he recalled that Wilson's adversaries had censured his asperity in unconventionally making a swift and direct answer to the Chamberlain charge through the medium of the public press.

"I think the country would have been pained and disappointed," he continued, "had not the President taken the quickest way to reassure the American people. It was a grave situation, one which could not endure hesitation or fine phrasing. Asperity! Yes; there was asperity; but there come occasions when benignity itself is challenged to aid the right by assuming an aspect of reproof."

Stating that his own earnest quest for the truth had carried him through nearly two thousand pages of responsible testimony, he announced:

"From the testimony I have turned away, not with tears nor with trembling apprehension for the well-being of my own sons or the sons of other fathers, but with a firmer faith in my country, praising God for the quiet courage of the men and the ineffable fortitude of the women of America who are to win this war."

In intervals between reiterant handclapping he reviewed the actual achievements of the War Department in mobilizing and transporting two million troops with a speed that had amazed the nations of the world. He defended Secretary Newton D. Baker's purchase of artillery and munitions from the already over-supplied arsenals of France, thus circumventing the delay that would have attended home manufacture.

"And merely because the Secretary of War and his expert military advisers thus used their plain common sense in a perplexing posture of affairs, it is not to be inferred that the Congress or the people of the country will be induced to credit the wild and foolish charge that the Government has broken down and needs to be frightened to its feet again by the distempered clatter of theatrical public men!"

He flayed the contention of captious critics that the Army

had been equipped with inferior machine guns. "Talleyrand tells us that language was invented to conceal our thoughts. I should hate to regard that as axiomatic. It is, of course, a witty French cynicism. But, at least, we do know that sometimes words are used to obscure the truth or skillfully employed to pervert it. The American Army in France has thousands of machine guns to go up against the enemy ; it is as well equipped with machine guns as any army in Europe – perhaps better equipped than the German army."

There had been delay, he granted, in equipping troops with rifles, but that delay had resulted in providing them with the finest rifles in the world. "It seems to be the idea of some distinguished gentlemen that we should have grabbed up any old instruments of warfare and sent a ragamuffin army across the Atlantic instantly to break the Hindenburg line ! . . .

"Who of us does not recall that the pictorial papers and magazines of this country for many months after Great Britain had gone to war teemed with illustrations portraying British recruits marching in silk hats, in shirt sleeves, and workman's blouse, and drilling on England's commons with broomsticks and walking canes ? Did any responsible public man in Great Britain, because of this, charge that the British military establishment was nonexistent ? Did the fact here cited betoken incompetence or slothful pace ? On the contrary, it seems to me that it signified an indomitable spirit – a spirit that found expression at Neuve-Chapelle and Passchendaele and other battle fields which will literally crowd the glorious pages of history."

He pleaded for frankness and honesty in American self-appraisal, and several times as he continued he was reminded by Speaker Champ Clark that his allotted time had expired ; and each time other Representatives yielded their own time that he might go on. Presently he moved his hearers to laughter and cheers with Shakespearean and Biblical analogies.

"I have been told that the severest of these criticisms of the Government have emanated from gentlemen who protest an unaffected devotion to this Administration. By that I am reminded that there was a lady in the play who protested too much. It also brings to me a vision of that memorable episode of the field of Gibeon, in the time of David, the King, when Joab met Amassa, whose face he caressed and whose body he despoiled. You remember the story. With the customary salutation of affection Joab, with his right hand, took hold of Amassa's beard and asked : 'Is it well with thee, my brother ?' And Amassa noted not the sword that was in Joab's other hand ; and Joab smote Amassa under the fifth rib and laid his bowels in the dust !

"The President of the United States has no beard, but he has eyes keen enough to perceive the sword in the other hand of those who would savagely slash him in public rather than confer with him in confidence.

"The other thing about this Biblical illustration which it is worth while to recall is the fact that pretty soon after that left-handed jab on the field of Gibeon Joab himself perished."

Allowing that there had been lack of military co-ordination, conflict of authority, and poutings and bickerings over rank and precedence, still, he averred, the machine was driving ahead. "Its velocity will not be increased, but rather impeded, by perverse politicians pounding at its vitals as it goes along."

Finally he turned from destructive attack to a constructive appeal for concerted efforts in the conduct of the war.

"I have in mind an incident which I shall remember to my dying day. When the Congress had under consideration the selective draft bill the governor of my State came to Washington for an interview with the President to protest against requiring Virginia boys to be drafted, instead of permitting them to volunteer. He also desired that State military units with a history and traditions dearly cherished should be permitted to retain their identity. A kinsman of J. E. B. Stuart, the great cavalry leader of the Confederacy, the Virginia governor, with all the sentiment and tenderness of an ancient Commonwealth in his vision, presented his case to the President with pathetic earnestness.

"When he had finished, the President, touched and gravely considerate, told Governor Stuart that the one thing we most needed to realize just then was the fact that this is a Nation. It is not Virginia's war, he said, nor New England's war ; not a war of the East or the West or the North or the South. It is America's war. There should be intermingling of troops from all the States. We should submerge provincialism and sectionalism and party spirit in one powerful flood of nationalism, which would carry us on to victory. The vision as the President saw and interpreted it was full of heart and inspiration.

"And, why may it not be so ? Why may not the fathers and mothers of sons who are going across the seas to fight the great battle for freedom have the precious privilege of feeling that their boys are flanked on either side by a brave American comrade ? What matter whether he be from Massachusetts or Virginia, from Maine or Mississippi, from the Atlantic seaboard or the Pacific, from the Lake region or the Gulf, just so he be a true American soldier, willing to die for his comrades and his country ?"

Among the legislators who joined in ovation there were many – fathers and brothers of men fighting in France – whose eyes were not dry. Glass added one sentence in conclusion.

"When in the providence of God they shall come back and

march in grand review, why may not all of us praise Heaven that, since they equally shared the perils of the struggle, equally they shall merit the honors and gratitude of this great united Nation?"

Later that year the President asked Glass to become a member of the Federal Reserve Board, to succeed Frederic A. Delano, who had resigned to enter the Army. Glass expressed reluctance.

"Well, think it over for a while," said Wilson. "Perhaps you'll change your mind."

Captain Powell Glass and Lieutenant Carter Glass, Jr. were now in combat service on the Western Front. Early in the autumn of 1918 their father, accompanied by two of his House colleagues, "Jimmy" Byrnes and "Dick" Whaley, both of South Carolina, went abroad and visited them on the Flanders battlefields. Since the boys served in separate divisions, Glass arranged, through General Pershing, for them to see each other for the first time since they had left the United States.

Glass was eager to see at first hand the ravages of war which had been preying so constantly on his mind. And he did. As he stood watching, a German shell fell and exploded within a scant two hundred feet.

He obtained temporary leave for the boys that they might spend several days in Paris. An amusing incident occurred at the café where they dined. Glass, not caring for the elaborate sweets on the menu, ordered a pear for dessert. After three evenings of this Byrne, whom they had appointed the common "pocket," or treasurer for the three tourists, blandly inquired if he had any idea what those pears cost.

"Oh, about a quarter, I suppose," Glass surmised.

"No," said Byrne, "they cost $2.50 each. In the past three days you have eaten three pears. Two dollars and fifty cents multiplied by three is how much?"

Glass decided to abstain from pears, and save the money.

After months of trench rations his two boys were famished for fruits. Between them they ate a dozen bananas a day. They were never told these cost 75 cents each.

In December, when Glass stepped off the gangplank at Halifax, Nova Scotia, the American Consul was there to greet him.

"Welcome home, Mr. Secretary."

Glass was momentarily alarmed.

"What's happened to McAdoo?"

"He's resigned, and they say that the President is certain to appoint you in his place."

And so it was. On his return to Washington he was summoned immediately to The White House. Wilson, worn with the strain of the great war now ended, on the eve of sailing for Paris and the Peace Conference, and conscious of the difficult task of reconstruction that now faced the nation, briefly tendered to Glass one of the most important posts in his Administration.

For his part the Virginia Congressman, though pleased and honored, was sober and unconvinced of his fitness for the job. He pointed out that his entire experience had been legislative, not administrative.

With something of a twinkle in his eye Wilson said, "I rather think, Glass, that we'll be able to manage the job together."

Glass mopped his brow, cleared his throat, looked at Wilson wistfully.

"Mr. President, if you will pardon me, there is one important person whose advice I want to ask before accepting."

"Who is it, if I may ask?"

"My wife."

"I have confidence in Mrs. Glass' judgment," said the President. "Go and ask her about it."

Mrs. Glass was in Lynchburg. That night he consulted her by long distance telephone. Next morning, after conferring briefly with McAdoo, he notified The White House of his acceptance. He was to become the first Secretary of the Treasury ever from Virginia, and the first cabinet officer from Virginia since John B. Flood was Secretary of War in Buchanan's administration.

CHAPTER TWELVE

Clemenceau and Lloyd George disagree with Glass; and Glass makes fateful prediction.

On the night of December 4, 1918, a message went out from the radio booth on the *George Washington*, far out on the Atlantic. Aboard was Woodrow Wilson, on his way to Europe, and the Peace Conference. The message, signed by the President, was in code. On shore, Navy Department operators received it and sent it to The White House. There it was decoded and turned over to Rudolph Forster, executive clerk, who dated it, and gave it to a messenger for delivery to the Senate.

Woodrow Wilson had placed in nomination for Secretary of the Treasury the name of Carter Glass.

The announcement was made on December 5, and that afternoon Glass received an ovation as his presence was discovered in the rear of the House of Representatives. To the questioning of newspapermen he had but one reply: "I will not have anything to say before the Senate has acted upon the matter."

There was no question as to how the Senate would act. On December 6 it confirmed the appointment with unanimous approval.

Weary under the load he had been carrying, McAdoo was glad, on December 16, to relinquish the post he had resigned with the signing of the Armistice. Accompanied by McAdoo, Glass went before Judge Hay, in the Court of Claims, where the oath was administered. With McAdoo he returned to the Treasury where further brief ceremonies were conducted under the inspection of motion picture cameras. Then McAdoo, with an audible sigh of relief, turned and walked out of the room, glancing up, as he was leaving, at a painting of Albert Gallatin, to remark: "That is how one Secretary of the Treasury looked when he retired – I am going to get out before I get that broken."

Glass had no illusions about the task now his. In many ways, it was an even more arduous job than the one McAdoo had so successfully completed. McAdoo's had been an exciting and dramatic experience of financing the war; for Glass there was the monotonous, but equally responsible and fatiguing job of cleaning up.

There was the responsibility of determining the terms of bonds, and certificates of indebtedness, for a new Liberty Loan.

There was the unhappy chore of convincing Congress that the tax program, which had been approved by Wilson before he sailed, should be passed. It was a program that called for the ratification of a revenue bill "to yield $6,000,000,000 payable during the year of 1919, and not less than $4,000,000,000 in the calendar year of 1920."

There remained the financial problems concerning the granting of loans to the Allies; and, accompanying this problem, the recognition that these loans should be discontinued as soon as possible.

There continued the foreign exchange situation, more difficult now because, during the war, exchange had become a question of trade balances between the United States, Great Britain, France and Italy.

Besides these, there were a multitude of foreign and domestic matters, all involving the Treasury – such matters as supplying funds, and transportation, in returning the expeditionary forces; the operation of the Federal Farm Loan Bureau; the War Risk Insurance Bureau. Hospitals had to be built, that being a Treasury problem along with the building of all other Federal structures ; and there was a President, and a Peace commission, to advise in financial dealings with nations around the Peace table.

Three days before Glass took over the post, William W. Rucker, a member of the House of Representatives, charged from the floor that "more than 300,000 letters, many of them containing allotments, applications for allowances, applications in behalf of widows and wives who had been deserted, and all that sort of thing, were dumped into a heap and left there without ever having been opened, and when some clerk discovered this and opened up three or four thousand of them someone higher in authority said that no more of these letters should be opened, because it was making too much work."

After saying he had received a report from the War Risk Insurance Bureau denying the charges and insisting that all mail in the bureau was promptly opened, and distributed, Glass requested the Congressman to give him the benefit of "any information you have on the subject."

Rucker had no information. Glass had some satisfaction.

Glass' first act upon becoming Secretary was to tell the Department "there will be no change in the Treasury policies, and I ask that all resignations, if any officials desire to be relieved, be deferred for several months. My reason for making the request is that my predecessor has built up an organization of unimpeachable integrity, sincerity and earnestness, and I choose not to disturb it. Without their support I would be unequal to the task of maintaining the standard of efficiency which Mr. McAdoo has established and which is the best the Government of the United States has had in its Treasury Department."

Among those he found in the Department were Russell Leffingwell, and Albert Rathbone, and Parker Gilbert, three men who soon were to become indispensable. These he called into immediate conference, asking for their confidence and promising his own. With them he went over the foreign loan situation, reached his own conclusions, and sent a wireless message to Wilson, then in Paris:

December 19, 1918.

Amembassy,
Paris.

For President from Glass.

First: On assuming my duties as Secretary of the Treasury situation regarding foreign loans gives me grave concern.

Second: Our loans to foreign governments now aggregate nearly $8,000,000,000 and will probably approximate $8,500,000,000 before declaration of peace an amount sufficient to pay all our government expenses for about eight years on the basis existing immediately preceding our entry into the war. Congress believes these loans are good and should be collected and the possibility that the debts may be forgiven or exchanged for debts not as good is fomenting opposition to extending the authority of Treasury within the limits of the existing $10,000,000,000 appropriation to make loans after the war to allied governments previously participating in the war against the enemies of the United States for purchases in the United States for reconstruction purposes.

Third: I judge from recent semi-official inquiries that European Allies may attempt to bring up at peace conference questions concerning our foreign loans. You will recall speeches which Wickersham and Beck have made advocating our cancelling foreign obligations. An Associated Press dispatch from Paris published December 17 announces probable presentation by French Government to Chamber of Deputies of bill to establish an international union to distribute the expenses of war already incurred between nations on basis of populations and power to contribute. Same dispatch states similar plan under consideration by British Government but no definite steps taken on it.

Fourth: While British loans to foreign governments exceed $7,000,000,000, including British loans to Russia of about $2,700,000,000, it might be that Great Britain would not be averse to cancelling war loans which it has made in consideration of cancellation of perfectly good debt of British to United States now about $4,000,000,000.

Fifth : French Finance Minister has indicated that he does not think it desirable to discuss at this time converting French demand obligations held by the United States into long time obligations as the maturities which French Government would consider as desirable and fair will depend upon moneys made available to them from Germany as a result of peace terms. As a few months ago Finance Minister strongly urged settlement of maturity dates he may have in mind the proposal of some plan permitting France to settle her debt to us by transferring a part of her claim for reparation against Germany.

Sixth : From Treasury standpoint it would be distinctly advisable to keep all questions regarding our foreign loans out of discussions at peace conference, in which event I can undertake definite settlement of these matters in Washington in such manner as to fully preserve the value of our foreign loans. If, however, Allied Governments are able to force discussion of these matters as a preliminary to or part of peace agreement, I recommend that Treasury be officially represented so that it may keep you advised of my views concerning these and any other financial questions arising and be prepared to participate in such discussions as may be necessary.

I feel that these financial questions are different in character from those with which Treasury representatives in Europe have been dealing and I agree with my predecessor's instruction to them not to participate in the pending peace discussions. If you should determine to have Treasury represented trust you will notify me as far in advance as circumstances permit so I may select and personally instruct my representatives and send them to Paris for this express purpose.

(signed) Carter Glass.

The response from the President came a few days later :

Paris, Dec. 23, 1918.

Tumulty,
White House,
Washington.

Message for Glass :

Hearty welcome to your new duties. I am trying to keep a close watch on the verdicts, plans and maneuvers about the loans to which you refer and shall continue to do so with the distinct determination that none of the things to which you refer shall be accomplished. I am confident it will be possible to prevent them. Many such things have once or twice to be exposed to be disposed of. There can be no proper basis for a discussion of our foreign loans in connection with the Peace Conference. At the same time it will be very serviceable to have some one in whom you have the utmost confidence sent over here to represent you in these important matters. When I left, Leffingwell seemed to be best posted but perhaps you need him at home.

Woodrow Wilson.

On December 19, Glass issued a public statement notifying the American people "the Treasury must issue another large loan before the end of the fiscal year," and cautioning holders of Government bonds against "exchanging them for other securities of very doubtful value. . . They have invested in the best security in the world and it is both to their own interest and to that of their Government that these securities be retained."

In a practical way, on December 30, he requested the Federal Reserve Board to continue its control over the money market for an indefinite date beyond January 10, 1919, the time previously fixed for the expiration of such supervision. He made this request "to aid the Government's financial requirements – on the one hand to prevent an increase in the rate for call money and on the other hand to prevent expansion of the loan market."

His reason for these words, and this action, was his anxiety over the increasing use of Government bonds as collateral for speculative borrowings. During the war the people had subscribed to $18,000,000,000 in bonds and certificates, and under the terms of the Federal Reserve Act such holdings were permissible collateral. A wave of stock market gambling had begun. He wanted it stopped before disaster came; and though it is getting ahead of the story, as early as October 25, 1919, there was an exchange of memoranda between himself and Leffingwell in which it was written:

". . . Although the New York Stock Exchange furnishes a valuable and necessary safety valve and barometer, its methods must be reformed so as to suppress manipulation and also as to the settlement and financing of transactions. These reforms should, of course, come from within. But if the Exchange cannot or will not reform itself then sooner or later the Government must undertake the task."

A little later we shall return to the detail of that prophetic memorandum. At the moment let us look at another, equally prophetic in the light of subsequent happenings in Germany.

Greatly concerned over the debates of the Peace Conference, on January 6, 1919, Glass cabled this message :

Ammission,
Paris.
The President from Glass.

I fear there is a great danger of confusion in regard to the matter of representatives of the Treasury in Europe. Colonel House has suggested that Norman Davis be appointed Commissioner in connection with the armistice discussions at Spa and I have recommended to you his appointment as such. Davis has also advised me of his appointment as one of the American representatives on Special Board created to deal with relief problems. Crosby has tendered his resignation and I have transmitted it to you for such action as you think proper.

Secretary Lansing has cabled me saying that the Peace Commissioners wish to have financial advice from some one other than the Treasury's representative and suggested Albert Strauss go over for that purpose if I approve. In view of these demands from various sources for financial representation, and the danger of conflicting councils and disorganization among the Treasury representatives I ask your approval of the creation of a Treasury Commission in Europe under the chairmanship of some one who will be my responsible representative. If you approve I plan to send Mr. Strauss over to head the Treasury's legation at as early a date as possible.

I have concluded to ask your approval also of sending Thomas W. Lamont of New York. He would be particularly useful in connection with the armistice discussions at Spa. You know he is a member of the firm of J. P. Morgan and Company and the owner of the New York Evening Post. The armistice discussions, it seems to me, are likely to involve the whole economic and financial problem of Germany. The British, the French and the Germans will doubtless be represented by their strongest financial men.

Our public opinion is by no means prepared as yet to welcome any effort on behalf of the United States or of the Allies to restore decent conditions in Germany. It is, therefore, peculiarly important that the financial representation of the United States in these discussions should be such as to inspire confidence in the ability of our representatives to hold their own in a contest with the most expert financiers of Europe and also that the men representing us should be men known to have been thoroughly pro-Ally and anti-German since the outbreak of the European War. Lamont combines these qualifications with a statesmanlike view of the requirements of the situation and recognition of the utter impossibility of preventing the spread of Bolshevism and enabling Germany to meet her indemnities without setting up some plan for the restoration of her economic life.

I quite recognize the possibility of objection to Lamont on the ground that he is a member of J. P. Morgan and Company and on the ground that he is the owner of a newspaper. I believe as to the first the advantage of his being a member of that firm for the reasons above indicated far counterbalances any disadvantages in connection with such a negotiation as this. As to the second I understand he has trusteed the ownership of the Post and takes no part in its direction. To summarize, my suggestion would be as follows:

That the Treasury be represented in Europe immediately by a commission headed by Strauss and including Davis and Lamont and Crosby, if you do not accept his resignation, and that they should retain the services of Goodhue, Loree and Harris and such organization as has been created in Europe under Crosby's direction. I should expect Strauss to act as the executive head and to be my responsible representative in Europe.

The plan and organization outlined in this cable are predicated upon the policy of excluding from discussion in Europe all questions concerning the making, the readjustment or the conversion of our loans to foreign governments. I may add that I assume you will agree with me that so far as the Peace Commissioners or Mr. Hoover, or others in Europe, are in need of financial advice, they should obtain it from an organization acting under my general direction and responsible to me.

(Signed) Carter Glass.

The President accepted Glass' recommendations and, in due time, the Treasury delegation sailed. Through five months Davis and Lamont argued with the British and the French against imposing penalties that would prevent Germany from "setting up some plan for the restoration of her economic life." To Glass, morality required decent conditions for the people of the beaten nation. France's Clemenceau and England's Lloyd George bitterly opposed this view.

Clemenceau hated Germany. He told the Americans they did not understand. Twice within his own lifetime France had had to fight for her existence against this invader. To Clemenceau, Germany, even a conquered Germany, was a menace. He wanted her destroyed, militaristically and economically. He wanted her prostrate before France – and he could not understand that a Germany prostrate before France was also prostrate before Russia. He could not see that unless Germany was allowed to restore her economic life, greater danger to France, and to Europe, was inevitable.

Clemenceau lived to see Bolshevism in Germany. Lloyd George has lived to see the chancellorship of Adolf Hitler.

This is not to imply that Glass foresaw the rise of the one who, at the time of these momentous discussions, was but a corporal in the Austrian army. It is to say he foresaw the consequences of communism. It is to say had the Allies recognized that statesmanship always accepts what morality requires, the future of Europe, and the world, would be vastly different.

And, at the time, morality in the name of humanity demanded that the starving nations of Europe be fed. Woodrow Wilson knew that, and Glass was in daily communication with the President, or with members of the American

Mission regarding loans for food purchases. As he cabled the President on January 14, 1919:

Ammission,
Paris
For President from Glass.

First: Your message regarding Roumania just received. Advance to Roumania will be made when essential requirements imposed by loan statute are met. Wired Davis several days ago particulars of requirements and that Treasury would make advance whenever put into position to do so legally. Understand State Department has cabled Lansing on subject.

Second: Appreciate importance of food supplies in relation to your policies and anxious to use powers of Treasury to support them. Treasury has uniformly recognized supply of foodstuffs to European allies as a purpose for which loans could be made under existing law and will continue to do so until conditions change or you advise to the contrary. In no case has it refused to make such loans.

Third: Appreciate desirability of marketing our surplus products, and this is a collateral advantage of the policy of supplying foods to Europe. The question of Treasury's attitude on prevention of loss to producers has been raised here. Treasury has taken position that artificial upholding of prices was undesirable because of burden thereby imposed on community in general and the disadvantage at which our industries would be placed in international markets. Since the armistice many claims for indirect protection of prices have been put forward in regard to commodities the production of which had been stimulated to meet war needs.

Treasury has maintained that any obligations of our Government to producers of such commodities should be met by direct appropriation and payment as is proposed by bills now pending in the case of certain minerals. I am convinced that to meet such obligations indirectly by using governmental powers granted for other specific purposes to prevent losses to the producers by artificial maintenance of price is both economically and politically objectionable. McCormick is familiar with, and I believe fully shares, my views on these questions, which I hope may have your approval.

(signed) Carter Glass.

The President was in agreement. On January 20, Glass cabled Norman Davis of the "Treasury's willingness to make advances to British, French and Italians for food purchases in United States for use in countries other than Allied countries to prevent anarchy," and pointed out "this government only to provide for its own needs is warranted by the urgent circumstances which exist."

At the same time Glass was completely opposed to the artificial maintenance of food prices by the Food Administration. He cabled Davis on January 16:

> It is the view of the Treasury that a fall in food prices, while causing some loss or loss of profits to the raisers and packers of food, would be a benefit to the general community and have a stimulating effect on industry. A general readjustment of prices is inevitable and industries will pursue a halting and timorous policy and be at a marked disadvantage in international trade until this fall has taken place. Food prices are largely the key to the whole situation, and in the interest of the country as a whole I am satisfied that a reduction in food prices would be advantageous rather than the contrary.

On January 20, he was again cabling Davis:

> It is the settled policy of the Treasury to discourage efforts to maintain high prices. Where legal or moral commitments exist to producers they should be met by direct appropriation by Congress and not by continuation of high prices through artificial means with resulting maintenance of high cost of living and other economic evils of utmost gravity. I am not willing to make loans to Allied Governments in order to assist other Departments of Government to continue artificial high prices in pursuance of a policy of which I emphatically disapprove. I am not willing to force upon Great Britain a loan for which she has not made application in order to enable Food Administration to force upon her the purchase of pork which she is unwilling to buy at artificial prices. Treasury has never refused loan to British required to meet their purchases in United States.

In the midst of these efforts, Glass sent a sudden warning through Colonel House to the President that it was "inadvisable to give any information which is confidential" to a certain Senator then in Europe because this "person, who urges removal of restrictions [on foreign exchange] is in cable communication with a notorious exchange speculator here." It is a matter of unofficial record that this Senator had a most uncomfortable ten minutes on his next visit with Wilson.

At home Glass also had time, in response to a request from the House Judiciary Committee, to recommend the passage of legislation which would provide that buildings used for selling liquor in violation of the wartime prohibition act could be treated as public nuisances, giving to the courts the power to prohibit the use of the property for any purpose for the period of one year – also, to provide in the bill, for the destruction of all seized goods, and for the seizure, sale or destruction of all vehicles used in the transportation of liquor.

Inasmuch as enforcement of the prohibition law was under supervision of the Treasury Department, Glass insisted if he was going to be responsible for the enforcement of the law "there must be legislation with teeth in it."

The corridors of the Capitol saw him often. The new revenue bill was his principal interest. On February 5, he was cabling the President:

> Conferees have agreed on provisions of revenue bill. Report will probably be approved by the Senate and House this week. Bill is great improvement over 1917 Act, structurally as well as from standpoint of administrative practicability. It will supersede several existing income tax laws and consolidates in one measure all income tax provisions. Practically all provisions for administrative relief in unusual cases are incorporated, as urged by the Treasury Department.

He also tried in vain to persuade the Congress to raise the salaries of his executive assistants from $5000 a year, telling the Chairman of the House Committee on Appropriations: "It is futile to expect the Treasury to retain for any great period or to obtain in the future men of the requisite ability to fill the responsible posts . . . of the Treasury for less than $10,000 a year."

To the anguish of many he kept John Skelton Williams as his Comptroller of the Currency, although he was not entirely happy in the matter, writing to McAdoo: "I fully agree with you that we should recognize the record Mr. Williams has made in office and that it requires exceptional courage and probity to make such a record. However, I could very earnestly wish that the record had been made with less friction."

But the French were returning to the question of settlement of their American debts, and were insisting on doing it at the Peace Conference. To this, as has been seen, Glass was unalterably opposed. On February 11, he sent a long cable to Davis in Paris in which he said:

> . . . It is advisable that Treasury representatives in Europe should discuss needs of the countries concerned and dimensions of their problems, and hear their proposals. Insist, however, that proposals involving advances from United States be submitted to Treasury in Washington by representatives of countries concerned.

But, again and again, in his cables, he kept returning to the plight of the people of Europe — and the need to do everything possible "to prevent anarchy." In his communication to Davis on February 28, he said:

> Food supplies purchased by British, French and Italians . . . may be used by them for Austrian relief. . . It must be borne in mind that Treasury is prepared to make these loans in order to make possible an agreement regarding general food distribution required as a military measure in order to prevent anarchy and not for the purpose of selling our wheat or pork products.
>
> . . . If it is essential to prevent anarchy prepared for some months, but not after peace, to establish credits in favor Czechoslovaks, Roumania and Serbia to purchase food in United States within following limits: Czechoslovaks, $9,000,000, Roumania and

Serbia each $5,000,000. Not sufficiently familiar with Czechoslovaks' status to be able to judge whether their obligations in circumstances preferable to French or Italian obligations. Should like combined judgment of Strauss, Lamont and yourself as to order of desirability of obligations of British, French, Italians, Belgians, Serbs, Roumanians, Czechoslovaks and Greeks.

In this action Glass kept well within the powers given to the Treasury by the Congress at the outbreak of the war. With Rathbone, he had gone before the Ways and Means Committee of the House, and the Finance Committee of the Senate, and explained at great length the reasons for continuing to make loans to foreign governments after the Armistice. His acts were approved. Congress confirmed and extended the authority, providing in Clause (2) of Section 7, of the Victory Loan Act, approved March 3, 1919, that the credits therein authorized were in addition to those authorized in Section 2 of the Second Liberty Bond Act ; and Clause (c) provided that nothing therein contained should be deemed to prohibit the use of the unexpended balance of the $10,000,000,000 appropriation, or any part thereof, for the purposes of Section 2 of the Second Liberty Bond Act.

Thus Congress, upon mature consideration and after full discussion unequivocally sanctioned the Treasury's interpretation of the law.

But the weight of responsibility, heavy though it was, also enabled him to become better acquainted with his fellow Cabinet members ; and the trivia concerning them gave him relief.

There was Acting Secretary of State Frank L. Polk, a hard worker who usually lunched at the Metropolitan Club and whose favorite pastime was quail shooting. . . Newton D. Baker, Secretary of War, whose pastimes were a pipe, a book, tennis and knitting. . . Josephus Daniels, Secretary of the Navy, who liked persimmon beer, preferred his own newspaper, *The Raleigh News and Observer*, to all others, who liked to appear on the lecture platform, and who found a bottle of milk and a slice of bread a satisfying and satisfactory lunch.

Attorney General A. Mitchell Palmer, who usually had lunch with Democratic leaders at the Shoreham Hotel, and whose delight it was to make irritating speeches to Pennsylvania Republicans. . . Postmaster General Albert S. Burleson, an incorrigible umbrella toter who wanted no pleasure other than fishing, and who knew every likely spot in the Potomac for miles around. . . Secretary of the Interior Franklin K. Lane, an early riser who ate his breakfast ham and eggs in the restaurant in the department building, who prided himself that he was on the job earlier than most of his staff and who spent his vacations visiting national parks.

Secretary of Commerce William C. Redfield, whose principal hobby was working out uplift schemes for business – ideas that business men never seemed to appreciate – and whose other hobby was driving an automobile. . . Secretary of Labor William B. Wilson, who had no hobbies except spending all his spare time at home and his vacations in Pennsylvania. . . Secretary of Agriculture David Franklin Houston, who was the story teller of the Cabinet, with a hobby of collecting inscriptions off headstones in country churchyards.

Into this group Glass found welcome. His hobbies were different from all the others. They were Jersey cattle, and molasses candy, the supply of which he replenished each day from a small shop that made it fresh every twenty-four hours.

CHAPTER THIRTEEN

"There are people who say the loan will fail . . . if I believed this I would despair of my country."

With the war ended, Glass was determined to discourage foreign borrowings. He was anxious to have trade return to its normal channels, and prices to their proper levels. He knew economic law would prevail; to him delay meant increasing penalties. And his insistence "it is the Treasury's settled policy to discourage efforts to maintain high prices," and that he was "not willing to force on foreign governments loans they did not need, and did not want," was most distressing to the Food Administration.

The Food Administration was in acrimonious debate with the Allied nations. With the signing of the Armistice, thus releasing shipping, food prices had dropped. The Allies, England particularly, no longer felt disposed to favor the American market. The Food Administration took the position that hundreds of millions of dollars' worth of food had been packed, and stored, awaiting European shipment. It maintained that inasmuch as the food had been processed for Allied consumption it should be bought at the stipulated prices, thus preventing losses to American producers.

Glass was insistent. He wrote to the Food Administration and also cabled Davis:

> The principle which the Food Administration suggests goes further than is legally possible, or, in my judgment, desirable. The Treasury has taken the position that the Allied governments should restore their trade with this country to the ordinary commercial channels as fully and as promptly as possible and should use other methods of providing dollars, which are reasonably available to them, besides loans from our government. Great Britain, for instance, has great financial resources and excellent

credit, and, with hostilities ended, I am confident and am advised that she could readily place a substantial loan in our markets.

An important part of this same problem of foreign loans, was the difficulty of financing a Victory Loan of not less than $5,000,000,000 "at a time," as Glass also cabled Davis, "when patriotic enthusiasm growing out of the war has largely abated ; when heavy taxation is being levied ; and when industries are in the difficult period of transition from war to peace activities.

"Our outstanding Liberty Loans are quoted at a discount which makes them compare unfavorably with first-class railroad securities. This condition is due not to any feeling that the railroads' bonds possess greater security, but simply to the enormous weight of Liberty Bonds resting on the market. Every hundred millions of foreign government expenditures in America which is financed by our loans adds to this burden. . ."

Caught between differences of opinion in his own Cabinet, several months were to pass before Wilson decided in Glass' favor. For, not only was the Food Administration an advocate of continuing the artificial price level, but the Industrial Board, appointed by Secretary of Commerce Redfield, was in favor of entering into a contract for high prices for steel rails, rails that were to be purchased by the Railroad Administration. Chairman George R. Peek, of the Industrial Board, contended he "would not approve a lower price" ; Director General Walker D. Hines, of the Railroad Administration, insisted he "would not consent to the price agreed upon between the steel companies and the Industrial Board."

The Cabinet was sharply divided in its opinions.

Unable to iron out the differences at home, Glass sent the following message to the President :

March 27, 1919.

VERY URGENT. NOT BY WIRELESS.

Ammission,
Paris.
The President from Glass.

Redfield has shown me his cable to you concerning disagreement between Industrial Board and Railroad Administration. Matter is very troublesome one and I suggest that you suspend judgment until you receive a further cable from me in which I shall give you detailed statement of my views.

(signed) Carter Glass.
Secretary of Treasury.

A few days later another message went forth from the Treasury Department:

April 3, 1919.

VERY URGENT. NOT BY WIRELESS.

Ammission,
Paris.
From Glass to the President.

Pursuing the subject of former cable, the Industrial Board appointed by Secretary Redfield, has proceeded along lines distinctly not approved by other members of Cabinet with whom I have conferred (stop) Its action involves a plain violation of Sherman Anti-Trust Law (stop) My opinion on this point concurred in by Palmer, Baker and Burleson (stop) Aside from this consideration, it is sought, in effect, to compel Railway Administration and other Government purchasing agencies to buy at figures established by Industrial Board in conference with certain industrial interests against protest of Railway Administration (stop) In my judgment the entire proceeding is contrary to the original proposal and is fundamentally wrong (stop) We are trying to extricate the Industrial Board from its predicament if it will consent to be rescued (stop) Meanwhile it is my judgment, concurred in by Baker, Burleson, Palmer and Lane that you should not be drawn into approval of the action taken by the Industrial Board.

(signed) Carter Glass.
Secretary of the Treasury.

Ten days more, and while in the midst of the Victory Loan drive, he returned to the subject, telephoning Leffingwell from Richmond, Va., and instructing him to send the following cable to Wilson:

April 14, 1919.

NOT BY WIRELESS

Ammission,
Paris.
President from Glass.

I have read the further statements of Secretary Redfield and the Industrial Board and Director General Hines, and I have reluctantly come to the following conclusions:

(1) That the Industrial Board allowed themselves to be unduly impressed by steel interests' talk of reduction in wages and fixed prices at rather a high level, which will not stimulate industry but, on the whole, will tend to prevent a revival of business, and, therefore, increase unemployment.

(2) That the Industrial Board have not proceeded along lines recommended to and approved by you which contemplated not price fixing but mediation between the industries and Governmental buying agencies and, on the contrary, have allowed themselves to be put in the position of sanctioning the practices which were first initiated at the famous Gary dinners and have given Governmental approval to a minimum price fixing plan effective for a year.

(3) That the sworn officers of the Government should not be ordered to make purchases at prices which in their judgment are too high and which have been fixed by men who are not sworn officers of the Government but are themselves interested in productive industry and whose natural, even if unconscious, bias is toward the side of the producers.

(4) That notwithstanding every effort to bring the Industrial Board to a realization of their mistakes they are disposed to persist in a policy which is fundamentally unsound economically and politically and that therefore the sooner the Board is dissolved the better.

(5) That you should not allow yourself to be drawn into this controversial matter and that the best solution is for the Attorney General promptly to announce the opinion, which he informs

me he has reached, that the lines on which the Industrial Board has been proceeding are contrary to law.

(signed) R. C. Leffingwell.
Assistant Secretary of the Treasury.

On the President's return Glass presented the matter personally and Wilson, by executive order, vitiated the contracts by consent of the other nations.

However, his arguments in reference to the reluctance of the United States Shipping Board to submit their accounts to the Treasury Department for audit, as required by law, did not need the attention of the President. He wrote Edward N. Hurley, President of the Emergency Fleet Corporation:

> The attitude of the Corporation has forced the Treasury to the point of considering what steps must be taken to induce compliance with the plain provisions of the statute with respect to auditing these accounts. Among the measures I have under consideration is the stopping of further payments from the Treasury to the Corporation until the law is complied with. Before taking this or other drastic steps, I shall give the trustee of the Corporation a reasonable time in which to reply to this letter.

Here, indeed, was something new! A Secretary of the Treasury threatening an independent agency with cutting off its supply money unless and until it complied with the law! The Corporation complied.

There were other immediately troublesome problems. From all sides, within and without the Cabinet, the Congress, and Wall Street, Glass was told it was hopeless to attempt to sell the needed $5,000,000,000 in Victory Bonds. The bankers advised him that the amount that could be raised was $2,000,000,000 or at the outside, $2,500,000,000. As for $5,000,000,000, they shook their heads and chorused "Never!"

Back to Washington he went, to talk with Leffingwell. But unlike the cabinet members, the Congressmen and Senators, and the bankers, Leffingwell was not pessimistic. Nor, for that matter, was Glass. They decided to go to the people, with Glass as the salesman; and as Glass told an audience in Norfolk, Va., so he told other audiences all over the country:

"There are people who say the loan will fail; that it must be approached in a cold-blooded manner; that the glamour of war is over and that you can't appeal to the patriotism of America in asking for more money. I have told these croakers that, if I believed this, I would despair of my country.

"Do we consider it a sacrifice to invest in safe and profitable American bonds? Will we refuse now to invest in the safest securities in the world to perpetuate the personal and property rights and security, making the excuse that the guns have ceased firing and the war is over?

"We should make this a national Thanksgiving Loan; thanksgiving that a million or more of our boys are returning home from the bloody fields of France. Some men hesitate to participate in the loan because of alleged extravagance in the expenditure of government funds. We have been extravagant. Millions of money have been wasted. But though we were unskilled in the art of war, we were able to put an end to it two years earlier than it was believed it could be accomplished.

"Everyone will admit that even the extravagance and waste through inexperience and even bungling in some quarters has been more than worth the money in the victory won and the comparatively light human sacrifice we have had to make. . ."

Glass went on to declare that all obligations must be met in some form . . . "and, it must come by these loans or through taxation. If you are taxed there is no money-come-back. If you lend your money to the government you get it back with interest and the additional benefits that come from habits of thrift."

For weeks he campaigned, spending his nights on trains, and

his days pleading with crowds wherever crowds gathered. Everywhere he went he encouraged the thousands of men and women who were working with him in hundreds of cities and towns. The people responded as all the time he was sure they would, and the loan was oversubscribed.

Never a day passed but what he was in communication with the Treasury, dictating communications to President Wilson, to Davis or to other members of the Treasury commission. But, even before the active work on the Victory Loan began he was again evidencing displeasure with the efforts of the French and Italians to bring the debt question into discussion at the Peace Conference.

On March 8, he cabled Davis:

> Greatly concerned regarding continuation of loans to governments which in effect are endeavoring to escape repayment of advances already made them. Please consult President or Peace Mission as to whether this is an opportune time to absolutely refuse to make further advances to countries in question while they are pressing these questions at Peace Conference.

In addition, he instructed Rathbone to write the French, and send a copy of the letter to the Italians, again warning these two nations "that the Treasury, as you are aware, is clothed by the Congress with full authority to deal with foreign loans which it has made," and that the Treasury "will not assent to any discussion at the Peace Conference, or elsewhere, of any plan or arrangement for the release, consolidation, or reapportionment of the obligations of foreign governments held by the United States. You will appreciate also that the Treasury cannot contemplate continuance of advances to any allied government which is lending its support to any plan which would create uncertainty as to its due repayment of advances made to it by the United States Treasury."

The debts of the Russian government troubled him. He

was convinced they would never be paid; and he cabled Wilson seeking authority to withdraw its unexpended balance of $137,275,250. On April 2, the President gave that authority.

But if there was responsibility, there also was relief. There had to be.

And so it was one morning, in the midst of Treasury matters, Glass found himself thinking not of bonds and debts, loans and currency, but of Jersey cattle. Picking up a telephone, he called Samuel Kaplan, a New York wool manufacturer, and a friend whose hobby, too, was purebred Jerseys.

"Sam," said Glass, "I want to see you. Come down here as fast as you can."

Dropping what he was doing, Kaplan hurried from his office in lower Manhattan, jumped into his always waiting automobile, and told the chauffeur:

"Washington."

Less than five hours later, Kaplan pulled up in front of the Treasury, and hurried into the building. As he was ushered into the Secretary's office Glass looked up at the clock, and remarked:

"You're late, Sam – thought you'd be here half an hour ago."

"I got here as quick as I could," responded Kaplan, thinking of the eighty and ninety miles an hour his speedometer had turned up along the open highway; and with concern covering his face, inquired: "Anything wrong, Mr. Secretary?"

"No," answered Glass, idling back in his chair. "I just wanted to talk about Jersey cattle. Sit down. Tell me, what do you know about that sale they are advertising for tomorrow at Mt. Kisco just beyond New York."

For an hour the two men sat talking their hobby while outside the Secretary's office waited the chairman of one of New York's largest banks, as well as others of lesser financial importance. With their conversation ended, Glass pulled his feet down from the desk, and grinned :

"Sam, stick around for a couple of hours. Then we will get out of here and go up to that sale together."

As Kaplan went out, the bank chairman came in. "Well, Mr. Secretary," he said, "that must have been a very important conference."

"It was," answered Glass. "Sam and I were talking about Jersey cattle and, to me, it was important that I get my mind off the same things that are on your mind, although I am sorry to have kept you waiting."

A burst of laughter greeted the explanation, as the banker sat down, for his hobby was dogs, and he understood perfectly.

The following day Glass and Kaplan were in Kaplan's car, racing along one of the parkways in Westchester County at the wool manufacturer's customary high speed – which was as fast as the automobile could go – when Kaplan broached the idea of buying a couple of the Secretary's Jersey calves. "I'll give you four thousand dollars for them," he offered.

Glass shook his head. "Not interested, but if you want them, I'll give them to you."

Through the remaining miles the two men argued, Glass refusing to sell and Kaplan just as stubbornly refusing to accept the purebreds as a gift. They attended the sale, made no purchases, but had the diversion each needed. As Glass was stepping into the automobile for the return trip, he turned to the stock raiser :

"I don't know whether you have ever ridden with Mr. Kaplan but whether you have, or have not, I want to give you these instructions. If, by chance, I am killed on my return trip to New York I want you to see the executor of my estate and tell him that under no circumstances is he to allow

Mr. Kaplan to gain possession of two Jersey calves he has been trying to buy from me."

"Yes, Mr. Secretary," agreed the stock raiser, staring with obvious hostility across Glass' shoulders at Kaplan.

Back in Washington, Glass turned again to the problem of restoring normal conditions in the United States. One of the important ways to do this was to remove controls over the export of coin, bullion and currency. On June 2, he cabled the President:

> In answer to your cable in response to mine recommending the removal of embargoes on the export of coin, bullion and currency, and of all control of foreign exchange operations with the exceptions * stated in said cable, and in a supplementary cable, permit me to explain the purpose of excepting that portion of Russia now under control of the so-called Bolshevik Government.
>
> 1. The Bolshevik Government is reported on good authority to be forging sterling notes and franc notes and, perhaps, also United States currency. Their avowed purpose is reported to be to flood with forged notes the markets of these countries in order to deprive all money in those countries of value.
>
> 2. The agents of the Bolshevik Government in the United States will, it is feared, be able to add largely to the funds at their disposal for propaganda purposes here if they are permitted to

* On May 28, Glass cabled the President as follows: "After full consultation with the Federal Reserve Board and with their hearty approval, I am prepared to recommend the prompt removal of all embargoes on the export of coin, bullion and currency and of all control of foreign exchange operations except so far as concerns intercourse with that part of Russia now under the control of the so-called bolshevik government. To make this effective a proclamation by the President is required. If this projected step meets with your approval the Secretary of the Treasury and the Federal Reserve Board would like to announce as promptly as possible that a recommendation to the above effect had been made to the President and that pending formal action by the President licenses for the export of gold in accordance with the recommendation will be freely granted on application. . .

"I should esteem it a favor if you will inform me as promptly as possible whether or not you approve the proposed course of action, in which case announcement as above will be made at the earliest possible moment and the formal papers on which your signature will be required will be cabled as promptly as they can be prepared."

draw rouble exchange or to bring rouble notes into the United States and to dispose of them here to Russians and others who are speculatively inclined and who believe or can be made to believe that rouble notes at their present prices are an attractive speculation. It is the control over exchange and over the importation of paper money and not control over the exportation of gold that is primarily intended to be preserved by the exception in question.

3. The proposed lifting of the embargo will not of course license dealings with enemy states. The Department of State and the War Trade Board are understood to share the views expressed above and which led to the inclusion of the exception in question in my cable to you. I have asked these bodies to express their views to the Secretary of State and to Vance McCormick, respectively, for submission to you, if you desire their judgment.

Wilson approved, and a week or ten days later the Federal Reserve Board announced the lifting of the embargo "except as to the exportation or importation of rouble notes, or exchange operations with that part of Russia now under the control of the so-called Bolshevik Government, and except as to exchange transactions with territories in respect of which such transactions are at present permitted only through the American Relief Administration."

Stock market speculation which had begun to assume sizable proportions, he wanted stopped before it could damage business. He saw then, as he kept emphasizing, repeatedly, through the years that led up to the collapse in 1929, the extreme danger in easy borrowings on Government collateral. He was fearful if the market continued to expand the demand for call money would take much of the available capital away from the needs of business; and, also, from the needs of government.

Along in April, 1919, he had requested Chairman William P. G. Harding, of the Federal Reserve Board, to direct each Federal Reserve bank throughout the country to send out a letter to each member bank in an effort to learn the extent to which banks were lending on Government obligations for speculative purposes. The survey disclosed that about nine-tenths of the loans were backed by Government paper, and then came the problem of what to do about it. He discussed it with his assistants and it was decided that while in normal times it would have been possible to regulate speculation by advancing discount rates, this could not be done and maintain faith with the institutions which had been so helpful – and were still being helpful – in financing the war. Instead of drastic action the banks were asked to co-operate in reducing the numbers of such loans. The understanding was that unless they did, drastic steps would follow.

The Federal Reserve System had financed the war. It was imperative, as Glass pointed out in his many communications to the President, the Peace Commission, the Food Administration, to other Governmental departments, and to the banks that abnormal strains be removed as quickly as possible; that "normal conditions in the United States be allowed to prevail," as he cabled Wilson in May, 1919; and that emotions of people be permitted to subside rather than to be shifted to market speculation, "to the inevitable ruin of these same people."

Writing Mrs. Ellis Meredith, of the National Democratic Committee in 1920, Glass said:

(1) It has successfully carried out the immense task of distributing, financing and supporting the great Liberty loans which were necessary to enable the United States to play its part in the war; and it has provided for the gathering of funds drawn from the public from all parts of the country at a minimum of expense and inconvenience.

(2) It has furnished an elastic currency which has responded to the needs of the growing business of the country at all times.

(3) It has been from the standpoint of earnings and dividends phenomenally successful.

(4) Its work has been carried on in such a way as to save the industrial and financial system of the United States from the shocks

and disturbances which would otherwise have come to it as the result of world changes in economic conditions, or as the result of periodic development of panic and depression.

(5) It has standardized commercial paper, stabilized and harmonized rates of interest and provided new and more economical methods of currently financing business.

(6) It has provided a uniform system for the collection of checks and drafts at a minimum of cost.

(7) It has furnished a democratic representation whereby the bankers, the business community and the public at large co-operate in the management of the underlying credit system of the country.

(8) It has economized gold and reserve money and rendered it possible to do a much larger volume of business upon a specified unit of reserve funds without danger.

(9) The Federal Reserve system was formed along the lines of recognized and sound financial and banking theory, conforming in the teachings of experience not only in the United States but in other countries. The Act made use of the ideas which had been presented in previously existing measures, but it went far beyond any of them in its rectification of banking methods and in its provision for the sound management of both public and private finance. It is not a copy or a duplicate of any previously existing measures and its characteristic ideas are not contained in any of the bills that had been presented to Congress during the quarter of a century preceding its enactment.

As the author of the Federal Reserve Act, Glass may be pardoned for his pride in it ; as Secretary of the Treasury, his great anxiety for the protection of the banking system which the Act created can be understood. Increasing market speculation and continuing high prices were threats to stability he could not ignore.

CHAPTER FOURTEEN

"If Stock Exchange does not reform itself, some day Government must undertake the task."

A newspaper paragraph in the financial section of the *New York Sun* of October 24, 1919, attracted Glass' attention and concern. It read:

> A coup that is becoming a favorite method of operation by large traders, that of dashing suddenly into a stock with a bushel basket full of buying orders and riding it with a strong whip for half an hour or so, was repeated yesterday morning in Lackawanna Steel. Exactly the same thing happened in Republic in the previous trading session. In both cases the bold operators were aided by a large short interest which had been accumulated in both stocks and which stuck tenaciously through the drives. Lackawanna opened at 89½ and sold up to 91, and at that figure was taken in hand. Within thirty minutes it had sold up to 103, up 13½ points. The move was so sudden and so fast and furious that at the moment the price of 91 was being printed on the type the market for Lackawanna on the floor of the exchange was 101. For this reason there was considerable complaint by traders who had orders to buy at the market and who expected to pay between 91 and 92 for their stock. They were surprised, to say the very least, when many report slips showed a price above 100.

It was Glass' view that market gamblers never think of yesterday, and have no regrets – never think of tomorrow, and have no plans . . . that their thoughts are centered on today, and today's minute, and what good, or ill, it will bring to their own pocketbooks. And he knew if the feverish gambling philosophy of "yesterday is gone and tomorrow never comes" spread from the few to the many there would be trouble.

After reading over the paragraph he called Leffingwell to his office for a discussion of the market situation. The conference lasted for some little time and at its conclusion Leffingwell was instructed to put into memorandum form their combined views. This was on October 25.

In this memorandum the Secretary and his assistant were agreed the methods of the New York Stock Exchange had to be reformed, "so as to suppress manipulation and also as to the settlement and financing of transactions," just as they were agreed if the Exchange did not do so from within, then "sooner or later the Government must undertake the task." They also agreed if brakes were to be applied to market gambling discount rates would have to be increased. Here, however, was a difficulty – how to increase rates so "as not to embarrass the Government's bond operations, and not to injure the holders of Liberty Bonds and Victory Bonds."

A mere change in rates would not solve the problem because, as they knew, "any increase would fall heavily upon legitimate borrowers who figure profits from industrial and commercial enterprise at a rate per cent per annum. An increase in rates, on the other hand, falls very lightly upon the borrower for speculative purposes, who figures a very large profit on the turnover in a day, a week, a month or some other short period."

Hence, the problem was:

(1) To protect Government, and its bond issues, and; (2) to protect the legitimate borrower so as not to curtail production at a time when the world was short of goods – and, while doing these two things, bring about effective action in curbing market gambling.

The solution, they decided, could be found in the same place where the solution to all such problems is found – in understanding of the mathematical factors involved; in recognition of the imperfections of humanity; and in co-operation between the Government, the Treasury, the Federal Reserve Board, and the individual bankers.

As pointed out in the memorandum:

"The Reserve Banks' rates should, of course, scientifically be above the commercial rate and not below it. That cannot happen until the independent resources of the banks suffice for the requirements of their customers for commercial, industrial and Government purposes. Banks cannot be expected to meet those requirements habitually or at a loss. Their dependence upon the Federal Reserve System should be seasonal or occasional and not habitual. Until that condition comes about as the result of the production and saving of wealth the tendency will be, as Reserve Bank rates are increased, for the rates to the Government and rates to the commercial borrower to be increased in turn. A game of leapfrog will be played between Reserve Bank rates and the Government and commercial rates indefinitely until a prohibitive rate is reached and business stops. This is practically what happened during the early part of the war.

"As fast as the Reserve Bank rates were increased the Government had to increase its rates for short borrowings and the commercial borrower had to do likewise until a truce was called. . . With the curtailment of export demand consequent upon the curtailment of foreign credits and with industrial production proceeding full steam ahead we should soon have reached an equilibrium. In the meantime, however, the labor situation has become so acute as gravely to threaten production and the speculative mania has been allowed to proceed to such an extent as gravely to threaten our credit structure. . .

"It is of prime importance that the Federal Reserve Board should insist upon and the Governors of the banks should exercise a firm discrimination in making loans and put an end to the abuse of the facilities of the Federal Reserve System in support of the reckless speculation in stocks, cotton, clothing, foodstuffs and commodities generally."

The two men were weary of the reiteration of copybook texts. "The bank governor must raise his mind above the language of the textbooks," they said, "and face the situation which exists. He must have courage to act promptly and with confidence in his own integrity to prevent abuse of the facilities of the Federal Reserve System by the customers of the Federal Reserve Banks, however powerful or influential."

Glass' point of view did not find complete appeal. On December 13, he was writing to Colonel E. M. House:

". . . The current borrowings of the government, the menacing attitude of the governor and directors of the New York Federal Reserve Bank and other grave problems have been a source of great anxiety for the last three months. Ben Strong and his board, which he thoroughly dominates, practically challenged the authority of the Federal Reserve Board, and I found it necessary to read the riot act to him and the entire outfit."

More than a little chastened, Strong wrote Leffingwell asking him to intercede in obtaining an interview with Glass for the purpose of removing "misunderstanding." Glass was willing to see Strong, and did see him. The Secretary's views remained unchanged. Directors of the New York Federal Reserve Bank lowered their resistance to the Federal Reserve Board.

Meanwhile other problems pressed. Glass, in a lengthy memorandum to the President on September 11, 1919, called attention to the vital need of fully stating the Treasury's position and general policy regarding foreign financing. It was imperative, as Glass saw it, that private enterprise be given immediate and real encouragement to go ahead on its own and that Governmental action be directed to that end.

He wrote the President:

"Since the armistice the United States has advanced to the Governments of the Allies, as of the close of business August 15, 1919, the sum of $2,141,996,211.55, and there remained on August 15 an unexpended balance of $780,889,038.45 from the total loans of $10,000,000,000 authorized under the Liberty Loan Acts. The Treasury sees no need of an additional appropriation for government loans, though, it may later have occasion to ask the Congress to make some further modification of the terms under which the existing appropriation is available.

"The Treasury asked and obtained power for the War Finance Corporation to make advances up to the amount of $1,000,000,000 for non-war purposes and the War Finance Corporation is prepared to make such advances.

"The Secretary of War is authorized to sell his surplus stores on credit.

"The United States Wheat Director is authorized to sell wheat to Europe on credit.

"The power which at present exists in the Government or Governmental agencies to assist in meeting Europe's financial needs is, therefore, considerable. This power must, of course, be exercised with extreme caution and with the most careful regard for the urgent needs of our own people for an ample supply of foodstuffs and other necessities of life at reasonable prices.

"The Treasury is prepared, at the convenience of the Governments of the Allies, to take up with their representatives the funding of the demand obligations which the United States holds, into long-time obligations, and at the same time the funding during the reconstruction period, or say for a period of two or three years, of the interest on the obligations of foreign governments acquired by the United States under the Liberty Loan Acts.

"The Treasury believes that the need of Europe for financial assistance, very great and very real though it is, has been much exaggerated both here and abroad. Our hearts have been so touched by the suffering which the war left in its train, and our experience is so recent of the financial conditions which existed during the war (when men were devoting themselves to the business of destruction) that we are prone to overlook the vast recuperative power inherent in any country which, though devastated, has not been depopulated, and the people of which are not starved afterwards. We must all feel deep sympathy for the suffering in Europe today, but we must not allow our sympathy to warp our judgment and, by exaggerating Europe's financial needs, make it more difficult to fill them.

"Men must go back to work in Europe, must contribute to increase production. The industries of Europe, of course, cannot be set to work without raw materials, machinery, etc., and, to the extent that these are to be secured from the United States, the problem of financing the restoration of Europe belongs primarily to our exporters. Governmental financial assistance in the past and talk of future government or banking aid to finance exports has apparently led our industrial concerns to the erroneous expectation that their war profits, based largely on exports, will continue indefinitely without effort or risk on their part. To them will fall the profits of the exports and upon them will fall the consequences of failure to make the exports. So soon as domestic stocks, which were very low at the time of the armistice, have been replenished, those industries which have been developed to meet a demand for great exports, paid for out of government war loans, will be forced to close plants and forego dividends unless they maintain and develop an outlet abroad. The industries of the country must be brought to a realization of the gravity of this problem, must go out and seek markets abroad, must reduce prices at home and abroad to a reasonable level, and create or cooperate in creating the means of financing export business.

"Since armistice day, the consistent policy of the Treasury has been, so far as possible, to restore private initiative and remove government controls and interferences. It has been the view of the Treasury that only thus can the prompt restoration of healthy economic life be gained. The embargoes on gold and silver and control of foreign exchange have been removed, as well as the voluntary and informal control of call money and the stock exchange loan account. The control exercised by the Capital Issues Committee over capital issues has been discontinued. Thus the financial markets of the United States have been opened to the whole world and all restrictions removed that might have hindered America's capital and credit resources, as well as its great gold reserve, from being available in aid of the world's commerce and Europe's need.

"There are those who believe that the dollar should be kept at par – no more, no less – in the market of foreign exchange. If effective action were taken to carry out such a policy, it could only be done by withdrawing gold out of the United States when the dollar would otherwise be at a discount, and by inflating credit when the dollar would otherwise be at a premium.

"The dollar is now at a premium almost everywhere in the world. Its artificial reduction and maintenance at the gold par of exchange in all currencies is quite unthinkable unless we propose to level all differences in the relative credit of nations and to substitute for our gold reserve, a reserve consisting of the promises to pay of any nation that chooses to become our debtor. Inequalities of exchange reflect not only the trade and financial balance between two countries, but, particularly after a great war such as that we have been through, the inequalities of domestic finance. The United States has met a greater proportion of the cost of the war from taxes and bond issues than any other country. Largely as a consequence of this policy, the buying power of the dollar at home has been better sustained than has the buying power at home of the currency of any European belligerent. For the United States to determine by governmental action to depress the dollar as measured in terms of foreign exchange and to improve the position of other currencies as measured in terms of dollars would be to shift to the American people the tax and loan burdens of foreign countries. This shifted burden would be measured by the taxes to be imposed and the further loans to be absorbed by our people as a consequence, and by increased domestic prices.

"United States Government action at this time to prevent in respect to foreign exchange the ordinary operation of the law of supply and demand, which automatically sets in action corrective causes, and to prevent the dollar from going to a premium when its natural tendency is to do so, would artificially stimulate our exports, and, through the competition of export demand with domestic demand, maintain or increase domestic prices.

"The view of the Governments of the Allies, I take it, is that if they, after the war control of their imports has been relaxed, attempted to continue to 'peg' their exchanges here at an artificial level by Government borrowing, the effect would be to stimulate their imports and discourage their exports, thus aggravating their already unfavorable international balances."

Continuing, Glass put Treasury approval upon legislation to authorize corporations privately to engage in foreign banking and the financing of exports, and to permit national banks, to a limited extent, to be stockholders therein ; and, also, approved amending the War Finance Corporation Act in order, among other things, to remove the fixed minimum on its interest rate.

Imports, exports, exchange . . . supply and demand . . . post-war reaction . . . Glass knew the facilitation of the flow of private capital into foreign channels to supplant Government lending could not be accomplished in a few swift administrative strokes – that there should be an exhaustive study of the needs and trends of a continent rising from the disaster of war – and American initiative could not be given complete assurance until political risk was measurably removed by the consummation of the Peace.

Wilson heeded his advice.

Glass also knew that Government spending and unbalanced budgets severely handicapped efforts to restore prosperity. In his annual Treasury statement * he warned Congress and the executive departments :

"All sense of values seems to have departed from among us. The departments, bureaus and boards, all inspired by a laudable enthusiasm for their work, but some by a less laudable instinct to magnify its importance, bombard the committees of Congress with projects, some more or less meritorious, some of no merit whatever, but all conceived in sublime indifference to the facts that the great business of Government is being run at a loss and that each one of these projects increases the deficit of the Government and consequently the burden to be thrown upon the great body of people, whether the deficit be met by increasing taxes or by floating additional loans. For no fallacy is more grotesque than the assumption that by issuing bonds or notes or certificates of indebtedness now we may

* For résumé of Treasury report see appendix.

pass on to future generations the burden of our own extravagance. The burden of these issues will have to be met today, not only in the interest and sinking-fund charges added to an already heavy load, but in the expansion of credit which is inevitable as a result of the issue of such securities, constituting as they do a prime basis for additional credit in the hands of the holders, whoever they may be. I shall not elaborate upon that point, but I want to say to you in all solemnity that a hundred million American people will pay for the extravagance of the Government, whether that extravagance finds its incidence in governmental waste or in the desire to accomplish real or fancied benefits for a portion of the community.

"Let us now get back to bedrock. Let us remember that there can be no spending by the Government without paying by the Government, and that the Government cannot pay except out of the pockets of the people. Let us remember, too, that in the last analysis taxes and the cost of government loans are borne by one hundred million people. The burden of taxation, the burden of credit expansion is inevitably shifted to the whole people of the United States. Some methods of finance are better than others. Some taxes are less readily adapted to being shifted from the backs of the people as a whole ; but in the long run the burden of governmental waste and extravagance falls more heavily upon the poor than upon the well to do and more heavily upon the well to do than upon the rich. By graduated income taxes we tend to mitigate this consequence, but we cannot wholly avoid it. Let us not fail to remember that the Government of the United States is simply a name for the people of the United States and that all of the people of the United States will pay in inverse order to their ability for extravagances of the Government perpetrated in the interest of a portion of the people or a section of the country. . .

"I have spoken of the initiation of appropriations in Congress. Let me speak also of the increase of appropriations. As you all know, and as I know after seventeen years in Congress and not more than half as many months in the Treasury, the processes employed in framing and passing public buildings and rivers and harbors bills lead to a great waste of the money of the people. The continuance of the United States Government's activities where they are not needed, whether those activities be army posts or sub-treasuries or hospitals, would have scant consideration in a real business budget submitted by a finance minister, duly empowered by law, and managed through Congress by a single committee under rules of limitation imposed by the Congress on itself. In my belief you cannot make a real budget unless you face these facts and deal with them. The Congress of the United States, in attempting this great reform in the interest of economy and efficiency, will fail and fail utterly if, while imposing the necessary firm control over the expenditures of the executive departments, it fails to exercise the sublime quality of self-control."

In his annual Treasury statement, Glass also dwelt on the borrowings of foreign governments from April 25, 1917, up to November 15, 1919. Advances made after the Armistice showed the following aggregate amounts:

Belgium	$ 162,900,000.00
Czechoslovakia	55,330,000.00
France	630,496,977.24
Great Britain	650,000,000.00
Greece	32,446,629.05
Italy	564,746,927.00
Roumania	25,000,000.00
Serbia	15,268,608.27
	$2,136,189,141.56
Less credit withdrawn	301,746,312.72
Net credits established	1,834,442,828.84

"and that cash advances had been made in the following aggregate amounts:

Belgium	$ 166,965,000.00
Czechoslovakia	52,690,000.00
France	917,477,800.00
Great Britain	581,000,000.00
Italy	579,922,872.99
Liberia	26,000.00
Roumania	25,000,000.00
Serbia	16,175,465.56
	$2,339,257,138.55

Some sixteen years later a Congressional committee investigating the causes and cure of war maligned Wilson's memory by implying that he not only carried the nation into the World War to collect Morgan loans but thereafter lied about the matter. Indignantly Glass leaped from his chair, vehemently he cried, pounding the desk until his hand was bleeding as tears filled his eyes:

"It occurred to me that, as a more or less intimate friend of the late Woodrow Wilson and as a former member of his official family, it would be pertinent if I should briefly respond to the shocking assault made upon his character and the attempted impeachment of his integrity and veracity.

"This I shall do in unmistakable terms and, but for the limitations of the rules of the Senate, in phraseology which I am not accustomed to use.

"If it were permissible in the Senate to say that any man who would asperse the integrity and veracity of Woodrow Wilson is a coward, if it were permissible to say that his charge is not only malicious but positively mendacious, that I would be glad to say here or elsewhere to any man, whether he be a United States Senator or not, because the charge would not only be destitute of decency, but it would be such a shocking exhibition as never has happened in the 35 years I have served in the Congress of the United States."

Afterward, looking at his bandaged hand, he added, "I fear I was a little emphatic."

The Morgan reference pertained to a matter of $400,000,000 loaned to Great Britain by J. P. Morgan & Co., and a group of sixty banks. Uninformed Senator Nye of North Dakota and equally uninformed Senator Lewis of Illinois had accomplished newspaper headlines by charging that many of the securities placed with the United States Treasury as collateral "had been removed from the Treasury."

As a matter of fact, the British paid the Morgan debt from their own resources. However, on February 1, and on September 1, 1918, in the critical period of the War, Secretary McAdoo advanced funds to the British to pay two other secured loans, falling due on those days. They were not loans held by the Morgans or the banks. They were loans widely distributed in the hands of the public. It was in respect to the collateral for these publicly held loans that McAdoo required, and obtained, subrogation. Attempts were made by Glass, and by his successor, to negotiate a debt settlement with Great Britain. Secretary Mellon succeeded, and released the securities, there being no point to keeping them after the settlement was effected.

On November 17, 1919, Woodrow Wilson wrote him "no President has had a more loyal, a more devoted, or more resourceful friend than you have been to me." The President was urging him to accept appointment to the United States Senate by Governor Westmoreland Davis, of Virginia. Senator Thomas Staples Martin was dead. To fill the vacancy Virginia newspapers talked only of Glass. In turn, Glass was unwilling.

Previously and briefly, he had entertained proposals by

friends that he run for Governor of Virginia. He had dismissed the idea. He wanted to remain in the Treasury post as long as the President required his services there. Then he wanted to go home. He had spent twenty-three years of his life in public service. It had been as he said, "no bed of roses." Now at sixty-two and worn with the strain of post-war finance, he was ready to conclude that career – to retire and return to his farm.

The social obligations of the Cabinet member had compelled him reluctantly to surrender the quiet of his hotel room for a large house on New Hampshire Avenue. There he was required to do a great deal of entertaining, which bored him. Mrs. Glass shared his distaste for the social limelight. She preferred the domesticity of their Virginia home.

She had become greatly interested in the restoration of the Quaker Meeting-House, just south of Lynchburg, and one of the oldest edifices in Virginia. Although shortly after their marriage she had dutifully transferred her affiliation to the Court Street Methodist Church, of which her husband was a member, it was always recognized among her intimates that her love for her own church was deep-seated. In fact, her husband often referred to her as "that Presbyterian wife of mine."

Incidentally, a rather odd whimsy, apparently characterizing the entire Glass clan for several generations, has been the complete banishment from the family vocabulary of the terms "Uncle" or "Aunt" or "Grandfather" or "Grandmother." All members of that big connection have to stand, or fall, in the estimation of the younger generation without the supporting props of titles.

Now in the closing months of his Treasury period, Glass' two boys, Powell and Carter Jr., were back from France, returning to their wives in Lynchburg and their work on their father's newspapers. The two daughters, Mary Archer and

Augusta, were in nearby schools, Mary Archer at Gunstan Hall School, in Washington, and Augusta at Mary Baldwin College, in Staunton, Virginia. For years Glass had envisaged a time when they could all spend their days together in the familiar surroundings they loved.

His farm, Montview, had come into his possession the previous year, and he had "had no time in the midst of pressing political activities, to rescue it from its primitive state." The orchard was neglected ; weeds and briars were taking possession of the meadows where, as a boy, he had watched the fleeting inscriptions of the wind on the waving grain. There was a ditch that needed digging to divert a stream around the base of a hill and drain a marshy section of the blue grass pasture. There were lanes to be fenced, trees to be planted, a new barn to be built. Attending to these varied details by correspondence was not only difficult, it was devoid of the pleasure of actual participation.

And there were the imported son of Sybil's Gambage, Bowlina, Oxford Majesty's Pearl, Floral Fancy and other prize beasts of his recently acquired foundation herd of pure bred Jersey cows. To a friend he wrote : "I had hoped to spend the balance of my years, certainly the remaining summers of my life, on my farm among the Jerseys ; but there seems little prospect of even getting in occasional contact with them while I hold this job. Perhaps it will be well to sell the herd and start afresh two years hence by buying another foundation." But the thought of parting with these animals he had selected with such care distressed him ; he could not give them up.

Then there was his ever-growing library, the scores of intriguing volumes he had bought and put aside to brighten contemplated hours of leisure. New material relating to the old Bacon-Shakespeare mystery had found its way into print ; some writers were attributing authorship to the Earl of Oxford. Glass had ideas on that, and it would have been a pleasure to articulate them in the scholastic arena. Altered viewpoints and conflicting philosophies were emerging from the aftermath of war. Glass wanted time to think, to reflect, and to read books which for years he had wanted to read, and which he had had time scarcely to skim.

It was not to be. The attractions of wife, family, farm, library, leisure and idyllic peace were to be subjugated by an inevitable compulsion toward public duty. "Virginia needs you in the Senate," Wilson told him, "just as the nation needs you. Of course, you must accept," he wrote. "Governor Davis has honored the old state of Virginia by paying tribute to so distinguished a son."

Glass finally assented, but on condition he should retain the Treasury portfolio until the work then piling his desk was completed. Also, the identity of his successor was one of his concerns.

Various names were being suggested to the President, with McAdoo and House favoring Daniel Roper, head of the Internal Revenue Department. John Sharpe Williams was also being mentioned. Glass' choice was his assistant, Russell Leffingwell.

He went to McAdoo in New York to press his choice, and followed the visit by writing both him and Colonel House. Of Roper he said that it would prove untimely for the President to select a Southerner; that sectionalism was "the only remaining asset of the Republican party," having nearly defeated Wilson in 1916 and having been responsible for the overturn in Congress in 1918.

"I have been told that the President, on this score alone, hesitated to designate me for the place, and I did not fail on this account to suggest the inadvisability of my selection," he continued in his letter to House. And, despite "every consideration of state pride," the same objection applied to Williams. Then Glass stressed the qualifications of his assistant.

"It is my settled conviction that the appointment of Leffingwell, from every standpoint, is the thing which should be done. As I see it, the very consideration which you present with respect to relieving the President of anxiety and the general burden of his office applies with conclusive force to the selection of Leffingwell. No man could exceed him in personal affection for the President and none in complete loyalty to the President's administration. . .

"It is my considered belief that his incumbence of the office of Secretary of the Treasury at this crisis would relieve the President of every particle of anxiety. . . His sense of responsibility, political and otherwise, to the President, would not only be punctilious but whole-hearted."

He summarized Leffingwell's political beliefs, and went on to remark :

"His appointment might not please men like Homer Cummings or Fred Lynch, who mistakenly conceive that political patronage availeth much in carrying elections ; but while Leffingwell's administration of the office would be unobjectionable to any fair-minded party-worker, it would be, in its efficiency and general good results, of inestimably more advantage to the party than the administration of some man less familiar with the problems themselves and of less intimate knowledge of this administration. . ."

In reply House wrote that he had talked with McAdoo, and that he himself was now persuaded that Leffingwell was the man. He expressed hope that Wilson would act soon for he was eager to see Glass in the Senate where, he said, he was sorely needed.

This was in mid-December. Six weeks later Glass received

a letter from The White House telling him of the appointment of David F. Houston as his successor.

On February 2, Glass' resignation took effect. The following day, escorted by Claude A. Swanson, his one-time political adversary, he appeared before Vice-President Marshall to take his oath as a United States Senator.

"In leaving the Cabinet for the Senate," he wrote Secretary Newton D. Baker, "I have no personal desires to serve. Indeed, public life never had any especial attraction for me; it has always been desperately hard work, and recently, human slavery."

He gave up the big house and moved back to his more comfortable hotel quarters, thinking his residence there would only be temporary – that his public career would be ended when his ad interim appointment terminated.

CHAPTER FIFTEEN

"It is with the utmost reluctance that the President turns away from any suggestion made by Senator Glass."

It was Glass' intention, when he became Senator, to maintain a studious silence relative to most matters up for debate, as he had done in his salad days in the lower chamber. But these were different times. He had scarcely taken his oath before he was fighting for his party, and his President, in trying to secure Senate ratification of the Peace Treaty.

On the Republican side, Henry Cabot Lodge of Massachusetts was the leader in the attack on the proposed agreement with its League of Nations Covenant; and joining him were a number of Democrats. Article Ten of the proposed Covenant read:

> The members of the League undertake to respect and preserve as against external aggression the territorial integrity and existing political independence of all members of the League. In case of any such aggression the Council shall advise upon the means by which this obligation shall be fulfilled.

The political firing was heaviest against this paragraph, although other provisions did not escape. Knowing the opposition was organized to defeat both the Treaty and the Covenant, Glass studied a substitute reservation William Howard Taft had drawn:

> The United States assumes no obligation under the provisions of Article X. to preserve the territorial integrity or political independence of any other country or to interfere in controversies between other nations, whether members of the League or not, or under any article of the treaty for any purpose to employ the military and naval forces of the United States except as, in any

particular case, the Congress, which under the Constitution has the sole power to declare war and to authorize the employment of the military and naval forces of the United States, shall by act or joint resolution so specifically determine.

Glass talked with opposition Senators, and found them willing to give ground if, in turn, Wilson could be persuaded to accept the proposal of a former Republican President. With this in mind, he communicated with Wilson :

February 9, 1920.

My dear Mr. President :

I am sure Democratic Senators now understand and quite clearly your determination never to agree to the Lodge reservations to the covenant and are convinced of the futility of any expectation of a conclusion of the matter on the basis of those reservations. They know that you would regard acquiescence in the Lodge reservations as a betrayal of the Democratic party and a betrayal of you. I agree with you.

If, however, we must go to the American people on the issue, it seems to me of supreme importance to the party and of the gravest concern for the treaty also that we should enter the fight fortified not alone by the righteousness of the cause, but able to convince the average citizen that we had exhausted every possible effort to conciliate the adversaries of the administration short of a virtual nullification of the covenant.

You are not more set against the Lodge reservations than Lodge is determined to reject anything which he may suspect you with favoring. Even if he were less implacable, Borah and Hiram Johnson would not let him accept anything which they could imagine would bring about a ratification of the treaty. This was indisputably revealed by Lodge's hasty and compulsory withdrawal from the conference table of the bi-partisan committee the other day when an agreement seemed imminent.

The analysis of the Taft reservation to article 10 which I ventured to make at my interview with you Friday meets the concurrence of Hitchcock, Underwood and every other Democratic Senator to whom I have submitted it, as well as of wary, discerning and uncompromising friends of the Administration on the outside. They agree that it does not in any particular impair the integrity of article 10 ; it merely states accepted facts and obvious constitutional processes. If offered by us and accepted it could do no harm to the treaty, but would drive Borah and Johnson into revolt against the Republican party for agreeing to it. But it would not be accepted. Lodge would not if he could and could not if he would. If his malignancy should not prevail to reject it, his fear of the Republican "implacables" would prevent him from accepting it.

Thus responsibility for defeat of the treaty would rest with Lodge and his Republican associates. We could go to the country pointing to our willingness to accept a reservation drafted by a Republican ex-President of the United States, but which was rejected by men willing to wreck the world to satiate their hatred of a Democratic President.

This, Mr. President, is my survey of the situation. I appreciate to the fullest extent your refusal to be drawn into making suggested modifications which might extricate Lodge from his dilemma or involve you in any appearance of assenting to any impairment of the real integrity of the covenant. At the same time your true friends who are uncompromising advocates of the treaty in its essential form would be embarrassed to present a modification such, for example, as the Taft reservation to article 10, if it should, perchance, be so at variance with your view as to cause a refusal to exchange ratifications in the unlikely event of its acceptance by the Republicans. If some word might come to some Senator in complete confidence, not to be directly communicated to anybody else, the matter could, I venture to think, go forward without in the least associating you with the legislative event. I submit the suggestion for what it may seem to be worth.

With warmest regards,
Cordially and faithfully,
(signed) Carter Glass.

The President,
The White House.

On February 11, by messenger, Glass received a note in Mrs. Wilson's handwriting. In it Mrs. Wilson represented the President as believing that Article Ten was the "backbone" of the Covenant; also, that Wilson questioned the "good faith" of Taft's proposed reservation. In addition she said it was the President's opinion that "absolute inaction" on the part of the

Democratic party was preferable to "mistaken initiative" ; and that any initiative "ought to be forced upon the Republicans."

Greatly disappointed, Glass acknowledged the President's note of refusal :

February 12, 1920.

Dear Mr. President :

I seem to have been rather unhappy in my note of Monday if I made the impression that I was proposing to initiate modifications of the covenant. On the contrary, as I tried to indicate at our interview last Friday, it is my considered judgment that Lodge has the treaty on his hands and the Democrats should originate no move to relieve his embarrassment. If I could direct the course of events, we should not budge from that position.

However, when the treaty comes up for consideration in the Senate next week and article 10 is reached, modifications will be proposed, possibly by Lodge himself ; if not, then by the so-called Republican "mild reservationists," and not unlikely by Democratic Senators who, willing to vote for the treaty as it stands, nevertheless would vote for modifications rather than have ratification fail.

When this stage is reached, with all the Republicans and certain treacherous Democrats set against taking the treaty as it stands, our side must determine whether, in the reservations submitted, our adversaries have proposed some other course which will meet with executive sanction. It is essentially desirable to send nothing from the Senate which would be rejected at the White House ; and yet there is danger of this unless, somehow, we may know how proposed reservations impress you. Hence the particular purpose of my note of the 9th was to draw some expression which would indicate whether the suggested Taft reservation or the bi-partisan committee draft was, either of them, impossible ; and the word which you have been good enough to send is perfectly clear on this point.

I agree, of course, that we must not, in any event, make any departure from principle, and it did not occur to me that anything of that sort was involved in the strategy of forcing the other side into either an acceptance or rejection of a reservation to article 10, drafted by a Republican ex-President, and which would not, if accepted, touch the integrity of the treaty, but would, if rejected, gravely weaken the opposition in an issue before the people. Very likely I am entirely mistaken about this and shall not pursue the matter.

With warmest regards,
Sincerely yours,
(signed) Carter Glass.

The President,
The White House.

The matter was not pursued. The Treaty, as it stood, was not ratified.

With the national conventions of the two major parties less than three months distant, Glass was aware of rumors that Wilson was toying with the idea of making an effort for a third term; nor was Glass unaware of efforts being made within the Democratic party to make him its standard bearer. Mentioned, also, as a distinct possibility for the Democratic nomination was Herbert Hoover. A "Make-Hoover-President-Club" was organized by California Democrats, to be quickly followed by a similar organization in Virginia.

William Cabell Bruce, of Baltimore, and later Democratic Senator, was asked to head up a Hoover group in Maryland. Instead, Bruce wrote Glass urging him to become a candidate.

Because Bruce was in a position to influence, if not completely control, Maryland's sixteen delegates, probably this was the first "Glass-for-President" delegation outside of Virginia. And, too, Bruce was influential with Democratic leaders in other states. Glass was mindful of the significance of the offer but ten days passed before, with characteristic candor, he answered:

My time has been so completely occupied since the receipt of your kind letter of March 12 that I have been utterly unable to give one particle of attention to personal correspondence until today. I am writing now to express again my very deep appreciation of the compliment you pay me in thinking that I should be considered for the Democratic Presidential nomination.

I have been the recipient of many letters of the same import;

but I have been utterly unable to bring myself to the belief that there is any possible chance of the nomination of a Southern man. Indeed, I have been unable to believe that the nomination of a Southern man would be wise.

I quite agree with what you say about Mr. Hoover. He is a man of unusual abilities in certain directions; but to me it seems most improbable that any man can be nominated by the presidential convention of either party who publicly avows, three months before the conventions are to assemble, that he is not prepared to say whether he is a Democrat or Republican.* It is literally certain, in my view, that the Republican convention will not dream of nominating Mr. Hoover, and I think totally unlikely that the Democratic convention will seriously consider doing so.

The whole Presidential situation is in a muddle, and I confess my own inability to discern the outcome of the many complications. In any event you may be sure that I shall always greatly appreciate your kind interest in me.

Meanwhile, there were frequent visits to The White House. Glass knew that many facets of Wilson's brilliant mind were beginning to cloud; that the mind, though still clear, had lost some of its quick perception and ready decision. They were trying meetings for both men, with Glass endeavoring to speak the words to fit the thoughts, thus sparing the sick man the effort; and, too, there was Wilson's impatience with himself.

Keeping a diary has never been a practice of Glass, but during this period he did make some notes; and these notes, though scant, tell the story:

June 10, 1920.

Grayson [Wilson's physician] told me President seriously contemplates permitting himself to be named for 3rd term and said it would kill him. Later in day Burleson told me he believed Presi-

* This "indecision" on the part of Mr. Hoover was a piece of political maneuvering inspired by Republican Senator Boies Penrose, of Pennsylvania. Disliking Hoover, but recognizing his strength, Penrose sought to make him unattractive to the Republicans and unavailable to the Democrats. By causing it to be published that "Hoover did not know whether he was a Republican or a Democrat," Penrose figured on shutting both doors on the Food Administrator. His political strategy turned out as he had anticipated.

dent wanted third term, saying he had told President latter or McAdoo would be nominated to which President made no answer. Both Grayson and Burleson told me President anxious for me to head Platform Committee, San Francisco.

June 12, 1920.

President asked me, by Mrs. Wilson, to come to White House at 2 P. M. Mrs. Wilson explained, when I got there, that President had forgotten prior engagement with masseur and was being at that moment treated. Said, however, President had commissioned her to say he wanted me to be Chairman Platform Committee, San Francisco. Told Mrs. Wilson President could not control such matters. Committee on Resolutions would elect its own Chairman. In her usual womanly way she professed ignorance of convention processes, but said that the President would like me to take Chairmanship if tendered, saying Cummings had wired President asking latter to get this assurance. I complied.

June 16, 1920.

Grayson at Executive Offices expressed to me greatest anxiety about President's third term thoughts, saying he literally impossible to measure up to exactions of campaign. Would probably kill him. Said President's sole idea was to lead fight for covenant; he was totally indifferent to all other considerations. Would resign after covenant adopted. I told Grayson I did not think convention could be induced to nominate man in President's disabled condition; and if President was in robust health, twas barely possible Democratic party and American people might submerge third term antipathies in their desire for permanent guaranty against war; but not in present circumstances. Grayson begged me to do all possible to guard against such an untoward development in San Francisco. Tumulty also today expressed concern about this third term manifestation.

June 17, 1920.

In response to long distance 'phone request made by McAdoo yesterday, met him at 11 A. M. today at his office.* Showed me letter he proposed to issue declining to permit use of his name for nomination at San Francisco. I remonstrated, telling him, aside from all graver considerations, he would leave his friends "in the air" with no man to whom they might turn. Replied that he

* At McAdoo's New York office

intended to ask his friends to support me. Told him twas nonsense; no man resident in the South would be considered. He talked about my case being different from average Southern politician; my connection with Federal Reserve legislation and my Treasury Administration had made me thousands of friends in North and West. Told him twas all moonshine. He insisted otherwise, and told me he wanted me to talk to Roper. He called Roper on 'phone and made appointment my room at the Biltmore. Roper came and talked same foolishness. Even said he would write letters asking McAdoo leaders to support me. Finally I said: "Roper, Mr. McAdoo nowhere says in that letter he would not accept a nomination; does he mean to go that *far?*" "He does not go that far. I persuaded him not to say that," replied Roper.

There was something in Roper's look which caused me swiftly to vision the whole situation, and I said: "Then you must think the publication of this letter will help, rather than eliminate McAdoo."

"I do," said Roper, smiling. "Then why this talk about turning McAdoo's friends to me?" I asked.

"Because Mr. McAdoo does not agree that the effect of his letter will be to keep him in the race; and he wants his friends to support you," said Roper.

June 18, 1920.

I came back to Washington decidedly puzzled. Jouett Shouse insisted on taking Mr. McAdoo's letter at its face and, altho' an ardent supporter of Mr. McAdoo, he issued today a public statement advocating my nomination. Indeed, Shouse almost convinced me, against my better judgment, that McAdoo's letter eliminated the latter. But I cannot forget that look on Roper's face when I questioned him in my room at the Biltmore. It seems like an attempt to trifle with me; but I have no illusions about a Presidential nomination. It is amiable nonsense, well intended, perhaps, but misdirected. I'm impressed by the obvious fact that we have nobody big enough to follow Wilson.

June 19, 1920.

Took noonday tea with President and Mrs. Wilson on south portico of White House. We talked about San Francisco convention. President expressed satisfaction at my willingness to take chairmanship of Resolutions Committee. Told him it remained to be seen whether Committee on Resolutions would be willing.

He said Cummings had assured him there would be no opposition to me; but said Colby for Chairman of Convention was being opposed. President asked me what I thought of McAdoo's letter. I said: "He nowhere says he would not accept a nomination." Very quickly the President responded with emphasis: "No, he does not; as I read it." We briefly commented on some of the men talked of for nomination. Of Mitchell Palmer, I said he would make a good President but a weak candidate having, in the performance of his duty, offended powerful groups of men. "Exactly," said the President, "hence his nomination would be futile." "As for Cox," I started, when the President broke in, saying, "Oh! you know Cox's nomination would be a joke," to which I fervently assented.

Grayson and Tumulty met me at the Treasury entrance to The White House and accompanied me to the Union Station. They were particularly anxious to know if the President was still thinking of a third term and whether he had charged me with any mission on the subject. I told them he had said no single word about it; also told them, in confidence, what he had said about Mr. McAdoo's letter and about Palmer and Cox. Grayson accompanied me to my sleeper and remained talking until the train moved, saying at last: "If anything comes up, save the life and fame of this man from the juggling of false friends." In our talk the President had asked me my impression of the Volstead Act and the advisability of declaring for its moderation. I told him whatever might be the severity or defects of the law it would be a fatal mistake to make a political issue of it before giving it a fair trial. He expressed the opinion that in ratifying the 18th amendment, the people had not supposed the statutory enforcement would be quite so drastic. "Maybe so," said I, "but any attempt to make modification a party issue would be interpreted into an effort to nullify the amendment in the interest of the brewers." "Perhaps that is so," said the President and dismissed the subject. He then handed me a paper saying: "I wish you would get this in the platform." After getting on the train, I found the paper to be a declaration for an Armenian Mandate written on the President's typewriter and initialed "W.W."

The plank suggested by Wilson did not reach the platform because of the intense opposition of Senator Thomas Walsh, of Montana.

It read :

Suggested platform declaration with regard to Armenia.

We hold it to be the Christian duty and privilege of our Government to assume responsible guardianship of Armenia which now needs only the advice and assistance of a powerful friend to establish her complete independence and to give to her distracted people the opportunities for peaceful happiness which they have vainly longed for through so many dark years of hopeless suffering and hideous distress.

Arriving in San Francisco, one of the first things that met the Senator's eyes was a banner stretched across a building opposite the railroad station – a banner which was lettered "WILLIAM G. McADOO FOR PRESIDENT." As his cab carried him through the streets to his hotel, he saw many other banners, all saying the same thing ; and they reminded him of a visit with McAdoo a few weeks before.

But Wilson, not his son-in-law McAdoo, was to be honored at that convention. As the sessions opened, a file of marines appeared to present a stand of colors. The great auditorium was hushed to break into wild applause as a giant American flag slowly unfurled and then lifted to disclose a portrait of the President. Immediately a stampede began, with delegates marching up and down the aisles, waving their state standards in wild acclaim. One standard alone (New York) remained motionless on the floor – then, it was suddenly lifted and with a wild yell a young man bounded from his seat, to join the others. It was Assistant Secretary of the Navy, Franklin D. Roosevelt, participating in what many thought was a third term stampede, instead of being, as it actually was, a tribute.

Following the demonstration, Glass was chosen Chairman of the Resolutions Committee over the opposition of Senator Walsh, who led the so-called Senate cabal in opposition to the Wilson Treaty, and it was Walsh, himself, who seconded the nomination to make the choice unanimous.

The important issue before the convention was the Peace Treaty and Glass, an advocate of the idealistic League of Nations, was incensed over the treatment accorded the President by Republicans, and "meekly followed by shallow Democrats." There was more than a little bitterness within the Resolutions Committee, with Glass arraigning critics of the President, and being arraigned by them. In the ammunition Glass had was a letter he had written to Judge Robert C. Jackson, of Roanoke, Virginia, a short time before ; the facts he had presented to the jurist were his arguments now :

"The wretched talk about the 'obstinacy' of the President over the Peace Treaty is purely an invention of adversary politicians, acquiesced in by a species of Democrat which has never sympathized with Mr. Wilson's ideals, or his policies. The President has not evinced one particle of obduracy about the Treaty. He negotiated the Treaty of Peace, which was agreed to by all the allied and associated nations in war against Germany, and by Germany also.

"It was not the President's business, when he brought this Treaty back from France, immediately to join with Mr. Lodge and other Republican haters of the President in their deliberate conspiracy to tear the Treaty to pieces, in order that they, and not a Democratic President, might have credit for the great achievement. It was not only not the business of the President to do this ; but for him to have initiated, suggested or assented to changes in the Treaty which would have substantially altered the nature of it, would have been a distinct breach of faith with his associates of the Peace Council. . ."

After four days of almost ceaseless wrangling, Glass won this fight, with the Committee approving the Treaty, as well as the League of Nations ; but leaving out, as previously stated, the one plank regarding Armenia that Wilson had personally dictated, changing it to read :

We express our deep and earnest sympathy for the unfortunate people of Armenia, and we believe that our government, consistent with its Constitution and principles, should render every possible and proper aid to them in their efforts to establish and maintain a government of their own.

As Chairman of the Resolutions Committee, Glass also beat off a proposal by Bryan to pay a bonus to the soldiers, sailors and marines engaged in the war. One of the first to recognize the vote-catching possibilities in the bonus issue, Bryan made an impassioned plea for "substantial recognition" of the men comprising the fighting forces, and in his plea included caustic references to the callousness of those who "had sacrificed nothing."

At the final word of the Nebraskan, Glass was on his feet, pointing out that "as Secretary of the Treasury I became intimately enough acquainted with the finances of the country to realize if ever we embark upon this thing it would bring us into such a serious situation as to jeopardize our security." He went on to say it would be an "invitation to group privilege to raid the Treasury year after year – something that once begun there is no telling where the end will be," and added: "I glorify the American soldier, and it is because I glorify him that I shrink from the idea of trying to compensate his services in dollars and cents."

With embarrassment coloring his face, he went on:

"I am going to say something here today that I have never repeated outside the confidence of my own family, and the confidence of the President of the United States. During the war I tried to enlist. I went to Mr. Wilson to express my desire for active service, in any capacity. He refused permission. He reminded me of my age, and told me I was more needed at home. In addition, he told me if I acted contrary to his wishes, and did enlist, he would see to it, personally, that my period of any such service ended abruptly.

"But I did give my two sons to the cause. I did give my two daughters to war work, one of them being in the Red Cross. Several of my nephews enlisted, and one of them was shot to pieces, and it will be a long time before he regains his health, if he ever does. Also, a great many other close relatives were in the service of their country. I tell you all this not to burnish my own shield because I am sure there are many others on this committee and elsewhere who can reply to this unwarranted aspersion better than I. I say it to indicate to Mr. Bryan that his references to those who 'sacrificed nothing' are not properly made when he seeks to apply them to those who are opposed to his bonus proposition. I repeat it because I shall be greatly interested to hear from Mr. Bryan's own lips if he can say for himself what, shamelessly, I have said for myself."

Stung by the rebuke, Bryan retreated into a corner of the room where he sat down, covered his face with his hands, and burst into tears. After a few minutes of emotion he walked back to where Glass was sitting. The two men shook hands quietly, and together they turned to the wording of the plank which, under Glass' direction, was written to say :

> The fine patriotism exhibited, the heroic conduct displayed by American soldiers, sailors and marines at home and abroad constitute a sacred heritage of posterity, the worth of which can never be recompensed from the Treasury and the glory of which must not be diminished by any such expedient.

He also wrote two other planks, one of which pertained to the "Cost of Living" and which stated, "The . . . high cost of living can only be remedied by increased production, strict governmental economy and a relentless pursuit of those who take advantage of post-war conditions." As for Tax Reform, his remaining contribution, the platform advocated "tax reform and a searching revision of the war revenue acts."

In balloting for the Presidential nomination the names of twenty-three candidates were placed before the delegates. Wilson's name was not among them. For the first time Glass heard his name entered into nomination for the Presidency of the United States. It was done by Representative Flood of Virginia. After thirty-eight ballots, the convention was in a deadlock over three men, McAdoo, Governor James M. Cox of Ohio, and A. Mitchell Palmer, Attorney General in the Wilson cabinet.

With Palmer's withdrawal after the 38th ballot, Glass appealed to the New York delegation to swing its votes to McAdoo. In that he was not successful. On the 44th ballot, Cox had 702½ votes, McAdoo, 266½ ; and on the 45th ballot the vote was made unanimous for Cox. The following day, without a ballot the tired delegates named, by acclamation, Franklin D. Roosevelt to be a running mate for the Ohio governor.

In the elections of the following November, Cox and Roosevelt were badly beaten, the Republicans electing Harding and Coolidge.

However, it should be stated that after the nomination, Wilson's attitude toward Cox changed, and he seemed to entertain considerable admiration, if not actual affection, for the Ohio governor.

CHAPTER SIXTEEN

"The day of reckoning for gambling cannot be escaped."

Post-war deflation held the world in its grip. Repeatedly the administration of the Federal Reserve System was attacked because it did not disregard its reserve requirements and float new billions of bank notes and credits. England did, in spite of her long tradition of financial soundness; and her foreign exchange became dislocated, her trade gravely impaired, her economic recovery retarded. France did, also to her grief. Germany did, and her mark became a grim monetary joke. Russia did, and it took a million roubles to buy a pound of butter. Glass resisted this ruinous tendency and assailed it as "printing-press economics."

Unwilling to tighten their belt in the lean years of getting "back to normalcy," there were those who, in many covert ways, were perverting the preventive provisions of the Federal Reserve System for their own speculative ends. In every move to convert reserve banking into speculative investment banking, Glass read signs of the future. Again and again, by these signs, he prophesied the economic collapse that came nine years later.

In December 1920, the Senate had censured the Federal Reserve Board, and professional "friends of the farmer" demanded that it mobilize the credits at its disposal for the crop-moving period. Glass demonstrated this had been done, that the censure was undeserved.

Senator Simmons, of North Carolina, was persistent in his criticisms of the board for withholding advance loans which would enable farmers to hold their crops for better marketing conditions. In a split second Glass was out of his chair:

"To 'hold' their crops! Now we are getting at the kernel of the whole proposition. The Senator would have the Federal Reserve banking system – which had its very inception in the idea of accommodating commerce, a system intended to be responsive to the commercial requirements of the country – transformed into a speculative and investment banking system, not a system designed to aid in the purchase of goods but a system designed to store goods, to keep them off the market.

"If that is what Congress wants to do, if it wants to wreck the Federal Reserve banking system . . . it should have the courage to do that act of unwisdom in the open. . .

"It was intimated here the other day that at one time the angle for expansion for a brief period was 45 degrees, whereas the angle of expansion for a later and longer period was but 2 degrees. Is there any sane human being who objects to the Federal Reserve Board putting a stop to the 45 degree angle, which meant ruin to the banking business of the country, ruin to the commerce and industry of the country, irreparable ruin to the farming interests of the country?

"It meant that speculation was running riot, and the only criticism I make of the Federal Reserve Board is that it did not begin to put a stop to commodity gambling soon enough. Had it done so, perhaps we should not have had so far to fall. It let the situation get almost out of hand, and it applied the brakes none too soon. It did not apply them to agriculture.

"The only suggestion of curtailment was as to non-essentials – automobiles, limousines, things of that kind. The day of reckoning for that sort of thing cannot be escaped. It must come, I do not care how soon it comes; how soon I am compelled to have one automobile instead of two, or no automobile instead of one, or how soon other people less able to have any shall be deprived of the privilege of mortgaging their homes and their futures for this sort of thing."

Early in 1922, in an exhaustive and fact-packed speech, *Truth about the Federal Reserve System,* Glass had occasion again to comment on the farmer's plight. He brought forth figures to prove that, instead of deflating credits and currency during a period of falling prices, the Federal Reserve Banks had enormously expanded bank credits and increased the volume of circulating notes . . . and that this was especially true in the agricultural sections.

"Why not tell the farmer the truth," he demanded, "and advise him, if he would escape the consequences of another such disaster, he should organize? Organize, not to be the plaything or the instrument of designing politicians, but organize for an intelligent investigation and pursuit of economics; organize for a cooperative marketing of his product; organize, if it may seem desirable, for the cooperative purchase of his requirements; organize for an intelligent understanding of the source and volume of demand for farm products. . ."

The following year, when real estate and agricultural loans were under discussion, that hoary recommendation that farmer representatives be allowed to have a direct hand in Federal Reserve management was revived. Glass had always opposed it. "I know it is unpleasant to tell farmers they are not bankers," he said. "I do not know whether I should be courageous enough to go among them and tell them that or not; but I say here that they are not bankers and they cannot manage banks as bankers can."

"They have sense enough to elect members of this body," countered Fletcher of Florida.

The Virginian's rejoinder was impersonal. "They apparently have had sense enough to elect United States Senators who have not, under the test, made very good Senators."

Connecticut's McLean asserted that there was a moral obligation, if not a legal one, for the Government to underwrite joint-stock land bank bonds in behalf of agriculture. To which Glass replied: "It has become fashionable when nobody has a legal claim that he can establish against the Government, to talk about the moral responsibility."

He pointed to the injustice of taxing the farmers of one state to give advantages to competing farmers in another.

"As the distinguished Senator from Georgia (George) said the other day, this is not even socialism. It does not approach in respectability the doctrine of communism. It is special privilege run mad. I am getting tired of seeing, even on this side of the Chamber, Senators in the guise of Democracy, professing the principles of Thomas Jefferson, voting to outrage every principle that Jefferson ever avowed in respect to government.

"I hold that taxation is solely for the purpose of insuring an effective and economic administration of the Federal Government. When funds are taken for any other use they are being improperly diverted."

Of this period there are several paragraphs in Glass' "diary," among them being:

April 14, 1921.
Senator Warren, Wyo. called me to his desk and said: "I hope some day a Democratic Senatorial Steering Committee will say as many fine things of you as I heard said of you today in our Republican Committee." I afterward learned that the Steering Committee had considered the desirability of increasing membership of B. & C. in order to put me on, and many kind things were said by my political adversaries.

April 15, 1921.
Swanson is trying to impress me with the idea that *he* is arranging to have me put on Banking & Currency. McLean, Chairman, has already told me that *he* induced his party Steering Committee to increase membership to put me on. I am sure Swanson wants me to go on; but I cannot restrain amusement at his eagerness to have it appear that *he* is managing the thing, when I know better.

Still, I am certain Swanson really wants me to have good assignments and desires to cooperate closely. He is bigger than I thought him when it comes to forgetting and forgiving. Why should not this be pleasant? *It is.*

December 18, 1921.

Grayson again told me War Department sent officer in person (Sassiter) to invite Mr. Wilson to parade on Armistice Day. Later Weeks wrote formal letter. Then Harding letter explaining. All exceedingly courteous. Siebold protested against publication of correspondence. Mayo asked Mr. Wilson if he was bothered by gases. Replied : "Yes ; chiefly from the Capitol."

December 3, 1922. (Sunday)

Called at 2340 "S." Didn't expect to see Chief or Mrs. Wilson as it was former's bed time. Mrs. Wilson sent word to come to Library and later Chief had me come to room. Looking well and in fine humor. Only the good sense of Mrs. Wilson saves the situation. She is simply great ; not divine, as we do often say in exaggeration, but with human qualities that are nearest akin to the divine.

Long and intensive studies in finance involving close scrutiny of countless columns and figures might easily shorten a man's vision, rendering him incapable of perceiving distant horizons. But no bookkeeper's myopia has ever shortened the gaze of Glass. In July, 1921, in a discussion of the Treasury's authority to deal with foreign loans, he made this foresighted statement :

"It is my belief that with respect to the major loans of foreign governments the Secretary of the Treasury has under existing law ample power to do this thing. It is only with respect to the miscellaneous loans, such as loans to Poland, Czechoslovakia, Lithuania, and a multiplicity of nations whose identity might disappear in six months or a year or a longer time, that the Secretary of the Treasury needs power to fund the loans."

Always an idealist, he supported Wilson in his fight to enter the United States into the League of Nations. After this monumental effort was wrecked and the League lacked the strength and moral support of the United States, the subsequent forced remaking of Europe's map and its ultimate menace were clear in Glass' comprehension.

Frequently his has been one of the most cogent and insistent voices in Congressional determination of American foreign policy. In March 1922, Underwood of Alabama was advocating the Four Power Treaty between Great Britain, France, Japan and the United States. He claimed it was not an alliance that could involve this country in a foreign war, but merely an innocuous agreement among nations. Glass took the opposite view. To him such a pact should be signed by all nations, not by only four. He asked Underwood if there were no implications of force in such a contract.

"I say that it is no alliance," reasserted Underwood, "but that it is an agreement by four great powers to keep the peace. I believe the great moving cause which made it possible for the world to sit at a table and agree on a League of Nations to keep the peace . . . came from the great heart-beats of Christian nations and Christian people."

"But it did not reflect itself in this great Christian nation," Glass said sardonically. "The Senator in his philosophizing about the doctrines of Christianity is getting away from my question."

Wisconsin's Lenroot entered the argument, avowing that under the treaty no representative of this country could involve it in the use of force, and that only the Congress possessed the constitutional authority to determine upon war. "That is a very fine argument," commented Glass, "which the Senator from Wisconsin took special pains repeatedly to controvert when the covenant of the League of Nations was before the Senate."

When Lenroot insisted that the treaty placed this nation under no moral obligation to fight, Glass replied: "When a man enters into a contract he is morally bound to observe the very purposes he avows in that contract at the outset, and the major purpose of this contract is to maintain the territorial integrity and rights of the contracting parties.

"We proceed to set up an agency for the purpose of carrying out the avowed object of this treaty. Then can we say that if our agent commits us to the use of force there is no moral obligation upon this nation to use force, but that under the covenant of the League there *was* a moral obligation? That is a legal refinement and quibble that is beyond the discernment or comprehension of a man of ordinary intelligence who does not belong to the legal fraternity."

Later he added: "The Senator said he could not argue this proposition, and I quite agree with him that he has not argued it. . ."

Two weeks later he again took the floor. "I have very earnestly desired," he stated, "to be among the supporters in the Senate of the four-power pact. I had hoped it would accomplish something in the direction of universal peace. Again, I am averse to exchange places with those Senators who are responsible for the defeat of the League of Nations purely upon partisan grounds. I have not desired to vote against a league for peace contrived by my political adversaries for no better reason than that they had voted against the league for peace contrived and presented by an administration of my own faith. I have very earnestly desired to ratify the work of the so-called Conference for the Limitation of Armaments if I could find it at all agreeable to my judgment and conscience to do so.

"It has been said that the four-power pact is in no respect akin to the League of Nations. I grant that it has none of the complete virtues of the League of Nations, but in one respect, at least, it has some resemblance to the league. It has been said and sought here today, by the most extraordinary species of casuistry to which a deliberate body ever listened, to show that this pact involves no exercise of force."

By quoting directly from the text of the treaty he demonstrated that it more specifically implied the use of force than the famous Article Ten of the League covenant to which the other side of the chamber had so strenuously objected. But, he continued, "I believe in force behind a treaty to insure peace. What I am objecting to is that there is not force enough behind this treaty. It is not too much force behind the pact that excites my hostility; it is too few member nations.

"In other words, instead of bringing us a treaty to preserve the peace of the world, the delegates have brought us a group intrigue, such as has disturbed the peace of Europe for two hundred years; a group alliance such as our forefathers denounced and against which this Nation has set its face since its existence; a group alliance pregnant with war itself. It is a misnomer, it is a travesty to speak of this pact as a treaty for peace.

"If you will put enough of the nations of the earth behind the force we shall have peace, instead of a menacing little imitation league, a four-ply alliance, destined to involve us in distress and humiliation, if not in actual war.

"I shall vote for that particular treaty which it is said will bring about, in some measure or degree, disarmament. . . If I could, I would banish from the high seas every man-of-war and every auxiliary vessel with great guns. I am for the measure of disarmament, although what we are doing is to scrap some obsolete battleships that would have the stuffing shot out of them before any one of them could reach a hostile vessel of modern type."

Senator Reed interrupted to point out that England and Japan were scrapping blueprints instead of battleships, and that in the end England would have a 20 per cent advantage on the seas.

"I have no fear of Great Britain," said Glass. "I am English by lineage. I believe in Great Britain, and I was willing to enter a world alliance with Great Britain for universal peace; but I am not willing to amplify the present Anglo-Japanese alliance. That is all this group treaty is – an amplification of the Anglo-Japanese menace – and we become a part of the menace to the balance of the world.

"We may be sure Japan knows what she is about. We are asked gravely to accept the wretched nonsense as to Japan having renounced her defensive alliance with Great Britain without deriving any compensatory advantage! Japan is not that simple, even if we in the Senate Chamber are. Japan knows what she got. She knows that in addition to Great Britain's powerful support she got a treaty that binds the United States to 'preserve and maintain' not only her territorial possessions but to preserve and maintain her 'rights,' as she may assert them."

Here his eye roved the chamber and met the gaze of Underwood.

"The Senator from Alabama," he said, "made a touching appeal to his colleagues to substitute the power of Christ for the menace of the sword. There is not a semblance of the spirit of Jesus Christ in this alliance with a pagan nation, not a semblance of it. It constitutes a quadruple alliance as the world's bully; it is an invitation to all the outside nations of the earth to hate us because we have deliberately excluded them from participation. Does that reflect, in any sense or degree, the spirit of Christ? I thought the spirit of the Saviour of mankind was all-inclusive. I have been taught that it means the brotherhood of man. . ."

Senator Hitchcock interposed that the opening prayer of the clergyman at the conference had been censored, and that he was not permitted to mention the name of Christ out of regard for Japan.

Glass said : "Oh, it is perfectly obvious that there is nothing about the pact suggestive of the spirit of Christianity. It is brutally exclusive. It was intended to be threatening, and is threatening. It is a challenge to the rest of the world.

"I will not vote for this miserable group alliance."

However, the pact was signed.

But there are times when his mind is far removed – times when fingers reach out from the past to turn the pages of the book that is never closed to him – times when he goes alone where only he alone can go, deep into the chambers of his own thought to travel through them in the roundabout way that is called contemplation.

His youth is in his thought now, and he doesn't know why ; and the day when, as in the terms of the Methodist Church, he was "converted." He didn't tell his father and sister Nannie what he was planning for fear they would be shocked at his entering the church because, just that day, they had called him "a wicked boy." Their shock was much greater, however, when they saw him get to his feet and accompany a group of young people to the altar. The minister asked if he had been baptized, and he said no. Not until after the ceremony did he learn he had been baptized in infancy, thus convicting himself, as he now recalls, of baptismal bigamy.

He thinks, too, of that Sunday morning in Lynchburg when, waiting for a street car, a girl and her mother came to wait, too . . . how he stared and the disdain in her single glance

. . . his own discomfiture . . . wonder who she was? . . . of the day when the handyman, Wyatt Johnson, stopped a press in his father's printing office just in time to prevent his hand from being mangled . . . the scars remain . . . of the loss of his sister Nannie in March, 1915 . . . the passing of his stepmother in January, 1912. . .

Of that day when he was just a little fellow and his stepmother was lying dozing, while under her bed were about a dozen pairs of shoes . . . how she laughed when he asked her if he could have a pair . . . and how the cobbler laughed when he asked him to cut them down so they would fit his small feet . . . of his wife, and their firstborn, Claiborne, who died in infancy . . . of Powell, Carter Jr., Augusta, Mary Archer . . . and now *he* was a grandfather . . . "Nonsense, I'm not old enough to be a grandfather!" . . . "Grandfather!" . . . "Pardner!" . . . "That's better." . . "Pardner it will be." . . Pardner it became.

That night in London, during the War, when he came into the room to find his friend, Congressman Dick Whaley, wrapped up in blankets, the room filled with steam from the hot-water faucet and the fireplace vacant and black . . . asking Whaley why he didn't light the fire, and Whaley telling him there was no wood while in an enclosed cubbyhole beside the fireplace there was wood aplenty . . . and Whaley's vigorous language at the secretiveness of the English.

And, now, Glass was defending England.

By invitation, early in 1923, Great Britain sent a commission to the United States to discuss ways and means of her repayment of wartime loans. Under the text of the Liberty Loan Acts the moral obligation of Great Britain was to pay no higher rate of interest than the charge at which America floated her own indebtedness to the buyers of Liberty Bonds. Now that America had reduced that rate from 5 to 4½ per cent, it was proposed to give Britain the advantage of a corresponding reduction. Many millions of dollars were involved and a number of Senators voiced their disapproval. To Glass this took the tone of an America demanding her "pound of flesh" from her former allies.

Among the dissidents was McKellar of Tennessee who, on February 1, made a most militant verbal attack against the English. In this he voiced the antagonism of that portion of the American public whose attitude toward the Allies had taken a pendulum swing away from the co-operative wartime fervor. Glass' feelings had undergone no such reaction.

"When it comes to casting up accounts and contrasting matters of indebtedness," he said, "I feel that there is a good deal to be said on the other side of the question. I had two boys on the firing line in France, and I cannot exactly repress a feeling of indebtedness to Great Britain that she buried about 1,500,000 of her sons to save the lives of my boys and other American boys. In short, the British fought three years for civilization before we took our place beside them in identically the same cause. . .

"I hate to lose poise; but I confess to some degree of irritation at certain things that have happened recently in this Chamber. I wish I might hear one kind word said of the people whom we joined, rather belatedly some think, in winning the World War. Instead we are treated day in and day out to 'poor Germany' this and 'poor Germany' that, and told how the people of Germany are suffering, as if no other people are suffering.

"Yes, I am a little exasperated that we seem so soon to have forgotten the men and nations with whom we were associated as to direct all our thought and all our generous sentiment to aiding those who a little while ago were trying to destroy our civilization. All our criticism seems now directed against those with whom we were comrades in arms."

Any criticism against the proposed reduction in interest, Glass maintained, should be directed at Congress and not against England. Doggedly McKellar tried to stand his ground, but when under the Virginian's constant thrusting and factual forays he realized his position, he complained he had been misunderstood. "I thought," he said, "I was able to make myself plain."

Glass heaved a rhetorical sigh. "Well, it was my fault. It was my stupidity. But I have now reached the conclusion that the Senator from Tennessee thinks that because our American Debt Commission is supposed to have proposed a different settlement of these foreign debts from that which the Congress had in mind, it is expedient to twist the British lion's tail."

He returned to the topic in an impassioned speech on February 16.

"It is my purpose," he began, "to vote for this adjustment of Great Britain's indebtedness to the United States, primarily because I am one of those who think that the indebtedness of the United States to Great Britain is quite as great as Great Britain's indebtedness to the United States. . ."

Referring again to Britain's debt, he said, "Every dollar of the $10,000,000,000 was expended in our own country, among our own people, for the wares and supplies which they supplied to Great Britain, sold at profiteering prices three years before we entered the war, sold at profiteering prices after we entered the war. . .

"We transported across the seas 2,000,000 American boys, not one of whom suffered death on the water at the hands of the enemy. We did this when hospital ships, under protection of the Red Cross, could not safely cross the English Channel.

Let us suppose that Great Britain's fleet had not held the German fleet behind Heligoland, cowering and afraid to venture out. Let us suppose that by our failure to loan the $10,000,000,000 the German fleet had come out and ranged the high seas; what would have been the story? Instead of transporting 2,000,000 troops without the loss of a man, hundreds of thousands of American soldiers would have found a grave at the bottom of the Atlantic Ocean, food for sharks and other monsters of the sea.

"It is set up in reply that had we not made the loan, had we not gone to the rescue, what would have become of Great Britain? The same thing would have become of her as later would have become of us. She and we would have been the prey of an autocratic barbarian power.

"I do not concede that there are no sentimental aspects of the question. I think there are. I think it is ungracious in a great American legislative body to forget some things that have happened in recent years. . .

"We won the war! Yes. We entered it opportunely. I conceive, as others conceive, that without our having gone in the war might have been lost. God pity America had it been lost, for the tyrant was impudent enough to tell the American ambassador at Berlin that it would be our turn next; and it *would* have been our turn next, when, instead of fighting side by side with Britain's sons and the sons of France and Belgium and Italy, we would have had to fight alone.

"Our contribution was money and theirs was lives. 'Nominated in the bond,' as the phrase of Shylock runs and as repeated here today. Under the Venetian contract there was to be no drop of blood shed in penalty of capital reprisal; but in this case, my God, British blood flowed in streams before the bond was executed and after the bond was made!"

Wearied with spent emotion, he moved toward his seat,

saying, "I believe I have, in very indignation, exhausted myself if not the subject of the moment."

Since January 1919, Woodrow Wilson had been a sick man. With his idealism of a League to bind all the nations of the earth in a covenant of permanent peace shattered, he had lain, for brooding years, an invalid in a third-story bedroom overlooking Washington. Glass was one of the few steadfast friends who came regularly to see him.

Early in 1924, the Virginian learned from his close friend, Dr. Cary T. Grayson, that the luminous spirit was visibly burning low. By February 1 the whole nation knew. From his large four-poster bed Wilson murmured to Grayson: "I am ready. I am a piece of broken machinery. When the machinery is broken . . ."

In his notebook Glass wrote:

February 1, 1924.

Reported in Senate Mr. Wilson dying. Randolph Bolling tells me on 'phone it is true. Spent two hours 2340 S. Street with Bolling, Swanson, Baruch, Axon awaiting report of Grayson and Ruffin. Mrs. Wilson in sickroom holding Chief's hand, so Grayson tells me. How worthily has this great woman acquitted herself as the wife of this great man! Physicians report, 10:20 P. M., Chief "steadily losing ground." I hardly expect him to last through night.

The following day an automobile inched its way through a silent throng that had gathered before the house in S Street. Slowly two men mounted the steps – gravely an aged Negro unbolted the double wooden doors for Bernard M. Baruch and Carter Glass. Late that night when Glass took his leave he saw the silent people still in the street. Some were on their knees, in prayer.

After church the next morning President and Mrs. Coolidge drove to S Street and sent in cards. Other early callers were Glass, Herbert Hoover and Cordell Hull. They sat awaiting word from the Admiral. Softly closing the door behind him, Grayson came from the bedroom. With eyes downcast he spoke to Glass.

"He smiled when I told him you sent your love."

In the eyes of both there were tears.

Outside, newsmen approached Glass with questions. He shook his head slowly and walked away.

A little after eleven the next morning, February 4, Admiral Grayson came out of the house and read a statement to the press. Few could hear his words, but they did not need to hear. For Glass, a great spirit was gone.

CHAPTER SEVENTEEN

David picked pebbles to slay Goliath.

Ordinarily, some eighty per cent of the members of Congress are lawyers. In Congressional debate Glass frequently makes bland apology for his lack of legal training. But the record does not show him inept in the use of lawyerlike strategy. One stratagem often employed with telling effect is to lure one's opponent, through apparently innocent inquiries, into a snare of his own words.

On March 14, 1925, Senator Ernst of Kentucky was advocating the assessment of additional income tax. Seeking to test Ernst's knowledge that such a tax was necessary, Glass asked, "Will the Senator give us any evidence that will assure us – ?"

"I have no knowledge upon that subject!" interrupted Ernst.

"Then the Senator is making a very specific statement without knowledge," Glass said gently.

"Yes," admitted Ernst, "but, like the Senator from Virginia, I do not know everything. Now let me continue."

But Glass persisted. "The Senator from Virginia, I will say, generally knows what he is talking about."

"I think I have demonstrated that *I* do," rejoined Ernst.

"No," came the Virginian's thrust, "the Senator admits that he does not."

Later in the discussion he took a firm stand against a move on the part of Secretary Mellon to collect from the minority stockholders of the Ford Motor Company additional income taxes for the year 1919.

"It happens that I was Secretary of the Treasury when this

valuation was made," he declared. "I do not desire to escape any responsibility whatever for it, though, in all frankness, I will say to the Senate that at the time I knew nothing about it.

"Those matters of detail are usually attended to, as everybody knows, by the under-Secretary of the Treasury in charge of fiscal affairs. At that time we had in the Treasury one of the ablest men associated with its operations since the day of Alexander Hamilton, who has never, in my judgment, received an ample meed of praise for his great accomplishments – Mr. Russell C. Leffingwell. I would be willing to say confidently that any transaction approved by him would receive my unquestioned approval.

"Therefore, I am not seeking to escape any responsibility for this valuation ; but it is not right, it is not just to the taxpayers of this country, it is a menace to the activities of this body, for the commissioner of Internal Revenue to reopen this case six years after the event."

Later, in response to a partisan intimation by Moses, of New Hampshire, that in behalf of men of great wealth he was trying to discriminate against the small taxpayer, Glass lost no time in recalling a good many previous visits with Secretary Mellon in the interests of the small taxpayer, among them, this one.

The year before a Virginia manufacturing concern had been notified it owed the Government a balance of $2,380 on its tax return for a given year. It had been required to waive the statute of limitations under threat of being charged with constructive fraud. It had been put to the necessity and expense of going to Washington and employing a high-priced attorney, familiar with such transactions, to present its case to the Internal Revenue Bureau. The bureau was compelled to admit that, instead of the Virginia concern owing the Government $2,380, the Government owed the concern a balance of $384.

"This was not the worst feature of the transaction," Glass

stated. "Those officials deliberately delayed for a period of three weeks making out and forwarding the check for that balance, and thereby deliberately maneuvered the United States Government into the attitude of pleading the statute of limitations against its own taxpayer.

"That was an offense so gross and so essentially dishonest that I took it up with the Secretary of the Treasury in person and he at once issued an order that the amount due that concern, which never had pleaded the statute of limitations, be paid.

"I hope that he kicked into the street the miserable little bureaucrat who deliberately maneuvered the Government into that position of evasion and dishonor. It is things like that that cause men who should love the Government actually to hate it.

". . . Why should not the Government refund the taxes that it has mistakenly or illicitly taken from American taxpayers, whether they be large or small? My complaint against the Government is that it deals with every taxpayer as if he were a rascal and as if it was his disposition to cheat the Government. My complaint against the Government is that if it ever gets a dollar of your money, it takes two dollars to get that dollar back."

Referring again to the bureau, he said, "They do not seem to understand at all that they are public servants and that it is just as much their official duty to protect the taxpayer against oppression by the Government as it is their duty to collect money for the Government."

At the time Mrs. Glass was at home convalescing from a serious illness. His mind was on her, and that day he received a letter that was both relieving and amusing. It was from Powell, and it told a story of his mother and of Annie, the Negro cook.

It seems Mrs. Glass had asked Annie to cook her an apple dumpling. Annie did, and proudly bore it into the bedroom. Mrs. Glass tasted it, and made a wry face.

"Annie," she said, sharply, "you can't make apple dumplings."

Annie quit.

She had been with the family for years, and Mrs. Glass regretted her going. She asked Powell to ask her to come back. Annie was willing – but only if Mrs. Glass apologized for criticizing the apple dumpling. When Powell brought back this news, his mother raised up from her pillows with considerable asperity.

"Never!" she declared. "That dumpling *wasn't* good!"

Powell pondered the problem. Back to Annie he went, saying his mother sent her apologies, but warned the cook against ever mentioning the matter again. Back Annie came to the Glass household, and to the Glass kitchen.

Because he has always stood tenaciously for certain principles pertaining to public service, it has often been assumed that Glass never changes his mind. He has, on a number of notable issues. But when he changed his mind in March 1925, partisan newspapers charged him with trying to embarrass the President. This was when he voted against the confirmation of a Coolidge appointee, Charles B. Warren, for the office of Attorney General.

He felt impelled to explain his vote.

"It had been my purpose from the first to vote for the confirmation of Mr. Warren. But if now I feel convinced that I should vote against the confirmation of Mr. Warren, what justification on earth can anyone have for the supposition that I am actuated by a desire to embarrass the President?

"I recall that I was responsible in the last Democratic administration largely, if not almost exclusively, for the appointment of a man to one of the most responsible positions in the Federal Government. . . Other people shared my confidence in his integrity and my admiration of his abilities to such an extent that he was appointed by a succeeding adversary administration to the same position, as his own successor."

But, Glass confessed, he had been disappointed.

"He never did divest himself of his early training or his environment. He was completely subservient to those interests with which he had been associated, so much so that I was positively distressed that I ever had any part in his elevation to his high and responsible position.

"So I have considered that it takes a man of more than ordinary strength of character and mind to turn from the saturation of his early ideas to a judicial consideration of the other sides of questions that may arise. I think a Senator may very readily conclude that a nominee who has been associated so constantly with the organization of trusts and the defense of trusts in litigation may be incapable of efficiently discharging the duties of the office of Attorney General.

"I think that a Senator may vote against that nomination without subjecting himself to the suspicion that he desires to embarrass the President of the United States."

A few weeks later the banking interests of the nation were in a state of apprehension. They needed a champion in Washington to defend their rights against Eastern aggression. From the governor of nearly every Federal Reserve Bank in the country letters of appeal were sped to Senator Glass.

The cause for their concern was the McFadden bill, passed by the House and sent to the Senate with the extraordinary Hull amendments attached. These were designed to eliminate branch banking in the United States. The bill proposed to contravene the existing statutes of twenty-two states which already permitted branch banking, and to serve notice on twenty-six other states that they might not thereafter change their systems of banking in that respect, except upon the penalty of exclusion from the Federal Reserve system.

The menace Glass instantly perceived in such a measure was the ultimate domination of all American banking and commerce by the Wall Street money centers. Bristling with indignation, he returned to the familiar battleground.

"Not since the foundation of this Republic," he declared, "was there ever before attempted, in any Federal legislation proposed, such a deliberate invasion of the rights of the States of this Union! That House bill proposes to do for banking what Mr. Lincoln said could not be done for slavery – to establish a nation one-half branch banking and one-half unit banking.

". . . I am not now speaking for branch banking. I am advocating the right of the States to establish their own banking systems, free from coercion by Federal Statute. Under these Hull amendments we would have the preposterous spectacle of national banks in the State of New York, which permits branch banking, confirmed in privileges, which hereafter would perpetually be denied to national banks in Pennsylvania, which does not permit branch banking now, but may sanction the system at some time in the future."

He charged that the proposition had originated with a small group of bankers which, while pretending they wanted to safeguard unit banking against monopoly, was actually appealing to Congress to give into their grasp a monopoly of the credits of their respective communities.

A high banking official, he said, had told him that certain bankers in the country had enough influence in one House of Congress to prevent any remedial legislation that did not contain the 22–26 coercion clause. He had asked a Cincinnati banker if he thought that these bankers were charged with the function of national legislation. "No," had been the reply, "but they exercise sufficient influence over members of the House to defeat, in my opinion, any bill that deviates materially from Section 9 of the McFadden bill."

Glass paused significantly.

"There you are," he said, "an open, unqualified admission that this is a premeditated attempt to coerce. There is the admission that it is proposed to perpetrate a wrong because in the conception of this gentleman and other bankers, one branch of Congress may not be induced to do right. The Senate is asked to confirm this admitted and gross injustice. There is not a board of trade, there is not a chamber of commerce, there is not an aggregation of intelligent farmers in the United States, in my judgment, who could be induced to approve such a legislative atrocity. . .

"The plea has been set up only by a small coterie of bankers within the American Bankers Association.

"I do not want to be disagreeable. I do not want to undertake in any respect to discredit the American Bankers Association. But every Senator here knows where this sort of propaganda originates and how it is carried on.

"I cannot forget the fact that it was the American Bankers Association at New Orleans in 1911 that unanimously approved the Aldrich central bank bill without knowing a thing in the world about it. It had so recently come from the printing press that it had not dried well enough to thumb its pages.

"I cannot forget it was the American Bankers Association at its annual convention in Boston, three weeks before the adoption of the Federal Reserve Act, that characterized it as a dangerous measure, which would create financial confusion, do a grave injustice to the banking community, and inevitably result in a constriction of credits. The association begged Congress not to enact the bill into law.

"Right now Senators are being deluged with telegrams and communications from this little circle of bankers, appealing to them to enact this monstrosity, this Federal statute that deliberately and avowedly invades the rights of the States.

"These propagandists have gone so far in their effrontery as to send one of their agents here to undertake to influence the appointment of conferees on this banking bill and to urge that a certain Senator in opposition be not appointed on the conference committee, and to pick out certain other Senators, whom they imagine they can control, to be put on the conference committee.

"Thus," he said in conclusion, "it appears that only this circle of bankers wants to perpetuate this injustice, whereas the commercial bodies of the country, those that have spoken, have spoken overwhelmingly in favor of equality in banking in all of the States."

The bill went down before his onslaught, but Glass did not stop there. Nine months later, after considerable personal inquiry he sent to the desk a resolution demanding a Congressional investigation of lobbying activities in connection with banking legislation.

On that occasion he said: "They have gone so far as to assert that a sum in excess of $100,000 has been expended by a certain group of bankers in behalf of what were known as the Hull amendments. They have gone so far as to suggest that a paid lobbyist of this group who, to my knowledge, has haunted the corridors and the doors of the Senate Chamber for months, had employed members of the Congress identified with this legislation to go out and make speeches in behalf of certain provisions of the bill.

"It has been definitely reported to me that this group of

bankers and their agents paid the way and the expenses of quite a number of delegates to the recent national convention of the American Bankers Association at Los Angeles.

"In view of these persistent reports, some of which I have good reason to believe, I am offering this resolution, because I think that the Senate owes it to its own integrity to have such matters investigated and determined." *

But if strenuous debate is his, enjoyment of laughter is his, too: Rabelaisian wit in the story repertoire of his boon companion Cary Grayson – the telling by Grayson of how King George, of England, induced him to shock the Queen, of how Jesse Jones took off his shoes in Buckingham Palace . . . of his own amusement in recalling his protest to Charles Francis Adams, Secretary of the Navy, because a young Virginian was being refused admittance to the Navy on the ground that two of his teeth had failed to mature. "Good Lord, Mr. Secretary," he argued with Adams, "do you train the Navy to bite the enemy?" And Adams' devastating rejoinder: "That's what we will have to do, Senator, if you keep cutting our appropriations."

There are nights, too, many of them, with his own depleted nerves constraining him to lie with sleep disdaining eyes while thoughts, like hounds, go leaping across his mind, or, like soft leaves falling, linger there. The strain, anxiety and activity of war years, the pride and pain, shared by his wife, of knowing their sons were in mid-Atlantic, the apprehensive scanning of daily casualty lists . . . then victory for armed force, and defeat for Wilson and the planners of permanent peace. . . Wilson's lingering sickness. . . Grayson coming from the sick-room in the last days, saying "he smiled when I told him

* Quietly, Glass did investigate. He obtained cancelled checks, proving his charges, but dropped the investigation because a principal involved was said to be dying. He did not want to bring disgrace to add to the family's sorrow.

you sent your love," . . . and the paradox of Wilson, plaintively yearning for the love of the people, like Gladstone, like Pitt – the finding its full rendition denied.

Wilson with a rueful laugh saying, "This Presbyterian face of mine frightens my enemies, but alas, it also cools the ardor of my friends" . . . and in the sleepless nights he recognizes that likewise to himself clings the gossip-born legend of forbidding austerity, ill-humor, testiness – the thorny harvest of a highly nervous temperament; but he knows, too, in the harvest of his years is gathered friendship, and deep love. Its nature, not its numerical spread, is to him the treasure; for, although the thought never occurs, in friendship, as in finance, he is not enthralled by a quantitive theory.

Sensitive in this matter of individual liberty and its protection, he finds it less wearying to meet the arguments of its enemies than the mistaken efforts of its friends; and soon, again, he is in militant foray on the Senate floor against the Haugen farm bill.

Under the guise of co-operative marketing to raise prices, the proposed bill empowered a board of twelve men, from whose judgment there would be no appeal, to levy a tax based upon estimates and speculation as to future crops. It contemplated the dumping idea – selling surpluses abroad cheap while arbitrarily raising the prices for consumers at home. Further, Glass saw it was a new invasion of State Rights by Federal authority.

In his speech of June 22, 1926, he called it "patent medicine farming," and branded it "a dangerous nostrum." He showed that it was clearly a delegation of the taxing power of the Government – which can also be the power to oppress – to a Federal board constituted for the avowed purpose of subserving private interests. He questioned its constitutionality, and deplored the fact that Democrats supported it.

"I am against the bill primarily," he said, "because it contravenes those fundamental principles of government to which I have always professed adherence."

He reviewed the legislation of the preceding twelve years designed to help the farmer, most effective of which had been the Federal Reserve Act. Also there had been the Farm Loan Act, the establishment of intermediate credit banks, and the extension of credit to agriculture by the War Finance Corporation for nearly eight years after the cessation of hostilities. He commented that there seemed to be a sort of fascination about borrowing money from the Government, getting what was miscalled "Government aid."

He was getting warmed up. He was pounding a desk when he said, "Nothing like this bill was ever before conceived or attempted in the tide of time!

"If you would strike an analogy between the Interstate Commerce Commission and this proposed price fixing farm board, you would have to establish a commission the members of which would be railroad men, selected by the railroads themselves, to fix the rates of the railroads. Under this Haugen bill we are to have a board selected not by the Government primarily, but by certain farmers themselves to fix the prices of certain commodities, of the foodstuffs and clothing which all of the people must have to exist, without any restraint whatsoever, but with the promptings of acquisitiveness saturating the very process itself."

He disposed of another false assumption, the claim that the same principle had been embodied in the Federal Farm Loan Act. Glass had been chairman of the joint committee which had passed that legislation. Then: "Senators have assumed to find some analogy between this proposed measure and the Federal Reserve system. 'Look,' they exclaim, 'what the Government has done for the banks!'

"Does anybody seriously imagine that the Federal Reserve Act was put on the statute books for the benefit of the banks? Bankers did not prepare or propose the law; bankers bitterly opposed the law. Moreover, no millions of dollars belonging to the taxpayers of the country were taken from the Federal Treasury to establish the Federal Reserve banking system. It was established at a cost of less than $50,000.

"The Government was not required to subscribe to one dollar of the capital stock. The Government owns not one dollar of proprietary interest in these banks. All the capital was supplied by member banks. So far from taking millions of dollars from the Treasury, the Federal Reserve banks in one year alone paid $62,000,000 into the Treasury, more than had been paid as a franchise tax by all the national banks of the United States put together for a period of twenty years theretofore. . .

"The principle of this bill has never found expression in any legislation of the Congress. Senators affect to see in it something akin to the protective tariff. It has the germ of that bitterly controverted principle, but it goes as far beyond the principle of the protective tariff as the protective tariff advocates have gone beyond the original conceptions of Alexander Hamilton. This bill affords a continuing subsidy to a restricted circle of farmers at the expense of all the people. It taxes more farmers than it pretends to aid. Senators can make nothing else out of it.

" 'Oh, but it is a compensatory process!' " he quoted in derision. "The tariff robs the farmer and everybody else, according to the doctrine which has been proclaimed from this side of the Chamber. And yet now we propose to let the farmer rob the tariff beneficiaries and incidentally rob everybody else – a dual system of robbery, united like the Siamese twins.

"After we have joined these twin evils, when and by whom is to be performed the surgical operation which will separate them in order that Democrats may get to be the Democratic Party again?

"They will never separate of their own accord, and they will never be separated. True, they will profiteer one another; but the advantage derived from profiteering the millions who neither manufacture nor farm, as well as the millions of farmers excluded from the sheltering folds of the bill, will largely more than compensate for picking each other's pockets.

"A vital objection to the bill is that it discriminates among classes of farmers themselves. It taxes the greater number of farmers for the benefit of the lesser number of farmers. It is proposed to tax all the farmers by withdrawing from the Federal Treasury, some say $250,000,000, others say $375,000,000, and ultimately it may be more than $1,000,000,000. This huge sum, taken in taxes from all the people, is to be devoted to the uses of a small class of people – not even to all the farmers, not even to the greater part of the agricultural industry. The money of the American taxpayer is to be used for the purpose of compelling the very man who puts the money into the Federal Treasury to pay more for his bread and meat and clothing."

He pointed to the hardships that would be imposed upon the cotton states, the tobacco planters. When he came to the tribute to be exacted from dairymen in the form of higher prices, he said, "I know whereof I speak. Some Senators, growing red in the face, talk about 'the poor farmer' in pathetic tones and with rhetorical flourishes, as if everybody who disagrees with their economic heresies is an enemy of the farmer.

"My pecuniary stake in farming would exceed my salary as

a United States Senator for ten years after I shall have died and been forgotten, and yet Senators who would not, except at election time, recognize a farmer if he would come down the road with a red flag attached to his person, suggest here that I am an enemy of the American farmer because I refuse to vote for this wretched makeshift!"

As he was proceeding to the lack of "compensation" in the bill for the growers of potatoes and apples, Vice-President Dawes banged his gavel.

"The Senator's time has expired."

But Jones of Washington rose to ask unanimous consent that he be permitted to conclude his remarks, and Glass continued. In reply to statements that the Haugen bill would protect one half of the American people, he demonstrated that it would not protect one fifth. He quoted statistics to show that farmers constitute less than one third of the population, and that only a decided minority of these would be benefited.

"I feel so sorry at times to sit here and have my section of the country described to the world as in a state of penury, finding it necessary, like mendicants, to come to Washington, hat in hand, for crumbs of subsistence from the Federal crib. While agriculture in the South is not advancing as I should like to see, while there are hardships and at times suffering, the Southern farmer is not the beggar of Federal alms. He is an upstanding, self-respecting, hard-pushing American citizen, not very attentive to the lamentations of the politicians. . .

"I do not pretend to believe that the farmers of the United States are prosperous. I simply contend that this bill will not remedy their plight. Their difficulty does not arise out of the prices they get for their produce, but must be ascribed to the prices they are compelled to pay for what they buy. The exchange of commodities is against the farmer, because he sells in an open market and buys in a protected market. While there are other disabilities, this is the real distemper, this is his vital disorder.

"The cure can not be had through legislative patent-medicine nostrums. It can not, as it should not, be had through illicit raids on the common Treasury fund, expressing the thrift, the toil, the sacrifice of all the people. We should go to the source of the malady. We should abate the excesses of the tariff. We should lower the wall that shelters privilege and not erect another beside it. . .

"I want to allude to another aspect of this discussion. What is the use of debating in terms of mysticism? Why all this unintelligible talk about the 'farmer's dollar,' a fad of those political economists who never look outside the pages of a school-book? Why make the impression that the 'farmer's dollar' is different from anybody else's dollar? Why confuse the farmer into the belief that he has a depreciated dollar instead of a dollar worth a hundred cents in gold on the domestic market and at a premium in every market in the world?"

Reiterating that the bill was but a new sort of subsidy, taxing all for the benefit of a few, he continued: "The Democrat who subscribes to that sort of doctrine will soon find himself on the probation bench of the Republican Party, cushioned with the fleece of Schedule K, bouncing on the springs of the Steel Trust, hat in hand, awaiting his time of admission to the status of that type of zealot which always exceeds the original apostles of a doctrine. If I were a Republican, I would not vote for this subsidy, because it goes, in the matter of special privilege, so far beyond anything that the Republican Party ever dared propose that I would be ashamed to vote for it. . ."

But with this assertion it was not his intention to bestow encomium upon the Republicans, for a moment later he added:

"With the Democratic Party subscribing to a doctrine like that, what issues would we have left to differentiate us from our political adversaries? Only the unhappy memories of reconstruction and the repellent official personality of the Republican Party in the South, where offices are sold and bartered. That is all!"

Again prefacing an attack with a panegyric, he paid tribute to the past achievements of Simmons of North Carolina, one of the most persistent advocates of the bill.

"But what an astounding thing happened yesterday!" he exclaimed, with reference to a speech by Simmons. "Following suggestively the example of William Jennings Bryan in the Chicago convention of thirty years ago, the Senator used a scriptural simile which would contrast the spirit of this Haugen bill with the immortality of a soul as expressed in the resurrection! As a young man I sat in that national convention and heard Mr. Bryan's stirring address, ending with the almost impious rhetorical gesture about the 'crown of thorns' and the 'cross of gold.'

"I have often felt that the people of America failed to discern the real inspiration of that occasion and of that speech. It was not so much the metaphor as it was the staging of the whole proceeding. David B. Hill had stood upon that platform and, as spokesman for vested property rights, in behalf of feasted privilege, had given a sordid, a narrow, a severely contracted definition to the term 'business men.' He had applied it to the great industries, to the merchant princes of his metropolis, to the men of enormous wealth, prospering beyond the dreams of avarice, while agriculture languished and the people were taxed.

"Seizing upon that reference, Mr. Bryan, in sharp, almost startling contrast spread the definition so that it might embrace every man who, in the sweat of his brow, earned an honest living. That was the magic of the speech. That is what nominated Mr. Bryan. That is what committed the Democratic Party to a candidacy and a fallacy which banished it from power for sixteen years.

"Not exactly alike, but some akin in principle, the Senator from North Carolina, blending the material with the sublime, undertook yesterday to circumscribe the name of 'farmer' to the comparatively small circle which will, it is conjectured, derive advantage from this setting up of an unconstitutional instrumentality of taxation without limit of responsibility. I reject his definition. I speak, in the name of many classes of farmers, in protest against this bill."

He arraigned the pending measure as providing for the private use of public funds. "Not for that was government instituted," he said. "It is a perversion of the taxing power. It enriches a part of the people and enslaves another part. Where favors are bestowed, rights are denied."

The high tariff he pronounced the undisguised enemy of the American farmer. He quoted Senator Cummings of Iowa as having warned that "just as surely as this bill is defeated the whole policy of protection is doomed to extinction."

"I could fervently wish so," Glass said. In sardonic vein he continued. "But the Senator from Iowa may take heart and quiet his apprehensions. The day is fair and the fight for privilege prospers when he finds on this side, ready at hand to avert the disaster of extinction, gentlemen who hitherto have preached against the Republican protective system and have denounced it in season and out.

"I have been pleased to follow the leadership of some of these gentlemen, notably of that David of the tribe who went out in the name of Israel and, pausing by the brook, picked pebbles with which to slay the Goliath of high protection. But methought on yesterday he cast his pebbles back into the water, flung his sling away, ripped his tunic from his body, and, waving it as a white flag of truce, capitulated to the Philistines !

"Much as I admire and love my colleague from North Carolina, far as I would follow his plume in real combat for the true philosophy and the genuine principles of Democracy, if it is my last utterance and last act in the Senate Chamber of the United States, I refuse, in the misappropriated name of the American farmer, to follow anybody in the effort to fasten upon the people this uneconomic, unequal, unjust species of privilege!"

The McNary-Haugen bill was vetoed by Coolidge. It was relegated to the ensuing years to reveal the accuracy of Glass' analysis.

CHAPTER EIGHTEEN

Some threw their hats into the ring ; Glass hung up his in a hotel room.

From his father Carter Glass learned that "truth provokes those it does not convert" – and many have cause to remember his words. There was that day in January 1922, when Senator Heflin of Alabama was orating on the Senate floor in criticism of the Federal Reserve Bank, in New York, with its gymnasium, its swimming pool. . .

As Heflin said "swimming pool" Glass sought the attention of the Chair : "Mr. President, may I interrupt the Senator for just a moment ?"

"Just for a minute," agreed Heflin.

"It will not take a minute," assured Glass. "I want to say to the Senator that the shoe factories in my town in Virginia provide a swimming pool for their employes. The cotton mills in Danville, as my colleague knows, provide swimming pools for their employes."

"Yes, I know that," condescended Heflin.

"Furthermore, the Senate of the United States provides a marble-bound swimming pool for the members of this body. . ."

"Yes, I know that, too," grunted Heflin.

"Is it possible, then," came Glass' smarting conclusion, "that the Senator from Alabama does not believe in people washing ?"

That other day, too, June 10, 1921, when Senator James Reed, of Missouri –no mean antagonist in his own right – was hammering away, also at the Federal Reserve Act, and in the course of his speech made a number of misstatements. Finally Glass interrupted with corrections, and Reed testily complained to Vice-President Coolidge:

"I do not intend to be diverted from this question to discuss the making of the banking and currency bill. I made an assertion so plainly within the facts that I did not suppose any living human being would have the temerity to challenge the statement. I know that the Senator regards that bill as the child of his brain, and he is unwilling to admit that anybody did anything to improve its condition, either before or after birth."

"The Senator does not know that, because it is not a fact," asserted Glass.

"That sort of statement is mere insolence," replied Reed, "the insolence of incapacity and defenselessness, and I insist that I shall not be interrupted any more by the Senator from Virginia on this or any other occasion while I am in the Senate."

"I shall respond to the Senator at the proper time," promised Glass.

At the proper time he did. As Reed concluded his remarks, Glass was on his feet, to sandwich his recital of the facts regarding the Federal Reserve Act with these challenging sentences:

"I was perfectly well aware, from my very brief observation in the Senate, that an interruption of the Senator from Missouri, even to correct a misstatement of fact, practically amounted to inviting offense. I had observed that the Senator was intolerant of differences of viewpoint and of opinion and quick to retort sharply upon any other Senator who might presume to bring in question his infallibility of judgment or his accuracy of statement. But I conceive that a Senator should not be deterred by things of that sort.

"I have never, in my twenty years of service in the Congress, been at all willing to seek the shelter of constitutional immunity to offend any man, whether a colleague, or some one outside the Congress. I do not think it is an evidence of courage any more than it is an evidence of civility.

". . . I conclude by putting the Senator from Missouri upon notice that whenever he makes a statement concerning me personally he will not avoid a proper answer by such a puerile performance as he ventured upon this afternoon."

Reed came to understand Glass because Glass was first to understand him ; and later the men became friends.

For Glass, the autumn of 1922 was a period of deep distress. For weeks he endured extreme anxiety concerning his elder and his only living brother, Edward Christian Glass, who had undergone a serious operation at Johns Hopkins Hospital, in Baltimore. Suffering himself from a state of depleted nerves, he kept in constant correspondence with the surgeons ; then he was subjected to a severe shock.

His elder son, Major Powell Glass, was accidentally shot while hunting with a friend. An eye had to be removed. "I am so thankful that his life is spared," Glass wrote to a friend, "that I hesitate to grieve too much over his misfortune." But he grieved, nevertheless.

A few months after the accident, the Senator was tendered a place on the commission President Harding was sending abroad for the readjustment of the Allied debts to the United States. Believing that any settlement in deference to political exigency would be a penny-pinching patchwork, Glass declined the appointment. He did not care to be a party to such action, reserving the right of independent action when the settlements should come before the Senate.

In declining, he wrote Harding :

My dear Mr. President:

I am just told that you have been good enough to nominate me as a member of the commission authorized to adjust the indebtedness of foreign governments to the United States and that the Senate has confirmed the appointment. Please be assured that I am keenly sensible of this expression of your confidence; but deeply regret to feel compelled to decline the distinction. There are circumstances which render it wellnigh impossible for me to assume this responsibility with any hope of requiting your kindness by taking a proper part in the work of the commission and I am unwilling to accept an honor and then evade the duties incident to it.

Had I known that you were seriously considering me for the commission I would have promptly apprised you of my inability to serve; but the mention of the matter to me by a colleague in the Senate and another in the House seemed so casual that I dismissed it with a word of deprecation.

I sincerely trust that I am not occasioning you any embarrassment whatsoever and, with renewed assurances of great appreciation and respect, believe me,

Sincerely yours,
(signed) Carter Glass.

To the President,
The White House.

Later, however, in his *Lest We Forget* speech when the work of the Commission was attacked by the "pound-of-flesh" extremists, Glass came to the defense of the settlements — not as being anywhere near ideal, but rather as the best that might be then negotiated and ratified by the Senate.

On the occasion of Harding's death in the summer of 1923, *The New York Times* asked Glass to make a statement. After an expression of grief, he said: "The whole sad episode to me assumes the guise of an intimate sorrow rather than a national calamity; for Mr. Harding was more a natural, kindly human being than he was an outstanding statesman or an indispensable public character."

Continuing, he sized up the traits of Harding and his successor, Calvin Coolidge :

"The reins of government will be held by President Coolidge with a firm hand and public affairs will be conducted by a clear mind and stronger will, with a more certain objective. Mr. Harding was warm and emotional. Mr. Coolidge has extraordinary poise : his sympathies and friendships are reasoned as well as felt. His judgments will be calculated and his decisions as to men and measures will never be whimsical.

"Nevertheless, former President Harding will be sorely missed. Right now 'in the shadow of a great affliction,' as Whittier suggests, 'the soul of the nation sits dumb.' "

And to President Coolidge at an appropriate time he sent this letter :

My dear Mr. President :

It is a fortunate circumstance that the pitiful death of President Harding does not leave the country totally without compensation. No person who has observed your conduct in public life, even in as limited a way as I, can fail to feel certain that the administration of the government in a firm and discerning fashion will ensue.

We do not congratulate but only pray for you on the assumption of the great responsibilities of the Presidency. We do, however, very cordially felicitate you personally on the great distinction which is your heritage.

In quite equal measure Mrs. Glass and I wish for Mrs. Coolidge all the happiness and genuine satisfaction which may be derived from a gracious acquittal of herself in trying days ahead. That all things will work together for the good of both of you and the security of the country is the confident expectation and earnest hope of

Sincerely yours
(signed) Carter Glass.

Many months of muckraking followed Harding's passing.

The following spring Governor Pinchot of Pennsylvania went to Washington and suggested to Senator Couzens of

Michigan that he privately employ Francis J. Heney, an attorney, to make an investigation of prohibition enforcement by the Internal Revenue Bureau. This elicited an angry complaint from Secretary Mellon, who wrote President Coolidge protesting that the legislative branch was seeking to perpetrate "government by investigation."

Coolidge sent Mellon's letter to the Senate with a note of stern rebuke. On April 15, Glass rose before a full floor and crowded galleries to answer the President.

He spoke from typewritten notes, but frequently departed from them to amplify his points. He had no criticism, he said, of the President's recent rebuff to the Senate when it had moved for the dismissal of Secretary of the Navy Denby. The President had a right to resent Senate encroachment on the Executive's prerogatives. He paid a tribute to Mr. Mellon's ability and honesty. Then in contrasting the rights which the President possessed with the language in which he had reproved the Senate, he demanded :

"Until now, when has any Executive of the nation, in a mood of uncontrolled irritation, abruptly faced the Senate of the United States with the official charge of having instituted a 'Government of lawlessness' ?

"Until now, when has it happened, if ever before, that the President of the United States, accepting the unauthenticated suspicions of an avowedly partisan Senator [Watson of Indiana], accentuated by the personal antipathies and apprehensions of a Cabinet Minister, has pointedly impeached the probity of the Senate by sharply charging it with subterfuge and insincerity, with intrusion upon the privacy of the citizen, and with the creation of a condition actually subversive of the most sacred guaranty of the Constitution ?

"It is all there, and more beside.

"The President intended to be vehement. The President intended to be threatening, and no Senator should risk his displeasure by any attempted interpretation in moderation of the plain English of it."

Here Glass himself grew vehement, pounding the desks about him with clenched fists. "No refinement of definition ; no misapplication of circumstances ; no artifice of sophistry ; no sort of casuistry can ever take from that Presidential message, with its attendant paper, the inherent nature of its amazing arraignment of the Senate of the United States as a menace to orderly government in the United States.

"Quite intolerable enough it is to have individual Senators go about broadcasting the accusations that their colleagues here are 'indecent' and engaged in 'dirty business' when they bring into the light of day the hidden offenses of maladministration. Bad enough it is, in this incendiary fashion, to apply the fagots of misinformation and vituperation to an already inflamed and poisoned public opinion which would stop pursuit of the actual criminals and punish the Senate for exposing crime."

After asserting his own disapproval of Couzens' employment of Heney, he stated that all this discussion would have been avoided had Coolidge and Mellon confined their comment only to that. But, he charged, both had wanted to project an issue ; their communications were directed, not against the Heney affair, but against "the entire business of investigation.

"May I not express the hope that in neither letter nor message is there the concealed purpose to arouse anew the abating bitterness against the Senate of the United States, so diligently propagated and nurtured among those misguided persons who persistently have been taught to believe that it is not possible, even if desirable, simultaneously to expel knaves from the high places which they have dishonored and reduce the excessive tax burden which the people too long have endured. . ."

Rather than be subjected to this "amazing imputation," he said, "the Senate should be commended by the President and the country for exposing a condition of lawlessness in government which had disgraced one Cabinet Minister, discredited another and confirmed the public detestation of a third. . .

"Had I not the highest respect for the President of the United States, I might be indifferent to his unwarranted aspersions of this body. It is because I highly regard him that I resent, that I deplore, his unprecedented strictures on a coordinate branch of the Government."

After pronouncing Mellon "the outstanding man of this Administration," Glass continued:

"'Government by investigation is not government,' the Secretary says. Conversely, government by suppression is not government."

Never in the history of the legislative branch, he asserted, had such an orgy of inquiry and search been indulged in as when the Republicans came into power after the war. They had fifty-one investigations "going in full blast at the same time." He mentioned that $150,000 had been spent in a single session of inquiry.

"Two million dollars were appropriated in addition," he added, "for the Department of Justice to continue its espionage. And what of their fifty-one investigations? What has any one of them amounted to? Where is a tainted dollar that was spent in the eight years of the Administration of Woodrow Wilson? Where is the culprit that you sought? Where is the Cabinet Minister displaced?"

He was thinking of the final months of Wilson's term, of Albert B. Fall, then a Senator, heading a Senate subcommittee's probing visit to Wilson to learn if he were in condition to transact public business. Glass mentioned no name; but as he resumed, the sadness of his tone was in itself a direct accusation.

"Let us not revive the wretched memory of the visit to the sickbed chamber. Retributive justice has laid its hand on the miscreant who cheerfully accepted the mission to peer beneath the counterpane.

"Let us not recall the persistent attempt to discredit the Administration of the sick man – how they hired neurologists to speculate upon the mental capability of the sick man as affected by his physical disorder.

"Better it were, perhaps, not to refer to the facts."

His mouth twitched sardonically in what might have been a smile.

"A senator from Pennsylvania from his place in this chamber made the unqualified declaration that upon the return of President and Mrs. Wilson from abroad they had brought in, free of duty, several million dollars worth of gifts from the crowned heads and people of Europe. They wanted to examine the pocket handkerchiefs and one or two lace coverlets that had been given in token of friendship.

"Government by investigation?"

And then, in conclusion, "I never should have spoken but for my conscientious conviction that this message, this letter of the President and the Secretary, constitute the most extraordinary breach of official etiquette that has ever occurred in the history of the Republic."

On front pages throughout the country were emblazoned such headlines as "Glass Flays President" and "Coolidge Assailed by Senator."

But one New York paper went beyond the facts. Next day in the Senate Glass said, "On the assumption that none of my colleagues on this side of the Chamber and none of the representative leaders of my party outside of the Chamber will want to be held responsible for the address which I ventured to make yesterday, I want to correct a newspaper statement with reference to it."

He quoted the caption: "Glass berates President in bitter speech after conference with party chiefs. Address considered significant as representing planned minority move."

And from the text he read: "It became known as the Senator was speaking, that he had decided on the major points of his address after a conference with a group of influential men of his party, both in and out of Congress."

"The only group that knew anything about my speech," avowed Glass, "was the group of women stenographers employed in my office, to whom the speech was dictated."

But the dream of a quiet country retirement kept pervading his thoughts. In the midst of bitter debate, he was planning the building of a new home.

The purchase of the Montview acres had greatly strained his resources. In 1921, when an adjoining property that would have extended his estate was for sale, he confessed to the hopeful realtor that "after building a barn on my place I haven't sufficient funds left to buy chicken feed."

For several months he had contemplated remodeling the old wooden house, but upon receiving from the architect an elaborate and expensive preliminary sketch, he decided to have the house pulled down and the material used for a cottage, wryly remarking that he did not think it would be satisfactory to spend $18,000 improving a $2000 dwelling. The following spring he began the erection of a new stone house on the site of the old building.

There were months of tentative sketching and planning before a single stone was raised, and, of course, he consulted Mrs. Glass on virtually every detail. They did not always see eye to eye. Where her cherished rose garden grew he wanted a swimming pool; it took a bit of coaxing and cajolery before she yielded.

By the summer of 1923 the reality began to resemble the dream, and he was ready to celebrate the completion of Montview Farms with a family reunion. To Mary Archer he wrote: "We are reasonably well pleased with the house and premises."

In the spring of 1924 the Democratic Party was looking longingly at the Presidential chair. With the G.O.P. escutcheon badly spattered by oil from Teapot Dome, the outlook seemed auspicious; with Woodrow Wilson dead, the banner of leadership was being bandied about among party lieutenants.

McAdoo had a potent organization in the East. So did Alfred E. Smith. If neither was chosen, whom would *they* choose? And would the selection meet the favor of Bryan who still was a power? There was talk of Senator Robinson of Arkansas, of Governor Ralston of Indiana. Unobtrusively but earnestly, a quiet "Glass-for-President" boom began.

Twelve men of high station held a meeting in New York. They were financiers and students of public affairs, the majority of them Republicans. They endeavored to agree among themselves on a candidate. After some half-dozen political balloons had been punctured, someone suggested they forget they were Republicans or Democrats, that they had likes or dislikes, and each write on a slip the name of the man he thought would make the best President in 1925, regardless of party.

The idea was adopted. Eleven of the twelve wrote down the name of Carter Glass. "And the man whom this story concerns most," commented the *Richmond News-Leader*, "has never heard it."

While Glass was drafting a Democratic platform for his state, the Virginia Legislature resolved they wanted him to be a candidate for President. He responded with no more than an acknowledgment, in which he said that he regarded this mark of confidence from them as a greater honor than any office.

Democratic bigwigs, and public-minded men in high places who were not Democrats, came to see him. And in May Glass told them : "I am not a candidate for President in any sense of the word. I understand that the Virginia delegation may go to New York instructed to vote for me, but that merely puts me in the favorite-son class, as many other men will be."

In *The World's Work* Mark Sullivan wrote :

"They go to see Glass and they labor with him. Glass squirms in his chair with the manner of a man who is torn between gracious consideration for friends who bring him a courteous communication, and the feelings of a man who is asked by well-meaning friends to do something he regards as approaching indelicacy. If Glass becomes the next President, he will cause the dictionaries to take account of a new meaning for the word 'run.' He will demonstrate that 'run' can be a transitive verb. Glass won't 'run' for the Presidency ; he must be run for it."

Political observers realized if Glass were to be President influential strategists would have to want him to be President – want him as much as Daugherty wanted Harding, or Stearns wanted Coolidge. Any such powerful indorsement seemed to devolve upon the shoulders of McAdoo, himself obviously not devoid of personal aspirations to the post . . . and Glass was repeatedly declaring himself for McAdoo.

When at the tumultuous Democratic National Convention at Madison Square Garden many a hat was sailed into the ring, Glass hung up his quietly in the Waldorf-Astoria.

Almost immediately a deadlock developed between McAdoo and Smith. A compromise candidate was sought. Governor Ralston of Indiana was suggested ; he declined the honor. The names of John W. Davis, of New York, and Carter Glass began to be heard, and Henry S. Morgenthau, Ambassador to Turkey in the Wilson administration, offered to underwrite Glass' candidacy for any amount up to $2,000,000. Fred W. Scott, John Stewart Bryan and Thomas B. McAdams, all of Richmond, were the driving powers behind the movement.

Dearer to the heart of Glass than the nomination itself was the question of standing by Woodrow Wilson and the League of Nations. He felt so deeply about it that when word came the Virginia delegation was going to vote for the Bryan proposal rather than support Newton D. Baker's forthright declaration, he abruptly informed them if they did so, he would withdraw his name from consideration by the convention.

As Baker had written him on June 4 :

> . . . Every passing hour shows me more clearly that our adversaries are going to call us the pro-League party, whether we put it into our platform or not. If we leave it out, they will call us cowards in addition, so that on the lowest ground of expediency I am convinced that no question to be decided in the coming election will compare in importance with that of the country's attitude toward international affairs, and so I am doing everything I can to urge a bold straight-forward, frank pro-League declaration.

Continuing, Baker pointed out there were those who

> desire our platform to declare for the League but promise that if returned to power, we will do nothing about it until a postcard referendum vote has been taken, by which we will be guided. To me this means that the party will ask to be given the jobs without any principles, and agree to find some principles by extra constitutional referenda after we get safely installed in office, which is not a very courageous attitude for a great and historical party.

Greatly moved by Baker's magnificent fight for a clear-cut pro-League plank, Glass sent his secretary to him with a note offering to step out of the race and come immediately to his aid. Baker paused in the heat of battle to write Glass he was the one man in all the world he would prefer to have by his side in such an hour, but it would be a futile and needless sacrifice.

Glass was not alone in his feelings that the Bryan plank on the League outraged the memory of Woodrow Wilson and the sensibilities of his followers. Davis felt so keenly about it that he called on Glass and proposed that they go before the convention and jointly withdraw their names in protest.

Meanwhile the battle raged. The scene in the Garden was no longer that of a convention ; it was a whirlwind of delirium. The Virginia delegation was sincerely pro-Glass, but there unity ended. Within themselves the delegates were divided between McAdoo, Smith and a compromise candidate – any compromise candidate. Glass could control them for himself, but not for anybody else.

If Glass' personal wishes and political judgment had prevailed, the Virginians would have cast at least two complimentary ballots for McAdoo at the height of his drive. It seemed perfectly apparent to Glass, that the McAdoo people, though lacking the votes to put over their leader's nomination, still controlled the convention and would dominate the eventual choice.

That this was not done, due to the bitter divisions in the delegation itself, gave rise to much rancor in the McAdoo ranks. As for McAdoo himself, when he sent a list of compromise candidates that would be acceptable to him and his followers, he omitted the name of Carter Glass.

Claude A. Swanson was head of the Virginia delegation, but Harry Flood Byrd, state chairman of the party, was active and powerful in its affairs. While ascribing to them both complete loyalty to Glass, any careful account of the affair cannot ignore the fact that Swanson's mismanagement and Byrd's dislike of McAdoo split the delegation wide open. When finally Swanson pulled from his pocket an undated letter from Glass asking the delegation to give McAdoo two complimentary ballots, the delegation became a scene of anger and riot which did not subside until the convention ended.

The undated letter read :

My dear Senator Swanson :

The more I have thought about the matter the more convinced have I become that the refusal of the Virginia delegation yesterday to regard my advice makes the present situation for me unendurable. As you and my other friends on the delegation know, I have never been in quest of a Presidential nomination ; but since my name has been formally presented to the Convention, there is an obligation upon me to insist that some consideration be given to my wishes as to matters of procedure. Inasmuch as members of the delegation do not coincide in this view, I am asking that you withdraw my name from the list of those who have been formally presented and cast my individual vote for Mr. McAdoo.

Thanking you and other friends for your fine devotion, believe me

Sincerely yours,
(signed) Carter Glass.

The Swanson action only made Byrd more determined in his opposition to McAdoo. Prior to the convention Byrd had declared himself publicly and had offered to withdraw as a delegate from Virginia if his presence as such was embarrassing to the Senator. Glass declined the offer, saying he thought Byrd was entitled to his own second choice as much as anyone else ; and assured him his presence would not be "in any way embarrassing."

Soon the party leaders at the convention decided Glass would be a better vote-getter than Davis. In their opinion, he was the more calculated to get his share of the farmer-labor vote then beginning to make itself effective in the Middle West. Moreover, as a Lynchburg publisher he was a successful "small business man." At the time when big business alliances with the current administration were being looked upon askance by the voting public, this was a distinct recommendation.

But Glass himself scotched the plans of the leaders by insisting that Davis be tried out first, and by instructing that half of the Virginia vote be delivered to him on the trial ballot. While Glass would have welcomed the nomination and made a valiant fight, he came quickly to the conclusion that this New York fiasco was killing whatever chance the Democratic party would have at the general elections to follow. When the Ku Klux Klan and religious issue could not be quietly compromised in the Resolutions Committee, when it was dragged out to the floor and into a veritable flood of passionate oratory, he told his closest friends the nomination wasn't going "to be worth the paper it was written on."

However, hopeless as the fight might be, he was well aware the Democratic nomination for the Presidency was a great honor, one not to be treated lightly nor set aside with indifference. For the gratification of many friends, if not his own, he wanted the nomination. He believed Davis would fail to get the required two-thirds vote on the 103rd ballot, and that he would be nominated on the next.

There never was that other ballot. The weary delegates stampeded to Davis and with them went the only real chance Carter Glass ever had for the Presidency of the United States.

It may be his small stature had something to do with the failure to get the nomination. When he appeared before the Convention as a Presidential possibility, the late Will Rogers took one good look, and exclaimed: "I didn't know they had trundle beds in The White House" ; and in similar vein, Isadore Dockweiler, Democratic national committeeman from California, observed : "A great little man ! A very great little man ! If he had been two inches taller he would have been President of the United States." The story was repeated to Glass. He smiled, saying, "my friend Dockweiler evidently has never heard of Napoleon, Julius Caesar and Alexander the Great."

After the convention, Byrd was strongly criticized in Virginia for McAdoo's loss of the nomination. Glass recognized the criticism and wrote Dr. F. S. Hope, of Fredericksburg :

> Whatever may be said of the refusal of certain other members of the Virginia delegation to vote for Mr. McAdoo, it is certain that no charge of bad faith can be properly made against Mr. Byrd, because his position in the premises had been publicly proclaimed before the Norfolk convention and at the Norfolk convention. And he had a perfect right to adhere strictly to the instructions of the Virginia State convention. This he preferred to do, notwithstanding my advice to the contrary ; but his action involved no disloyalty to me and no breach of faith with the Democrats of Virginia. He was firm enough and man enough to do at the convention what he had said beforehand he would do if sent to the convention.

Because he has never been willing to accede to the arbitrary dicta of titled consequence, whether of high or humble degree, the long life of Glass has been studded with lively combats. Not all have been in Washington. Late in 1924 his attention shifted from the Presidential race to his own farm lot, and to a legal fight in the Virginia courts. Personal property worth about $1000 had been jeopardized, and he spent more than $10,000 to protect it.

The property consisted of two heifers of his prize Jersey herd.

Three years earlier an inspector from the state sanitary board had examined his herd and declared the two animals tubercular. They were summarily condemned to be slaughtered. Glass refused to let them be killed pending an application to Judge R. Carter Scott of the Circuit Court of Richmond to compel the sanitary bureau to retest them, claiming that the test had been made in an improper, unlawful and unsanitary way.

Dr. J. G. Ferneyhough, the State Veterinarian, had refused to have the work of his inspector reviewed by anybody, notwithstanding that the bureau of animal husbandry and other recognized expert authorities to whom Glass appealed had said the heifers should be retested. This, he asserted, "violated neither any regulation nor professional ethic." Dr. Weaver declared the animals perfectly healthy, without a sign of tuberculosis . . . whereupon he was promptly disqualified by the State Veterinarian and the state sanitary board. Judge Scott, however, enjoined these officials from interfering with Dr. Weaver.

Glass resorted to the pen. He wrote an appeal to the Governor of Virginia. He dictated a letter to the Secretary of Agriculture in Washington. And he wrote a pamphlet, entitled *A Tale of Two Heifers*, which was given wide circulation.

He charged that the state board had slaughtered numerous animals in other Virginia herds, which had proved by autopsy to be perfectly sound. He cited evidence that out of thirteen allegedly tubercular cows condemned and killed by Dr. Ferneyhough's agent, twelve had been proved by post-mortem to be entirely sound, and only one dubious.

"After the court shall have decided the suit now pending," he said, "I intend to take further steps to safeguard the breeders and dairymen of Virginia against the chance of reckless depredations by incompetent and arrogant State agents.

"The official record speaks for itself and will be presented to the court. It confirms the validity of my protest against the wanton mutilation and slaughter of my cattle. It demonstrates the accuracy of Dr. Weaver's private test, for making which he has been hounded and his professional business injured.

"It shows that the State Veterinarian, by his refusal to permit men of high professional skill to review the bungling work of his agent, caused the slaughter of one of the great dairy cows of Virginia, progeny of a bull that sold at public auction for $65,000. It makes one wonder how long the higher authorities of the State will subject the stock breeders and dairymen of Virginia to a menace that threatens great damage to an industry representing an investment of over $150,000,000."

Meanwhile the two famous animals had been segregated from the rest of the herd, awaiting the court decision. Far from succumbing to the tuberculosis ascribed to them three years previous, they grew into excellent cows, capable, as Glass pointed out, on ordinary farm care, of winning the American Jersey Cattle Club's gold medal for high production. The court directed a retest and after applying every test known to veterinary science the cows were pronounced clear of disease.

A final chapter was written to the dispute when a horse kicked one of the cows, breaking its leg so that it had to be killed. It was the animal Dr. Ferneyhough had pronounced the worse infected of the two. Glass immediately notified the Federal and state authorities that he intended to have an autopsy made to discover whether or not the cow had tuberculosis.

He summoned five of the outstanding veterinarians of the region. Their searching post-mortem was supplemented by a

MONTVIEW AND THE JERSEYS

microscopic examination of the animal's glands at the United States Bureau of Animal Industry in Washington.

All agreed the slaughtered cow showed not the slightest trace of disease.

CHAPTER NINETEEN

A Yale professor paraphrases Genesis.

By opposing his wishes as to the 1924 Democratic nominee for the Presidency, and firmly standing his ground, Harry Flood Byrd gained the increased respect and friendship of Glass.

In 1925 Byrd was seeking the Governorship of Virginia over State Senator G. Walter Mapp. As a United States Senator representing Virginia, Glass had always remained aloof from indicating nominees in state primaries ; and he announced at the beginning of the campaign that his support of Byrd was largely personal. He introduced Byrd to a Lynchburg audience as a recognition of a long-standing friendship with the candidate's father, Richard Evelyn Byrd, as well as a conviction that the son was the proper man for the office.

Glass would have stopped here in the campaign had he not been provoked by the Mapp supporters who demanded that he state his reasons more fully, and discuss the issues involved. One of these supporters, C. O'Connor Goolrick of Fredericksburg, challenged Glass to a debate. The challenge was accepted immediately, but the terms could not be agreed upon. By this time Glass was thoroughly aroused. Taking the stump for Byrd he made a number of speeches – and Byrd was overwhelmingly elected.

For Glass it was a wish, long deferred, come true. Years before, at an apple picnic, he had said to young Byrd in his father's presence, "Some day, I hope to see you Governor of Virginia."

During Byrd's incumbency, and especially when his reform program was getting under way at the beginning of his administration, the two men were in close touch.

On December 20, 1925, Glass wrote:

I could have wished that you had put a little more emphasis on the desirability of reducing public expenditures and combining bureaus and offices; but I assume this will come later.

On February 28, 1926, this letter:

. . . Let me repeat what I tried to say to you in Richmond about the recommendations contained in your inaugural address. Just stick to them and fight for them. If I have any discernment at all or any familiarity with the feeling and judgment of the Virginia people, I am perfectly confident that such a course will make your administration notable. There will be opposition. Every little fellow whose job is threatened will get every other little fellow busy to oppose your plans of reformation; but the people of Virginia are behind you and will applaud your fighting qualities.

I have been gratified, as I am sure you must be, at the favor with which your inaugural address and subsequent messages have been received by the press of the State. Almost without exception the newspapers have given unqualified assent to the various proposals which you have made. I think there can be no question of a very wide approval of your suggestion that the administrative powers of the State government should be lodged with the executive, who should in turn be held accountable to the people for honest and efficient service. Fight for this and your real friends will aid you along the line.

I do not think it would be the part of wise friendship to pester you with suggestions concerning official patronage. In a general way I venture to express the wish that you may act always from a clear conviction of the entire worth, capability and sobriety of the man named in each instance, because on the personal qualities of the comparatively few appointees which the Governor now has to name will largely depend the success of your plan to have the executive charged with greater powers and larger responsibilities with respect to official appointments.

Be good enough to acquit me of any desire to give you gratuitous advice. Any suggestions that I shall ever venture will be prompted by my desire to have you succeed, and succeed brilliantly, in giving Virginia an executive administration such as it sorely needs, but has not had for a long time — indeed, such as cannot be had under existing statutes and constitutional limitations.

On January 17, 1927, Governor Byrd surprised and pleased Glass by notifying him :

This is just a line to advise you that I am looking forward to the pleasure tomorrow of voting for your brother, Mr. E. C. Glass, as a member of the State Board of Education.

And in reply this revealing letter from the Senator :

Responding to your note of the 17th, I am sure my brother, Ned, will be glad to know that he has your approval for a position on the State Board of Education. I frequently think of the inequalities of this life. This finds no better illustration than in the fact that Ned Glass, with infinitely more culture, learning and real ability than I, with vastly more real work to his credit, has given forty years of his life to Virginia at a comparatively paltry wage, whereas the Commonwealth has loaded me with distinctions which he might more appropriately have received.

The only compensation I can think of for such inequalities is the fact that my brother's work has been of a more enduring nature than mine and will be remembered by succeeding generations long after I shall have been forgotten. I am grateful that you are about to give it the sanction of executive approval.

Having formed a great attachment for Richard Evelyn Byrd, it was natural that Glass' affection should extend to the sons of his friend. Speaking for Harry Flood Byrd in the gubernatorial campaign he had said : ". . . when no man dared to run for office without first going to Washington and there getting consent ; when that campaign to break down the political machine was raging, the opponent of Harry Byrd in this campaign was an outstanding figure in the political machine, voting against me and against William A. Jones. . ."

In 1926, Commander Richard Evelyn Byrd, Jr., invited Glass to lunch with him in New York and inspect the ship in which he was sailing to the Arctic ; and, later, a public statement from Glass :

Virginians must be highly gratified at the success of Commander Byrd in his great adventure around the North Pole. . . The predominating thought in my mind and feeling in my heart is pleasure at the fact that he will safely return to his mother and his wife and his children. The North Pole seems to be a great lure. In my conception nothing about it could compensate for the human agony which family and friends must endure when there is no return from its frozen embrace.

1933. Supporting Harry Flood Byrd for the United States Senate.

1937. Commander Byrd to Glass:

I am sending you a rock, mounted on mahogany, from the range of "Carter Glass mountains" I named after you, in recognition of your great contribution to the progress of this nation, and because of my very high regard for you. I am sorry it is not larger but these mountains, which had never been looked upon until we discovered them, are within the shadow of the South Pole and it is extremely difficult to transport by dog sled, 500 miles, anything but the barest necessities. . .

I don't want you to answer this letter. Writing a letter takes time and I am determined, as I promised you, not to require you to do things that will take up your time.

* * *

"This one thing I do know and assert, in whatever degree the statement may seem to lack proper reserve, that there is no man living who, from beginning or in the progress or at the ending of federal reserve legislation, was more closely or constantly than I privy to and identified with the consideration and enactment of the law under which the federal reserve banking system was set up."

When he wrote that Glass, as he expressed it, was motivated by "a sense of indignation subordinate only to a desire to tell the truth." This was in 1926; in his library at Montview he was intensively at work on his book, *An Adventure in Constructive Finance*.

The library at Montview is a long, paneled, bookcase-lined retreat, in which the Senator is never bored. There, principally among the English classics, he finds what Dr. Johnson called "his most unchanging friends and supporters," "still telling men's hearts," in the words of Clarence Day, "of the hearts of men centuries dead" – Burke, Hume, Bagehot, Gibbon, Addison, Steele, Carlyle, and a favorite, *Letters of Junius*, which he regards as the supreme political satire of the ages. That great Elizabethan seer, Francis Bacon, is to Glass the climax of Anglo-Saxon genius.

As to Shakespeare, there is a preponderance of evidence accrediting to Bacon, at least in part, the authorship of the immortal plays and sonnets. "Imagine a man who wrote *The Merchant of Venice* and *Hamlet*," Glass has said, scornfully, "leaving a will in which he bequeaths his second-best bedstead and never mentions a book!"

"Ever since the enactment of the Federal Reserve law," he wrote, "it has been my intention to write, some day, a story of the many inside events. . . Very likely my desire to tell the dramatic story would have abated, and even faded away, as so often happens with cherished intentions, had not there recently issued from the presses a work by Doctor Charles Seymour, a professor of history at Yale, in which the paternity of the Federal Reserve Act and its particular management are placidly ascribed to Colonel E. M. House, whose *Intimate Papers* are presented as the source of this astounding pretension.

"Often I have remarked that a person acquainted with the details could, if endued with a fertile facility of expression, write a history of Federal Reserve legislation which would read like a romance. Little did I dream that any person would venture upon the task of writing a romance on the subject and calling it history."

With a pen dipped in caustic he proceeded to demolish the

professor's claim, the fabrication of which he styled "literary legerdemain." Although he refrained from dealing harshly with Colonel House, who was pictured by Seymour as the "unseen guardian angel" of the Federal Reserve Measure, nevertheless this allegedly heavenly visitant does not emerge from Glass' marshalling of incontrovertible facts with completely unsullied raiment.

"An exceptionally pleasant personal contact with Colonel House and consequent estimate of his character would make me hesitate to believe that he could be willing to assume one particle of responsibility for the manipulation practiced by his editor in the use of scanty data or for the meanings attached thereto. . . For this false compound Professor Seymour seems primarily responsible, albeit Colonel House cannot escape a share of culpability as long as he gives to this book the sanction of his silence."

The Yale professor, according to Glass, was paraphrasing Genesis : " 'Let there be a Flexible Currency ; and there was a Flexible Currency !' – this for Dr. Seymour was crowning evidence of Colonel House's marvelous perspicacity and his gift for legislative detail. And the professor is simple enough to imagine that there is nobody left, after Mr. Wilson's death, who might be expected authoritatively to reveal the childishness of such fudge !"

In later pages he went on to shower scorn upon bankers who nurtured the hallucination that they might penetrate The White House through the medium of "the President's stealthy friend." "I venture to fathom the fatuity of those who, failing to escape the magic of Colonel House's illusions, in the final exigency even magnified him into a financial 'Moses' and craved the distinction, as the Colonel himself says, of officiating as his 'Aarons.' Their failure to sense the real status of things was beyond all comprehension."

But any reader who fancies that in *An Adventure in Constructive Finance* Glass claims for himself paternity of the Federal Reserve Act, either by admission or inference, will search those pages in vain. Speaking ten years earlier to a public assemblage, in Washington, from a table at which sat Woodrow Wilson, he said all he has cared to say on that point, and he quotes those remarks in his book:

"As to the Federal Reserve Act itself, there has been occasional speculation as to who most deserves credit for its conception and its enactment into law. Its paternity has curiously been ascribed to men who were savagely hostile to the act; to men who never saw a sentence of the original draft; to men who could not write its title in a month's trial."

In modest reference to himself, he continued: "I know very well the chairman of the House Committee on Banking and Currency has been given an undue share of the praise. . . But, gentlemen, the serious fact is that the master mind of the whole performance was Woodrow Wilson's. It was his infinite prescience and patience; it was his courage and wisdom; it was his patriotism and power – his passion to serve mankind – that gave zest and inspiration to the battle for financial freedom."

Completing the manuscript he sent it to Newton D. Baker for criticism and comment. On November 14, 1926, Baker wrote Glass:

> . . . As I read this manuscript in as detached a spirit as I can command, I have the feeling that you are doing two things: first, setting right the truth of history with regard to Colonel House; and second, setting up the almost romantic history of the enactment of the Federal Reserve legislation.

Baker went on to suggest that the first three chapters which confined themselves to demolishment of House and a refutation of the Seymour claims be confined to a prefatory note because then, "it seems to me, the House incident would assume a more normal position in the permanent volume."

Glass disagreed. As he wrote Baker on November 17:

> . . . I find myself unable to agree with you about eliminating from the book publication the first three chapters of my narrative and for this reason, that one of the primary purposes of my Chronicle is to destroy the credibility of House, not merely with respect to that feature of his book which attempts to appropriate credit for federal reserve legislation, but concurrently with respect to all other achievements of the Wilson administration which, by the same inference and implications, he would take unto himself. This being my purpose I felt obliged to analyze and expose in detail the absurdities of his Diary and Seymour's deductions. Only in this way, as I conceive it, could I effectually discredit both House and Seymour in their preposterous claims. . .

As to the ascription of major credit for the legislation, there need never be any conjecture comparable to the Shakespeare-Bacon controversy or the authorship of the *Letters of Junius*. History will survey all that actually occurred and write its opinion, just as it will write its opinion, if it writes at all, of politicians who acquire prestige and votes with talk of "doing something for the farmer" and who generally are not oblivious to similar advantages to be accrued through talk of "doing something for the Negro."

When such talk was revived by the White House secretariat in the early autumn of 1938, and when President Roosevelt expressed an opinion favorable to the abolition of poll taxes in the South, Glass' terse comment was "the President displays a very superficial knowledge of the subject." It was Glass who had largely drawn the suffrage article in the Virginia Constitution, and he had reasons for the provisions he had inserted therein.

In January 1928, the Eighteenth Amendment was under fire in the Senate. Glass believed in the enforcement of the law so long as it was on the statute books. Bruce of Maryland implied if he was too stubborn in his stand he might bring upon the South the full weight of the Fourteenth and Fifteenth Amendments. Both humor and heat enlivened the discussion that ensued.

"I ask the Senator," said Glass, "if he is among those who threaten the South with universal Negro suffrage unless the South shall quietly sanction the violation of the Eighteenth Amendment to the Federal Constitution. . . The South does what it does within the provisions of the Federal Constitution, and if the Senator from Maryland can get his liquor within the limitations of the Federal Constitution, let him get it."

Laughter rippled through the chamber.

Then, in serious vein, he challenged Bruce to point out the inequity of any of the Virginia suffrage resolutions, or any discrimination between the white and colored races.

"We provide in the first place," said Glass, "that a man shall be 21 years of age, whether he be white or black. We provide that he shall have had a certain length of residence in the State, whether he be white or black. We require that before he shall have the privilege of a voter he shall register, whether he be white or black. We require that he shall make out his application for registration in his own handwriting, without memoranda or assistance of any sort, whether he be white or black. We require that he pay $1.50 poll tax, to be devoted to the public school fund of the State, whether he be white or black. We require that he shall pay this poll tax six months in advance of the election. . . I want to assert for Virginia that the laws there apply with perfect equality between the whites and the blacks."

Bruce deplored that prejudice should hold sway in the South. Glass made pertinent response.

"Let me ask the Senator how long it has been since the end

of the Civil War. Let me ask the Senator if he believes that a Southern man could be nominated for President of the United States? He is talking about prejudice."

"Certainly I think so," answered Bruce.

"Why has not one been nominated in the last 65 years? That is not prejudice, is it?"

"I think we will have a Southern man in The White House again in the future."

"Yes," Glass concurred, "but the Senator's great-great-grandchildren will not live to see it."

A week later the same two Senators found themselves on opposing sides of another argument. This was after Bruce had offered an amendment to the Civil Service law. Glass expressed contempt for the evasion, pretense and patronage he had encountered in the law's enforcement.

"I had one experience within a few weeks when a boy – he bears a very distinguished name; his name is Jefferson – who had gone across the ocean and offered his life for his country and was shot to pieces, and had, in a competition for a position as rural carrier, stood first on the list, but was turned down for a bomb-proof artist, the lowest man on the list, by the Civil Service Commission and the Post Office Department.

"Then Senators talk to me about the enforcement of the Civil Service law! It is not enforced half as well as the Prohibition law!"

Because he is a newspaperman, and more particularly because his utterances can bristle with phrases that make excellent copy, many editors are quick to solicit Glass' opinion whenever controversy flares in the Capitol. In 1926 the *Baltimore Sun* wired for his "instructive comment" on the dispute between President Coolidge and Frank Smith of Illinois. It was reported that Coolidge had quoted the *Chicago Tribune* as opposing Smith because of campaign contributions from

Samuel Insull, a utility magnate. Tartly Smith retorted that the President, endowed with arbitrary power to alter tariff rates, nevertheless cheerfully received campaign contributions from tariff beneficiaries.

"Was there no way," queried the *Sun*, "for a President to protect himself from having such questionable contributions forced upon his party?"

"Mr. Coolidge is not to be blamed," responded Glass, "because Congress was foolish enough to charge the Executive with the unconstitutional power to advance or lower tariff taxes. He is culpable only because in the exercise of this extraordinary power he has consistently refused to lower excessive tariff rates.

"A Republican Congress is responsible for lodging with one public official this power; the power itself is subject to the exact criticism Smith directed against it. . . Congress should repeal this monstrous provision without a day's delay and the President himself should urge the repeal. In the hands of a corrupt or excessively partisan President it is susceptible to inconceivable abuse.

"Neither the President nor his party should accept campaign contributions from protected interests while this wicked provision remains a part of the law."

In February 1928, a stymied investigation of the public-utility corporations brought the Federal Trade Commission into the Senate limelight. A resolution by Norris, of Nebraska, had ordered the probe. It had not been carried out because the Federal Trade Commission did not have sufficient funds to pursue the inquiry. There had been some pretense of investigation, discreetly lenient to the corporations, which pleased Glass not at all.

"I am no longer to be frightened, as once I was," he said, "by the vehemently expressed hostility of some gentlemen to municipal ownership of public utilities. Like most people of my temperament and nature, I get my preconception of things, and it is exceedingly difficult to alter opinions when once they are fixed. For years I capitulated to the idea that it was a horrible heresy to talk about community or public ownership of public utilities. I began to recover my senses when we entered upon the discussion here of Muscle Shoals, when some people actually wanted to give away a great property, costing the Government of the United States more than a hundred million dollars. Then, by actual personal observation and inquiry I was confirmed in my dawning belief that a seriously debatable question was involved, and that no intellectual or moral stain attaches to any man who may advocate, in certain conditions and to a certain extent, public ownership of public utilities."

Probably Newton D. Baker, more than any other person, influenced Glass "to alter opinions . . . once fixed" ; and in 1924, when the controversy over the leasing of the Muscle Shoals property to Henry Ford was raging in the Senate, the Senator received a letter from the former Secretary of War which said :

> . . . as I was responsible for the selection of the Muscle Shoals site and the building of the dam, I have felt a strong interest in the project, and therefore venture to submit some observations about it. Needless to say, I have no interest whatever in the subject, represent nobody but myself and do not even know the names of the companies or individuals submitting the various proposals.
>
> . . . it seems to me that as coal is growing daily scarcer and scarcer, industry in America will come more and more to depend upon water power, and the control of these great powers will, in a few years, give an industrial dominance to their owners more absolute than the ownership of the soft coal deposits, as in the past.
>
> I have no desire to see the government of the United States enter the field of industry in competition with private initiative and am still old fashioned enough to believe that the government

ought not to undertake to do anything that can be better or even as well done privately, but the ownership of these sources of power is an ultimate resource. It is quite impossible now to calculate their value twenty-five or fifty years from now, and any contract which could possibly be drawn now would fall far short of a true valuation of these powers or true estimate of their influence on the future of industrial America.

I have, therefore, earnestly urged since 1920 that the government retain these power sources in its own hands, operating them either directly or through some such agency as the Panama Railroad Company (a corporation of which the government owns the stock) producing power and supplying it wholesale as a dominating element in the super-power district, roughly within the circle two hundred miles in radius from Sheffield or Florence.

. . . I cannot rid myself of the feeling that safety lies alone in the government's retaining this property and others like it, rather than passing it . . . to any private corporation whatsoever.

Replying to Baker's letter, Glass said:

. . . As a member of the Appropriations Committee of the Senate I four years ago voted to appropriate $20,000,000 to proceed with the work at Muscle Shoals as a government enterprise and favored going ahead with the work as such to completion. Without an intimate knowledge of the details of Ford's offer, I have felt that no acquisitive individual or corporation should have exclusive proprietary control of so tremendous an enterprise as the Muscle Shoals power plant. It is true that in time of war – God forbid that it may ever recur – the government could commandeer the plant; but such procedure invariably leads to bitter and protracted controversy and I have thought it would be better for the government to complete and operate the plant. . .

And, in the spring, 1928. Hoover and Smith had not yet sprung into the headlines which were now relating stirring tales of action in Nicaragua, where terrified natives, mostly unarmed, ran screaming, some falling, before the guns of United States Marines.

On April 25, when Glass was absent from the capital, the Senate voted on amendments to a naval appropriations bill, providing fresh funds for the Central American excursion. But next day Glass was back in the Senate.

"I think that in sending troops to Nicaragua the President has no constitutional or statutory warrant. I think he made a very grave mistake, which, had it been made with respect to one of the major nations of the earth, might and very likely would have resulted in dangerous and disastrous consequences."

When a Senator sought to compare the Government policy with that advocated by the League, Glass snapped: "Under the terms of the League of Nations it would not be necessary, it certainly would not have been imperative, that we should send our naval force there. . . There is such a thing as moral force in the world. . ."

CHAPTER TWENTY

Here was a call to battle.

In June 1928, Glass was busy completing the draft of the Virginia platform for presentation at the state meeting in Roanoke. Remembering the futility of the 1924 Democratic National Convention, and fearful of a prolonged party row over prohibition, he had half made up his mind not to attend the gathering in Houston. His own choice for the nomination was Newton D. Baker, and in letters to the former Secretary of War he had expressed that desire. But Alfred E. Smith, Governor of New York, seemed the certain candidate.

While debating the advisability of going to Houston, he received a letter from Senator Swanson urging his attendance because "if Smith is nominated it is of the utmost importance that the platform be not injurious and accentuate the fact of his nomination."

In replying to Swanson, Glass mentioned

> I ran into Cordell Hull. I infer from what he told me the Tammany crowd will not only assail the immigration policy of Congress, but is dead set upon a protective tariff plank that will not be distasteful to Massachusetts and New Jersey. I am disposed to agree with Hull that, if the Democratic party is to embrace Republican doctrines, and permit certain Republican States to nominate its candidate, it had as well disband and go over to the enemy. It is to be hoped things are not as bad as that.

As expected, the Democrats nominated Smith. Glass returned to Lynchburg to write an unburdening letter to his close friend, Robert L. Ailworth, of Eastville, Va.:

> . . . Politics not only makes strange bedfellows, but it does some amazing things beside. At Houston we denounced the Republican party for its failure to enforce the prohibition laws

and pledged ourselves to do better. Then we nominated a wringing wet candidate for President and a theoretically bone dry candidate for Vice-President. The wet candidate for President proceeded immediately to slap his platform in the face and to insist that the liquor question be made the supreme issue of the presidential campaign! The protection and subsidy planks of the platform went far beyond the declarations of the Republican National Convention. Indeed, in this respect we picked up the cast-off garments of the Republican party. But for my two planks denouncing Republican corruption, one could read the Houston platform and readily think it was adopted by the Republicans at Kansas City. . . Nothing was left for us but to come home and appeal to the South for party regularity.

Predicting defeat for the Democratic party at the November elections, Glass continued:

Forgive me for "blowing off" in this way to you; but there are so few persons to whom I could be willing to trust my innermost thoughts that I have picked on you to unburden myself. It may be that, as the campaign proceeds, I may feel in a better humor.

Glass was fearful the Democratic candidate would persist in his purpose to come out openly for repeal of the Eighteenth Amendment. He was convinced, if this happened, that Virginia's electoral vote would go to Hoover; in fact, he said it in a letter to Senator Pat Harrison, of Mississippi; and sent a copy of the letter to the Vice-Presidential nominee, Joseph T. Robinson of Little Rock, Arkansas.

In this letter he pointed out that while he was no prohibition zealot, he was a steadfast antagonist of the open saloon and "both practically and theoretically against whiskey." He admitted the Volstead Act would bear modification. But he warned Smith would only sacrifice votes that, otherwise, would be his, by making liquor a leading issue.

On the evening of August 14, he went to Albany and gave Smith his frank opinion. The trip was futile. Smith, feeling the South was obliged to vote the ticket whether it wanted to or not, had made up his mind to risk the election on what Glass described as "an impossible proposal." "While our interview was entirely civil and friendly," he wrote Harrison, "it did not lack in spirit or even vehemence."

Looking back to the previous Presidential campaign, he had made only one or two speeches in behalf of his personal friend John W. Davis. And yet, into this campaign he plunged with a passion without precedent in all the years of his political life.

Why did he allow himself to get so worked up?

There can be only one answer. The question of religious liberty as guaranteed in the Constitution was at stake.

In Virginia was a slight, stooped, pale-faced, bespectacled man, partly bald, with graying hair – of his appearance Frank Kent wrote in the *Baltimore Sun* "he might have been a Congressman or a clerk." This man was Reverend James Cannon, Jr., a Bishop of the Methodist Church South and leader of the Anti-Saloon League. Heading a coalition of prohibitionists and Southern Republicans, Cannon was loudly assailing Smith on religious grounds. When he spoke, it was the "moral forces of America" that thundered; when he was answered, it was by "wet and Roman Catholic press."

Glass took his stand in the squarest opposition. He did not deny the churchman's right to argue for prohibition; but he did denounce the attempt to drag the Methodist Church, of which he himself was a life-long member, into politics and use its agencies for political purposes. He adhered to the principle of Edmund Burke that "the religionist in politics and the politician in religion are equally a curse to human society."

He remembered that Virginia was the very cradle of civil and religious liberty; that Thomas Jefferson was the author of the Federal statute for religious freedom; that he himself had written such a statute into his state constitution; and that the

Methodist Church, with its history of persecution, had particular reason to stand for the separation of church and state. He objected to religious interference with government just as he would object to government interference with religion; and he especially condemned appeals to religious prejudice. Intolerance and bigotry were to him anathema.

Out of this campaign grew a long-drawn-out and exceedingly bitter battle into which the Virginia Senator poured every ounce of his strength and wrath.

In October, answering an invitation to speak in Mississippi, he reported to Harrison: "If I were twenty men instead of one I could not respond to the calls from various parts of my own State."

Belatedly, from the ballots of the people, Smith discovered the validity of the Glass warnings. The coalition of religionists and prohibitionists prevailed, and for the second time since the Civil War Virginia voted Republican.

The net gain was in electoral votes Hoover did not need. The net loss to the nation was morally great. The sweeping victory of 444 to 87 was dimmed because Hoover was the beneficiary, however innocent, of a discreditable appeal to religious prejudice.

Flushed with temporary triumph, Bishop Cannon now regarded himself as a decisive power in Virginia politics. Glass was warned that Cannon was after his scalp and the scalps of Senator Swanson and Governor Harry Byrd. It amused him. Annoyed him, too. But by election time in 1930 the Cannon machine was stalled.

Alleged bucket-shop manipulations, into which the ecclesiastic, it was charged, had diverted thousands of dollars of campaign contributions entrusted to his care, for use in stock gambling, became a national scandal in 1929, and for years later a matter of bitter litigation, only recently terminated by a decision of the Supreme Court. Significant of Glass' single-minded focus on the issue of religious freedom was the fact that he had been among the first to learn of the alleged bucket-shop dealings, but refrained from injecting this matter into the Presidential campaign.

Early in the fateful year of 1929, before Hoover took office, Glass was concerned with the growth of bucket-shop practices to a national scale of alarming magnitude. For years he had predicted ultimate collapse of the economic system if prodigal stock and commodity gambling were not checked. Now he saw the dark clouds of disaster directly ahead.

The Federal Reserve Board was not charged by law with the supervision of stock-exchange activities, except as speculative activities might relate themselves to the facilities of the Federal Reserve Banks. "These processes in the money centers have gotten far beyond that," Glass warned the Senate in February. "The great corporations of the country have acquired the habit of throwing their surplus funds into the vortex of stock speculation, instead of distributing them among their stockholders in the nature of dividends, and individuals are doing the same thing.

"Member banks of the system have manipulated their deposit accounts so as to transfer from the demand deposit account, requiring a reserve of 7 per cent, to the time deposit account, requiring a reserve of only 3 per cent, thereby releasing enormous funds to be thrown into the maelstrom of stock speculation.

"When I presented a bill here last week to restore the reserve behind time deposits to the figure which obtained in the original set-up, banks all over the country began to write me letters of protest. That alone would withhold from those speculative activities at least $300,000,000 ; but banks are not willing to desist. . .

"Unless some man be wise enough, and have wit enough to give a statutory definition of investments as contra-distinguished from stock gambling, I do not see how we are to curb these gambling activities. That ought to be done."

He demonstrated if a man invested $10,000 in General Motors with a view of deriving therefrom the dividends a prosperous company is supposed to pay annually, that constitutes an investment. But if he bought $10,000 of stock with a view of selling it even before delivery physically could be made, the next hour, or with a view of anticipating the future of tomorrow or the next day, that was nothing in the world but pure gambling – "just as much gambling as if Senators were to sit at a roulette table and bet on the outcome of the game."

Senator Caraway likened it to a poker game and added that, unlike poker, in stock transactions the gambling is done with other people's money.

"They sell things they do not possess," agreed Glass, "and they buy things they never expect to get, and thereby disturb the whole commercial fabric of this country, and it ought to be stopped. But they have done it too late."

Also up for consideration by this "lame duck" session of the 70th Congress was the Multilateral Peace Treaty. Glass declared he would vote for it, but added, "I am not simple enough to suppose that it is worth a postage stamp in the direction of permanent international peace."

Lamely enough, as time has proved, this treaty – the Kellogg Peace Pact – was drawn up to substitute negotiation for the use of armed force. "I think we are about to renounce something as a national policy," Glass said, "which no nation on earth for 150 years has ever proclaimed as a national policy.

"I had purposed speaking on the pact, but when I sat here and reflected that in the twenty-eight years that I have been a member of one or the other branches of Congress, I have never known a speech to change a vote, I decided that I would not encroach upon the time of the Senate.

"I am going to vote for the treaty for the simple reason that I think its defeat will psychologically be a bad thing. I have come to the considered judgment that Mr. Lincoln's most popular aphorism needs amending, wherein he said that 'you cannot fool all the people all the time.' If the word 'time' may be applied to an epoch or a period rather than to eternity, I say that all the people all the time for nearly the last ten years have been fooled."

He branded the pact a mere conscience-penny proffered as a solace to the awakened conscience of those who had kept the United States out of the League of Nations. He predicted it would fool many people into thinking peace may be secured by polite professions of neighborly and brotherly love.

"That did not fool Theodore Roosevelt; it did not fool Henry Cabot Lodge; it did not fool Taft, the present Chief Justice; it did not in any respect or degree fool the President-elect of the United States. Every one of those men is over and over again on the record as saying that no peace pact between nations will ever amount to a thrip that has not behind it the potential use of the military power of these nations combined.

"I agree with that. But I am going to be simple enough, along with the balance of you, to vote for the ratification of this worthless, but perfectly harmless peace treaty."

For Glass this was predominantly a year of protest. Two months after President Hoover had been inaugurated, and when farm relief was again under debate, he protested against Federal encroachment upon private enterprise, saying, "The people who have built up a successful industry want to manage their own business affairs. They do not want any strutting satrap of the Federal Government nosing around in their business. That is one of the most annoying and exasperating things I can think of. I have had experience with it."

And in June, protesting against high money rates, he said, "Not only are commercial enterprises and industrial business heavily taxed for their essential credits, but even States and communities have been obliged to defer necessary public improvements because they cannot get accommodations at reasonable rates ; and they cannot get them because the gamblers have run away with the money market in New York.

"While I am on my feet let me say to the credit of the Federal Reserve Board – which is, as the Senate knows, an altruistic body ; it has no interest whatsoever in banking or in credits – that it has vainly but persistently been trying for the last six months to establish a policy that the law itself makes mandatory upon the banks and the board, and that should have been established long ago, and if established long ago, would have averted this difficulty."

He stated that ever since mid-February the directors of the New York Federal Reserve Board had been persistently pounding the Federal Reserve Board every week to permit them to penalize legitimate commercial transactions by upping its rediscount rate. And as he arrayed his facts his anger increased.

"By every influence, legitimate and illegitimate, by threats and otherwise, that New York crowd has been trying to compel the board to raise its commercial rediscount rate ; and it has refused by a very narrow margin within the board. As I pointed out publicly six or eight weeks ago, when an outstanding director of the New York Federal Reserve Bank – the President [Charles E. Mitchell] of the largest bank in the Western Hemisphere – defied the board and publicly avowed that his obligation to the stock gamblers was superior to his obligation as a sworn officer of the Federal Reserve system, what the board should have done was to have incontinently kicked that fellow out of his position before noon of the day upon which he made that announcement."

Letters and clippings littered the Senator's desk . . . call money on the New York Stock Exchange had advanced to the startling figure of 22 per cent; brokers' loans had increased to nearly $7,000,000,000! . . . headlines . . . "Orgy of speculation checks improvement programs of cities" . . . "Sustained wave has lured billions into market as brokers' loans, diverting credits from business and agriculture" . . . "Effect of high money rates on business causing concern."

"To say this is wholesome," wrote Glass, "is to betray a case of intellectual astigmatism that requires the curative skill of a physician.

"I own stocks and proprietary interests in newspapers, banks, hotels, farms, foundries and other productive enterprises, but I have never acquired the habit of betting at one hour that the value of these interests will be greater or less the next hour or the next day or the next month. I didn't cast dice on the better wit of the 'bulls' or the duller wit of the 'bears.' I invested my money; and I do not have to listen at the ticker or watch the tapes for profits."

In October came the debacle Glass had long foreseen. For ten years he had known, as apparently few economists had seemed to know, that after the expansive prosperity of the war years a constriction was certain to come. Knowing the piper would have to be paid, he had consistently advocated payment in a graduated, orderly and fiscal fashion. But the spurious, speculative paper prosperity had blinded men in the mass, and those in high places in the financial realm, intoxicated with pyramiding profits, had at last upset the precarious balance and brought, in one great crash, what Glass had hoped to see spread over sane and necessarily sober years.

He was not surprised when it came. It is not on record he ever rose to remark, "I told you so." Rather, he began seriously to consider the methods and means of remedial legislation.

In February of the following year President Hoover put the name of Charles Evans Hughes before the Senate for confirmation as Chief Justice of the Supreme Court of the United States. Glass took the floor to tell why his vote would be a negative one. His admittedly futile objection to this nominee, he said, was based first on Hughes' "lack of sensibility." In theory and expectation Glass believed that a person appointed and confirmed to the highest court in this land should serve for his lifetime, or until he is himself convinced that he has reached that point of service and age in life when he finds himself disqualified for the position.

"That is why Supreme Court judges have life tenure, and it has always seemed to me an exhibition of the severest indifference to that theory and that consideration for any Justice of the Supreme Court of the United States to contemplate for a moment discarding the ermine and coming down from his exalted station to participate selfishly in the turmoils and disputes of partisan politics. I believe this whole country felt a shock, as it was grievously distressed, when Mr. Justice Hughes resigned his place on the Supreme Court bench to be a candidate for President of the United States.

"I think the offense, if such it be – and such, in my conception it was – is frightfully accentuated when he is nominated for a position upon that same bench and indicates a willingness to accept such nomination. For that reason alone I could not in conscience or judgment vote for his confirmation because, as I have said, perhaps rather severely, such action indicates an insensibility that does not become a man who is to pass in the last stage and final analysis upon the great concerns of this nation."

He gave further objections, particularly his disapproval of Hughes' previous Shreveport decision, which he viewed as a rank invasion of States' Rights, since it arrogated to the Interstate Commerce Commission discriminatory powers which the Congress itself did not possess. But, of course, he was speaking in a predominantly Republican Senate, and his "Nay" was merely for the record.

But humor was not lost in the seriousness of the times. An appropriation bill came before the Senate. It was proposed to expend $65,000 of the public funds to eradicate mosquitoes in the District of Columbia. Glass pounced upon it.

"It appears that an attaché of the White House," he said, "discovered some mosquitoes in a bush or in the lawn grass and immediately assembled a council of war."

As though he were weightily impressed, Glass listed the doctors and dignitaries who had been summoned into conference. He quoted one of them as saying that for the first year the expenditure would be higher because it would be necessary for the Health Service to buy some automobiles.

"Automobiles," chuckled Glass, "to hunt mosquitoes with!

"Of course, mosquitoes are annoying – when one discovers any mosquitoes; but . . . I have never been bitten by a mosquito in all the years I have been in Washington."

Seeing only the bait, an unsuspecting colleague rose to remark his experience had been different, whereupon Glass replied: "I am perfectly willing that the Senator should go on record as having been bitten by a mosquito."

At three score and ten many may say, "I have lived my Biblical allotment of years; now I shall rest from my labors, for I have earned peace." But for Glass 1928 and the following years were to become the most strenuous of all: Drafting the Virginia platform . . . called to the national convention . . . urging Newton D. Baker to become a candidate for the Democratic Presidential nomination; Baker's appreciative reply . . . Smith nominated and forebodings of failure if the candidate went "wet" . . . Cannon making his own church a bitter partisan . . . here had been a call to battle. . .

Writing, speaking, stumping his state from end to end, up to the eve of inevitable defeat . . . but sustained by the conviction that he was championing an inalienable right . . . that churches are holy things, not to be debased into political machines . . . that religious liberty deserved staunch defense regardless of who won that year, or any year. . .

The vengeful efforts to unseat him from the Senate . . . and Cannon politically discredited. . . Stock speculation riding for a fall . . . his efforts to apply the brakes . . . the "lame duck" session and its lame peace pact. . . And then – Black Thursday . . . crash and consternation . . . and, a little later, $65,000 to chase mosquitoes. . .

The comic and tragic blend in the years; the great and grotesque link hands; the contrasts go into the record and the record goes on the shelf. But, under the contrasts, ever the consistency of fair play . . . indignant salvos against executive scoldings of the Congress . . . interspersed, properly, by indignant defenses of the President against partisan aspersions. . .

Constitutional rights, bitterly fought measures, farm relief, tariff, the seating of Justices on the high-court bench . . . emergency measures, appropriations running into the hundreds of millions . . . and then . . .

May 21, 1930. The senior Senator from Virginia addresses the Chair.

"I submit a resolution and ask that it may lie on the table."

Whereas dial telephones are more difficult to operate than are manual telephones; and whereas Senators are required, since the installations of the dial telephones in the Capitol, to perform the duties of the telephone operators in order to enjoy the benefit of telephone service; and whereas dial telephones have failed to expedite telephone service;

THEREFORE, BE IT RESOLVED:

That the Sergeant-at-Arms of the Senate is authorized and directed to order the Chesapeake & Potomac Telephone Company to replace with manual telephones, within thirty days after the adoption of this resolution, all dial telephones in the Senate wing of the United States Capitol and in the Senate Office Building.

Next day Glass followed through: "I ask unanimous consent to take from the table Senate Resolution 274, directing the Sergeant-at-Arms to have these abominable dial telephones taken out of use on the Senate side. I have not seen a Senator who does not say he is in favor of the resolution. Many of them have voluntarily come forward and told me that the system is a perfect nuisance to them."

For once Glass was not opposed on any partisan front. A Senator across the aisle called attention to the dial telephones resulting in the discharge of a number of telephone employees.

"I object to that phase of it," said Glass, "and I object to being transformed into one of the employees of the telephone company without compensation."

The resolution, later amended to make the choice of dial or manual telephones optional, was passed.

The period was a time of anxiety, too. Mrs. Glass was seriously ill. For a time, the attending physicians were none too hopeful.

In many things Mrs. Glass supplemented her husband, in others she had little share. The problems of government were never on her horizon and she had little patience with politics.

But where her husband was concerned she was always on guard to shield him from assault. She never set foot in the Court Street Methodist Church after Bishop Cannon accused the Senator with having sacrificed moral principles to political expediency in the 1928 campaign.

With Glass immersed in legislative affairs, she was thinking of their Lynchburg home. Even while convalescing in the hospital, she was writing domestic instructions to Annie, the cook; and always appended a postscript, "Be sure you take care of my roses."

CHAPTER TWENTY-ONE

Conversation with a turnip.

As has been shown, long before the stock market collapsed in October 1929, it was apparent to Glass, and other thoughtful men, that abuses had come into finance.

For years improper use, by a greedy few, had turned the credit machinery set up to protect the nation's enterprise into a juggernaut that flattened wherever it rolled; and now it was rolling almost everywhere. Conscious of weaknesses in the structure where the people kept their savings, as in the preparatory work for the Federal Reserve Act, Glass had taken years to investigate facts, and to form his own conclusions. He was almost ready to begin writing a new banking reform bill out of the printed information and penciled notes that, in scattered profusion, covered his desk.

When he had written the Federal Reserve Act he had made many provisions to prevent inflation of the currency, as well as provisions that, on occasion, could be used to deflate the currency.

Under the Act the Federal Reserve Board was permitted to influence interest rates. It could lower them (*a*) by lowering the rediscount rate to member banks; (*b*) by lowering open market rates; (*c*) by lowering reserve requirements; (*d*) by issuing Federal Reserve bank note currency against United States bonds; (*e*) by actively buying bills, notes, acceptances, etc.; and (*f*) by not paying interest on excess deposits and letting out money freely.

It could raise interest rates (*a*) by raising their rediscount rate to member banks; (*b*) by raising their open market rates; (*c*) by raising reserve requirements, which the Federal Reserve Board can do indirectly ; (*d*) by purchasing Government bonds with circulation privilege but withholding the issuance of Federal Reserve bank notes against them ; (*e*) by selling bills, notes, acceptances, etc. ; (*f*) by paying interest on excess deposits (i. e., above legal minimum) and hoarding the money.

What Glass did not foresee, when writing the act, was that the provision permitting the use of United States bonds would be used by speculators as security for loans, an opening which was made much wider by the extraordinary borrowings to prosecute the war. In 1920, the Federal Reserve Board while acting late had acted, and had succeeded in halting an inflationary boom.

But in the years between 1920 and 1929 other factors had come into the banking picture.

In the summer of 1927 business began to slacken and the speculative fever increased. With the spell of gambling on the country, the unemployment went almost unnoticed, but Glass was one of those who did notice. On the Senate floor in 1927, he warned against "growing speculation" ; and off the Senate floor discussed with the head of a New York investment banking organization the advisability of legislation which would compel stock-market gamblers to pay a tax of five per cent on sales of stocks held less than sixty days.

"That would ruin the market," declared the investment banker.

"Supposing it does – it is better to 'ruin the market,' as you say, than to ruin the country, as will surely happen if this gambling fever continues to spread."

The investment banker smiled tolerantly. "My own opinion, Senator, is that the people of this country are just beginning to realize on the prosperity to which they are entitled."

"I hope you are right, but common sense tells me you are

wrong. The day of reckoning for gambling cannot be escaped. It must come. I think something *should* be done to deprive people of the privilege of mortgaging their homes and their futures to buy stocks on margin and to keep blowing up bubbles that are certain to break in their faces."

Then, too, there were other factors which all contributed to the factor of gambling. Trying to get back on the gold standard, European countries discussed various ways for reversing the flow of gold. In the years from 1922 to 1927 gold stocks in the United States had increased by $780,000,000. In the summer of 1927 a number of bankers from different European countries visited Washington and New York, holding conferences with members of the Federal Reserve Board, as well as with prominent New York bankers.

It was decided to reduce the rediscount rates of all Federal Reserve banks to 3½ per cent, in addition to making heavy purchases in the Government bond market as well as acceptances in the open market. With news of this impending policy Federal Reserve Banks in cities other than New York began telegraphing and telephoning objections, especially to the rediscount rate of 3½ per cent. The board, instead of heeding these objections in their entirety, decided to make a test of one district.

Summarily, and without precedent, it ordered the Chicago Federal Reserve Banks to lower their rediscount rate to 3½ per cent, and the thing Chicago bankers said would happen, happened. Funds began flowing to New York and speculation, instead of being discouraged, was encouraged. Easy credit came in. Gold began flowing out, almost $600,000,000 being exported between the summer of 1927 and the summer of 1928.

Before the end of 1927, however, it became apparent to the Federal Reserve Board that the policy was too liberal. It began selling securities to contract credit and did sell, in its open market operations, within a period of six months, more than $400,000,000 worth. It was late and, as proved, too late. The fuel it had added to a blaze already started had intensified the fire. Successive increases in the rediscount rates to 4 per cent, then to 4½ per cent and, finally, on July 13, 1928, to 5 per cent came too late. At the time the board did discuss the advisability of raising the rate to 6 per cent, but thought better of it, fearing for its effect on agriculture and industry. As events turned out likely enough it would have been wise.

By February of 1929 there came a division of opinion on the board. In the beginning it was fairly unanimous in the belief that pressure should be brought to bear on Federal Reserve Banks to force them to reduce their loans, and curb, as well as liquidate, speculative and investment loans. While these discussions were in progress Charles E. Mitchell, President of the National City Bank of New York, as well as Owen D. Young, argued against this action, declaring it better policy to have a succession of increases in the rediscount rates.

In the end the board did both. In February the board issued a public warning, requesting member banks to refrain from making speculative loans. Five days previously, and privately, it had sent a letter to Federal Reserve Banks, requesting them to bring pressure on their member banks to reduce such loans, or stop making them entirely. The Federal Advisory Council, which opposed raising rediscount rates, approved the board's action.

A week following the public warning by the Federal Reserve Board, the Federal Reserve Bank of New York made formal application to the board to increase the rate of rediscount to 6 per cent. The request was declined. Nine more times did the New York Federal Reserve Bank make the request; on August 9, the board granted it. Then, it certainly was too late. The crash came about two months later. It was the Federal Reserve System that prevented a complete collapse, not only of all security markets but the entire banking structure. Where men's judgments had failed, the system itself stood.

With the withdrawal and liquidation of brokers' loans, banks had to find protection for stocks in which they had become interested. This necessitated calling upon the system to furnish large sums of immediate money ; and, in addition, the Federal Reserve Banks provided new credit by going into the open market and buying, between October 1929 and December 1930, $560,0000,000 worth of Government securities. Up to this time it was the largest credit expansion program of this type the reserve banks had been called upon to execute.

Looking over this history which, necessarily, has been greatly briefed, Glass knew legislation had to be written to tighten control over speculative credit. In preparing the original bill, he had provided prohibitory clauses covering speculative loans – but had failed to include penalties that would make such prohibition effective. He wasn't so naïve to believe there were not people then, and there would not be people in the future, who would violate this spirit of the law, if not its letter. But, as already said, he did not anticipate the huge borrowings of the Government during the World War, a debt which in 1929 amounted to $16,742,800,000, which in 1920 amounted to approximately $26,000,000,000 ; and which in 1913, when the Federal Reserve Act was written, amounted to $1,028,600,000.

Under Section 13 of the act, Federal Reserve Banks were permitted to rediscount paper of member banks under the stipulation that "such definition shall not include notes, drafts or bills covering merely investments or issued or drawn for the purpose of carrying or trading in stocks, bonds or other investment securities, except bonds and notes of the Government of the United States." From this wording it can be seen it was easy, considering the enormous amount of Government securities outstanding, for the banks to borrow from the Federal Reserve, thus diverting funds into speculative borrowings.

Also, where there are regulations there are always those who will find their way around them, thereby requiring additional rules.

With the growth of business, and the more rapid growth of speculation, security affiliates for banks had come into the financial picture; and, according to Adolph C. Miller, Federal Reserve Board economist, "if we had not had these affiliated institutions in 1928 and 1929 we should not have had as bad a situation, speculatively, as we have had – some of these affiliates have been little more than market operators."

Glass was determined to separate these appendages from the banking structure.

In that determination he knew he would be opposed by powerful bankers and powerful banking interests. To prepare for that opposition, he had begun assembling data showing the increase in security investments by national banks, state banks and trust companies. He learned that in 1930 security investments and loans, together, represented 40 per cent of the total banking resources; and that security loans had increased by more than 50 per cent, while security investments by banks and trust companies had increased by 63 per cent.

In 1930 his only remaining brother, Edward, died. From Washington came a telegram from Edith Bolling Wilson. In response Glass wrote: "I am sure you will know how deeply I appreciate your kindness when I tell you how devotedly I loved my brother."

On the floor of the Senate, also in 1930, he was defending President Hoover in discussions over the Emergency Public

Works bill. "I do not think the consideration of this discussion necessitates either the applause of the President or that bitter criticism should have assumed an aspect of calling in question the integrity and honesty of the President of the United States."

However, by no means did Glass approve all the administrative acts, nor fail to censure Hoover when he thought his dissent was justified.

Early in 1931 the Senatorial minority approved of relief measures for the drought-afflicted areas of the country. The majority, influenced by The White House, sought to modify the appropriations. "The President of the United States," said Glass, "ventures to translate the proposal of the Senate, involving the kindliest attribute with which God ever graced human nature, into a bitterly disparaging epithet, applied to Senators through the medium of the public press. He calls governmental benefaction a socialistic 'dole.' I stand here to controvert any such shocking misconception. . .

"I happened to be Secretary of the Treasury in January, 1919, when the appeal came from the American mission abroad, signed by Mr. Hoover, imploring this Government to take a foremost part with the other nations in relieving the starving populations of Europe. Mr. Hoover was importunate ; President Wilson, then in France, was peremptory, and I myself had occasion to come to the Capitol in an endeavor to abate opposition, in the attempt to persuade Congress to act promptly and to the fullest extent. We appropriated $100,000,000 to be expended through the agency of Mr. Hoover to relieve the hungry and destitute of Europe. . .

"I recall to his credit that as chairman of the American commission abroad, notwithstanding the fact that the Congress in terms prohibited the use of one dollar of this $100,000,000 in the central empires of Europe or in enemy nations, Mr. Hoover sent ton after ton of American food and supplies into Germany, saying that when women and children were suffering for food, he would recognize no line of demarcation and would feed the enemy population as well as others.

"Were any of these European sufferers 'degraded' by accepting the benefaction of the American people? Then, why should American men and women and children experience any degree of shame when, afflicted in this manner, they accept from the Treasury of the United States assistance to which they are richly entitled?"

Glass then pointed his attack at Arthur M. Hyde, the "kindly soul who presides over the Agricultural Department." "This compromise," he said, "graciously permits the Secretary to feed cows. That is all – as if the Secretary of Agriculture should not have known in the first instance that it was necessary to feed cows in order to feed babies. . . We are going to 'rehabilitate' the farms. Let us strike out 'rehabilitation' and put in its place the simple, well-understood English word 'food.'

"It is a farce. At least, it would be a farce were it not a tragedy."

This time Hyde escaped easily; on January 26, 1932, Glass was addressing the Senate:

"Mr. President, some days ago I had occasion in the Senate to characterize a statement made by the Secretary of Agriculture charging the late President Wilson and two of his Secretaries of the Treasury with making enormous loans to foreign governments after the termination of the war and 'without the legal right to do so.' I termed this accusation a 'malicious fabrication.' In a statement given to the press Secretary Hyde appears to imagine that he has acquitted himself of my imputation and established the truth of his wretched misrepresentation. He has done nothing of the kind."

Glass went on to point out that Hyde had been taken in by the deductions of a clerk who prepared "an irresponsible paper" quite at variance with the historical facts and the law. Producing document after document to prove his points he concluded in sardonic tones by referring to a letter written by the English playwright, Henry Arthur Jones, to H. G. Wells. In this letter Jones, in criticizing Wells, told of having a long and futile argument with an excessively dull person.

"I produced more facts, more evidence, more arguments," wrote Jones. "He merely vociferated – the round head waggled and shook with obstinate denial of fact and argument – I paused for a moment and looked at that round waggling head – by a sudden illumination I became aware that it was not a head at all, but a turnip, a veritable turnip placed on the top of his neck and shoulders.

". . . After a shock of surprise which took away my breath, I rushed out of the room. I had wasted a good hour arguing with a turnip. . ." Glass affixed his own postscript to the Jones letter by adding, "As old Bishop John Early, of Virginia, used to say, the Senate 'may note the phraseology and mark the application.' "

Meanwhile, in the spring of 1931, Glass began writing his proposed banking reform bill.

He talked it over with his subcommittee and the members were quite in agreement that much more severe restrictions should be written to curb the use of Federal Reserve funds for speculative purposes. Hearings were started to which all interested parties were invited to give their views.

By the time these meetings were ended Glass' course was pretty well charted ; and he began putting the finishing touches on the first draft of his bill, of which these were some of the principal features :

1 – To provide the Federal Reserve Board with greater con-

trol over speculative credit by giving it power to impose penalties, one penalty being to suspend credit facilities of the System to any member bank which ignored official warnings against increasing outstanding collateral loans while obtaining 15-day advances from a Federal Reserve Bank on its promissory note.

2 – Security affiliates of banks were to be brought under strict supervision by the Federal Reserve Board ; and it was required that they be completely divorced within three years.

3 – To keep open market operations under control, and under the close supervision of the Federal Reserve Board, it was to be required that a Federal Open Market Committee consisting of one member from each of the twelve Federal Reserve districts be appointed.

4 – The bill eliminated the Secretary of the Treasury as ex-officio member of the board thus removing the board from Treasury influences in its policies.

5 – To safeguard the System from foreign banking interests, it required that all such relationships be brought under the board's supervision.

6 – To give further protection to depositors, branch banking was encouraged. It provided that national banks with a minimum capital of $500,000 should be permitted to operate branches within the states and regardless of state laws ; and, in exceptional cases, state lines could be crossed, providing a branch was within fifty miles of the parent institution.

7 – Because inadequate capital was found to be the cause for many failures minimum requirements for capital of banks particularly in smaller communities were raised on a graduating scale based on population. Increased reserves were also required by these smaller institutions.

8 – A Federal liquidating corporation was to be formed, the capital of which would be supplied by an appropriation from

the Treasury and from assessments against member banks as well as Federal Reserve Banks surpluses. This capital was to be used in purchasing the assets of closed member banks, thus speeding up payments to depositors.

The bill was introduced into the Senate on January 22, 1932; Glass, the Congress and the Administration were immediately flooded by protests. Five days later it was returned to the subcommittee for revision. On March 18, it was again before the Senate. Once more it was bombarded with protests; once more it was returned to the subcommittee. On April 9, it came before the Senate for a third time; and, on April 27, it became "privileged business." The opposition continued to assail it, maintaining it was too deflationary, with the result that on June 16, the Senate removed it from the calendar.

Meanwhile, in November 1931, Glass discussed with President Hoover the suggestion that all banks engaged in interstate commerce be compelled to join the Federal Reserve System. He wanted a legal opinion as to whether commercial banking was interstate commerce. Hoover referred the matter to the Attorney General; and an informal opinion, later forwarded confidentially by the President to Glass, was in the negative.

In May of the following year letters of protest and denial passed between Attorney General William D. Mitchell and Glass. Newspapers reported the Senator, in a Senate speech, as charging an opinion by former Solicitor General Frederick W. Lebmann declaring banking affiliates absolutely illegal had been suppressed by the Attorney General of the Taft Administration and by a later Democratic Attorney General.

That twenty-year-old opinion, Glass was quoted as saying, was "as good law now" as when rendered. And concerning the suppression: ". . . few things have ever happened in this country that better illustrate the power and blandishments of inordinate wealth. . . The institutions declared to be engaged in illicit practices were perhaps the greatest contributors to this riot of credit and inflation, with the result that the country is now almost in an irreparable condition."

Mitchell protested he had supplied the opinion only for use in pending banking legislation, and not as a basis for any attack upon his predecessors in office. Glass responded that he was not responsible for newspaper reports of his Senate speeches, and suggested to the Attorney General that an examination of his actual speech would reveal he had made no such attack. The affair subsided.

And, though it has not been previously mentioned, devious controversy reminiscent of the old Federal Reserve fight flared early in 1932 against the proposed reforms, to "improve the facilities of the Federal Reserve System for the service of commerce, industry and agriculture, to provide means for meeting the needs of member banks in exceptional circumstances and for other purposes." The *Literary Digest* wired Glass for a written rejoinder to adverse criticism by certain influential Eastern bankers.

He telegraphed :

> The hostile comment was so entirely concerted, if not actually tutored, as to have constituted an utter waste of time. I cannot better indicate what I mean by this than to say that one of the most intelligent of the bankers who testified told me today that as soon as he reached Washington he was called on long-distance telephone from New York and explicitly told to join in the assault on every provision of the bill and to contribute his part toward the defeat of the measure. This he declined to do. . .

And of those who did obey instructions :

> Each succeeding witness repeated the comment and enmeshed himself in the misconceptions and mistakes of the preceding wit-

ness. Most of them appeared to have gone to a bankers' hostile night school in Washington.

To newspapers he stated the bill was not intended, and should never be used, for inflation of the currency. It should have the effect, he said, of assuring the 7600 member banks of the Federal Reserve System that they might proceed to use their great volume of eligible and acceptable assets by rediscounting at the Federal Reserve Banks without fear of embarrassment, since they would be free, should they exhaust their eligible assets, to use other assets not then eligible under existing law. Thus the nation's banking community would be granted a new lease of confidence and induced to stimulate commercial and industrial activities with timely and suitable loans. This should lead to expansion and mean freedom for business of all kinds without the danger of unbridled inflation.

In the spring of 1932, however, other issues were forcing their way into public attention – and, one issue, in particular. The national conventions of the two major political parties were directly ahead.

Glass went to the Democratic convention in Chicago with two purposes in mind. One was to write a plank in the platform regarding currency – a plank that would state "in plain English," as Roosevelt later said, the pledge of the party regarding the monetary policies of the new Administration, for he was completely confident his party would win in the November elections. He was aware of the presence within his party of currency tinkerers, and was bent on shutting that door before they could open it.

His other purpose was to obtain for Newton D. Baker the Democratic nomination for the Presidency of the United States.

As Secretary of War in the Cabinet of Woodrow Wilson, Baker had earned Glass' admiration and confidence. A scholar, and a statesman, Baker, in Glass' estimation, more nearly approached the Wilson ideal than any other man. Baker, through experience, he knew to be one who would grace the Presidential office, one who would never grovel before political expediency, one who would bring to The White House a mind that was too steady to be wasted by hate, but a mind so clear that the unfinished social task would be a challenge – a man who was an idealist both to the duties of public office and the morals of government.

His second choice was his fellow Senator from Virginia, Harry F. Byrd, and to Byrd he gave his first votes, waiting for the time when the tumult for another – Franklin D. Roosevelt – would subside. It never subsided, due to the political management of "Jim" Farley.

The vote of the Virginia delegation did not go to Roosevelt until the final and decisive ballot.

Regarding Roosevelt Glass had an open mind. He liked the candidate personally, although he often had wondered what lay behind the attractive personality. There had been two experiences to which he reacted with distaste. One was the practice of Roosevelt, when Governor of New York, in stopping over in Washington on his way to and from Warm Springs, Georgia, and indulging in political pow-wows with Democratic Congressmen and Senators. All his life Glass had been opposed to men seeking public office – and, to him, the Presidency, or a Presidential nomination, was one honor that should always seek the man. He was often invited to these meetings. He never went.

The other experience was when he was Secretary of the Treasury, and Roosevelt was Assistant Secretary of the Navy, under Josephus Daniels.

During the World War the Coast Guard, which had been under the jurisdiction of the Treasury Department, was shifted to the authority of Secretary Daniels. With the war ended, Glass wanted it returned because its principal duty was the prevention of smuggling and chasing rum runners, the enforcement of the Eighteenth Amendment being under the jurisdiction of the Treasury.

He discussed the matter with Secretary Daniels, but could not persuade him to relinquish control. Agreeably they decided to leave the decision to President Wilson. The following day, at the close of a Cabinet meeting, the two men remained with the President, each arguing his case. Wilson decided in favor of the Treasury Department, and issued an order returning the Coast Guard to its jurisdiction.

Two days afterward Glass received a letter from Roosevelt. The letter was a fretful communication, accusing Glass of "taking advantage" of the "absence of the Secretary of the Navy from Washington," to recapture control of the Coast Guard.

To that false accusation, Glass replied in clear language. The Assistant Secretary of the Navy made no response.

So these two experiences – one a quest for the highest office and the other a question of fact – remained in Glass' mind, even as Virginia's twenty-four votes went into the column for Roosevelt; and Virginia's standard became one of the last to mingle with the other standards marching around and around and around the immense hall in nomination of the Governor of New York.

With Roosevelt now the candidate, the Senator's two disappointments were unimportant. He had pledged his support. He would give it. He had wanted Newton D. Baker as the nominee or, if not Baker, his colleague, Senator Byrd. That wasn't to be. He accepted it.

But if the convention brought disappointment, it also brought amusement. One evening Glass' New York friend,

Samuel Kaplan, suggested relaxation, and undertook to arrange the entertainment. Unwittingly he succeeded far better than he had intended.

"Look," he said, "let's get away from the hurly-burly of politics. Let's go to a movie."

"All right," agreed Glass. "Where do you want to go?"

Kaplan had not the faintest notion. He did not know much about Chicago, but had no intention of confessing it. Recalling a newspaper advertisement he had glanced at, he suggested the Avalon Theatre, and added vaguely: "We'll take a taxi."

And so they did, Kaplan directing the driver to take them to the Avalon. The cab rolled north along Michigan Avenue. As they entered Lincoln Park and swung into the Outer Drive both men were peering about in search of the destination while Kaplan kept up a running fire of irrelevance.

"A beautiful lake front, isn't it?"

"Um," grunted Glass.

"Lovely park. Wonderful view."

Glass nodded in agreement, then asked: "Where is this Avalon?"

"Oh, just a little way," reassured Kaplan.

Northward they went, then west over to Sheridan Road, with Kaplan continuing to comment on the passing scenery. Finally Glass could stand it no longer, and he tapped on the window to ask the driver how much further they had to ride. It was forty more blocks, or nearly five miles.

Trapped, Kaplan wanted to turn back.

"Oh, no," said Glass. "You wanted to go to the Avalon, Sam, so we're going to the Avalon."

When they reached the neighborhood theatre, they saw the name of Joan Crawford over the entrance. "Nice picture, beautiful actress," commented Glass, "but I've already seen it."

"So have I," returned the crestfallen Kaplan. "Senator, I'm

sorry to have hauled you all over the city like this. Let's go back downtown."

"No, no," disagreed Glass. "You said you wanted to go to the Avalon."

They did.

With the convention over Kaplan evened the score by taking Glass for another ride.

"Look," he suggested, "let's drive back to Washington."

Glass shook his head. "No, I'm going back by train." But Kaplan persisted until, finally, the Senator asked: "How long does it take by train?"

"About eighteen hours."

"How long will it take to drive?"

"Not much longer – perhaps twenty hours."

Glass thought a moment, then agreed. Kaplan's chauffeur stowed their bags in the car and they were on their way. But as soon as they were free of the city limits Kaplan took over the wheel, with Glass in the front seat with him.

Up shot the speedometer to seventy, eighty, ninety, and on the open stretches to more than one hundred miles an hour. Onward they sped, skirting the larger towns wherever possible. Glass could not understand why they were not arrested, and fervently he hoped they would be.

As they streaked across Indiana and Ohio an occasional policeman waved them on much to Glass' annoyance. In West Virginia his hopes rose. Trailing them was a motorcycle policeman. He said nothing, but Kaplan, watching in the rear vision mirror, slowed down. The motorcycle shot past and slowed down also. Then, to Glass' consternation, the policeman looked back and waved "Come on! come on!" Kaplan pressed down his foot. Glass, who had been chuckling in anticipation, fairly shrieked: "That officer is not doing his duty."

Kaplan grinned.

"You wouldn't grin if that policeman had done his duty and arrested you," fumed Glass.

"It wouldn't have made any difference," beamed Kaplan. "He couldn't have held me."

"What?"

"He couldn't have held me," repeated Kaplan. "All I would have had to do was to tell him who you were, and that it was a felony to stop a United States Senator on his way to official business in Washington."

"It's no such thing," barked Glass.

"That policeman might not have known it wasn't."

When they arrived in Washington and the car rolled to a stop, Glass, who had been doing some serious thinking, got out and with never a word walked to the front of the automobile. Then he walked to the rear. Conspicuous, both fore and aft, were his own Congressional license plates, the reasons for the solicitude of the highway police of several states. Prior to the convention, Kaplan had secretly borrowed them from the Senator's secretary in anticipation of exactly what had happened.

CHAPTER TWENTY-TWO

A Challenge Answered

Close to the Democratic candidate were advocates of currency manipulation. Men such as Henry A. Wallace, later to become Secretary of Agriculture; Professor George F. Warren of Cornell University; Senator Elmer Thomas of Oklahoma; Professor James Harvey Rogers of Yale University – these, with a number of others, seemed to have preferred proximity to Mr. Roosevelt's ear.

Republican speakers, including President Hoover, noted their presence, suspected their influence, and made political capital. To offset their accusations, the candidate repeatedly pointed out that the "democratic platform specifically declares 'we advocate a sound currency to be preserved at all hazards' and I accept that platform in every plank."

Offhand, it would seem this was sufficient assurance. It wasn't. More than one employer, and more than one labor leader, was beginning to be anxious and to wonder if there was not something more than political propaganda behind the oft-repeated Republican charges that, if elected, the Democrats would tamper with the currency.

Knowing Glass' position of integrity in the public mind, Roosevelt made frequent appeals to him through Chairman Farley to refute the charges. But, always, the doctor's orders prevailed, although from his bed at home the Senator kept close watch over the progress of the campaign.

However, there came a time.

Propped up in bed on the night of October 4, he was listening to President Hoover speaking over the radio from Des Moines. Hoover was relating some of the difficulties that confronted the Administration and, finally, his address turned into a discourse of "the third peril . . . that of being forced off the gold standard."

"I believe I can make it clear," he said, "why we were in danger of being forced off even with our theoretically large stocks of gold. I have told you of the enormous sums of gold and exchange drained from us by foreigners. You will realize also that our citizens who hoard Federal Reserve and some other forms of currency are now in effect hoarding gold, because under the law we must maintain 40 per cent gold reserve under such currency. Owing to the lack in the Federal Reserve System of the kind of securities required by law for the additional 60 per cent coverage of the currency, the Reserve System was forced to increase their gold reserve up to 75 per cent. Thus with $1,500,000,000 of hoarded currency there was in effect over $1,000,000,000 of gold hoarded by our citizens.

"These drains had at one moment reduced the amount of gold we could spare for the current payments to a point where the Secretary of the Treasury informed me unless we could put into effect a remedy, we could not hold to the gold standard but two weeks longer because of inability to meet the demands of foreigners and our own citizens for gold. . . In the midst of this hurricane the Republican Administration kept a cool head and rejected every counsel of weakness and cowardice. . ."

Inasmuch as Democrats, including himself, had worked with the President in averting the disaster, Glass thought this transfer of all "strength and courage" to the Republicans and, by inference, allocation of all "weakness and cowardice" to the Democrats too big a dose of political speech-making to swallow.

Swinging his legs out of bed, he called for his pants. In

turn, his nurse called for the doctor. Hurrying into the room the medico found the nurse trying to convince the Senator he should stay in bed ; and the Senator just as convincingly arguing he was going to get out. With no little diplomacy the doctor persuaded him to remain where he was, swallow Hoover's bitter political medicine and let Nature handle the whole proposition.

A little more than three weeks later he was again listening to the radio and again to Hoover, this time talking from Indianapolis.

"Tampering with the currency has been a perennial policy of the Democratic Party," declared the President. "The Republican Party has had to repel that policy before now. In the absence of any declaration by the Democratic candidate on this subject for seven weeks of his campaign no delayed promise now can effectually disavow that policy. The taint of it is firmly embedded in the Democratic Party. The dangers of it are embedded in this election. . ."

The challenge rang in his ears, while before his eyes was a newspaper containing an excerpt from a speech by Secretary of War Patrick Hurley in which it was charged "Should the Democratic Party succeed at the November election the United States will be driven off the gold standard."

This time no amount of persuasion could influence him. Reaching for a telephone, he called Democratic National Headquarters to inform it he was willing to make a reply to the President, and added "Please notify Governor Roosevelt accordingly." Next he got his secretary on the wire, instructing him to put together certain needed material without the slightest delay.

With these preliminaries out of the way, he immediately went to Washington and dictated his proposed speech. He finished it at two sittings without altering a sentence. By this time he had received word that "Governor Roosevelt would be delighted to have him speak," and that arrangements had been completed for a broadcast over a nation-wide network. A full hour was set aside for him.

He had an argument with his physician. "I forbid it," declared the doctor. Glass pleaded and stormed until, at last, the doctor wearily acquiesced :

"Well, go ahead. If it means that much to you you're probably better off talking over the air than staying here talking to yourself."

With Dr. Cary Grayson accompanying him he went to the broadcasting station on the evening of November 1 to deliver one of the most damaging blows the Republican cause received during the entire campaign.

He said : *

"Anybody who says this country was within two weeks of being 'driven off the gold standard,' actually impeaches the official integrity of the President of the United States and of the Secretary of the Treasury. The latter official, from January 1, 1932 to June 30, 1932, with the approval of the President, sold to the banks and private investors in the United States $3,709,213,450 of Treasury notes and certificates of indebtedness, redeemable in gold at the Treasury. Of this amount $2,014,224,050 represented one-year certificates, and $1,034,152,000 were redeemable in ninety days from issue.

"If the President and the Secretary of the Treasury had knowledge of the fact that this country was faced with imminent disaster by being 'driven off the gold standard in two weeks,' and failed so to advise the banks and private investors who purchased nearly four billions of dollars of these federal securities they were guilty of amazing dishonesty ; they were cheating the investing public ; and could not even appropriate

* See appendix for full speech

to themselves the solace of future oblivion, because their names would have been remembered in terms of anathema for a century to come.

"Despite this suggested infamy, the authentic figures and facts show that no such situation existed as that which politicians have conjured up for discreditable campaign purposes in order to exaggerate the executive powers of a candidate for the Presidency. The figures are conclusive; and persons who repeat this campaign hoax do not seem to realize that they are impeaching the common honesty of the President of the United States and the Secretary of the Treasury.

". . . In this connection, the newspapers report that Secretary Hurley, of the War Department, has openly proclaimed from the public rostrum that should the Democratic Party succeed at the November election 'the United States will be driven off the gold standard.' For the sake of decency, it must be hoped that Mr. Hurley did not say that. If he did say it he was guilty of a dangerous calumny. If he said it, he is totally unfit for official responsibility, and the President should have booted him out of office before breakfast time of the following day. Indecency, even in a political campaign, has its limitations. This alleged declaration, if made . . . was not far short of treason to the country.

". . . Franklin D. Roosevelt as Governor of one of the largest states of the Union, clean of body and clear of mind, dealing promptly with almost insuperable difficulties, is amply prepared for the tremendous task of reconstruction which will face the next Federal administration. He will not go to sleep at his post. The Congressional contacts and understanding and plain common sense of John Garner preeminently equip him for helpful service in promoting the legislative program of a Democratic administration.

"We shall not make impossible promises and then proceed

to break them. We shall not employ Lydia Pinkham political pills nor psychological poultices as a cure for the maladies of the country. We shall not rely upon transient devices and mere temporary remedies for serious situations ; but holding fast to sound Jeffersonian principles and applying tested orthodox processes, we shall hope to rescue the government and the country from the unendurable confusion and distress into which the Republican maladministration has thrust us. So serious is the situation that only by the help of Almighty God can this be done."

The response was immediate. Before he had even finished speaking telegrams began coming into the broadcasting station, and the following day the newspapers of the country were hailing the effort as one of the greatest speaking contributions in our political history. Even Republican New England was impressed while from Republican Pennsylvania came a telegram rejoicing that "your rapier still carries its pristine lustre, and the amenities customary among gentlemen receive added honor in your employment of them." And, too, from Mr. Roosevelt this telegram :

Hyde Park, N.Y.
November 2, 1932.

Honorable Carter Glass,
Washington, D.C.
Heartiest congratulations and sincere appreciation for your wonderful speech last night. I listened to all of it and was thrilled and inspired.

Franklin D. Roosevelt.

The Republicans called upon Senator Watson, of Indiana, to answer Glass and to remind him of "a two-hour confidential conference . . . called last February . . . for the immediate enactment of legislation . . . to prevent imminent jeopardy of the gold standard in the United States."

"I well recall," continued Watson, "we had at that time

only about $350,000,000 of free gold, and that losses to foreigners and hoarders were going on at the rate of $150,000,000 a week. . ."

Glass wasted no time in giving an answer :

"The Senator suggests that I may remember a confidential conference with the President and others last February in which the President recommended legislation 'to prevent imminent jeopardy to the gold standard of the United States.' I very distinctly recall every detail of that conference, at which not one word was uttered as to the jeopardy of the gold standard in the United States. . .

"The announced purpose of the conference with the President was to discuss proposed legislative expedients to stop the alarming flood of bank failures by broadening the rediscount rate of the Federal Reserve Act. . . The President regarded the banking situation as filled with imminent peril, telling the assembled company that many of the larger banks of the country were in a desperate state and the failure of any one of them might precipitate widespread disaster. The President suggested that the Senate Sub-Committee having charge of banking legislation might be willing to lift several provisions out of the so-called Glass bill and incorporate them in an emergency bill for immediate passage. . . The 'imminent jeopardy' mentioned by Senator Watson had reference to the domestic banking situation and to the frantic withdrawal of deposits for hoarding purposes."

In his statement Glass went on to point out that "as of February 1st, the amount of gold held by the Federal Reserve System was $579,000,000, and the withdrawals per month were not one-third of the figure mentioned by Senator Watson. . ."

He also confronted Watson with a statement by Secretary of the Treasury Mills, on February 12 (the day following the

White House Conference) and given before the Banking and Currency Committee of the House of Representatives, in which Mills said :

"I am here as a responsible government official, supposed to give you facts, and I say to you that I am perfectly confident of our ability to meet all demands that may be made upon us. We have on hand sufficient gold resources at home to permit us to meet all such demands."

Then the Republicans said no one could speak for Mr. Roosevelt in the matter of currency manipulation excepting Mr. Roosevelt himself. Mr. Roosevelt did speak. On November 4, from Brooklyn, he told the nation :

". . . It is worthy of note that no adequate answer has been made to the magnificent philippic of Senator Glass the other night, in which he showed how unsound this assertion was. I might add, Senator Glass made a devastating challenge that no responsible government would have sold to the country securities payable in gold if it knew the promise – yes, the covenant – embodied in these securities was as dubious as the President of the United States claims it was. Why, of course, the assertion was unsound. . .

"One of the most commonly repeated misrepresentations by Republican speakers, including the President, has been the claim that the Democratic position with regard to money has not been made sufficiently clear. The President is seeing visions of rubber dollars. But that is only part of his campaign of fear. I am not going to characterize these statements. I merely present the facts.

"The Democratic platform specifically declares, 'We advocate a sound currency to be preserved at all hazards.' That, I take it, is plain English.

"In discussing this platform on July 30, I said 'Sound money is an international necessity; not a domestic consideration for one nation alone.' In other words, I want to see sound money in all the world.

"Far up in the Northwest at Butte I repeated the pledge of the platform, saying 'Sound money must be maintained at all regards.'

"In Seattle I reaffirmed my attitude on this question. The thing has been said, therefore, in plain English three times in my speeches. It is stated without qualification in the platform and I have announced my unqualified acceptance of that platform in every plank."

From the hospital Glass listened with intense gratification. The effort he had made for his party, and for its candidate, had taken a lot out of him. But he felt well rewarded. The sincerity in Mr. Roosevelt's voice – his assurances – his pledge – his "unqualified acceptance" of the Democratic platform. . .

Carter Glass went to sleep on the night of November 4, 1932, knowing Franklin D. Roosevelt had been chosen by the people . . . and his eyes closed on thoughts of Woodrow Wilson, Thomas Jefferson, and the coming March 4 when, once more, a member of his party would stand before the Chief Justice of the Supreme Court and take his sacred oath to "uphold, protect and defend the Constitution of the United States."

For a few brief weeks after the elections, the banking situation showed continued improvement. The Federal Reserve Board figures of January 1, 1933, as compared with the spring of 1932, showed these gains:

Monetary gold stock (increase)	$580,000,000
Member-bank Reserve balances (increase)	500,000,000
Deposits in member banks subject to reserve (increase)	700,000,000
Deposits returned to banks from hoarding	150,000,000
Borrowings from Federal Reserve Banks (decrease)	137,000,000

In the same period the value of industrial stocks had increased by some 30 per cent, while the bond market had shown a 15 per cent improvement. Doubtless, the currency pledge of the Democratic party and the additional pledge to balance the budget had something to do with the improved feeling.

Then rumors began circulating that the President-elect was planning "some sort of devaluation, inflation or reflation of the currency." Glass heard these rumors, and placed no stock in them. Hadn't the Democratic platform specifically stated: "A sound currency to be preserved at all hazards"? Hadn't Roosevelt pledged himself "unqualifiedly" to that plank, and to every plank, in the platform?

"You're impugning the honor and integrity of the next President of the United States," he rebuked his worried friends. "I will not listen to such malicious gossip. It is nothing but hangover propaganda from a disgruntled group that has lost public confidence."

The rumors persisted.

Those who were skeptical of Roosevelt's good intentions were buying foreign securities and foreign currencies – in other words, exporting their capital. Others were buying gold bullion, and leaving it on deposit abroad. These, of course, were people with money who stood to make handsome profits if the rumors turned out to be true; and who were in no danger of loss did they turn out to be untrue.

It was apparent, in December, that the budget could not be balanced without increased taxation. Word came from The White House that Hoover was considering a sales tax. Congressional leaders, Glass among them, discussed the proposition with the result that Vice-President-elect Garner and Senator Harrison conferred with the President and worked out a plan by which some $500,000,000 in additional revenue would be procured. It would provide for a balanced budget in the first fiscal year of the new administration. They assured Hoover the legislation could be passed, and Garner told newsmen: "We must balance the budget. . . I feel we must carry out our promises."

The following day – December 28 – the President-elect denounced the plan. Garner returned to The White House to make his apologies. The fact that later a sales tax was imposed, although it was called "a processing tax," probably is beside the point. On January 4, with Garner in the Chair, the House passed a resolution requiring all loans by the Reconstruction Finance Corporation to banks and corporations, prior to July 21, 1932, to be made public. This was an extension of a previous enactment by the House which covered only loans made by the RFC after July 21, 1932.

On November 11, 1932, Glass had dropped a note to his friend R. L. Ailworth, of Eastville, Virginia:

> The victory Tuesday was almost too overwhelming to be safe. I hope Roosevelt will have the good sense to select a strong Cabinet; otherwise, he is lost. . .

Executive power was shifting from The White House to Hyde Park. Some sixty days before the inauguration the people began to ponder Roosevelt's silence regarding the rumors of tampering with the currency. And the more the people pondered, the more they listened to and the more they believed the rumors. Regaining confidence with Roosevelt's election they soon became a doubtful people, then a frightened people . . . worried over their savings . . . worried over their money. Events began running swiftly.

January, 1933. Twenty noted economists send open letter to President-elect urging that "gold standard be unflinchingly maintained." Committee for the Nation begins chorus for inflation, led by Vanderlip (banking), Bendix (airplanes), Rand (typewriters), Cord (autos), and Professor Warren (monetary theories). . . Borah plans dollar reduction. . . Europe raids American dollar . . . rumors, headlines, opinions, by-lines. . . Mark Sullivan, columnist: "Hardly any responsible Democrat believes that Mr. Roosevelt, as party leader, would encourage inflation, or that as President, he would fail to veto it." Walter Lippmann, columnist: "To suppose that he [Roosevelt] has secretly scrapped his pledges is to believe that there is no honor left in our public life. . ." Washington dispatch: "The whole question of inflation, which has been stalking the Capitol for weeks and so far has been held behind cloak room doors, boiled out on the floor of the Senate today . . . to remonetize silver . . . to devalue the gold dollar" . . . Senator Huey P. Long: "Inflate . . . Roosevelt's 'controlled currency inflation.' . . ." Henry A. Wallace: "The smart thing would be to go off the gold standard a little further than England has."

February: Senator Elmer Thomas calls on Wall Street to back inflation . . . Professor Warren explained "the compensated dollar" . . . Hoover's plea to Congress to cease publication of Reconstruction Finance Corporation's loans to banks and corporations, called by RFC Chairman Atlee Pomerene (Democrat) "the most damnable and vicious thing ever done" . . . bank crisis in Michigan . . . spreading from Michigan . . . panic. . .

March: The inaugural address. . . The *New York Times:* "It seems a pity that he [Roosevelt] let slip the opportunity to utter some assurance of the fundamental soundness and safety of our financial system so that frightened people will take hope. . ."

History, day by day.

It is difficult to say precisely when Glass began to have doubts concerning the monetary policies of the incoming Administration. He was not one of the tight-lipped few who had been taken into Roosevelt's confidence about what he planned to do, if elected.

Certain it is, however, he had no doubts during the campaign. To him a party platform meant what it said, "a covenant with the people to be faithfully kept by the party when entrusted with power." Up to January he continued to brand the persistent rumors as "malicious and inspired gossip," but with each passing day of silence after the first of January, he began to wonder, and then to worry.

In a similar situation in 1885 and in 1893, another Democratic President-elect, Grover Cleveland, had publicly avowed his intentions, thus removing apprehension, over the maintenance of gold payments. Glass wished Roosevelt would do likewise – and because the President-elect did not, the Senator made up his mind to find out, if he could, and at the first opportunity, what truth, if any, there was behind the now common talk.

CHAPTER TWENTY-THREE

The Treasury post is offered, and declined.

In the main, as Glass saw them, certain things were in combination in bringing about the hollow Paradise in which the country reveled when Hoover took office in March, 1929; and the chaos which prevailed when Roosevelt took office in March, 1933.

1 – The failure of the Coolidge Administration to take steps to put a stop to stock-market gambling; and, after Coolidge, the failure of the Hoover Administration to realize, fully and quickly enough, what was actually happening in the 1929 collapse.

2 – The action of the House of Representatives in compelling the Reconstruction Finance Corporation to make public the borrowings of banks, and of private corporations. With Senator Robinson, of Arkansas, and other Democratic leaders, Glass had tried to stop this vicious ruling.

3 – The growing public belief that the Roosevelt Administration, when in office, would devalue the dollar, and go off the gold standard; and the failure of the President-elect publicly to disclaim these rumors.

Desperately trying to break the legislative log jam that had piled up with the elections, and failing in his appeals to Roosevelt, Hoover sent word to Glass, in February, that he would like to see him.

With that summons Glass found himself in an ironical position. A Republican President whom he had assailed only a few months before was asking him for help. Also, a Republican President was seeing eye to eye with him in the importance of the Glass banking bill. Hoover wanted to know if there was not some way in which he – a President of the

United States! – could help in getting the proposed legislation enacted into law. Glass thought of other days when other Republicans had tried to sabotage his Federal Reserve Act; but this day a Republican and a Democrat saw the same thing.

They discussed the banking bill for a long time, and then Hoover outlined something that was on his mind. It was a plan by which the Reconstruction Finance Corporation could come to the aid of the banks by temporarily buying the assets of such institutions as were closed.

Glass thought that over, then asked: "Do you seriously contend that the Government has any responsibility whatsoever for the indebtedness of these closed banks?"

"From one point of view, no," answered Hoover. "From another point of view, yes." Glass listened as the President explained: "I believe the Government has a real responsibility because of publicizing loans from the Reconstruction Finance Corporation it has caused runs on these banks – runs that have resulted, directly, in the closing of the institutions. Furthermore," said Hoover, "the purchase of their assets would be but temporary, and I am confident there would be no loss to the Government. I am confident of this because I am certain in my own mind that practically all these banks are solvent."

Glass was in agreement that, for the most part, the closed banks were solvent notwithstanding their inability to meet the demands of their depositors for cash. Finally, after considerably more discussion, he suggested:

"It is possible the House might be coaxed into doing something. Supposing we use your idea as bait on the banking bill?"

It was done. The amendment excited some interest in the House of Representatives, but no action. On February 20, Hoover tried to force dislodgment of the bill by appealing to Congress:

. . . There are certain measures looking to the promotion of economic recovery which have been under consideration by the Congress and are so advanced toward completion or understanding as to seem possible of enactment during the present session. . . The enactment by the House of the general principles embodied in the Glass Banking Bill, which has already passed the Senate, will greatly contribute to re-establishing confidence. It is the first constructive step to remedy the prime weakness of our whole economic life – that is, organization of our credit system. . .

With changes, the Glass bill was passed when the new administration came into power. The delay was one of the real contributing factors in accelerating the forces speeding toward disaster.

Meanwhile, there was a great deal of speculation in the newspapers as to the make-up of the new Cabinet; and the greater part of this speculation concerned the post of Secretary of the Treasury.

James Farley, Postmaster General and Chairman of the Democratic National Committee, in his recently published book *Behind the Ballots* has written:

"One of the first moves made by the President-elect was to indicate to Senator Carter Glass, of Virginia, that he would like to have him as Secretary of the Treasury, a position the elderly Virginian had filled under President Woodrow Wilson. Glass took the offer under advisement, but before he reached a decision it became evident to the President-elect that the approaching banking and financial crisis demanded measures far more radical than were at first anticipated. Roosevelt entrusted me with the task of communicating his ideas in this respect to Senator Glass.

"Glass was courteous and kindly and expressed sympathy with the President-elect in the overwhelming burden of duties ahead. He asked me to tell F. D. of his appreciation of the thoughtfulness of letting him know the probable attitude of the new administration. However, some time later Senator Glass informed the President-elect, in a personal interview, that he would be unable to assume the grave responsibilities of the Treasury. He felt that the strain would be too much for a man of his age, but there was no doubt also that both men realized their conflicting views on financial questions would soon lead them far apart."

Farley's recital is incorrect in several important details :

1 – He was not the one instructed by the President-elect with carrying on the negotiations with Glass. Raymond Moley was the man. At no time during this period did Glass and Farley meet for any such discussions ; and if they did it is in Farley's recollection and not Glass'. Nor, in Glass' notes of that period is there mention of such a meeting. Further, one of the authors (Smith) of this biography, as Secretary to the Senator, has no record of such a conference. It would seem there would be a record of such an important matter.

2 – At no time during this period did Glass know that "measures far more radical than were first anticipated" would be needed ; and, at no time during this period did Glass have any knowledge of "his [Roosevelt's] ideas in this respect."

3 – Having no knowledge that Roosevelt intended to depart from the Democratic platform, it would have been impossible for Glass to have "realized their conflicting views on financial questions would soon lead them far apart." Throughout the campaign the Democratic candidate had repeatedly said : "It [the monetary plank] is stated without qualification in the platform and I have announced my *unqualified* acceptance." So, how could there be "conflicting views" over something already agreed upon ?

However, Raymond Moley did come to see Glass, and did discuss with him the appointment to the Cabinet post. Previously, Roosevelt had made the offer and soon afterward went on a fishing trip in southern waters with Vincent Astor, leaving Moley to continue the negotiations.

Concerned over the many rumors that the new administration was planning to experiment with the currency, Glass wanted these rumors squelched before giving a definite answer. Moley, no more than Glass, knew Roosevelt's plans, or intentions regarding money. Whatever suspicions he might have had Moley kept to himself. He quizzed Moley at close range, firing questions at him, but elicited no answers for the reason Moley could risk no answers. It would not have been proper for him to have voiced suspicions, even if he had them.

There were a number of meetings between the men, with each meeting as fruitless as the others.

On February 3, Glass handed Moley a letter he had received that day from Dr. A. W. Terrell of Lynchburg :

Feb. 2, 1933.

Dear Mr. Glass :

Touching our conversation over long distance phone, I must again advise you that a continued depletion of your nervous system by excessive overwork would inevitably prove disastrous The exudate of serum, now causing numbness in your left hand, leg and foot, would thereby be accentuated rather than abated and might lead to distressing results. You should be admonished not only by what I have said to you, but by what has happened to you. I have marvelled at your ability to endure the legislative ordeal of passing your bank bill in the Senate.

Should you assume responsibility for the tremendous problems with which you tell me the Treasury Department must immediately deal, I feel, knowing your temperament as I have for 40 years, that the work would consume your activities in the day and occupy your thought into the nights. To the plea "your country at this time needs your service," I would answer : that your country should not be willing to use your service to the point of certainly impairing your health, if not endangering your life.

I do not think it necessary for me to come to Washington or for you to come home in order to determine this matter, as far as my professional judgment may be needed to decide the case ;

hence, I feel obliged to advise you not to go to the Treasury. You must know that I reach this conclusion reluctantly, because I would like to see you thus honored and would like to see the country have the advantage of your administrative experience and your knowledge of financial problems.

Sincerely yours,
(signed) A. W. Terrell.

On February 8, he wrote Moley saying:

My dear Mr. Moley:

I am sending you the letter to the President-elect, under seal and registered, and will be obliged if you will communicate my decision to Mr. Roosevelt. You have been very kind and patient to hear my story and I derive infinite satisfaction from the fact that you seem to concur in my conclusions.

Hoping for you the best of good fortunes and happiness, believe me,

Sincerely yours
(signed) Carter Glass.

Professor Raymond Moley,
Columbia University,
New York City.

Moley met the President-elect at Miami on his return from the fishing trip. The college professor from Ohio breathed in relief as he turned over to the President-elect the sealed and registered letter which contained Glass' refusal; and with it, Dr. Terrell's communication.

The letter follows:

February 7, 1933.

My dear Franklin:

I shall never be able to tell you the measure of my appreciation of the honor which you have done me in inviting me to take the responsible post of Secretary of the Treasury in your cabinet. It grieves me to find that I am unable to requite your confidence and kindness by complying with your wish. I have very earnestly considered the matter in all its important aspects, prompted by a compelling desire to be of service to you and to the country. You may be sure it has caused me genuine distress to reach the decision indicated.

Aside from the fact that the reaction to the suggestion among my colleagues in the Senate has been positively averse to me leaving this body, the unanimity of protest from Virginia by press and representative men has been emphatic. Without any intimation from me as to my own concurring conviction, my associates in the Senate and public sentiment in Virginia unite in the judgment that I can better serve you and the country where I am than by a transfer to the Treasury. I trust you may, upon mature reflection, reach the same conclusion, keeping always uppermost in mind that I shall ever be ready to serve your administration to the full extent of my capabilities.

That you may clearly realize that I have tried hard to overcome various difficulties of an almost insuperable nature, I may state that, at the last, hoping to allay the fears of my immediate family as to the effect of the proposed transfer on my health, I sought the frank professional opinion of my regular physician. His letter I am sending to you in strictest confidence.

I am sure you will experience no difficulty in securing a Secretary of the Treasury upon whose vision, courage and strength you may confidently rely.

With fervent good wishes for you and your administration and a further expression of gratitude for your kindness, believe me

Faithfully yours,
(signed) Carter Glass.

Hon. Franklin D. Roosevelt,
Miami, Florida.

Roosevelt read it, and commented, "I will see Glass on my way north."

However, there was a great deal more to the negotiations between Roosevelt and Glass than the efforts of Professor Moley.

The offer was first tendered by the President-elect on the night of January 19 when Roosevelt stopped over in Washington on his way to Warm Springs. This meeting was brief, lasting no longer than fifteen minutes, but during it Glass repeatedly asked Roosevelt for his views on currency matters and, in reply, received no satisfactory answers. At the close of the interview Glass said he would have to think it over, explained he was not in the best of health, and would like to get in touch with his doctor for his advice. Roosevelt pressed the offer, requesting an answer the following day so "my mind will be at rest with this important Cabinet post filled."

The following day they talked again ; and once again Glass sought answers to the same questions he had asked the preceding night regarding the currency . . . and, as on the preceding night received no answers that, to him, were satisfactory. He then told the President-elect of his doctor's advice : "My doctor strongly urges me to decline the honor ; and I am just as strongly inclined to follow his advice."

To this Roosevelt, in somewhat exasperated vein, retorted : "It's your duty to your party, and to your country, to assume this post. I won't take 'no' for an answer," and went on to say that no man, by training or by experience, was so well fitted for the position.

"You make it difficult for me to decline but if you insist, you will have to give me more time," responded Glass. Roosevelt reluctantly agreed.

Upon receipt of the letter from Dr. Terrell, Glass turned his attention to the situation in Virginia. When the subject of entering the Cabinet was broached to him thoughts reached out as to a successor in the Senate should he accept. There was one man he wanted most. It was former Governor Harry F. Byrd. And so, on February 4, he wrote the following revealing letter to Byrd :

February 4, 1933.

(PERSONAL AND CONFIDENTIAL)

My dear Governor :

None of a multitude of newspaper conjectures ever disturbs me and I trust you will not permit any of them to bother you. . .

I have given very serious thought to the invitation to go to the

Treasury ; but, in strictest confidence, I have been unable to convince myself that it is the wise thing to do. Over long-distance phone my family physician, who has known me for forty years and understands the congenital impossibility for me to treat grave problems indifferently or to avert serious worry over them, advised me day before yesterday that it would certainly impair my health, if it should not endanger my life, to assume responsibility for the tremendously important problems with which the Treasury must now deal.

Aside from everything else, I am far from being convinced that, if I retain my health, I cannot be of more help to the new administration in the Senate, where, God knows, it will need friends more than at the Treasury. This seems to be, almost without exception, the considered opinion of my colleagues on both sides of the Senate chamber.

Apart from the natural desire to be of service to the country, the one thing that has made the invitation to the Treasury desirable was the certainty of being succeeded in the Senate by you. In this connection I took the precaution to ask the President-elect if there was any probability, in the event I should feel compelled to decline the Treasury portfolio, of the appointment of any other Virginian to the cabinet. You will observe that the form of this inquiry covered the talk about you as well as that about Swanson. In strictest confidence, which I know you will respect, he frankly said there was a strong probability of the appointment of the latter to the Navy. I think this will ensue, and that, therefore, the Senate will be open to you. This greatly relieves my anxiety, and makes rather certain my own action unless some unforeseen circumstances shall change my mind. This I do not think will happen.

I am glad to hear about George Peery. I think he will easily get the nomination and will make a fine governor.

Thank you for sending me the editorial from The Lexington Herald. The unanimity and generosity of the public, regardless of party division, have so touched me that I cannot, without great emotion, speak or write of this kindness.

Sincerely yours,
(signed) Carter Glass.

Hon. Harry F. Byrd,
Winchester,
Virginia.

Meanwhile, the newspapers were carrying stories from Washington – some saying "Glass has accepted" ; others saying "Glass has declined" ; and still others predicting "if Glass does decline, the result will be a general reshuffling of the Cabinet." Of Professor Moley's visits the newspapers said little, or nothing, which was not surprising, because Moley was extremely discreet in his visits. On his way north, Roosevelt telegraphed Glass to meet his train.

With Senator Bronson Cutting, of New Mexico, Glass went aboard at Washington. Almost immediately he joined the President-elect. The offer of the Treasury post was renewed. Before answering Glass tried, for a third time, to learn Roosevelt's views regarding currency matters. Failing to elicit satisfactory responses, he brought up the matter as to choice of assistants, in case he did accept. He mentioned one or two names. Roosevelt shook his head. A little more conversation, and Glass became convinced that his own views regarding assistants in the Treasury Department could not be reconciled with those of the President-elect.

For several minutes the two men sat without a word between them, Roosevelt watching the passing countryside, Glass deep in thought. Then addressing the President-elect by his first name, Glass said :

"Franklin, I have made up my mind. I appreciate . . ."

But before he could conclude the sentence, Roosevelt interrupted to again declare he would not take "no" for an answer.

"In that case, then the best answer I can make is that I will give the offer my prayerful consideration," returned Glass.

That ended the conversation. With Cutting, Glass left the train at Baltimore.

Through the following three days all manner of pressure was put on the Virginian to accept the post. At the end of that time he telephoned the President-elect, and gave a final "no."

Then came the problem of wording a public statement. Convinced though he was that the many rumors were correct, still he did not want to give his own thoughts for fear their publication would add to the damage already done. His statement released to the newspapers on February 20, read :

"There are being printed so many speculative reports concerning my declination of the post of Secretary of the Treasury and the reasons thereof that I think it both pertinent and desirable that I should make an authoritative statement on the subject. I have not refused the transfer from the Senate to the Treasury on account of my age or the state of my health.

"All reasonable persons should agree that if I am too old for the Treasury post, I am too old to remain in the Senate, and that my health could not more certainly be impaired in the contemplative post of the one place than in the active and tempestuous duties of the other.

"Most important is the mischievous report that I declined the Treasury on account of differences with the President-elect on fundamental economic issues. This is not so. The simple fact is that I prefer to remain in the Senate because nobody has shaken my conviction that I can be of more usefulness there to the country and to the incoming administration than at the Treasury. This conviction, urged to President-elect Roosevelt at the outset, has persisted to the end and prompted my final answer. It was confirmed by the unanimity of expression in the Senate and in Virginia. I deeply regret that I could reach no different conclusion."

Glass phrased and rephrased one sentence again and again before he had it precisely as he wanted it. That was the sentence : "Most important is the mischievous report that I declined the Treasury on account of differences with the President-elect on fundamental economic issues." In that sentence, Glass told the literal, if diplomatic, truth. There were no differences between the President-elect and himself because, as has been seen, there were no discussions regarding "fundamental economic issues."

CHAPTER TWENTY-FOUR

"I have not deserted anybody, or any party, in opposing this bill."

With Glass' definite refusal of the Treasury post, Roosevelt named William H. Woodin. The appointment was intended as encouragement to business. Woodin, as President of the American Car & Foundry Company, was known as a good executive, honest and able. With his appointment, Woodin was commissioned by the President-elect to represent him in whatever meetings were requested by the Secretary of the Treasury, Ogden L. Mills. Woodin's instructions, judging by what Mills reported to The White House, were "not to agree to anything," on the theory that "not being in power the incoming administration is without responsibility."

With less than two days remaining before the inauguration, Hoover sent for Glass and Senator Joseph Robinson, Majority Leader of the Senate. Hoover, Glass and Robinson discussed possible steps that, even at this late date, might be taken to allay the panic. They talked of the possibility of getting the Glass Banking Bill through the House. Hoover suggested this could be done in a few hours – "and it would be of paramount help if the Democratic majority would agree."

He pointed out if the bill were passed by the House without debate, it could go to conference and all that would be necessary then for its quick ratification would be the agreement of the Senate to a conference report, and the Presidential signature.

"For my part I will promise that signature without the slightest delay," he said.

Neither Glass, nor Robinson, could make promises.

"I regret to tell you, Mr. President," said Robinson, "that as much as Senator Glass and myself desire to co-operate in restoring confidence, it is hopeless to try to do something without the approval of Mr. Roosevelt."

Their search extended to proposals for the issuance of clearing-house script, Federal government control of withdrawals from banks, and other expedient measures. When the long conference ended nothing feasible had been proposed because, as Robinson again said:

"In the little time remaining before his inauguration, I do not believe the President-elect will agree to any steps whatsoever – and, without his consent – " The Senator expressively shrugged his shoulders.

The following night a telephone rang in a room in the Mayflower Hotel. It was 11:30 o'clock. In the room was the man who within a few hours would become President of the United States. A secretary answered, turned and with one hand cupped over the transmitter, said:

"Mr. Hoover is calling."

Roosevelt picked up the telephone, listened, and replied:

"I understand, Mr. President. Senator Glass is here now. We are discussing the banking situation. . . No, he does not think it is necessary to close the banks – my own opinion is the governors of the various states can take care of the bank closings wherever it is necessary. . . No, I prefer that you issue no proclamations of this nature."

The conversation ended, and Roosevelt turned to Glass.

"The Federal Reserve Board telephoned The White House this afternoon with a request that a proclamation be issued tomorrow morning, closing all banks before they could open."

"What did Mr. Hoover say to this request?"

"He told me he told the Federal Reserve Board he did not think such a step was necessary. Thinks most of the banks that are still open are solvent. I told him, as you heard me say, that you thought the same way."

Glass grunted.

"This is the second time the Federal Reserve Board has made that same request within the last three days."

"Yes, I know."

"The previous time I sent Woodin to Mills to tell him I would not give my approval to such a proclamation."

"I see. What are you planning to do?" asked Glass.

"Planning to close them, of course," answered Roosevelt.

"You will have no authority to do that, no authority to issue any such proclamation," protested Glass. "It is highly questionable in my mind if you will even have the authority to close national banks – and there is no question, at all, that you, even as President, will lack the authority to close banks chartered by the states."

"I will have that authority," argued Roosevelt. "Under the Enemy Trading Act, passed during the World War and never rescinded by Congress, I, as President, will have the authority to issue such an emergency proclamation 'for the purpose,' as the Act says, 'of limiting the use of coin and currency to necessary purposes.' "

"It is my understanding that President Hoover explored that avenue a year or two ago – and again during recent days," said Glass. "Likewise, it is my understanding that the Attorney General informed him that it was highly questionable if, even under this act, though it has never been rescinded by Congress, the President has any such authority. Highly questionable because the likelihood is the act was dead with the signing of the Peace Treaty, if not before."

"My advice is precisely the opposite."

"Then you've got some expedient advice," returned Glass.

"I am not a lawyer, but it is my understanding that the Attorney General advised Mr. Hoover that even if Congress ratified such a proclamation, such an action would probably be deemed unconstitutional by the courts. The point he made, and I think it a proper point, is that by such a proclamation the President would be unwarrantedly closing solvent banks. If all the banks were known to be insolvent – well, that might be a different matter ; but, even then, I am sure such a proclamation could not legally include banks chartered by the states."

"Nevertheless," declared Roosevelt, "I am going to issue such a proclamation."

Glass left the Roosevelt suite that night, dreading what this portent of the future seemed to him to mean.

The next day Franklin Delano Roosevelt was inaugurated President of the United States.

At eleven o'clock, the following night, without benefit of Congress, he issued a proclamation, the main points of which were :

(1) A national bank holiday from March 6 to March 9, inclusive.

(2) An embargo on the withdrawal of gold and silver for export or domestic use during this period except with permission of the Secretary of the Treasury.

(3) The issuance of Clearing House certificates or other evidence of claims against the assets of banking institutions to permit business to carry on.

(4) Authorization to banking institutions under regulations of the Secretary of the Treasury to receive new deposits and make them subject to withdrawal on demand without restrictions or limitations.

Surrounding the President were advisers who had never come to grips with the realities of a nation's currency and a nation's credit ; in the Congress, which had been called into emergency session as of noon, March 9, were many who in their hurry to harvest votes had cultivated within themselves little knowledge of the problem, and no restraint for their public acts. These things, too, Glass knew.

The 73rd Congress convened at noon on March 9; before it was a message from the President:

> Our first task is to reopen all sound banks. . .
>
> In order that the first objective . . . may be accomplished, I ask of the Congress the immediate enactment of legislation giving to the executive branch of the Government control over banks for the protection of depositors; authority forthwith to open such banks as have already been ascertained to be in sound condition and other such banks as rapidly as possible; and authority to reorganize such banks and reopen such banks as may be found to require organization to put them on a sound basis.
>
> I ask amendments to the Federal Reserve Act to provide for such additional currency, adequately secured, as it may become necessary to issue. . .

Convinced though he was there had been no need for closing the banks and certain, too, the President was without constitutional authority for his act, those convictions were lost causes. The thing to do now was to get the banks open. Glass had spent two sleepless nights in efforts to restore a semblance of order to the situation so precipitously expanded. He had been at The White House a great deal, and when he was not there he was in conference with other Senators in his office, and in his hotel room. So when the Emergency Banking Bill came before the Congress he was familiar with its contents, and despite his misgivings, was co-operating.

Addressing the Senate he said: "Congress is dealing in an unprecedented way with an extraordinary and desperate situation in the country.

"Under the proclamation of the President and of the Governors of many of the States, all the banks in the country are now closed. The proclamation of the President automatically expires at midnight tonight; and, unless some remedial legislation is enacted before that hour, we will have an indescribable condition in the United States tomorrow.

"This bill undertakes to apply, in the emergency, remedial powers fixed in the President of the United States, the Secretary of the Treasury and the Comptroller of the Currency. It broadens – in a degree that is almost shocking to me – the currency and credit facilities of the Federal Reserve Banking System, and largely extends these facilities to State banks which are not members of the Federal Reserve Banking System, that have never endured one penny of the expense of the establishment of the system or of its maintenance, and do not do so today.

"This talk of closing all the State banks is based upon a total misunderstanding of the provisions of the bill. We do not close, by act or implication, a single, solitary State bank in the United States – not one. These banks are within the jurisdiction and under the authority of the respective States, and every one of them may be reopened at daybreak tomorrow by authority of the respective States.

". . . I have never known in the history of this country, except in time of war, such nonpartisan concert, such a desire upon the part of every reasonable man to cooperate and relieve the situation. At The White House last night we had assembled there the leading representatives of both political parties in both Houses of Congress. With one voice they agreed, almost if not without qualification, in saying that they would unite to enact this legislation before midnight tonight, and that if there might be discovered in it any difficulties, they should be remedied later. But let us do today what will result in the opening tomorrow or within the next few days of 5000 member banks of the Federal Reserve System, which banks in turn will give out their facilities in an indirect way to their correspondent non-member State banks and thus help the whole banking situation in the country.

"There are provisions in the bill to which in ordinary times I would not dream of subscribing, but we have a situation that invites the patriotic cooperation and aid of every man who has any regard for his country and for its public interests. I appeal to you, Senators, not to load it down with amendments. Let us accept the bill, almost, if not unanimously, as passed by the House of Representatives, and not alter it and have to go into controversial conference that might take us beyond the time when aid is imperatively needed."

In response to questions from the floor of the Senate, Glass promised if the legislation was passed that "the banks would be opened the following day."

The bill was ratified within seven and one-half hours after Congress went into session. The vote was 73 to 7. Before the day was over, it carried the signature of the President, making it law.

March 10, 1933, fell on Friday. The banks were not open. March 11, 1933, was Saturday. The banks were not open.

And on March 11, in the Senate, Glass was called to task because "the legislation was rushed through as a result of statements made by those who were charged with knowledge that it would permit the banks to open the next morning."

Answering, Glass said: "I simply want to say that when I made the statement just quoted it was as explicit as I felt authorized to make. I had definite information from the Treasury that the banks would open the following day, else I should not have made that statement."

On the same day, Saturday, a Presidential statement was issued. It announced "a definite program consisting of successive steps by which banks throughout the country will be opened progressively on Monday, Tuesday and Wednesday mornings."

Roosevelt acted, presumably, on the theory (as he had written Hoover on March 1) "that the real trouble is that on present values very few financial institutions anywhere in the country are actually able to pay off their deposits in full, and the knowledge of this fact is widely held." In his proclamation, Roosevelt also declared no banks would be permitted to reopen until they were proved to be solvent. On Wednesday, March 15, when "the successive steps" had been taken, it was discovered that banks holding 92 per cent of the nation's deposits were reopened, proving they were solvent when closed. The constitutionality of the proclamation was never put to the test of the courts.

It was during the debates on the banking situation that Huey Long felt the full lash of Glass' vocabulary.

Long had been grieving over his submergence in the rush of events, and had been advised he could recapture newspaper headlines by "picking on Carter Glass." He thought the advice good, and followed it by nipping at the Virginian with interrupting jibes and sarcastic references to "our financial prophet." To the comments Glass, at first, paid no attention. He considered Long "a demagogic screech owl from the swamps of Louisiana rather than the Kingfish of its bayous," and, as such, beneath his notice as well as his contempt.

But when through day after day of momentous debate, Long persisted in his favorite annoyance of wandering over to Glass' desk, to breathe his long-winded outrecuidances down the back of the Virginian's neck, anger began to smolder. The time came when Glass served notice on the Louisianan, in a few terse words:

"The Senator from Louisiana has such ignorance of the

whole problem and such a lack of appreciation of things that he wants the President of the United States to cover 14,000 state banks into the Federal Reserve System without knowing a thing in the world about them."

Long failed to heed this rebuke, and continued his sputtering fire of financial argument, interlarding it with increasingly frequent personal observations until, finally, Glass' deadly little figure emerged from its aloofness. Walking over to where Long was sitting, Glass leaned over. . .

Twisting and turning in the hot frying pan of words, the Kingfish finally buried his head in his arms, hands over his ears to shut out the scorching fire. But Glass was determined he would hear. He moved closer and delivered a final passage. What he said was only for Long to hear. Long did hear. An instant later, with his hands still tightly clamped against his ears, he was running in a lumbering gait off the Senate floor, and to the protection of the cloak room.

His voice was scarce heard above the Senate floor as he began to speak. A few minutes before he had walked in slowly to take his accustomed seat. He sat there, eyes lowered. Around him other Senators laughed and joked while from crowded galleries came the murmur of voices, scuffling feet, smothered coughs. It was Thursday, April 27, 1933, the day of final debate on the measure creating the Agricultural Adjustment Act establishing the Farm Credit Association and authorizing the President to devalue the gold content of the dollar.

His thoughts went back to that night just a few months before when, in referring to Hoover's statement that the United States was "within two weeks of going off the gold standard," Roosevelt had charged "no responsible government would have sold to the country securities payable in gold if it knew the promise – yes, the covenant – embodied in those securities was dubious. . ."

Yet, a week after assuming authority, his party and his President had sold $800,000,000 in securities of the United States Government, payable in "United States coin of the present value."

The words kept repeating themselves as he sat, waiting . . . "no responsible government would have sold . . . if it knew the promise . . . embodied in those securities . . . was dubious" . . . and his party, and his President, had done that – all the while aware that the $800,000,000 which the people subscribed, in good faith, would not be redeemed as the contract with these same people said it would.

Up to now hope had flattered him into believing his party would not dishonor itself . . . and his President would not dishonor himself. "I have not deserted anybody, or any party, in opposing the bill." This sentence kept running through his mind ; and he was to say it. In his mind, too, were his visits to the White House . . . pleading with the President that the act was unnecessary and indefensible – but the President, though listening, would not believe . . . and those who surrounded the President had even come to him with their persuasions. He thought of them contemptuously and personally – "you play the spaniel, and think with the wagging of your tongue. . ."

All his public life, in serving his people, he had given careful study to these questions of currency and banking . . . "today my lessons confront me" . . . "today I must be true or false, honest or cunning, faithful or unfaithful" . . . he thought of Senator Lucius Q. C. Lamarr, of Mississippi, and of what Lamarr had said, and how Lamarr had voted on the silver question in this very chamber nearly fifty years before. . . "I will vote against this bill" . . . "my reasons for my vote shall be given to my people. . ."

And now, the Senate was in order. The senior Senator was on his feet:

"Mr. President, it has been my desire to make a somewhat complete exposition of the pending bill in order that I might indicate to the Senate and to the country precisely why I feel impelled to vote against it. I find myself physically unable to do that, however; but I cannot refrain from briefly indicating my objection to the measure.

"The newspapers of yesterday and today have stated that the senior Senator from Virginia has created a sensation by disagreeing with the President. The implication is, of course, that any Senator who now preserves his intellectual integrity and consistently maintains the views which he has privately and publicly expressed for many years is creating a sensation. I wrote with my own hand that provision of the national Democratic platform which declared for 'a sound currency to be preserved at all hazards.'

"I was unable because of illness to make more than one speech during the entire Presidential campaign. In that one speech, with all the righteous indignation that I could summon and in terms, perhaps, of some bitterness, I reproached the then President of the United States and the Secretary of the Treasury for saying that this country was within two weeks of going off the gold standard. The reaction to that speech – and I do not say it in a boastful way – was that I now have bound in excess of 5000 telegrams and letters, from people mostly strangers to me, commending that utterance. The first telegram in the first bound volume is one from Franklin D. Roosevelt, now President of the United States, who said the speech was to him an inspiration. In his public utterances at Brooklyn and at other places he textually commended that part of the speech which so bitterly criticized his political adversary and competitor for suggesting that the country was in imminent danger of going off the gold standard.

"This simple recital will indicate that I have not deserted anybody or any party in opposing the bill. I am simply consistently maintaining an attitude of earnest conviction on public questions, which is more important to me than the favor of party or potentate.

"I object to the first section of the bill because, as I said yesterday, it degrades the Federal Reserve Bank System into a servile agency of the Treasury Department. It was not instituted for that purpose. By law we took the reserve funds of the national banking associations of the United States out of the money centers, rescued them from the hands of the stock gamblers, and impounded them in regional Federal Reserve banks for the avowed use of commerce and industry and agriculture. Giving the Federal Reserve Board the right to define eligible paper, within certain limitations, we expressly denied to it the right to comprehend in its definition those who were engaged in stock gambling and speculation ; and we set up this system, not as an adjunct to the Treasury Department – which has used it as a doormat – but to respond to the requirements of the tradesmen and of the industry and of the agricultural interest of this country, the agricultural interest being given precedence in the maturity of its paper. The first section of this amendment transforms it from a system of that kind into a mere agency of the Treasury Department, to be dominated by the Secretary of the Treasury, and to be used, not for business purposes but to enable the Government to float its term and time indebtedness.

"Today, the Federal Reserve System has a gold supply on the 40-per cent reserve basis that would enable it to expand its credits nearly four billions of dollars ! It has choked its portfolios with nearly two billions of dollars of Government bonds, practically by direction of the Secretary of the Treasury and the board here, not a dollar of which is required in its business. It did that in a financial adventure upon the principle of the Representative Goldsborough bill, which assumed that by an inflation of the currency the commodity prices of this country would be increased. It has today every dollar of those bonds, without any use. It cannot dispose of them without utterly demoralizing the entire bond market of the United States ; and yet here we have a proposition to accentuate that disastrous condition, and further to imperil the Reserve System, by adding three billions of dollars more of United States bonds to its portfolios !

"What does that mean to the business interests of the country ? It means that just in that measure the Federal Reserve banks of the United States will be unable to accommodate their member banks, and just in that measure their member banks will be unable to accommodate trade. That is what it means. It does not mean inflation ; it means deflation of business and all that was accomplished in that transaction, I may say to the limited credit of the Federal Reserve Board and banks, was to release nearly $2,000,000,000 of reserve indebtedness of the member banks to the Federal Reserve banks, with the vain idea that the member banks thereupon would release credits to business, which they did not do and are not doing ; and there is nothing in this bill that compels them to do it, and there is nothing in any law that can compel member banks to loan the deposits of their depositors to anybody, for any purpose.

"I think the first section of the amendment is vicious. The authors and proponents of it thought it was ineffective. They did not dare make it imperative, because it would have been confiscation and unconstitutional. They made it permissive ;

and the distinguished Senator from Idaho [Sen. Borah] thinks that means impairment. If he could know as I know the influences at work that have applied themselves to the activities of the Federal Reserve Board and banks, he would know that it means $3,000,000,000 more of United States securities in the portfolios of the Federal Reserve banks, and an almost literal paralysis of the facilities of those institutions to accommodate trade.

"Very likely I shall surprise some of my colleagues by the statement that the least objectionable feature of the amendment is the so-called 'greenback feature.' It is, perhaps, the only feature of the amendment that will get any so-called 'money' in circulation above that now in circulation. It means simply to transform time obligations of the United States bearing no interest; and those who hold to the gold standard have said to us that it would wipe out every dollar of the reserve gold in the United States Treasury overnight – and it would if people should demand redemption. Experience over a long period of years, however, has determined that even less than four per cent is required to meet the redemption bonds in ordinary times, unless people should be unpatriotic enough to raid their own treasury; and this feature of the amendment provides a four-per cent redemption fund for the retirement of those greenbacks.

"While I do not advocate that section of the Amendment, I again say it is the most defensible provision of the amendment. I do not advocate it primarily because the Federal Reserve System is now, with its gold reserve, prepared to expand to the extent of a billion dollars more than the proposed $3,000,000,000 in greenbacks. Because business is not being transacted it does not expand; and because confidence has not yet been restored, it does not expand; and are we doing anything to restore confidence?

"Why, we have literally destroyed the mortgage-bond market of this country. The Federal land banks, with all the millions of assistance the Government has given them, cannot sell their tax-exempt bonds today – not to save their lives. There is no market for them. We have destroyed the mortgage-bond market."

The sharp rap of a gavel broke in on the Virginian's words, as from the chair Vice-President Garner was saying: "The Senator's time on the amendment has expired."

Wearily Glass turned his eyes toward his audience, then his voice went on, this time stronger:

"I will take the balance of my time on the bill.

"We are proceeding upon the assumption that nobody hereafter will desire credit; that farmers hereafter will not want credit, or need it, because we are destroying credit, and largely have done so. No man outside of a lunatic asylum will loan his money today on farm mortgages, because we have destroyed the market for farm mortgages, and for almost all types of mortgages.

"I cannot in any circumstances, painful as it is to me to differ from the occupant of the White House and from my party colleagues, support the second section of this amendment, relating to the devaluation of the gold dollar.

"England went off the gold standard because she was compelled to do so, and not from choice. She had less than a million dollars in gold left after paying her indebtedness to the United States. Of course she went off the gold standard; and her going off has not resulted in increasing the prices of commodities. There was a temporary flurry then, as there has been in this country now; but the inevitable reaction came.

"Why are we going off the gold standard? With nearly 40 per cent of the entire gold supply of the world, why are we going off the gold standard? With all the earmarked gold, with all of the securities of ours that they hold, foreign governments could withdraw in total less than $700,000,000 of our gold, which would leave us an ample fund of gold in the extremest case to maintain gold payments both abroad and at home.

"To me, the suggestion that we may revalue the gold dollar fifty per cent means national repudiation. To me, it means dishonor. In my conception of it, it is immoral. All the legalistic arguments which the lawyers of the Senate, men of eminent ability and refinement, may make here or have made here have not dislodged from my mind the irrevocable conviction that it is immoral, and that it means not only a contravention of my party's platform in that respect but of the promises of party spokesmen during the campaign.

"Mr. President, there was never any necessity for a gold embargo. There is no necessity for making statutory criminals of citizens of the United States who may please to take property in the shape of gold or currency out of banks and use it for their own purposes as they may please.

"As I remarked to the Senator from Pennsylvania the other day, we have gone beyond the cruel extremities of the French when they made it a capital crime, punishable at the guillotine, for any tradesman or individual citizen of the realm to discriminate in favor of gold and against their printing-press currency. We have gone beyond that. We have said that no man may have his gold, under penalty of ten years in the penitentiary or $10,000 fine.

"An expansion of the currency? Federal Reserve notes outstanding today exceed by nearly $3,000,000,000 the outstanding Federal Reserve notes in 1929, in those days of prosperity on paper, prosperity in the orgies of the stock gamblers who have ruined this country. Yet we have not been willing to pass a bank bill in the Congress of the United States designed and effectively framed to avert a repetition of that sort of thing. If there were need to go off the gold standard, very well, I would say let us go off the gold standard ; but there has been no need for that. If there were need for currency expansion, I would say let us expand, though I fail to comprehend how much better off one is with $2 which will purchase no more than the dollar which he had yesterday.

"The history of inflation has been recited. Bacon, the wisest philosopher since Christ, the author of the inductive system, from which we have drawn all of our inventions, valued experience. Edmund Burke, the greatest rhetorician of all times, was logician enough to magnify experience. Patrick Henry, the greatest advocate of human liberty, said that his feet were lighted by the lamp of experience. Yet here today we are flying right in the face of human experience, rejecting it all.

"My colleagues talk about serving the public. What public? The men who work for a wage, the neediest of all classes of the public, the clerks and the stenographers and the professional men, constituting, in the aggregate, half, yea, more than half, of our laboring population, will be the people to suffer under this unbridled expansion. That is what it is, because the rein is so loose that the steed will never stop until he goes over the precipice, killing his rider.

"Mr. President, I find that I must desist. I regret to disagree with my colleagues. It is painful to disagree with the ocupant of The White House, whom I love and respect, and who has exhibited unparalleled courage in trying to bring the Government within its budgetary requirements. But whether it be a commonplace or whether it be sensational, I am one Democrat who is going to vote against this inflation amendment even if every one of the 94 other Senators vote for it. I may have regrets, but shall never make apologies for acting upon my own convictions and conscience."

As he concluded, applause swept down from the crowded galleries. Senators, some with tears in their eyes, crowded about him, to reach for his hand – and to leave him, after a brief moment, to hazard their consciences in the keeping of a President's expedient will.

CHAPTER TWENTY-FIVE

"Gentlemen who persist in questioning the motives of others should not be supersensitive when . . ."

But the debates over money, the gold standard and banking continued. Congress was being importuned by telegram, by telephone, by letter, and by Administration pressure to write into law the guaranty of bank deposits by the Federal Government.

To this Glass was opposed, pointing out:

"Is there any reason why the American people should be taxed to guarantee the debts of banks, any more than they should be taxed to guarantee the debts of other institutions, including the merchants, the industries, and the mills of the country?"

His calm logic was to go unheeded.

In anticipation, however, of a request for emergency legislation affecting the currency he had permitted Lew Douglas and Dean Acheson of the Treasury Department to appear before the Banking and Currency subcommittee. Douglas and Acheson assured the committee members: ". . . the likelihood is, the Administration will remain on the gold standard as presently interpreted but, in the event of the unexpected, the President is considering three steps; and in the order named:

1 – The Federal Reserve System to buy $3,000,000,000 in Government bonds:

2 – Adoption of Senator Elmer Thomas' amendment to issue $3,000,000,000 in greenbacks; or

3 – Devalue the currency.

"The President does not anticipate any of these things will be done," agreed the Treasury representatives, "but, if he is forced to take any steps, he will take them in an orderly way, and will ask the Congress to consider the steps in the order named."

Doubtless Douglas and Acheson were authorized to give such assurances. Doubtless, too, neither Douglas nor Acheson knew the Administration was looking for money – quick money. The net balance in the General Fund, as of February 28, was $221,480,376. The gold account on the daily Treasury statement for the same day showed assets of $931,000,000 in gold coin, and $2,361,000,000 in gold bullion, or a total of $3,292,000,000. Liabilities offsetting these assets included $1,351,000,000 in gold certificates outstanding, $1,760,000 in the gold fund of the Federal Reserve Board, and $156,000,000 for the reserve against United States notes outstanding, and Treasury notes of 1890. The balance of approximately $125,000,000 consisted of gold in the general fund.

Action to get "quick money" was taken suddenly; and not by the orderly process promised through Douglas and Acheson.

One night, on summons, Glass went to The White House.

The President disclosed he was planning to capture the gold stocks owned by the Federal Reserve Banks. He explained by buying these gold stocks at the then price of $20.50 an ounce for gold, and immediately revaluing the gold at $35 an ounce, the Treasury would have a "profit" of $2,800,000,000; or, as he said, "nearly $3,000,000,000."

Glass was shocked. For a moment he said nothing, scarce believing his ears, then protested:

"That isn't a 'profit,' as you call it – it is nothing but a bookkeeping mark-up. Furthermore, that gold you are proposing to confiscate belongs to the Federal Reserve Banks, and the Treasury of the United States has never invested a penny in it. You are proposing to appropriate something that does not belong to the Government, and something that has never belonged to the Government."

"The Treasury will pay the Federal Reserve Board for the gold at its present market value," returned Roosevelt.

"And confiscate the difference, setting up a fictitious 'profit' on a fictitious price?"

Not equipped to argue problems of finance, or currency, or banking, or economics with Glass, Roosevelt refrained from discussion. Rather, with a smile, he inquired:

"What do you think of it?"

"I think it is worse than anything Ali Baba's forty thieves ever perpetrated," angrily snapped the Virginian.

Bursting into laughter, Roosevelt counseled Glass against losing his temper.

In January 1934, by Executive order, the United States went off the gold standard. A few weeks previously – December 20, 1933 – and in response to a query, Glass had written Walter Lippmann:

"Responding to yours of December 19 – it coincidentally enough happens that I have just returned from a two-hour talk with the President on the problem about which you write. It is perfectly obvious that the Federal Reserve Banks and member banks of the system now have excessive reserves, which in itself offers an irrefutable argument against the inflationists, since these banks are adequately prepared to meet every requirement of a revival in business. Apparently that is what the wild inflationists don't want; they appear to want to start the printing presses and stand criers on the street corners with bell and trumpet to invite people to take the inflated currency.

"In the present state of mind of Congress I think it would be difficult, if not impossible, to tighten up the reserve requirements of the Federal Reserve Act. Indeed, I think we shall be fortunate if these reserve requirements, by recommendation from The White House, are not considerably reduced. Why they should be reduced in the present situation is something that nobody can satisfactorily explain.

"I note that Professor Warren and Senator Thomas advocate seizure by the government of one-half of the gold stocks of the banks, to be appropriated to the uses of the government on a basis for currency issues or for other purposes. If you can differentiate this from legislative theft, you are considerably more of an expert lexicographer than I. . . The Federal Government has no more right to seize the gold holdings of the banks and appropriate the money thus obtained to its own uses than it has to seize and sell the bank buildings for the same purpose. The government never appropriated a dollar toward the establishment nor the maintenance of the Federal Reserve Banking system, and could not under the terms of the Constitution confiscate the system's property.

". . . In addition to the gold reserves of the Federal Reserve banks, these banks have more than two billions of dollars of government securities in their portfolios. You suggest that these may be sold, enabling the banks with the acquired revenue from such sale to retire outstanding notes. Normally this would be true, but as a matter of fact the Federal Reserve banks cannot sell these securities without utterly demoralizing the entire bond market of the country. Federal Reserve banks should never have been permitted, much less compelled, to acquire these securities ; but as soon as they can be sold that should be done and outstanding notes in the same amount retired, and the system thus required to return it to the original purpose of responding to the demands of commerce and industry."

Meanwhile, and following the enactment of the amendment to the Agricultural Adjustment Act had come a phantasmagoria of new laws, among them the National Industrial Recovery Act. This law, with its price-fixing features, would provide, so its advocates proclaimed, the bootstraps by which Uncle Sam would lift himself up from Depression. Once again, Glass took his place among the few Senators opposing the measure. Once more those who were in opposition were hopelessly outvoted.

Immediately with the passage of the act, the nation was plunged into a hurried, harried, helter-skelter hullabaloo, with ten thousand pages of rules and regulations – codes for business, codes for coal miners, butchers, clerks, pants pressers, bakers, undertakers, codes for crazy-quilts and crazy-quilts for codes ; with blue eagles, symbols of political domination, flying high over office and factory.

To General Hugh S. Johnson was given the authority of enforcing the act. To Carter Glass was given the pleasure of resisting it.

One of the codes affected newspapers. Glass saw in this code an attempt to destroy the freedom of the press. He wasted no time in communicating with General Johnson.

"I just want to tell you, General," he said, "that your blue buzzard will not fly from the mastheads of my two newspapers."

Taken aback, Johnson sought to mollify the Virginian. "We will make an exception of your case," he said. "If your newspapers do not wish to display the Blue Eagle they will not be disturbed."

Instead of placating, Johnson's concession angered Glass. Bitterly excoriating the National Industrial Recovery Act as an unconstitutional invasion of individual liberty, the Senator told the Administrator : "I do not appreciate your willingness to make exceptions of my newspapers. If this act is constitutional, you have as much authority to enforce it against me as you have against any other person but because it is not constitutional you have no right to enforce it against anyone."

Johnson tried to explain it was not his job to inquire into the constitutionality of the measure – but only to enforce it.

"That is precisely my point," declared Glass. "And because your job is to enforce the act, you have no authority to make exceptions. I want you to try and enforce it on me. I invite you to send your assistant * to Lynchburg with orders from you to enforce it. But before you send him I want to tell you that when he comes he will be requested to leave, quietly. If he refuses to leave quietly I will see to it, personally, that he is thrown out."

It is a matter of record that the invitation was not accepted. It is also a matter of record that the Supreme Court of the United States, by unanimous decision, declared the act unconstitutional.

There was more than one tilt between Glass and Johnson.

Early in December 1933, Johnson wrote a letter to Glass complaining about an editorial in which Professor Oliver M. W. Sprague, of Harvard University, was defended for his action in resigning as a Treasury adviser to the Administration. In reply, Glass said:

December 5, 1933.

Dear General:

I infer that your letter of December 4, just now brought to my attention, was written on the assumption that an editorial appearing in my morning paper in Virginia and reproduced conspicuously in The Washington Post was written by me. That would be a not unreasonable conjecture from the way in which the article was presented in the Washington paper. However, without apologizing for anything of real consequence contained in the article, I desire to say that I did not write or suggest the editorial in question nor did I see it until the paper came to my hotel apartment

* Donald Richberg

in Washington. Moreover, I do not recall that I ever had a conversation with the editor on your general attitude toward current administrative events ; I am quite certain I never discussed with him directly or indirectly the resignation of Dr. Sprague.

I may say that the comment of the newspaper which I happen to own was in no degree different from the editorial reaction of nearly all the important newspapers of the country and was freer of disagreeable personal criticism than scores of editorials in the metropolitan press. Had I written the article of which you complain, it is pretty certain that I would have refrained from any sharp personal criticism ; but this would have been due solely to my long-time personal affection for you. Gentlemen who persist in questioning the motives of others ; who vituperate respectable citizens as Tories and accuse them of a lack of patriotism merely because they disagree with the extraordinary methods being pursued in Washington ; who revile persons who have spirit enough to protest against tyranny and to resent threats of reprisal and resist the destruction of their business under a system of unprecedented experimentation – gentlemen who pursue this course without the sanction of law and, as some think, far beyond the intent of Congress, should not be supersensitive when other persons and newspapers assume the role of critic. Had my newspaper, even in any small degree, said half about you that you have said about those who disagree with you, it would have said many things which my deep personal regard for you would have restrained me from saying had I written the article which you obviously impute to me.

I have no disposition to enter into any defense of Dr. Sprague nor could I do so within the range of this personal communication. Nevertheless, I would not be frank should I assent to your charge that Dr. Sprague "made an assault on the Federal credit." This, I think, was done when the Congress repudiated a sacred national debt incurred for war purposes, and has frightfully been accentuated by other devices since. Notwithstanding this very intense conviction, I have purposely refrained, although repeatedly urged, from making any public statement on the subject, because I do not covet newspaper notoriety and further because I have not desired to seem resentful toward an Administration that sought to honor me above my deserts ; but please understand it was distinctly not because I had any fear of being characterized as a Tory or because I had the remotest idea of tamely submitting to tyranny from any source.

I may add that if you and Bernie Baruch are in no disagreement I have simply been in a trance for the last six months. With most cordial regards.

Sincerely yours,
(signed) Carter Glass.

Honorable Hugh S. Johnson,
National Recovery Administration,
Washington, D.C.

Nor was Johnson the only person to whom Glass expressed his views on the NRA. Writing to Walter Lippmann, he said :

. . . You have stated the case succinctly and with startling vigor ; but I have come to the conclusion that the nation is in a state of hysteria and that there are few men of discernment and courage left.

Of course, it was supremely desirable that there should be complete cooperation with the federal administration in the effort to restore prosperity and to abate the wretchedness of the prevailing depression ; but, in my view, the methods employed have been brutal and absolutely in contravention of every guaranty of the Constitution and of the whole spirit of sane civilization. The government itself has restored to blackmail, boycott and to a species of threats that will forever mark a black page in the history of the country.

. . . Unless I am frightfully mistaken in my conception of things, I shall always be glad of having voted against the wretched law. . . I am glad, as I am sure you will ever be, that you have the courage to pungently describe the utterly dangerous effort of the federal government at Washington to transplant Hitlerism to every corner of this nation.

The Agricultural Adjustment Act was another example of the theory that prosperity could be summoned by law.

Contrary, very likely, to popular supposition, neither Secretary Henry A. Wallace, of the Department of Agriculture, nor the President of the United States, should be accredited with the paternity of the idea of "scarcity of production" as a cure for the depression. The credit for this peculiar notion should go to Huey P. Long. Apparently Long was the first person formally to project this policy of recovery in this country. On August 17, 1931, he sent the following telegram to Senator Glass, among others:

New Orleans, La.

Honorable Carter Glass,
United States Senator,
Lynchburg, Virginia.

We can restore the prosperity of the South and materially the balance of the world within less than two weeks if the cotton-producing states have Governors and other officials who have the courage to act now and decisively. The only way that this can be done is to prohibit by law at once the raising of a single bale of cotton in all cotton growing states during the year 1932. The farmers yet have their cotton and if action is immediately taken along this line they will get the benefit of the price that will result from this move. If such action be taken by all the states immediately the farmers will get more money for this year's crop alone than they will get for this and the next two cotton crops they raise. A condition of near bankruptcy to a large part of our population and industries can be avoided if the officials of the southern states are willing to act now.

New Orleans is the official domicile of the American Cotton Co-operative Association and the leading port of the South and center of the cotton producing and marketing area of the whole world. The business is largely financed through her. I am issuing this call to ask all the Governors, Lieutenant-Governors, Congressmen and Senators of the cotton growing states to meet here in New Orleans on this Friday, the twenty-first of August, to organize for immediate steps to avoid cotton raising in America next year. Meeting at the Roosevelt Hotel at 10 o'clock in the morning.

With this year's crop we will have a surplus to carry over of 15,000,000 bales for next year. With this condition we are going to have no market at all. If we will stop the cotton raising altogether we will afford a market for what we have now and next year we will still have all that the world can use. The Lord told us to lay off raising these crops one year out of each seven to let the people have time to consume them.

Louisiana will pass this law if other states will join us. Wire me at once that you will attend.

I think I am lawyer enough to tell you that the laws I have in mind are valid and sound and will do the work that will save your State. Will you not come here and lets get to work on something that actually settles the cotton trouble.

Please issue notices to your farmers to gather their cotton and sell none of it until the results of this meeting is accomplished, because we want the benefits to go to the farmer. When that is accomplished all business prospers.

Huey P. Long,
Governor and United States Senator-elect.

Glass would have nothing to do with this strange theory of economics. He was utterly opposed to the theory, as he continued to be. Being a strict adherent to the principles of Jefferson, he recalled that the latter had written: "Were we to depend on Washington to tell us when to sow and when to reap we should soon want for bread." Glass refused to attend Long's proposed meeting; and, in the beginning of the Louisiana Senator's career in Washington slight attention was given to his theories by the new Administration.

However, a little later the public authorities evidently became disturbed over Long's persistent advocacy of a redistribution of wealth and other things that would appeal to the unthinking, and actually adopted the Louisianan's theory of "scarcity of production," carrying it to the extremity of plowing under crops and slaughtering a million or more pigs.

Uncompromisingly opposed to the policy of the Federal Government assuming to control such matters from Washington, Glass voted against the AAA. And in this, and other respects, Glass insists he did not leave his party, but that the party left him and the fundamental principles advocated by Thomas Jefferson.

The thought of a man alone in the hills castigates with silence the far clamor of mediocrity. Upon his shoulders the mantle of understanding falls again. Inevitable is the truth he apprehends – in the discernment of Nature's cycles irrevocably recurring, seedtime and harvest, night and day, the wheel of the stars.

In such a mood the statesman is able to see beyond the exigent moment to that certain hour for which the many voices cry – life, liberty, the unending pursuit ; and his gaze is fixed directly on the way they must go, and on the goals the many vainly try to circumscribe with numbers and catch with words.

Yet, the efforts of such a man searching for integrity in government are called Quixotic. And so they are – with so many windmills in the legislative halls where he works.

From the Virginia hills wherein stands Montview, Glass can see the tracks of the Southern railroad, and they recall his own many train rides, shuttling back and forth between home and Capitol ; and the rails monotonously click out an accompaniment for reflection.

The easy optimism of political adventures flaunting their impossible promises and cocksure plans. And the times he has drenched such rose-tinted dreams with cold water accurately thrown . . . believing, with Thomas Hardy, that "if way to the Better there be, it exacts a full look at the Worst."

The many trips to party conventions, every four years for forty years . . . that first ride to Washington as a member of Congress . . . the Christmas night journey to Princeton, the tentative plan that gave birth to the Federal Reserve Act snug in his pocket . . . the ride with Roosevelt from Washington to Baltimore, when he tacitly declined the Treasury post. . .

And another ride with Roosevelt, in 1934, en route to the dedication ceremony at Roanoke. The President's broad smile, "Carter, for once I have you going along with me." And his own reply, "Yes, Franklin, for once you are going in the right direction." Going south. . .

From Washington to Richmond with Wilson in 1911 . . .

the long trip from Washington to the Democratic convention in San Francisco, Grayson's parting words as the train was moving out of the Washington station: "If anything comes up, save the life and fame of this great man from the juggling of false friends." . . .

And always coming home again – where Annie has everything in order, where "Mr. Elliott" flashes white teeth in welcome, where his books stand familiarly on his library shelves, where his dogs wait, where "Mac" is bantering and gently scolding . . . he *is* home again.

CHAPTER TWENTY-SIX

"An outrage upon constitutional morality."

The fact that the New Deal carried all but two states in 1936 failed to impress Carter Glass except with the conviction that "it is well nigh impossible to beat a five billion dollar campaign fund."

Prior to the elections, however, there was more than a little speculation as to whether Glass would support Roosevelt. The Senator gave heed by saying: "It is distinctly distasteful for any one to infer, or even think, that I will not support the nominee of my party. The mere fact that I have not always voted for New Deal measures does not mean I will not vote for Mr. Roosevelt. I will vote for him."

This statement was heartening to the Democratic National Committee; and heartening, too, to Roosevelt; and, as is the case with many public utterances, what was not told was of more significance.

Remembering the great effect of Glass' speech in the 1932 campaign, Roosevelt was anxious to have him speak again.

Three times effort was made to have Glass make two radio addresses.

Glass listened respectfully to Roosevelt's persuasive suggestion – but made no address.

"Since I must vote for a New Dealer," he told the President, "I prefer to vote for a first-rate one rather than one who is distinctly second-rate. That means I will vote for you"; and left The White House to issue his statement.

In the early summer of 1936 Glass again seriously considered retirement from public life. Knowing how tired – and disillusioned – he was, Mrs. Glass assented to it. But he pondered the times, the condition of the country, the prospects for the future. He consulted his conscience. He tried fairly to fathom whether to go in the direction of his own desire, or in the further service of Virginia and his country. There came a time when he had to make up his mind.

Suddenly in the midst of discussion one evening, he said to his wife : "Mac, this issue has to be decided here and now." He paused, then continued : "It is your decision. I will do what you say for me to do." His wife's decision sent him back to the Senate.

Glass declined to participate in the writing of the 1936 program. It was the first time in years he had failed to play a prominent rôle in the formulation of his party's national policies.

Talking with Democratic friends on the day following the election, and while the avalanche of votes was still rising, he did not agree when some said "this is the end of the Republican Party."

"The very foundation of our political system is in two-party government," he pointed out. "The fact is, the elections would have been much closer had my party not had a four billion, eight hundred million dollar relief bill as campaign fodder."

To that a short time later he added :

"Talk of coalition between the parties is not based on sound thinking. In the first place, the traditions of the two parties are too deep for such easy change ; and, in the second place – but more important – there is no room in America for two such parties as are indicated by such talk – one party having as its purpose, when in power, the privilege of destroying American institutions of government ; and the other party having as its purpose, when in power, the privilege of protecting American institutions of government. The thing to do is for each party to clean its own house. So, whichever party is in power our American form of democracy, with its checks and balances, and its freedom for the individual, will be secure. The way things are now there are too many thoughtless and careless persons reaching for, and carrying, the banners of both parties.

"As for my own party, I am reminded of an incident of a number of years ago. Colonel Laurence Marye, an old Confederate soldier, used to come into my newspaper office with General Jubal Early and one day, during the Spanish-American War, Marye said to me :

" 'Carter, I had hoped to repent my sins in the hope that when I died I would go to Heaven and again see Robert E. Lee. But I have changed my mind. I want to go to hell to see the devil burn those Yankee uniforms off Joe Wheeler and Fitz Lee.'

"For myself, I had thought I would like to go to Heaven and commune with the spirits of Patrick Henry, Clay and Calhoun, Grover Cleveland and Woodrow Wilson ; but, like the old colonel, I seem disposed to change my mind and go, temporarily, to the other place to see the devil burn those strange uniforms off some people who think they are Democrats, but don't believe in the reserved rights of the States or the checks and balances provided by the Constitution of the United States, but who are mere opportunists and think the majority is always right.

"I am not calling any names, nor am I pointing unerringly to any figure in public life, but I would like to see this performance of his Satanic Majesty. Very likely, the gentlemen whom I have in mind think the same about me.

"It is more than likely, though I don't admit it, that I have been wrong more than I have been right. But whether I have been right or wrong, I have spoken my own mind and voted my own way and did not permit any one to do it for me. If I have been wrong, I regret it. In all events my purpose always has been to serve Virginia and my country, and I could wish that when some modern Diogenes passes his lantern through the political cemetery, he will pause at my sepulcher and give me an approving nod."

As Glass sees it, the proposition of defending American institutions of government is not a partisan political matter at all. It is a proposition of principle. And he feels that history has its certain way of taking care of those who think in terms of all for power and nothing for honor – and he says "in any battle for principles the names of all such 'will be found not among the dead, nor the wounded, but among the missing.' "

Certainly, he did not regard the 1936 elections as any mandate to plunge the country still further into debt.

When the subject of relief appropriations came before the Senate in June, 1937, he was more determined than ever against them. Refusing to take seriously the Robinson and Byrnes amendments to reduce the amounts by percentages, he went the whole way and voted against any lump sum relief "to be expended by irresponsible spendthrifts."

"More economic blunders, if not in some instances economic crimes," he maintained, "have been perpetrated by Congress in the name of starving people who never starved, and freezing people not one of whom has ever frozen, than the imagination can conjure up."

He said the notion that the states and cities and small political units of the country could get these funds without ever paying them back was utter nonsense. "In nearly every community in this country," he said, "public officials are taxing their ingenuity to think of and devise projects, a large proportion of which are of no use on earth.

"Federal money! Where does the Government get any

money which it does not first pick from the pockets of the taxpayers of the various States and their subdivisions?" And then he proceeded to point a warning finger at the structure of government credit, by declaring:

"We boast of the credit of the Government; we see it announced in the newspapers that subscriptions to the Treasury issues are tremendously over-subscribed. As a matter of fact, they are not subscriptions at all; they are allocations. The Treasury certificates are allocated to the banks, and the banks are compelled to take the bonds, for they have been maneuvered into a position where they cannot refuse to take future issues because they must protect the enormous amounts of Federal securities which they already hold; and a reduction of ten per cent under the par value of Federal securities would practically bankrupt ninety per cent of the banks of the country.

"If we keep on constituting ourselves legislative spendthrifts for the Government, pretty soon such a depression in Government securities is going to occur, and when it does occur, and when the banks with their millions of depositors and stockholders have to meet that issue, we are going to have precipitated upon us a disaster of which none of us can conceive."

In other words, it is Glass' conviction that government credit, so called, is an illusion, and will end as illusion always ends – in disillusion. He knows, although not enough people do, that the money Government spends is the people's money, and the debts it contracts are the people's debts. To him repudiation of debt is dishonor, but he sees that dishonorable course ahead for the American people – repudiation, inflation or unbearable taxation, the result of "economic blunders, if not economic crimes."

On January 4, 1938, the Senator observed his eightieth birthday, by commenting:

"Several things worry me a great deal. I suppose I shouldn't permit them to worry me, but they do. For one thing, everybody who meets me exclaims, with the most obvious air of astonishment, 'Why, Mr. Glass, how well you are looking!' thus intimating that I should be looking like the devil. For another, everybody, consciously or unconsciously, accidentally or deliberately, treats me as if I were perfectly helpless. I can't get in or out of a car, off or on an elevator, or up and down a step that somebody doesn't reach out to assist me. And here lately, many women I meet have taken the liberty of kissing me, not, perhaps, realizing that in so doing they are accentuating, at least to me, my too many years."

Having rid himself of that penetrating and ironical observation, he went on to recall that on his seventy-ninth birthday he had said he wanted to live to be eighty, because in that event he would have lived longer than any member of his family. On his eightieth birthday, he said he regretted to have lived to see the principles in which he believed eclipsed and his country distressed. For it was not long after his seventy-ninth birthday that the President announced his intentions to "pack" the Supreme Court.

Glass was not one of those approached by White House emissaries for his support on the measure. No one has ever dared to approach Glass with any sort of proposition in return for his vote. In fact, he has never permitted anyone to talk with him about pending measures. There was nothing behind his Court packing stand except his own infuriation at the suggestion; and his belief that what he had to say would be more effective if delivered over the radio than if said in the Senate.

Knowing of Glass' indignation over the President's demand, Admiral Cary T. Grayson came to urge strongly against any active participation in the debates. "Husband your strength," he advised, "and content yourself with voting against this proposal when that time comes."

Glass was obdurate. "I must speak," he said. "On my desk are thousands upon thousands of telegrams and letters protesting against this invasion of the Courts. I must do what I can, and the best I can, to represent these people, and to represent myself."

"The effort may be serious for you," declared the doctor significantly.

Glass was quiet for a moment, then looked up to reply: "I understand what you mean, but it is my duty to speak."

After writing his speech he read it to Admiral Grayson and Jesse Jones for their criticism, as Democrats. And, following them, to Senator William E. Borah for his criticism, not only as a Republican but as an authority on the Constitution. Borah's comment echoed what the others had said: "I would not change it, even to the crossing of a 't' or the dotting of an 'i'."

On the night of March 29, 1937, he went on the air to deliver a speech * that lasted a full hour. It was a speech in which he advised his millions of listeners that "never in my career until now have I ventured to debate before the public a measure pending in the Senate and awaiting decision there; but the proponents of the problem to which I shall address myself tonight seem fearful of a deliberate consideration of the proposal to pack the Supreme Court of the United States; they have literally avowed their purpose to take the discussion into every forum, with the unconcealed intention of bringing pressure to bear on members of Congress to submit obediently to the frightful suggestion which has come to them from The White House. The challenge has been accepted by those who oppose the repugnant scheme to disrupt representative

* See appendix for full speech

government in the Nation; and the battle is on to the end.

". . . The Attorney General in inaugurating 'organized propaganda' in behalf of the project undertook to identify the names of Washington, Jefferson, and other eminent Americans with expedients akin to the unprecedented proposal of the President. Already I have publicly pronounced the assertion as an indefensible libel on the fame of these great men, and was glad to note that the Attorney General omitted in his statement before the Senate Judiciary Committee to repeat the aspersion. The White House proposal is without precedent in the history of American jurisprudence. Its consequences portend evils beyond the anxiety of any person concerned for a decent administration of justice in this country. . .

". . . We are simply given to understand that the President has 'a mandate from the people' to so reconstitute the Supreme Court as to have it sanction whatever The White House proposes to an agreeing Congress, particularly if it involves no 'check upon unauthorized freedom,' to quote Grover Cleveland, or 'restraint on dangerous liberty.'

"But we know there has been no such mandate from the people to rape the Supreme Court or to tamper with the Constitution. The Constitution belongs to the people. It was written by great representatives of the people, chosen for the purpose, and was ratified by the people as the Supreme Charter of their Government, to be respected and maintained with the help of God. With the consent and by mandate of the people their Constitution provides how it may be amended to meet the requirements of the ages. It has always been so, and no administration in the history of the Republic has attempted to flank the Constitution by a legislative short-cut so vividly denounced by Woodrow Wilson as 'an outrage upon constitutional morality.'

"The people were not asked for any such mandate. They

were kept in ignorance of any such purpose. They were told that the liberal aims of the President could very likely be achieved within the limitations of the Constitution ; and if not, we could suggest to the people amendments that would authorize such certain things to be done. When once it was intimated by political adversaries that the Supreme Court might be tampered with, the insinuation was branded as a splenetic libel.

"No word in the platform of the prevailing party could be interpreted into advocacy of any such abnormality as that now in issue. Quite contrary, every platform declaration on the subject gave promise of the customary constitutional procedure. But somebody badly advising the President was evidently afraid of the people. The Attorney General apparently feared to 'ask a mandate from the people' for his wretched scheme, defended so weakly in reason as to invite expressions of contempt. Convicted by his own official reports of inaccurate assertions about congestion of the Supreme Court calendar, and now flatly contradicted on this and other points by the Chief Justice and associates, there is nothing left of his bitter assault on the Court more notable than the brutal contention that six eminent members 'get out' and give place to six others of a compliant type, in the selection of whom the Department of Justice would probably have a cunning hand.

"It will do in this case particularly what Thomas Jefferson pungently deplored when he declared 'the multiplication of judges only enables the weak to outvote the wise.' The fact is their proposed bill will cure none of the alleged evils which offend their ideas of judicial reform.

". . . The predominant question is whether the practice of a century under an independent judiciary is to be abruptly terminated by authorizing the President to seize the Court by the process of packing in order to compel agreement with the

Executive views. Should this be done without 'a mandate' from the people? Should the people be ignored and, without asking their consent in the usual way, submit helplessly to having their Constitution tortured into meanings which have been declared in contravention of the fundamental law? If Andrew Jackson was right in asserting that 'Eternal vigilance by the people is the price of liberty,' God knows that never before since the establishment of the Republic could the people better be warned to preserve their priceless heritage. The talk about 'party loyalty' being involved in the opposition to this extraordinary scheme is a familiar species of coercion.

". . . Should the iniquitous scheme go through, the intelligence and character of the Nation will be interested to know what lawyer of notable attainments or independent spirit would be willing to go on the Supreme Court bench in such circumstances or could regard such an appointment as an honor. Doubtless there are practitioners eager for such recognition; but are they men whom the Nation would prefer or who could feel comfortable in association with those now constituting the Court?

"I am but an unlearned layman, untrained in the ethics of the legal profession; nevertheless, I cannot escape the conclusion that any man of approved sensibility who should accept such a distinction would experience trouble in outliving his mistake. Moreover, I have a distinct premonition that the people of America would not confidently trust to the supreme decision of such a Court the life, liberty and pursuit of happiness guaranteed by the Constitution.

"I am far from intimating that the President of the United States is incapable of selecting suitable men for the Supreme Court. I am simply accepting his own word and that of his spokesmen to the effect that he wants men 'biased' in behalf of his legislative and administrative projects, who may be counted on to reverse the Supreme Court decisions already rendered and give such other decisions of policy as may be desired. . .

"The assumption of the proponents of this scheme to tamper with the Court and the Constitution that only they are the President's real friends has no justification in fact. . . Rather is he the real friend of the President who will commend to his serious attention the ringing words of Thomas Jefferson when he proclaimed himself 'against writing letters to judiciary officers' because he 'thought them independent of the Executive, not subject to his coercion, and therefore not obliged to attend to its admonitions.' "

The physician accompanied Glass back to his hotel, remained with him for some time, to return the following morning and find the Senator sitting up, immersed in reading telegrams that were stacked high on the tables. Sweeping aside the messages, the doctor ordered his patient back to bed – "and to remain there for the rest of the day," leaving acknowledgment of the nearly thirty thousand communications to the secretarial staff.

Soon thereafter the Court packing scheme was beaten off in the Senate ; and a little later when announcement came from The White House that the President had filled a vacancy on the Bench, Glass was in committee meeting. The name of the appointee was written on a piece of paper that was handed from one committee member to the other. Without his spectacles, Glass could not decipher the name but after studying it a moment, he passed along the slip of paper, with the observation : "I don't know what it says on there, but whoever it is, his name is 'Charlie McCarthy.' "

Federal subsidy is a subject to which he continually returns. He sees it as an attempt to break down the rights of the states, and pleads for Americans to "place an inestimable value on freedom" because when "the rights of the States are sacrificed the nation itself is gone." And, in recognition of the vastly increased numbers of persons on Federal payrolls, he recalls Lincoln's words, "if ever this free people – if this government itself is ever utterly demoralized, it will come from this incessant human wriggle and struggle for office, which is but one way to live without work."

He views, with contempt, the opinions of men who have never had experience in anything but mob incitement – and he considers with dismay the empiric decisions of such office holders in problems they have not studied, rendering decisions that become laws affecting agriculture, business, economics, and the Constitution itself. Because he is a student of history, Glass knows the recordings of time are crowded with illustrations of men who have persuaded other men to give up protection for bread, to the end they lost both. And he thinks the reason history repeats itself so often is because people have such short memories – forgetting, too easily, that when they begin to prize political subsidy, they really have begun to despise their own political freedom.

Very early in the first session of the 75th Congress he started in to work on appropriations. On January 27, 1938, the Senate had under consideration crop production and harvesting loans.

Quietly, in the midst of debate, Glass skipped a reminder across the surface of the arguments; in a matter of seconds, the United States Senate was transformed into a whirlpool. The reminder was simply an executive message from Grover Cleveland, dated February 16, 1887, vetoing a somewhat similar measure on the grounds that he could find no "warrant for such an appropriation in the Constitution, and I do not believe that the power and duty of the general government ought to be extended to the relief of individual sufferers which is in no manner properly related to the public service or benefit," and the conviction that "people are supposed to support the Government and not the Government the people."

In amusement Glass listened to the torrent of oratory that instantly began pouring from legislative throats – and when, after a time, it had abated, he arose in satirical conclusion :

"I distinctly stated, when asking consent to have the message of a great Democratic President read from the desk, that it was a relic of constitutional government. I had not the remotest idea that it was going to affect the question pending before the Senate. I had not the faintest notion that it would control the vote of a single, solitary Senator.

"Perhaps I am a relic of constitutional government – I am rather inclined to think I am. I entertain what may be the misguided notion that the Constitution of the United States, as it existed in the time of Grover Cleveland, is the same Constitution that exists today, and that if Mr. Cleveland, with his clear conception and courage, could find nothing in the Constitution then which authorized appropriations for special purposes and not for the general welfare, I cannot today find anything in the Constitution warranting such action.

"Incidentally, I may express the greatest astonishment that any Member of the Senate should appeal to decisions of the Supreme Court, whether actually involved or incidental, at the very time when arrangements are going forward to tear down the Supreme Court, when so many people have no conception of its establishment or its uses in constitutional government.

"The reference to the general-welfare clause simply provokes the statement that whenever Congress desires to appropriate money for any purpose it is at liberty to appeal, and does appeal, to the general-welfare clause. Latterly, the interpretation of the general-welfare clause by the Congress of the United States differs as widely from the interpretation of it by the man who wrote it, James Madison, as our attitude now differs from the constitutional conceptions of Grover Cleveland. . .

"So far as Mr. Cleveland's message being related to the great disaster now afflicting the country is concerned, everybody knows that this is a national disaster. Everyone knows that when we deal liberally and generously with a situation of this sort, we are dealing with the general welfare of the country. So the vehement and rhetorical address to which the Senate has just listened has no application to my attitude or to that so succinctly and courageously expressed by Grover Cleveland and overwhelmingly sustained by the Congress of the United States at that time. Of course we should appropriate funds to alleviate the afflictions and to abate the distresses resulting from a great national disaster which affects not merely the unfortunate people immediately involved but affects the entire Nation, and I have no patience with oratorical efforts in commendation of such appropriations. I have no respect for them either.

"Nor am I hiding my face in shame at the suggestion of the Senator from North Carolina or at that of the Senator from Arkansas. I am in favor of the 'horse and buggy' age, if that means respect for the Constitution of the United States and of the Supreme Court acting under the Constitution of the United States.

"I am not willing to tear down that Court because I may disagree with some of its decisions. I wish some of them had never been rendered, such as that which has destroyed intrastate commerce, and that which said we might swindle our own people but not foreigners in the matter of our contractual relations. However, although I, a layman, disagree with those decisions of the Court, I am not willing under my oath as a United States Senator to contribute in any degree at any moment to the effort to tear down the Court and make it useless.

"I had not purposed to raise a riot of oratory here in the Senate. Simply as a matter of amusement to myself and, I trust, of interest to the Senate, I wanted to indicate how far we had gotten away from some constitutional bases when we contrast them with what we now think about the Constitution and the Courts." Then dryly he ended, "I think Mr. Cleveland's reputation and that of James Madison will survive both the condemnation and praise which we have heard here today."

On his eightieth birthday friends of the Senator, notably Admiral Grayson, Eugene Meyer and Colonel Edwin A. Halsey, wanted to organize a nation-wide dinner as a testimonial, but Glass shrank from such a public demonstration as an "unendurable ordeal." If his friends wished to honor him, they could do so behind his back, and without benefit of food or fanfare.

But on the evening on that day, after having received hundreds of letters and telegrams and cables, as well as many personal calls, he marked the end of the eighth, and the beginning of the ninth decade of his life by a family gathering and dinner in his apartment in the Mayflower Hotel. The following day, the Senate stopped all business for two hours to pay him tribute. At the very outset and as his colleague from Virginia, Senator Harry Byrd, began to speak, Glass bolted from the Senate. His absence did not halt the felicitations, joined in by Democrat and Republican alike. The tenor of their remarks being expressed by a Republican Senator, Vandenberg, of Michigan:

". . . Admiration for Carter Glass is not limited to his own side of the aisle, or to his own section of the country, or to his own political group in the public life of the United States.

The Senator from Virginia will always be remembered as one of the great public servants of his or any other age."

And shortly after his eightieth birthday, he lost, in death, his friend Admiral Cary T. Grayson of whom he sadly wrote, "Our companionship was almost sacred."

And, too, a few months before his eightieth birthday . . .

Ill, Mrs. Glass was sitting up in bed when her husband entered. Bending over, he kissed her, smoothed out the pillows, brushed her forehead, his fingers lingering in caress while for a deep moment his eyes searched into hers, and his lips smiled :

"Feeling better today."

"Yes, dear, much better," she smiled back – and she knew, as he knew, the words each spoke were for the encouragement of the other.

Pulling up a chair, he slapped his hands on his knees, relating an amusing happening of the day, and picked up the newspapers to read to her.

For a long time he went through the news, selecting with care those items he knew would interest her. Finally, he put down the papers to find her eyes still on him. She was smiling again.

"My dear," she said, "I was thinking about those other days, when we were young and newspapers weren't the bustling, hustling things they now are . . ." she paused . . . "I was thinking, too, of something else."

"What was that, Mac ?" he asked.

"It was something that happened – oh, a long time ago and, still, it doesn't seem so long ago. Do you remember a Sunday morning in Lynchburg when you were a young man and – and, you were waiting on a corner for a street car to take you to church . . . a girl and her mother came to wait . . .

and you stared at the girl, and kept staring at her until you almost stared her out of countenance – remember ?"

"Yes, I remember that," chuckled her husband, after a moment of thought. "I recall it very well, now that you've brought it to my mind. I remember, because she slapped my face."

"She 'slapped' your face ?"

"Well, not exactly that, but she slapped it mentally. I was so flabbergasted that I didn't have the nerve to get on the street car. How did you happen to be thinking of that ?"

"Oh, I was just thinking about it."

Glass mused. "She certainly was a pretty girl" – and then, teasing, "she was an awfully pretty girl, Mac. Wonder what ever became of her ? Wonder who she was ?"

"You never saw her again ?"

"No, not that I remember. You see, Mac, you came across my vision not long after that, and I forgot all about her. But, say, how did you know about that girl ? Did I ever tell you about her ?"

"No, you never told me."

"Then, how did you know what happened ?"

"I was the girl," softly returned the sick woman, her face radiant in the confession of a secret she had kept for more than fifty years.

Two weeks more and Aurelia McDearman Glass was dead.

He wept with loneliness for himself without her ; and with loneliness for the years ahead, if there were any. He did not weep because their relationship was ended, or their friendship over. They were safe and secure now. He knew she was aware – and that she understood much better than if she were here, and he had only his clumsy words to try to explain things to her.

CHAPTER TWENTY-SEVEN

The Privileged Class

As a public office holder, Glass maintains that the greatest protection for democratic institutions of government is a people vigilantly suspicious of public office holders. Unless watched, he knows government by permission soon becomes government by compulsion.

As Glass sees it, the people are well governed when their public officials obey the Constitution. "The people should keep in mind," he says, "that the Constitution is a set of written rules designed to control the desires of public officials. The people should realize, fully, when public officials continually propose, or continually do, unconstitutional acts, or continually inveigh against the provisions of the Constitution that these same public officials are really seeking the destruction of constitutional government in appeasement of their own desires. Such public officials do not wish to govern – they seek to rule!

"We hear much of 'privilege' and 'privileged classes,' but I should like to remind the people there is no class more privileged than those who occupy public office. Today, by breaking down constitutional barriers, public officials in many parts of the world have succeeded in extending their privileges, making them exclusive. In their own safety there is one privilege the people of the United States should keep for themselves. That is the privilege of final decision, both as to legislation and administration, as well as the final decision as to who shall legislate and administer.

"This is what Daniel Webster meant when he said 'Nothing will ruin a country if the people themselves will undertake its safety ; and nothing can save a country if they leave that safety in any hands but their own.' "

Being, as he has said, "a relic of constitutional government," Glass has been critical and, at times, caustic, when speaking of the New Deal. He has been critical, or he has been caustic, not because he disagrees with Government spending for relief, not because he disagrees with bettering conditions for agriculture and labor, not because he disagrees with any humanitarian objective of government. He believes in those things. Nor is he a recent believer, as his long public life attests. What he does not believe in is the use of public money to serve partisan political ends, the waste of public money to accomplish partisan political ambitions, and the assumption of powers constitutionally denied, with the subsequent distribution of such powers among transient political favorites.

He believes Congress was wrong in extending these powers to the President – and he believes the President was wrong in accepting them.

In the summer of 1936 he was given another opportunity to state this belief. William C. Bullitt, at the time ambassador to Russia, was in the United States. In the course of his political duties Bullitt delivered an oration in Ashland, Virginia, and in his remarks implied that "the lamp that lighted" Patrick Henry's feet in the quest for liberty was the same lamp that lighted the steps of the New Dealers. The following week, in Ashland, Glass corrected inaccuracies in Bullitt's speech regarding Henry ; and, at the same time, called the attention of his audience to the "unconstitutionality" of the trade treaties being arranged by the State Department. A few days later he received a letter arraigning him for his remarks. The letter was from the Department of State, and was signed by Secretary Cordell Hull.

Glass replied :

Lynchburg, Virginia,
August 3, 1936.

STRICTLY PERSONAL

Honorable Cordell Hull,
Secretary of State,
Washington, D.C.

My dear Cordell:

I am just in receipt of yours of July 28th and am indebted to you for writing me so fully. However, I am afraid you share in the misapprehension of the meaning of my impromptu speech at Ashland ten days ago.

I had not intended speaking there at all, having made that a condition of going to Ashland; but the day before leaving home I noted from newspaper reports that your Mr. Bullitt had undertaken to conjure with the name and fame of Patrick Henry in justification of certain principles of government to which, in my view, the Democratic party, since the days of Jefferson, had consistently condemned. The plain inference was that Mr. Bullitt had condemned the two Virginia Senators for voting against certain measures which they regarded as unconstitutional. I also noted that, contrary to our understanding, I was advertised as "the principal speaker" for the following Friday. I did not think and do not now think there was anything inappropriate in contrasting the real views of Patrick Henry with the assumptions of a gentleman universally regarded by the conservative sentiment of the country as an extreme radical.

In the hurried process of doing this, I mentioned Henry's inveterate antagonism to governmental paternalism and to privilege and discrimination. I recalled no measure of privilege more monstrous than the Smoot-Hawley high protective tariff act, denounced in both houses of Congress and from every platform in America by every Democratic speaker from the time of its adoption to the day of election in 1932. In this connection, I deplored the fact that the Democratic party, with a President in The White House and with two-thirds majority in both branches of Congress, had not repealed or radically modified this measure instead of merely authorizing an executive official to mollify its dangerous features piecemeal. On this point I recalled the fact that Patrick Henry was inexorably opposed in principle to the failure of the Constitution to include the House of Representatives, as well as the Senate and the President, in the making of treaties with foreign governments and wondered if the Democrats of the country would be willing "to clothe Joe Grundy with the authority now being exercised alone by an executive official." Judging from his attitude and expressions Patrick Henry would never have consented to this.

Of course you know that if there is any one man in the United States to whom might properly be committed the drafting and enforcement of tariff legislation, I would pick you above all others; but I think that the levying of taxes, whether tariff or internal, is a function for Congress and not for executive officials. If this is not sound Democracy, essential to representative government, I have misread the principles and practices of the Democratic party since its foundation. But the whole point was "what Patrick Henry thought and said about this," and there can be no mistake about that. His entire viewpoint was, as it seemed to me, misrepresented by your Mr. Bullitt and correctly stated by me.

As to precisely how you are discharging the dangerous undertaking confided to you, without knowing the details (but knowing you) I have assumed that you were doing everything possible in the interests of the consumers of the country and in behalf of our trade with foreign nations; but, then again, suppose the Republicans should unhappily get possession of the government and put Joe Grundy in your place!

The wretched talk in some quarters about my having "assailed the President" is simply malevolent. I did nothing of the sort. The only time I mentioned the President in my hurried remarks was to deprecate certain bitter criticism of him and to deplore the fact that Congress had delegated unconstitutional authority to him and to other executive officials.

Sincerely yours,
(signed) Carter Glass.

Hull made no reply.

Nearly two years previously, or in December 1934, Glass was indignant over a ruling by the Federal Reserve Board and the Federal Deposit Insurance Corporation requiring nonmember state banks, as well as member banks of the Federal Reserve System, to reduce to two and one half per cent interest payments on savings and time deposits. This, too, as he saw it, was assuming and extending unwarranted authority.

Promptly he made inquiries as to the authority of the two groups for their action ; and wrote, in part, to C. S. Hamlin, of the Federal Reserve Board in Washington :

Your general counsel unhesitatingly stated, of course, that the Federal Reserve Board had no such legal authority ; and, off the record, as it were, said he had been unable to find any legal justification for such action by the Insurance of Deposits Corporation. The chairman of that Corporation frankly admitted to me that he could cite no legal authority for such action and confessed that the Corporation, in so resolving "was skating on thin ice." The Comptroller of the Currency, another member of the Corporation board, could refer me to no provision of the law authorizing any such action by the Corporation ; and I conjecture he had no part in the performance.

The Corporation's general counsel disclaimed responsibility for advising such action by the Corporation and frankly said the action was "subject to serious question." In my view, there can be no possible question of the illegality of the action, which plainly constitutes assumption of legislative authority ; and I venture to think the Federal Reserve Board made a grave mistake in lending the force of its prestige to such illicit action by making itself the medium of the public announcement. . .

. . . We seem, my dear sir, to have reached a stage in public affairs where every little sub-professor brought to Washington, however destitute of practical business acumen, is supposed to know more in a fortnight about banking and financial problems than the President of the United States, the seasoned officials of the Federal Reserve system and members of Congress who for many years have been keen observers of banking practices and intimately identified with financial measures. I note hastily in the papers today proposals from one or two of these supremely wise men to strike from a certain federal statute, which has had but a few months' test, a provision which the President urgently asked to have incorporated ; also a provision drawn by former Governor Black, of the Reserve Board, and by him earnestly pressed upon the Banking and Currency Committees of Congress, together with a provision which you and other members of the Federal Reserve Board thought to be a major contribution to the code of regional banking legislation. Possessing the merit of reasonable precaution, I assume these provisions of law are comprehended in the sneer at banking "righteousness" continued in this remarkable report. Apparently the embryonic Solons responsible for the report are cheerful believers in the wanton use of bank trust funds, the very vice that so recently plunged the country into an era of bank wreckage unprecedented in the history of America. Apparently they think resort now to the unwise banking practices which helped to bring on disaster would facilitate recovery from the evil consequences of such practices. There is scarcely a phase of banking touched by this report which has not repeatedly been traversed by the Banking and Currency Committees of Congress without the assembling of a costly staff of employees to furnish data and make suggestions.

Speaking as chairman of the Senate Committee directly in charge of the legislation condemned without adequate trial, I think the sooner Washington is rid of impatient academicians whose threatening manifestos and decrees keep business and banks alike in suspense, if not in consternation, the sooner and more certain will we have a complete restoration of confidence and resumption of business in every line of endeavor. *Terram coelo miscent;* or as Cicero has it : *Damnant quod non intelligunt.*

In the "Ickes file" in Glass' records are several signed letters from the Secretary of the Interior expressing his appreciation of the "many courtesies and kindnesses" of the Senator – these, in spite of "differences" in their views. In the spring of 1935, Glass disagreed sharply with Ickes regarding the spending of PWA allotments ; and once more the Virginian was protesting unconstitutional interpretations. In reply to a message from Ickes he dictated a communication which, like the letters to Hull and Hamlin, portrays his point of view. This letter, too, speaks for itself :

Sunday, March 31, 1935.

Honorable Harold L. Ickes,
The Secretary of the Interior,
Washington, D.C.

My dear Mr. Secretary :

Last night I received by messenger your letter having reference to a certain provision of the conference report on H. J. Res. 117, and have managed, after much delay, to reach one of my office stenographers today in order that I may promptly respond to your communication.

The provision of the conference report to which you object is classification of projects (g), Senate amendment (3) as amended in conference, as follows:

> "(g) loans or grants, or both, for projects of States, Territories, possessions, including subdivisions and agencies thereof, and self-liquidating projects of public bodies thereof, municipalities, and the District of Columbia, where not less than one-third of the loan or the grant or the aggregate thereof is for expenditures for direct work, $900,000,000;"

Your objection seems founded (1) upon the theory that by restricting loans and grants to projects where not less than one-third of the loan or grant, or the aggregate thereof, is for expenditure for "direct work," only work "at the site of the project" may be credited as "direct work" within the meaning of the provision, and (2) because "the more desirable the project from a social and economic point of view the less chance will there be of its qualifying under the language" of the amendment as agreed to in conference.

The President, in his message to Congress, assured us that there are many millions of unfortunate persons out of employment, some of whom are in serious circumstances, and, accordingly, the clear legislative purpose of the conference report on H. J. Res. 117 is to make available nearly five billions of dollars of public money to "provide *relief*, *work relief* and to *increase employment* by *providing for useful projects*;"

Apparently you do not agree with this clear legislative purpose, but feel that the public moneys involved should be made available – first, for any social revision or upheaval determined upon by those selected to administer the legislation, and – second, for such employment as their "social and economic" program may permit.

In my view, shared by my colleagues, any plan for accomplishing a marked change in our social structure, especially through Federal direction and uses of public moneys, should be considered by the Congress as such and not under the guise of merely providing work for millions of persons out of employment.

As to your objection (1) you mistakenly read into the amendment language not appearing therein by adding the words "at the site of the project." These words, specifically rejected in conference, nowhere appear in the report. Hence, "direct work" as used in the amendment means actual work on the loan-project—and not necessarily "*at the site of the project.*" Such was the understanding of every member of the conference. For instance, in a loan-project for construction of a municipal water system, or electric lighting plant, or gas plant, or other public utility, there would be for crediting as "direct work" not only the work of constructing the plant, installing the machinery, laying the mains, etc., (all of which would be, of course, at the site of the project) but the work involved in the construction of pumps, motors, other machinery, etc., if actually constructed for the particular plant, even if constructed far from the site of the project; also, the work actually involved in the transporting, trucking, and unloading thereof, etc. There is nothing in the amendment limiting "direct work" to "labor directly employed *at the site of the project.*" To be sure of this the conferees called in the Comptroller General and by him were assured he would so hold in any matter submitted to him for decision.

The public moneys, as we understand, are being provided, in the joint resolution, to "increase employment" and a project that does not involve direct work to the extent of at least one-third of the expenditures involved, may not fairly be considered one designed to materially increase employment. It is not difficult to think of projects for which money might be loaned, if there be no reasonable restriction, which would not involve the employment of a single one of the 3,500,000 employable persons now on relief.

As to objection (2) that under the amendment "the more desirable the project from a social and economic point of view, the less chance will there be of its qualifying," I respectfully submit that there is a distinctive conflict between this and the expressed legislative purpose of the joint resolution. Apparently, you think the purpose of this joint resolution is to accomplish revision of the social structure, whereas the legislative purpose, it seems to me, is to increase employment in the interest of the millions of persons out of work.

The amendment is designed to prevent loans for purchase of existing plants with no appreciable amount of new or direct work involved and merely or largely to effect a change in ownership or management.

As to the possibility of courts holding that the required amount of direct work is not shown to be involved in a loan-project, and, if such be the fact, enjoining prosecution of the project, it would seem that the courts might feel it their duty to so give effect to the law; and why not if there should be attempted an evasion of the law?

In this connection, I venture to suggest that, should the Congress state no minimum requirement for direct work in connection with loans-and-grants projects, the courts might feel it their duty to enjoin in all cases where the direct work shown to be involved fails to bring the project, in the judgment of the court, within the basic purposes of the enactment — to "provide relief, work relief and to increase employment by providing for useful projects."

Stating in the joint resolution a minimum requirement of one-third, for direct work, discloses the legislative purpose to raise no question for the courts in cases fully meeting such statutory requirement.

With respect to any administrative duty to "certify" that a loan-project will provide "direct work" to the extent of one-third of the expenditures, it may be pointed out that under the amendment any such project may not be the subject of a loan until the amount of direct work involved is established as a fact. . .

Of course, I completely understand that you have no personal interest in the matter and can readily comprehend that you have not greatly enjoyed the disagreeable duty of making P. W. A. allotments. I certainly could not suppose that you would covet the task of further doing this critical work. But I would not have you imagine that is any criticism of your official activities or of you. Personally, I have omitted no proper occasion to commend you, and, frankly, I should regret to see your functions turned over to any other person attached to the Washington administration. I am always glad to oblige you; but in this particular instance I think you are clearly wrong and the conference report clearly right.

With very genuine respect,
Sincerely yours
(signed) Carter Glass.

There is no record of any reply to this letter in Glass' files.

The next sharp difference of opinion between the two men occurred in the early fall of 1938. This time there was no courteousness. Returning from a trip to Alaska, Ickes ventured upon a platform in Tacoma, Washington, to say that

Glass was typical of "political hypocrites that bite the hand that feeds them."

"The reactionary press hails this 'rugged individual' as another Horatius at the bridge because of his bitter attacks on economic policies of the government," said Ickes. "Yet no Senator comes oftener and with more insistence for W. P. A. grants than does this same Senator Glass."

When Ickes' charges were read over the telephone to Glass, the Senator made an immediate reply for the newspapers :

"Secretary Ickes has become a confirmed blackguard, saturated with hate for every member of Congress who voted against spendthrift practices of the New Deal authorities and against projecting the government into every conceivable species of business. . . Horatius at the bridge stood and fought ; he did not go 3000 miles across the continent to lie about his adversaries . . . but assuming the Secretary's assertion to be true, instead of maliciously false, why should I not advocate so-called 'grants' to Virginia projects and in what respect is such advocacy 'hypocritical ?'

"Over my protest and contrary to my vote, Congress decided on this fatuous policy of doing business and inasmuch as Virginia must repay on foolish borrowings, why should not Virginia Senators and Representatives ask Federal 'aid' for her projects without being offensively and falsely accused of hypocrisy by one of the most prolific spenders of the taxpayers' money ?

"The only reason I have not advocated PWA projects is that I have not believed in Federal 'grants,' every dollar of which, with accrued interest, Virginia taxpayers must repay."

Early in 1939 the President's long pent-up resentment broke out against Glass. In an effort to discredit not only Glass but Virginia's other Senator, Harry Flood Byrd, the President named Floyd H. Roberts to a place on the federal bench in Virginia.

Months previously intimation of what Roosevelt was planning to do came from a newspaper account in the *Richmond Times-Dispatch*. The newspaper article told of a meeting between State Senator Charles J. Harkrader, of Virginia, and Roosevelt in The White House. At this meeting it was decided, so said the newspaper, that Governor James H. Price, of Virginia, should have "veto power" over all federal appointments within the state.

The story was called to Glass' attention, and he wrote the President inquiring as to its authenticity. In reply Roosevelt was evasive. Again Glass posed the question. A second time the President declined a direct answer.

Biding his time, Glass waited for the matter to come before the Committee on the Judiciary of the Senate. There he reviewed the history of the case, and in the course of his remarks insisted:

"The President of the United States did give to the Governor of Virginia the veto power over nominations made by the two Virginia United States Senators. He was given ample opportunity by me personally to deny the accuracy of that statement, and he has not done so. He has confirmed it by taking from the six applicants for that position, all of high character and capabilities, the only man who is personally offensive to the two Virginia Senators – offensive to them in that he lent himself to the conspiracy to discredit and dishonor their recommendations to the President. Any man would be personally offensive to me, whoever he might be, however near he might be, how much he may have supported me politically, if he would be a cheerful and willing recipient of the benefits of a proposal that the two United States Senators from Virginia, charged by the Constitution with the duty of advising and consenting to Federal appointments, should have their recommendations vetoed by the Governor of Virginia, who has not disputed his connection with the proposition."

Threatening Glass and the Senate by announcing he intended writing "an interesting letter" in case the nomination of Roberts was not affirmed, Roosevelt awaited developments. They were not long in coming. The Senate rejected the nomination by a vote of 72 to 9.

A few hours later the President released a letter he had written to Roberts. Glass wasted no time in answering. Saying he thought "it pertinent to summarize the relative facts in order that the public may determine the exact truth," he continued:

"The President in his unprecedented letter to his rejected nominee expresses the opinion that 'every person of common sense knows' that 'no Governor, no Senator has at any time had or ever will have the right of veto over Presidential nominations.' This is as inaccurate as many other statements and inferences made by the President are. Ninety-six Senators have the right of veto over Presidential nominations in specified cases, and on last Monday seventy-two of them against nine to the contrary exercised their right of veto on the President's nominee for Judge of the Western District of Virginia, and I am assured that others would have done likewise had they been present at the vote."

Continuing, Glass declared he and Senator Byrd were "prepared to accept any capable man who was not deliberately intended to be offensive . . . by willingly making himself the beneficiary of an attempt to dishonor us in our State and among our colleagues," and he closed his statement by saying:

"This is no fight for patronage. I do not care a tinker's

dam for patronage. I do not recall that I ever met Judge Buchanan.* I do not know nor have I ever inquired whether or not he approved my course in the Senate. I inferred his appointment would not get either Senator a vote he would not receive anyhow, because I know Buchanan has too much character and too great a sense of propriety to be a judicial 'sniper' or to permit politics of any description to enter his court.

"I was looking for a judge, not for a job. I was not seeking a man under my political patronage nor one under the patronage of any politician. Buchanan would have been an ornament to the federal bench as he has been to that of the state; and it is to be deplored from every point of view that he should have been rejected by the appointive power merely through a desire to 'purge' the junior Senator next year and the senior Senator of Virginia later should I live longer than the intriguers hope."

Glass is not impressed by threats of "discipline" because he disagrees with acts which violate fundamental Democratic principles.

In 1934 an influential politician warned him that the President intended to separate the sheep from the goats; and admonished the Senator to beware of being grouped with the goats.

"I will take care of my own classification when the separation takes place," said Glass, "but I know, sir, you will be in neither classification, for your advice discloses you to be a beast of burden of another species."

It is his belief that no single man is going to decide the destiny of all the people in this nation; just as it is his belief that no single man is going to decide the membership of this nation's major political parties. Being more than superficially informed in the history of nations, and the history of political

* A. C. Buchanan, one of Glass' nominees.

parties, Glass knows there must be meeting places for the latter – and he conceives of the Democratic Party as having been anchored in the traditions of the American form of government ; and not built on the shore where the sand piles up under the eaves, or the house comes down in the first high wind.

He does not believe because any one man is successful politically that such success anoints him with the virtues of omniscience and omnipotence ; and he is confident that he who so deceives himself is certain to end up in the dreary waste places of his own ego.

Thousands of letters come to Glass each year. In them, frequently, he finds the friendly cordial that cheers ; and, more often, the selfish quest that arouses. Some are from friends long gone, some from Presidents, many from farmers, workers at benches, clerks at desks, mothers, fathers, people he has never seen but has come to know, from editors and reporters, from business men and from bankers, doctors, lawyers, clergymen, from people everywhere. . .

A letter from an editor who, while expressing trepidation for inquiring, sought his opinion of a certain gentleman the mere mention of whose name causes the hackles of Glass' mind to stiffen ; and the instant response : "That man is a disgrace to the Methodist Church to which I belong, and he is a disgrace to the Christian religion to which I adhere, and dad bum it, he is a disgrace to the human race of which I am a member."

To a newspaper reporter there was a confirmation of what he had said to a certain Congressman who had made a blatant speech in a Senate and House conference committee meeting, and who had protested when Glass observed "that is a completely mendacious statement" by threatening to leave the room. "Very well," said Glass, "that is fine. Go back to the body that sent you here and see if they can send someone in your place with the rudimentary instincts of a gentleman and an elementary conception of the truth."

From Mrs. Edith Bolling Wilson, the President's widow, thanks for a copy of *An Adventure in Constructive Finance.* A note from his half-sister, Meta, now President of Sweet Briar College ; a letter from another half-sister, Marian, now assistant treasurer of the United States. . .

A note from the evangelist, Billy Sunday, and his own comment in reply, "I venture to derive some comfort from the thought that no man can effectively serve his government without being inspired by God." A letter to a self-seeking climber who was pestering him for an invitation to a White House reception : "What ! Ask a gentleman to invite a stranger into his home. Never ! I would as soon think of asking him to let me pick out his wife."

In July 1919, a long letter seeking his views on woman suffrage, and his answer : "I have not changed my conviction that thrusting women into the tumult and demoralization of party politics is going to have a frightfully unhappy consequence for the women themselves ; nevertheless I believe the question of ratifying the proposed Federal amendment should be fairly and honestly dealt with. . ." May 8, 1919, a note to William P. Platt, of White Plains, N.Y., in thanks for a Great Dane pup, "which I have sent to Montview where I am sure it will be a joy to Red," his grandson.

And the summation of him in a letter by Frank Kent and which was passed along by a mutual friend for his reading ; and which pleased and amused him : "I very greatly like and admire Senator Glass. . . I do believe that he is as able and sincere a man as there is in the public life of any country today . . . nevertheless, I believe he is the most testy, irascible, outspoken, short-tempered and sharp-tongued little individual who ever held a public office in our country. That with his disposition he has remained in politics all these years is a political marvel I can't explain."

CHAPTER TWENTY-EIGHT

"When equality of opportunity is assured, government should interfere as little as possible."

"In time of crumbling standards" Carter Glass has refused to hazard his conscience to the keeping of anyone but himself.

"I have a distinct distaste," he says, "for a modern-day interpretation of the phrase 'public servant.' To me it was never intended to mean abject subservience to the public will, however uninformed or misdirected. I prefer to think of a United States Senator as a representative of the sovereignty of his State and subject every moment of his service to the promptings of his conscience and the preservation of his own intellectual integrity.

"He has no moral right to sacrifice either to the clamor of the multitude or to the decree of 'titled consequence' wherever it may be enthroned. Long ago I learned – indeed I did not have to learn; it is a self-evident proposition – that the public man who permits himself to pause long enough to inquire whether a thing is popular or unpopular, instead of seeking to know whether it is right or wrong, it not only useless, but dangerous to his country. He is a coward to begin with and a menace always."

To that he adds:

"The people of my state, I think, understand when they send me to the Senate, they send me to exercise my own best judgment and heed my own conscience. I would rather go out of the Senate and spend the few remaining years of my life where I was born among my people, and without their favor – but possessing still my intellectual integrity – than to surrender my convictions."

To understand how he came by this independence of thought, and action, all one needs to keep in mind is this:

Carter Glass is a Democrat.

And, what is a Democrat?

A Democrat is one who holds to the historic principle of his party, "equal rights to all and special privilege to none." He is one who pledges his fealty to the Constitution of the United States; and one who, while recognizing that Government is a necessary instrument for the common good likewise recognizes that the most constant danger to his individual freedom is the very instrument he creates to protect it. For this reason he knows Government can never be trusted and must always be watched.

And, he is a Democrat who finds anchorage for his political creed in the words of Thomas Jefferson, as stated in the first inaugural address, March 4, 1801:

. . . All, too, will bear in mind this sacred principle, that though the will of the majority is in all cases to prevail, that will, to be rightful, must be reasonable; that the minority possess their equal rights, which equal laws must protect, and to violate which would be oppression.

. . . But every difference of opinion is not a difference of principle. We have called by different names brethren of the same principle. We are all republicans — we are federalists. If there be any among us who would wish to dissolve this Union or to change its republican form, let them stand undisturbed as monuments of the safety with which error of opinion may be tolerated where reason is left free to combat it. I know, indeed, that some honest men fear that a republican government cannot be strong; that this government is not strong enough. But would the honest patriot, in the full tide of successful experiment, abandon a government which has so far kept us free and firm, on the theoretic and visionary fear that this government, the world's best hope, may by possibility want energy to preserve itself? I trust not. I believe this, on the contrary, the strongest government on earth. I believe it is the only one where every man, at the call of the laws, would fly to the standard of the law, and would meet invasions of the public order as his own personal concern. Sometimes it is said that man cannot be trusted with the government of himself. Can he, then, be trusted with the government of others? Or have we found angels in the form of kings to govern him? Let history answer this question.

. . . With all these blessings, what more is necessary to make us a happy and prosperous people? Still one thing more, fellow citizens – wise and frugal government, which shall restrain men from injuring one another, which shall leave them otherwise free to regulate their own pursuits of industry and improvement, and shall not take from the mouth of labor the bread it has earned. This is the sum of good government, and this is necessary to close the circle of our felicities.

About to enter, fellow citizens, on the exercise of duties which comprehend everything dear and valuable to you, it is proper that you should understand what I deem the essential principles of our government, and consequently those which ought to shape its administration. I will compress them within the narrowest compass they will bear, stating the general principle, but not all its limitations. Equal and exact justice to all men, of whatever state or persuasion, religious or political; peace, commerce and honest friendship, with all nations – entangling alliances with none; the support of the state governments in all their rights, as the most competent administrations for our domestic concerns and the surest bulwarks against anti-republican tendencies; the preservation of the General Government in its whole constitutional vigor, as the sheet-anchor of our peace at home and safety abroad; a jealous care of the right of election by the people – a mild and safe corrective of abuses which are lopped by the sword of the revolution where peaceable remedies are unprovided; absolute acquiescence in the decisions of the majority – the vital principle of republics, from which there is no appeal but to force the vital principle and immediate parent of despotism; a well-disciplined militia – our best reliance in peace and for the first moments of war, till regulars may relieve them; the supremacy of the civil over the military authority; economy in the public expense that labor may be lightly burdened; the honest payment of our debts and sacred preservation of the public faith; encouragement of agriculture, and of commerce as its handmaid; the diffusion of information and the arraignment of all abuses at the bar of public reason; freedom of religion; freedom of the press; freedom of person under the protection of the habeas corpus; and trial by juries impartially selected

— these principles form the bright constellation which has gone before us, and guided our steps through an age of revolution and reformation. The wisdom of our sages and the blood of our heroes have been devoted to their attainment. They should be the creed of our political faith — the text of civil instruction — the touchstone by which to try the services of those we trust ; and should we wander from them in moments of error or alarm, let us hasten to retrace our steps and to regain the road which alone leads to peace, liberty and safety.

Glass stands with the historic principles that are inherent in good government. Looking about him he sees little resemblance between the New Deal and the Democratic party in which he has spent his long lifetime. It is these fundamental principles he sees violated and, recalling Jefferson's words, "should we wander from them in moments of error or alarm," he thinks only to summon his party, and his people, to "hasten to retrace our steps and to regain the road which alone leads to peace, liberty and safety."

Glass has hatred for excessive secrecy in government, just as he has contempt for ignorance on the part of those who administer it. If he insists on making public the underhand methods of government officials, it is because he believes in a democratic state.

Through a life that spans half the history of the nation, and through a public career that covers one-fourth of the history of the nation, he has come to realize that the collective integrity of government is far less than the individual integrity of the citizens who comprise it. This knowledge offends him. Admitting the frailties of human nature, and frankly confessing his own, still he can see no reason why men in the attainment of public office should thereupon become public deceivers. And here, again, he takes his place beside Jefferson in the "sacred preservation of the public faith."

"It is sinful," he says, "for anyone to feel as I feel about the present administration of our governmental affairs. The deceit being practiced upon the American people by men who have no purpose but to satiate their appetite for power is shameful.

"The elections of 1936, in many cases, were carried by people who were getting favors from the government, people who were subsidized by the government, people who were on relief rolls, and people who were sanctioning the invasion of private property and its occupation. In nation, and in some states, government has surrendered to group privilege."

Carter Glass believes, as Jefferson believed, "in equal rights to all and special privilege to none." He believes, as Jefferson believed, in a strict check on the powers delegated to the Federal Government, insisting "the support of the State governments in all their rights form the surest bulwarks against antirepublican tendencies."

He looks with apprehension upon the seizure of powers by the Federal Government; and is deeply resentful of the Federal bureaucracy that has been set up to administer relief.

"We talk about 'aiding' the States," he says, "but it has puzzled me to determine just precisely how it is 'aiding' the States if we tax the people in the States, bring their revenues to Washington and impound them in the Federal Treasury, and then erect a dangerous and costly Federal system of distribution of money we have taken from the States, doling it out to States as the judgment of these Federal minions may dictate. That is bribing the States with their own money to surrender their sovereignty.

"These temporary expedients providing so-called 'relief' have merely deferred the agony, and postponed the payday. We have been hurried into the passage of measures tendered for curative purposes, but which in the end are proving, and are going to continue to prove, worse than the disease sought to be cured.

"Various of the officials of government are not motivated by charity, by patriotism, or by any other high motive – no matter how much they prate about their tenderness for the poor. What they are doing is making millions of our people unserviceable to themselves, their families, and their country in order to make them obedient.

"This is nothing but the old theory of tyranny which beggars its subjects into submission. These public officials do not realize that, when they have come to the end of their system of impoverishment, nature still prevails; and that discontent will increase with misery. When that time comes – and it will! – those who are too weak to contribute to a nation's prosperity will still be strong enough to complete its ruin.

"To my mind, a President of the United States, no matter who he may be, is the unfittest person on earth to argue another American into accepting pittances from the brazenest politician among us.

"My authorities for that point of view are Thomas Jefferson, who called for 'jealous care of the right of election by the people,' and Edmund Burke who, as I have often said, was the 'greatest rhetorician of all time.' I have done no more, because I could do no more, than paraphrase what Burke said to the English Parliament in 1775 in his famous speech on 'Conciliation with the Colonies.'

"At that time Burke warned his King, and his countrymen:

> . . . when I consider that we have colonies for no purpose but to be serviceable to us, it seems to my poor understanding a little preposterous to make them unserviceable, in order to keep them obedient. It is, in truth, nothing more than the old and, as I thought, exploded theory of tyranny, which proposed to beggar its subjects into submission. But remember, when you have com-

pleted your system of impoverishment, that nature still proceeds in her orderly course; that discontent will increase with misery; and that there are critical moments in the fortune of all states, when they who are too weak to contribute to your prosperity, may be strong enough to complete your ruin.

The temper, and character, which prevail in our colonies are, I am afraid, unalterable by any human act. An Englishman is the unfittest person on earth to argue another Englishman into slavery.

"So what I dread is the setting up of an oligarchy, instead of the continuance of our democratic processes of government. Already growing luxuriantly in our American soil are all the discredited theories, past and present, of Europe and Asia. What we need here is organized propaganda in the sense that men and women of America who value the liberties they have enjoyed for 150 years, should, with unexampled spontaneity, exercise their constitutional right of petition, and with all the earnestness of their souls protest against this attempt to replace representative government with an autocracy.

"No government, and particularly no democratic government, can be better than its citizenship. A people must not only be capable of self-government but must have the spirit of self-government if they are to progress toward better things. No single man can do it for them. It is just as Jefferson said:

Sometimes it is said that man cannot be trusted with the government of himself. Can he, then, be trusted with the government of others? Or have we found angels in the form of kings to govern him? Let history answer this question.

"Take the National Industrial Recovery Act as an illustration. Its administration was confined to one man, long a respected friend of mine, exceptionally able, and with no selfish interest to subserve; but in circumstances he was as ruthless and harsh as human nature ever gets.

"In his first speech his chief lieutenant denounced every American citizen as a 'slacker' who should not volunteer obedience to the NRA. . . He urged the women of the country to pin white feathers on every person who would not willingly cooperate with enforcement; thus he would have put the badge of disgrace on all men and women who would not submit to the atrocious exactions of an Act of Congress which all nine judges of the Supreme Court, young and old alike, pronounced unconstitutional.

"It is this tyranny I would, if I could, save my country from experiencing. It is this error that I would keep the Democratic party from making. It is this horrible mistake I would keep the President from pursuing. Well-intentioned as they may be, men cannot be given such power over other men, and remain sound. Inevitably, and as Kipling wrote of an autocrat:

> We shall take our station, dirt beneath his feet,
> While his hired captains jeer us in the street.

"We have seen enough of these 'hired captains' and we have heard them jeering at us too often. They have whittled away at our constitutional barriers – barriers erected to protect a free people; they have forced us into debt from which there is no escape save through repudiation, inflation or excessive taxation. They must not be permitted to complete our ruin.

"Nor am I insensible of the fact that there are Senators and Representatives with so little spirit and so devoid of self-esteem as shamelessly to plead guilty to this shocking indictment. I have said that before, on another occasion. That, too, I say again. Unhappily, there are representatives of the people who seem to derive peculiar satisfaction in the confession of their own degeneracy.

"I did not think, and you did not think, when the Democratic party came into power in 1932 we would be led so far astray from the principles that made us an independent people and a great people. None of us even suspected the path along which we would be asked to travel. I had high hopes then that things would be done to help people and, as the record will show, every outstanding legislative problem upon which I have sharply differed with the Administration has been declared by the Supreme Court of the United States, or inferior courts throughout the country, to be clearly unconstitutional.

"Prior to these decisions the agencies administering these invalid laws were cruel and insufferably insolent. I refuse to believe that the people of Virginia want me, as their representative, or the people of other States want their representatives, to vote for things unconstitutional and oppressive.

"Thomas Jefferson never said a truer thing than that those people who are best governed are least governed. The American people must work out their own problems, and their own salvation. There is entirely too much running to Washington by business, by agriculture and by labor. That way lies paternalism, with socialism just beyond.

"There are certain things necessary to be done, of course, which the people in their private capacities lack the power to do, and in such cases the public must operate through the government. Privileges which are entrenched and greedy must be curbed, and it is the proper function of government to prevent the erection of any unnatural barriers to the equality of opportunity. But when equality of opportunity is assured government should interfere as little as possible with the normal activities of the people, and the normal processes of trade and industry.

"Government should not in any artificial way attempt to assure the man of poor ability a reward equal to that of a man of good ability ; but government should, in every possible way, afford to every citizen an opportunity to better his ability. This includes the opportunity for education for every one according to his capacity and his willingness to strive for it. The dullard still would lag behind and the unthrifty know times of want, but this would be because of the imperfections of humanity, not because of the injustice of our social system.

"The United States is the best earthly place of which we have knowledge. But it can be, and must be, made better. I often think that we who are of old American stock hold the privilege of American citizenship too lightly. It is a case where if familiarity does not breed contempt it does appear to breed at least a lack of appreciation and indifference. Because it became a part of our heritage at birth and an accompaniment of our manhood as a matter of course, we are apt to value it too lightly and lose sight of the thousand years of struggle upward which made American citizenship the thing it is.

"And because we, the heirs of a decade of centuries of struggle for self-government share our patrimony so readily with those who have not in their fiber the discipline of that struggle, the gift is cheapened in the eyes of the recipient. They are not to be blamed if they reason that a thing so lightly bestowed cannot have in it much of intrinsic value.

"I said that in a short article I wrote for *The Washington Star* a number of years ago. It is doubly important today.

"I have often thought it might be well to consider placing severer limitations than those that now prevail upon all participation in the government by the foreign born, both as to holding office and as to the exercise of the franchise. If the Anglo-Saxon race struggled a thousand years to win the liberties we enjoy today, it would not seem unreasonable to ask the coming tide of other races, who had no part in the struggle and who are untrained in its traditions, to wait an adequate time before being admitted to share in the responsibility for their maintenance.

"This would be no denial of free government to those who

shall be admitted within our gates, only the protection of our institutions against those who in their hearts might harbor other allegiances. A man who really loves a country which he technically has renounced better than the country which he formally has embraced is not an ideal citizen. He is not altogether an honest man.

"We can make better Americans, and thereby make America better, by placing the relations between those who toil and those for whom they toil upon a better and more equitable footing. The toiler must be more content if he is to be a better citizen. He ought not to have any cause to feel that he is being deprived by any unfair means of the just reward of his labor. He cannot be expected to have reverence for American institutions if he feels that American institutions permit him to be made the victim of an injustice, but he should sedulously guard against permitting his crusade for justice to degenerate into an intolerable campaign for privilege.

"Social justice is the thing upon which right-thinking Americans have set their minds. It will be won in time. But it will never be won by disorder. It will never succeed in a tumult. Neither strikes nor lockouts will hasten the events. Violence and threats and lawless activities will long postpone it. Nor will it ever be attained by the adoption of a 'scarcity of production' theory as a remedy for depression.

"I know it is unpleasant to tell government officials they are not thinking in the best interests of the people, as a whole, when they squander the people's money, rich and poor alike, but it is the truth.

"I know it is unpleasant to remind the people that it is to their own best interest that they look with genuine suspicion on all acts of government, and to completely satisfy themselves that all such acts as are proposed are to the people's permanent best interest, and not put forth in the transient best interests of political office holders. That, too, is the truth.

"No government of privilege, high or low – no government which always thinks first of whether a thing is popular or unpopular, instead of seeking to know whether it is right or wrong – no government which denies to its citizens any measure of prosperity – no government which has as its principle the unprincipled purpose of making millions of people unserviceable to themselves, their families, and their country in order to make them obedient at the polls, can ever bring a better and a more prosperous nation.

"Social justice can no more be won overnight than can political liberty. And the certainty of attaining social justice depends, completely, upon the retention of political liberty. Surrender political liberty and the struggle for justice ends immediately in disastrous defeat."

Glass asks, as did Jefferson :

"Would the honest patriot . . . abandon a government which has so far kept us free and firm, on the theoretic and visionary fear that this government, the world's best hope, may by possibility want energy to preserve itself ?"

And, as did Jefferson, he adds :

"I hope not."

It is evening. Down Lynchburg way from Montview, lighted windows – over there, a vagrant cloud, fringed in red and yellow and violet as it catches briefly, and holds eagerly, bright streamers of the departed sun – against the horizon, the mountains, their trees silhouetted sharply now, to be lost in speeding minutes in the deeper, darker blue of the sky. The air is brisk ; Elliott has a fire blazing. Glass goes indoors, switches off the lamp, sits down. Friendly flames draw his mind away from pressing duties and depressing distractions into the nowhere which is everywhere. . .

Sometimes there is music, low-tuned, from his radio. Now the only sound is the fire-crackle . . . "Mac" used to enjoy such hours as these. His thoughts turn on the momentous, the casual, the intimate . . . his eighty-first birthday, with the reporters asking how he felt . . . "I feel like the devil" . . . Why? . . . "There are eighty-one reasons why" . . . Then those days, during the World War, when to forget casualty lists and daily destruction he put on denims and painted his barn. . .

And now, once more, war madness, defense hysteria, rehearsals for slaughter . . . in contrast to what the League might have achieved . . . what might have been . . . the ignoble deeds men do for power; and worse, what power so often does to ignoble men . . . man's inhumanity . . . his scrabbling for power under vaunted symbols, hammer and sickle, swastika . . . in place of friendly handclasp the clenched fist raised and the goose-step ordered . . . ancient greeds, old as primal fire. . . He pokes the fire with vigor, the red sparks fly, an ardent flame embraces the log. . .

Fire is good, too . . . warmth, light . . . and still watching the ramparts, as in Plato's day and ancient Palestine, in Burke's day and Patrick Henry's, are men of good will. Theirs the eternal vigilance; in them, hope . . . the flames dance cheerily . . .

He recalls reading of Henry Adams in the '90s, gazing first at the old world splendor of Chartres cathedral, then at this thing called a dynamo . . . deploring the barren hardness of a new machine age, yet confident that in another forty years man would have mastered it, would have achieved human dignity, outlawed war . . . Well, today the machines are improved. . .

His own voyaging, in fancy and in fact . . . engine throb and throated whistle . . . white flash of gull's wing and wind-tossed foam . . . London, Paris . . . the moon and the vast sea, restlessly rolling . . . And the good feel of firm native earth . . . other days . . . fishing and swimming in the James . . . cool, heavy clay dust squirming beneath his brown bare feet. . .

The fire burns low, the flames recede ; the wine-red embers put on white mantles. . .

CHAPTER TWENTY-NINE

"My appeal is to the patriotic masses who have an inherited right to value their liberties and a traditional incentive to assert them."

The evolution of ideas, as of species, is a slow and painful process. It is possible our prehistoric ancestors stayed in the caves too long ; and certain it is, democracy wallowed blindly in the mires of time.

Thousands of years were needed to bring the democracy of the Greek states, and Aristotle's dictum that the reins of power continually shift among the hands of the one, the few and the many. The collapse of the Greek states he predicted, and diagnosed the cause : The two extremes of luxury and rags creating mutual hatred and dissent ; and the remedy – mitigating the evils of economic inequality by the formation of a strong middle class. The Greek states perished chiefly because his warning fell on barren ground.

From Greece's cultural ashes, Rome rose and set up her proud Republic. Greed grew as the Romans feasted, and the letter of the law was fabricated at the expense of the people. Power passed from the many to the few, and from the few to the one. Under the Caesars liberty languished, and Rome went down.

Western culture bled as tyrants led devastating hordes over feudal Europe. Soldiers and slaves swarmed where once free citizens met in forum. Instead of the council chamber came the armed camp, ready to resist or raid. Substituted for reason, sympathy, equality, justice and the poetry of life were rape, robbery, the sword – all led by lawless lust for power. Because moral evil inevitably sows material evil, it was democracy's dark age.

But always, when the yoke of tyranny grows too heavy,

power passes to other hands. Aristocracy waxed as autocracy waned ; the rule of the one gave way again to the control of the few, and hope came for the many. Oppression has never sat comfortably on Anglo-Saxon shoulders, and when upon baronial demand in the 13th century King John at Runnymede put his seal to the Magna Charta, English constitutional liberty was born. Soon after, Simon de Montfort allowed municipalities to send members to Parliament, laying the foundations for the House of Commons.

Like a dawn no dam can stay, the rising light of liberty overflowed to other lands – from these struggles by Anglo-Saxons for representative government, and after centuries of growth and reform, American democracy was born.

Such brief search of changing skies may be inadequate but, though brief, it should give us a glimpse of a spiraling eagle, and it should enable us to distinguish it more easily from the vultures that are always sweeping directly overhead to cast moving shadows on the land – for ours is a heritage not to be hazarded lightly. It is not yet secure. It is still fresh in the soil, and until its roots clutch with unbreakable hold, it is threatened by the too brief experience that always besets the years of youth.

Edmund Burke pointed to democracy's peril before encroaching despotism, when he said : "They will leave us as much liberty as they are unable to take away."

Patrick Henry knew it when, before Virginia burgesses, he hurled defiance at the British Crown.

Thomas Jefferson knew it when he wrote "eternal vigilance is the price of liberty."

And Carter Glass is in key with his political ancestry when he says, "My appeal is to the patriotic masses who have an inherited right to value their liberties and a traditional incentive to assert them."

Note well, however, this is not the demagogue's vote-hungry mass oratory.

The statement is qualified – "patriotic," "inherited right," "traditional incentive" – and the qualifications set him apart from politicians obediently attentive to the vacillations of the public pulse. He is obedient to the popular mandate only when he believes it to be wise and good.

Not that he is oblivious to the popular will. In the mass, as history attests, the good generally triumphs over the evil – hence the expression "*vox populi, vox Dei.*" Glass is deeply concerned with public opinion, and dwells apart in no ivory tower. Ben Jonson remarked that "he that is only taught by himself had a fool for his master." Talleyrand stated it succinctly when he said "there is one person that is wiser than anybody, and that is everybody." But like all aphorisms, these may be savored, each with a grain of salt.

For the voice of the people is not always right. From earliest times error and superstition, ignorance and idolatry, passion, prejudice and avarice have sounded – the voice that sang "Hosanna" also cried "Crucify!" It has shouted for liberty and tolerance – and shrieked above Salem fires.

Glass has not always had the people's transient favor, but he has always had their lasting support. He has had it because he has fought for his ideals – because he has "never sold the truth to serve the hour," – because, like Woodrow Wilson he strives for a state "where justice and mercy are reconciled, and the judge and brother are one." Such men serve democracy because they conceive of tradition as something more than the dry bones of their forefathers.

In the full idealistic sense of that worn word, these men are democrats, and their hands are never ready for incendiary torches lighted by the ideologies of communism, fascism, socialism, or that most ambiguous blaze, "liberalism," so currently ascendant. Politically and intellectually as well as literally, Glass was not born yesterday. He sees the experience of the past as the harness of the present. Under that harness he knows there will always be some who will feel free to forage in the acres of spurious utopianism ; likewise, he knows that when leaders throw off that harness there will be many who will kick high heels in the stampede toward visionary fields of a collectively secure Nirvana.

Secure from what ? Secure from inherited independence, from responsibility and from self-planned enterprise – of course ; but not secure from hunger, struggle, strife and despotism.

With the perspective of public comprehension narrowed by emergency planning and replanning, Glass is concerned because the American citizen has so complacently witnessed, during recent years, an enormous drift of governmental functions away from the states to the Federal capital. And, since the voice of the governed has always been diminished as the distance lengthened between it and the seat of power, it can be said that democracy in the American tradition stands in the dark door wherein enter the few to govern that from it may emerge the one who will rule.

History, both ancient and recent, emphatically reveals that great concentrations of power result inevitably in loss of personal liberty and the denial of justice and freedom of spirit by a bullying bureaucracy. The word despotism seems a little out of fashion since the dethronement of kings, but dictatorship is the same thing in modern dress, with one slight difference. For the former, force was the forthright weapon of subjection ; for the latter, force is screened by the opium vapors of a promised economic security. The greatest security this, or any other, nation has known has been achieved through liberty, and not through its denial.

Another adjunct of inordinate centralization, aside from the debasement of a citizenry rendered dependent on the power it has surrendered, is the corruption of "hired captains" given authority over regions and functions which they cherish no more than they try to understand. Jefferson spoke with greater prescience than he knew when he said: "What an augmentation of the field for jobbing, speculating, plundering, office building and office hunting would be produced by an assumption of all the State powers into the hands of the general government."

That venerable form of corruption known as patronage has been greatly centralized of late, now that the states are compelled to pour the money of their citizens into the Federal Treasury. Glass detects here an order of buying something that should never be for sale, for when a vote becomes a commodity it becomes immoral. And here, supplanting the mailed fist of old, is Federal power over a nation's purse strings as the chief weapon of authoritarianism into the hands of the few. Federal assumption of the administration of relief weights the weapon.

Those who wield this weapon proclaim it is necessary they do so because "life has grown complex." There is this to be said for their argument. No government can bestow morality upon the citizenry, only the citizenry can infuse it into the government. Until they themselves feel not "what can we get from the government?" but "what can we give?" there is little hope for a people . . . and, until they compel understanding on the part of their public officials that morals are not complex there is less hope.

Any survey of democracy, here and abroad, reveals that liberty and the doctrine of free enterprise have co-existed together harmoniously, each an element of the other. Such societies granting their members this right have delegated to their governments, local and national, the authority to regulate human industry to the point of preventing abuse, special privilege and restraint of trade by the vested interests, thus affording equality of opportunity to all citizens.

This is what Glass means when he says "when equality of opportunity is assured government should interfere as little as possible with the normal activities of the people, and the normal processes of trade and industry. . . If the dullard lags behind, or the unthrifty know times of want, this would be because of the imperfections of humanity, not because of the injustice of our social system."

To him, because a Federal Government enacts a highly beneficial Food and Drug Act, it does not follow that Government further serves the interests of its people if it establishes Federal drug stores, as well as Federal grocery stores. Private property that serves the public interest is still private property, the creation of individuals who have devoted their labors and their savings that society may be better served, and that men of ability may have their just reward.

He sees it as an inevitable tendency of centralized governments, heady with the old wine of power, and on the pretext of acting in the public good, crossing the line between regulation and participation. Here, again, power is wrested from the many into the hands of the few – the few who always practice more flagrant abuses than those they accused.

Having read and understood history, Glass knows, too, that becoming masters of men's labor, unsatisfied ambition drives dictators into becoming attempted masters of men's thoughts. The religion of the leaders of the State becomes the religion of the State, and its people. The charred stakes of ten thousand martyrs attest to that. . .

It is in the revitalization of local and state governments, and their vigilant and stubborn resistance to Federal encroachments on their native terrains that Glass sees hope for the future.

The fate of the nation at large is always primarily a local problem. Not beneath the dome of a distant Capitol, but in the homes of common citizens must the course of government be charted. Thus does democracy bring squarely to the citizen in his home the responsibility for public policy.

The real dignity of the individual is too frequently submerged because he is one among many. Deluded with the falsity inherent in this point of view, he finds it easy to evade his public duty. In every general election millions of potential votes, capable of protecting the citizen against autocratic subversion, remain unused weapons. Every citizen, on election day, should remind himself that the great weakness of democracy is the failure of all its citizens to vote – and by this failure, exposing democracy to another weakness . . . the weakness of, by their ballots, spewing into public office the second-rate, whose only desire for public office is the desire to enrich themselves. Glass has long favored the imposing of fines on those too indolent to vote – and he would compel all such to pay their fines at their polling places, on election day.

He believes that only in the way of morality does true freedom lie. He believes an honest people, spiritually alive, will not tolerate dishonesty and oppression. He believes democracy is rooted in the principle that people in the mass are good. He conceives government as did Aristotle – not as the expressed power of plutocrat or proletarian, but of the strong middle group constituting in a democracy, the majority.

And so when democracy falters, and all the powers are seized by latter-day Caesars, he says it is the citizen who cherishes freedom who must first put his own house in order. But while he is doing it, he will be distracted by hotly conflicting views. Special pleading, passion and propaganda will lure him to stairs not his own. He will have to take his stand against greed, hate, privilege, dishonesty, fanaticism. He will be suborned by weaklings who would vote away their own liberties for a mess of patronage. Because the evil minority is ever articulate, he will be flattered, cajoled, threatened and deceived. And if, in such a bedlam, he is bewildered, he will turn again, as Glass predicts, to the traditions of democracy.

He will proceed according to the essential, not the transient or accidental. He will strip away the deceptive furbishments of political structures and mark for himself the foundation stones planted in the bedrock of moral good. He will, as men have done before, return to the simplicities of liberty and justice, reaffirm them and translate them afresh. He will have learned again that he, himself, is his own best protector of his own freedom . . . and that contentment comes only from the workshop of his own mind, and the labor of his own hands.

CHAPTER THIRTY

No Room For Despair

To those whose work is to chart and administer along the crowded way that is human destiny, it is helpful to know something of both ends of the road. For such men it is needful to go again and again back along the worn path – back from city and council chamber to the quiet land for understanding.

Carter Glass' love of the land, acquired when the fields lay fallow in days of war, has never diminished. Like it, he has weathered many storms and endured, patient and undefeated. In legislative halls through four decades he has adhered to his Miltonic concept of duty as "the eldest daughter of the voice of God." Almost incessant labor has taxed his strength, battles have left him broken in health, but the frailty of his body has never dimmed the hard crystal of a sternly unswerving mind. He has not won all his battles, he frequently has been bitterly opposed, harassed, disappointed, and sometimes deceived, but even when humiliated he has never been humbled.

Although he never completed public school, he holds more degrees from American colleges and universities than any other member of Congress. The honorary degree of Doctor of Laws has been conferred upon him by Columbia, Hamilton, Tufts, LaFayette, Washington and Lee, University of North Carolina, Wesleyan, Princeton, Yale, Dartmouth – all in the same vein as the citation conferred on him by John Stewart Bryan, President of William and Mary College:

In time of crumbling standards he has stood like a rock in a wasted land. An eternal foe to ignoble compromise, undeterred by demagoguery, unblinded by fallacy, unanswered by specious-ness, with the courage of a soldier, and the devotion of a patriot, he has brought to his high responsibilities the statesmanship that became a Secretary of the Treasury, a Senator of the United States and a son of Virginia.

He has been honored by his country in the placing of a bronze plaque in the Federal Reserve Building in Washington whereon is inscribed "Defender of the Federal Reserve System" ; and by the minting of a silver half dollar, with his features in profile. He has been honored by his city as "the first citizen of Lynchburg," by the planting of an oak tree there as symbolic of his character, and by a plaque marking the place of his birth. At the School of Business at Harvard University there is a Carter Glass Hall. . .

These, and a great many more tributes have come to Glass but the following is the one that pleased him most :

November 22, 1922.

To Mr. Glass :

Those of us who have been employed by The News and The Daily Advance for more than twenty years have sent to your office a simple gift, a framed map of old Lynchburg, to serve as a vehicle for the conveyance of our sentiments.

The very simplicity of the offering is a tribute to your understanding, for it is intended to be a symbol of an intangible, spiritual regard and reverence we find it difficult to translate into words.

As an adequate token of faith, admiration, pride, respect, and above all, appreciation and love, we hope that you will find in the gift all that we would have it express.

Frank A. Lovelock	M. P. Tanner
Herbert F. Miley	Edgar Ferrell
M. K. Duerson	Owen Rush
C. D. Candler	Howard Shaner
R. Chess McGhee	Robert Berry
Ruby Roberts	Martha Adams
	W. H. Ferrell

Modesty is not unusual, but true humility is rare. Repeatedly Glass has said : "I am genuinely embarrassed by being praised for such things as integrity, independence and courage. I regard those as virtues to the common man. In all my life, day in and day out, I have never done anything but what I would expect and what should be expected of the average man of good sense and good character."

His colleagues in public life have not always been "average men of good sense and good character." He has seen many of the cherished tenets of his political philosophy abandoned and trampled in ignoble jockeying for political gain. Believing, with liberty-loving Virginians of an earlier day, that the best government is the least government, he has seen centralization of paternalistic power spread its dominance over a people, many of whom are only too willing to yield of their personal freedom for crumbs from the table of politics.

Yet, whatever his thoughts, they are not tinged with rancor, and they permit no room for despair. As he stands upon his land watching the sun sink westward in benign valediction, there is in his soul, too, a benign serenity, nourished by the enduring strength born of an intrinsic rectitude and sustained by convictions he will never abandon.

Guided and enriched by the philosophers and statesmen whose works he has treasured since youth, one man has climbed to a peak in Darien and acted according to what he there saw, and seeing, believed. As dusk deepens, at his elbow are Plato, Bacon, Jefferson, Wilson – and within, greater than all these, the knowledge that in the end he must stand alone with his conscience open for his God to see.

APPENDIX

BANKING AND CURRENCY REFORM

Speech of the Hon. Carter Glass, of Virginia, in the House of Representatives

Wednesday, September 10, 1913.

The House in Committee of the Whole House on the state of the Union had under consideration the bill (H. R. 7837) to provide for the establishment of Federal reserve banks, for furnishing an elastic currency, affording means of rediscounting commercial paper, and to establish a more effective supervision of banking in the United States, and for other purposes.

Mr. Glass. Mr. Chairman, I desire to present to the House, as in Committee of the Whole, a brief explanation of H. R. 7837, reported from the Banking and Currency Committee, with immaterial amendments, and to give the reasons which actuated the committee in its construction and consideration of this measure. I would ask the kind indulgence of my colleagues as I make this presentation of the bill, and would especially request that the continuity of my speech be not interrupted, as the topic is technical and as I am unused to addressing the House. When we come to consider the bill paragraph by paragraph under the five-minute rule the chairman of the committee and other members who have collaborated with him will be glad to answer all questions, if they can.

I think it is pretty generally agreed that there is a pressing necessity for currency legislation in this country. The country itself thinks so if any significance may be attached to the thousands of letters received by the Banking and Currency Committee of the House within the last six months or to the resolutions passed by hundreds of commercial bodies throughout the United States calling for immediate consideration and action by Congress. From every quarter and from all classes of citizens the demand has proceeded; and, in the judgment of the Banking and Currency Committee, Congress should no longer evade an imperative duty.

"A BARBAROUS SYSTEM"

For more than a quarter of a century there have been strong symptoms of an intense dissatisfaction with the prevailing national banking and currency system; and this spirit of discontent has been accentuated as, from time to time, the utter inadequacy of the system has been made manifest in periods of financial peril. While the existing system has operated satisfactorily under ordinary business conditions, and while the administration of the system for the 50 years of its history furnishes a high tribute to the integrity and efficiency of those concerned in its operation and oversight, its very best friend is bound to admit that, in time of stress and storm it has broken down utterly. This has occurred so often and the ensuing disaster has been so dreadful as to cause the banking experts of other nations and practical financiers everywhere to marvel at our continued failure either to adopt a better system or correct the evils of the one we have. Financial textbook writers of Europe have characterized our American system as "barbarous," and eminent bankers of this country who, from time to time, have appeared before the Banking and Currency Committee of the House, have not hesitated to confess that this bitter criticism is merited. While we may boast that no note holder has ever lost a dollar, and that the losses of depositors constitute an inconsiderable percentage of the total liabilities of the banks, nevertheless the failure of the system in acute exigencies has caused widespread business demoralization and almost universal distress. Five times within the last 30 years financial catastrophe has overtaken the country under this system; and it would be difficult to compute the enormous losses sustained by all classes of society – by the banks immediately involved; by the merchants whose credits were curtailed; by the industries whose shops were closed; by the railroads whose cars were stopped; by the farmers whose crops rotted in the fields; by the laborer who was deprived of his wage. The system literally has no reserve force. The currency based upon the Nation's debt is absolutely unresponsive to the Nation's business needs. The lack of cooperation and coordination among the more than 7,300 national banks produces a curtailment of facilities at all periods of exceptional demand for credit. This peculiar defect renders disaster inevitable.

EFFORTS AT REFORM

For years the business and banking community has been casting about for a remedy. In 1898 the Indianapolis Monetary Commission met and offered suggestions which were ignored. Later the American Bankers' Association at Atlantic City drafted an emergency currency bill which was introduced by Mr. Fowler, referred to the Banking and Currency Committee, but never reported or enacted into law. Several years thereafter we had the Lovering bill, and next the Fowler bill, consideration of which latter measure was rudely interrupted by the action of the Republican congressional caucus in May, 1908. Ignoring the Banking and Currency Committee, the party caucus agreed upon the Vreeland bill for an emergency currency and caused the discharge of the House Banking and Currency Committee from further consideration of currency matters at that session of Congress. Meanwhile, Mr. Aldrich had introduced a bill in the Senate and, by an act of legislative miscegenation, the two became one, and in hyphenated form we have the Vreeland-Aldrich law, which soon will expire by limitation. Not one dollar of currency has ever been issued under its provisions, thus literally confirming the prediction made at the time by those who opposed the measure. However, the commission for which the bill provided was duly appointed and for three years, at a cost of nearly $300,000 to the Government, prosecuted the work of investigation, making its report and recommendations to the Sixty-second Congress.

THE ALDRICH SCHEME

I do not desire at this time to make any comments upon the work of the Monetary Commission. It is treated in some detail in the report of the Banking and Currency Committee which accompanies the bill now under consideration. It is sufficient to say that those members of the Banking and Currency Committee peculiarly charged with the responsibility of recommending legislation felt precluded from considering the so-called Aldrich bill by reason of the fact that the platform of the Democratic Party adopted at Baltimore explicitly denounced that proposed legislation. It is interesting to note also that the platform of the Progressive Party likewise denounced the plan of the Monetary Commission, while the platform of the Republican Party was silent on the subject. The wisdom of these platform declarations has since been justified by the fact that thousands of bankers have abandoned the Aldrich bill and even some of those whom it was most intended to benefit have publicly confessed that the measure contains some exceedingly dangerous provisions.

The proponents of the bill now under consideration did not hesitate to appropriate any suggestion of a meritorious nature made by the Monetary Commission, just as the so-called Aldrich scheme embodied many of the provisions of the Fowler bill and the Muhleman central bank plan. We also made a careful study of the branch banking system of Canada and while we found that it had admirably served its purpose in that country we came to the conclusion that it would not be possible to apply it to the American system without vital alterations which would run athwart the banking principles and the business habits to which the American people have been so long accustomed. Hence, after exhaustive investigation and hearings, extending over a period of many months, the pending bill was drafted and, after full consideration as to every detail, is reported to the House with the recommendation that it be passed. Thus, Mr. Chairman, the Banking and Currency Committee feels that it has fully discharged its own duty and that further responsibility is with this body.

TIME TO ACT

I venture to express the sincere hope that the House will not delay the enactment of this bill. The chief and everlasting curse of attempted banking and currency legislation in this country has been the proneness of public men to procrastinate. When the Vreeland-Aldrich makeshift was adopted ex-Secretary Lyman J. Gage warned the committee and Congress that the bill was "merely a dangerous narcotic to lull the Nation to sleep, from which slumber it would some day awaken in agony." Remembering that financial panics in the United States are decennial, and that we are fast approaching the time-limit from 1907 to 1917, it seems to me that the obligation to legislate is immediate. We should no longer, from habit or timidity, gravely shake our heads and insist that we "will not be hurried in this matter" ; that we want further time for consideration ; that we must have other hearings and additional information. Sometimes I am brought to wonder, Mr. Chairman, what sort of information is wanted by the public men who eternally plead for delay. There is no theme on earth upon which information may more readily be obtained than upon the currency question. There is no topic upon which we have more authoritative expert expression and there are few subjects upon the general principles of which expert opinions are in greater accord. If it did no other good, the Monetary Commission, at a cost of approximately $150,000, assembled a great library on the subject of banking and currency reform, which for two years has been accessible to every Member of Congress. Less than six months ago the Banking and Currency Committee of the House closed exhaustive hearings on the subject, at which the best selected representatives of every known national group testified – big bankers and little bankers, merchants and farmers, credit men and manufacturers, currency experts, laboring men and textbook writers. And there is scarcely a provision of this pending currency bill which may not be related to these hearings. They took the widest range and reflected every conceivable variety of opinion ; and there is absolutely no excuse for further delay.

THE PLEDGE OF PARTIES

All parties are committed to the solution of this problem. When the Vreeland-Aldrich bill was passed five years ago the Republican Party in Congress solemnly pledged itself to speedily replace that temporary expedient with a permanent and comprehensive statute, while one of the latest public expressions of the last Republican President was upon the necessity of banking and currency reform. Mr. Taft declared that –

> It is more important than the tariff, more important than conservation, more important than the question of trusts and more important than any political legislation that has been presented.

The last national platform of the Democratic Party committed us to "a systematic revision of the banking laws of the country," and the Democratic President of the United States who was elected on that platform appeared at the Speaker's desk of this House more than two months ago and urged Congress not to wait until "the demands of the country shall have become reproaches." The President recommended the lines upon which we should proceed, saying :

> We must have a currency, not rigid as now, but readily, elastically responsive to sound credit, the expanding and contracting credits of everyday transactions, the normal ebb and flow of personal and corporate dealings. Our banking laws must mobilize reserves ; must not permit the concentration anywhere in a few hands of the monetary resources of the country or their use for speculative purposes in such volume as to hinder or impede or stand in the way of other more legitimate, more fruitful uses. And the control of the system of banking and of issue which our new laws are to set up must be public, not private, must be vested in the Government itself, so that the banks may be the instruments, not the masters, of business and of individual enterprise and initiative.

REGIONAL RESERVE BANKS

Upon these precise lines this bill is cast. Guided by the lamp of experience, taking note of the fact that, in time of emergency, clearing-house associations in the great money centers, and even in smaller communities, repeatedly succeeded in arresting financial disaster, the House Banking and Currency Committee conceived the idea that regional organizations of individual banks throughout the country might effectually prevent disaster. Hence, the fundamental idea of the bill now presented is the creation of a new class of banks to be known as Federal reserve banks. The country is to be divided into twelve parts, having reference to capital and the existing course of business; and in each of these regions is to be organized a Federal reserve bank. The minimum capital is to be $5,000,000 and the bank is to be owned and operated by the stockholding banks of the district, both National and State. The capitalization of the reserve banks is to be 20 per centum of the capital of the stockholding banks, one-half paid in and one-half subject to call. The business of the reserve bank will be the rediscounting of paper presented by member banks growing out of commercial, industrial, and agricultural transactions, with a maturity in some cases of not more than 90 and in others of not more than 120 days. These banks may also buy and sell Government securities, gold and silver bullion, foreign coin, foreign exchange, and open-market bills of given maturity. They are also to conduct, without charge, the fiscal operations of the United States Government.

Under this bill there is vastly less interference with the existing independent banking system than was provided by the Aldrich scheme. Each member bank is to deal directly with its regional reserve bank in securing rediscounts, and in no case is its paper to be guaranteed by other banks. While subject to limited control by the Federal reserve board, the regional reserve bank is given an independent status as well as exceedingly important functions. It has the initiative in fixing rates of discount within its territory and the exclusive determination of the amount of paper to be rediscounted for member banks. It is operated by a board of nine directors, two-thirds of whom are selected directly by the member banks and one-third by the Federal reserve board. Three of the nine directors must fairly represent the commercial, industrial, or agricultural interests of the community.

SMALL BANKS PROTECTED

In order to provide against control by the larger banks of a given district, the member banks of each region are divided into three groups equal, as nearly as may be, in number and of similar capitalization. Each bank, regardless of its size, is given one vote in the selection of directors. Notwithstanding the care which has been exercised to protect the rights of the small banks in the selection of directors, fears continue to be expressed that the larger banks of the district may control the system. By reference to the last annual report of the Comptroller of the Currency anybody who entertains a doubt on this point may readily have his apprehension quieted. I shall embody the table taken from the comptroller's report in my remarks :

Number of National Banks, Classified by Capital (Paid In), on Sept. 4, 1912.

Class.	Number.	Per cent.	Amount.	Per cent.
$25,000	2,004	27.09	$50,069,730	4.79
Over $25,000 and less than $50,000	381	5.15	12,849,335	1.23
$50,000 and less than $100,000	2,321	31.38	124,452,200	11.90
$100,000 and less than $250,000	2,006	27.12	254,053,385	24.29
$250,000 and less than $1,000,000	498	6.73	195,282,230	18.67
$1,000,000 and less than $5,000,000	169	2.29	234,305,700	22.40
$5,000,000 and over	18	.24	175,000,000	16.72
Grand total	7,397	100.00	1,046,012,580	100.00

It will be noted that of the 7,397 national banks 2,004 have not more than $25,000 capital ; 2,321 have less than $100,000 ; 2,006 have less than $250,000, while only 685 banks exceed a capitalization of $250,000. Thus of the 7,397 national banks in the system 6,712 may be classified as small banks, making it next to impossible for the larger banks to control.

NUMBER AND RESOURCES

The question has repeatedly been asked as to why the number of Federal reserve banks is fixed at 12, to which I reply that the number adopted is a compromise between the extreme suggestion of 50 on one hand and 3 on the other. The great central reserve city bankers advocate but 3 regional reserve banks, to be located, of course, in their central reserve cities, while a distinguished member of the other branch of Congress advocates 1 for each of the 48 States. The committee in fixing the number at 12 gave consideration to the amount of available capital of all the national banks, which aggregates $1,046,012,580. Three competent actuaries have made suggestive divisions of the country into 12 regions, and there can be no possible doubt, if all the national banks go into the system, that the minimum capital can be secured in the weakest of the 12 districts. The New York bank will have approximately $20,000,000 capital; the Boston bank more than $10,000,000; the Chicago bank nearly $11,000,000; the St. Louis bank $9,000,000; the Cincinnati bank $10,000,000; the Pennsylvania bank $12,000,000; the Washington bank $8,000,000, and, as previously stated, the weakest bank in the system, located experimentally at New Orleans, $5,500,000. This, of course, is merely a suggestive division of the country; the actual division is to be made by the Federal reserve board after painstaking investigation.

The resources of the Federal reserve banks can only be approximated. Basing the calculation on the aggregate capital of the national banks, the Federal reserve banks will have a capital of $104,000,000; about $400,000,000 in reserve funds and, perhaps, $200,000,000 of Government deposits, making a total of $704,000,000, giving them an aggregate credit-extending capacity of great proportions. That such additional facilities are needed for the development of the country can not seriously be questioned. In this connection I shall ask leave to insert in my remarks at this point an Associated Press dispatch from Sacketts Harbor, N. Y., under date of September 5, 1913, containing the testimony of Frank A. Vanderlip, president of the National City Bank of New York City, who asserts that $2,000,000,000 can be profitably invested within the next five years in developing the electrical industry of this country alone:

COULD USE BILLIONS

Sackets Harbor, N. Y., *September 5*

Eight million dollars a week for five years — $2,000,000,000 in all — can profitably be invested in developing the electrical industry in this country, in the opinion of Frank A. Vanderlip, president of the National City Bank, of New York. Mr. Vanderlip so declared to-night in addressing representatives of the electrical industry in the United States, meeting at Association Island. He said in part:

"In making such an estimate one does not need to draw on one's imagination. Little more is needed than a grasp of present-day statistics, compared with those of 5 or 10 years ago, to give the basis for such an estimate."

LARGER USE OF ELECTRICAL POWER

"When we think what is certain to be done in the way of electrification of steam railroad terminals and heavy mountain grades; when we reflect on the larger use of electrical energy for industrial power, in agricultural uses, and in continued growth of necessary interurban lines, we do not need to look further into the possible development of the industry to see a requirement for $400,000,000 a year of new capital.

"That means an $8,000,000 new capital issue every week for the next five years. It is such a capital requirement that you gentlemen are facing, and which must be successfully met if your energies are to have an adequate field of display. Can you get it?"

OTHER DEMANDS FOR CAPITAL

"To get a full appreciation of the difficulties, you may well glance outside of your own field, however, and note that there will mature within that five-year period well over $1,000,000,000 of steam railroad securities. The railroads in five years will need, say, $4,000,000,000 for refunding and fresh capital. States and municipalities will absorb in the neighborhood of $1,500,000,000 more, so with the $2,000,000,000 your industry will need there should be provided between now and the end of 1918 between $7,000,000,000 and $8,000,000,000 for these three purposes alone, to say nothing of general industrial and other needs.

"These are bewildering figures. They sound more like astronomical mathematics than totals of round, hard-earned dollars. The raising of these sums, however, is the practical problem that financiers have directly in front of them."

FEDERAL RESERVE BOARD

I do not desire to weary the House, Mr. Chairman, with too detailed a description of the provisions of this bill; therefore in the balance of my time I shall deal only with its several vital features. Overseeing the whole new system of Federal reserve banks, as a capstone of the scheme, is created a Federal reserve board, consisting of seven members. Three of them, the Secretary of the Treasury, the Secretary of Agriculture, and the Comptroller of the Currency, are members ex officio, and the other four members are to be appointed by the President of the United States for a term of eight years each. As set out in the report of the committee, the reasons for the selection of the two Treasury officials is self-evident. The Treasury Department not only is, but will continue to be, a fundamentally important factor in the financial organization of the country, while the Comptroller of the

Currency, in charge of the national banking system, will be a necessary adjunct in the management of the reserve bank system proposed in this bill. The Secretary of Agriculture has been added because of the belief that conditions in the producing regions of the country would deserve special consideration at the hands of the Federal reserve board, and that the Secretary of Agriculture is the natural representative of these interests. It is further thought that the presence of this official on the reserve board will give its deliberations a broader character than if it were composed altogether of members primarily equipped for the technical details of banking. The bill provides that not more than two of the presidential appointees shall belong to the same political party, thus emphasizing the view of the committee that the board should be a nonpartisan institution.

NO CENTRAL BANK

By not a few persons of intelligent observation and long experience the confident belief is entertained that no necessity exists for any central body of control. They contend that we might safely limit the operations of the new system to a given number of regional reserve banks with the function of divisional clearing-house associations and distinctively independent of one another. But the best expert and practical banking opinion insists that the first essential of banking and currency reform is a correlation of all the national banks at least, so as to render possible a quick mobilization of reserves at any threatened point in time of emergency. On this latter theory was based in large degree several currency plans considered by the Banking and Currency Committee of the House prior to the adoption by Congress of the Vreeland-Aldrich Act ; and altogether based on this theory was the proposal of the Monetary Commission to establish a single reserve association, which in reality would have provided a central bank of banks. Indeed, in its final analysis this scheme of the Monetary Commission, more familiarly known as the Aldrich bill, falls short of being a central bank in the broad sense of the term only because it contains no provision which would authorize the transaction of business with the public. There was method in this omission, it being part of the general contrivance to avoid every semblance of competition with the great banks of the country.

I have observed, Mr. Chairman, that certain eminent bankers, appearing recently before a legislative committee of the other branch of Congress, have spoken consistently and vehemently in favor of a central bank; but if you will carefully examine the hearings had by the Banking and Currency Committee of this House last winter you can not avoid the conclusion that these gentlemen do not mean exactly what they say. They do not want a real central bank. They simply want to establish a central banking institution which they may control and use for their own convenience, but to which the American people may not resort for any business purpose whatsoever. These gentlemen, when appearing before the Banking and Currency Committee of the House, were distinctly asked if they should be understood as advocating a national central bank with branches throughout the country, doing business with individuals, firms, and corporations, as well as with individual banks, whereupon they very promptly replied that they were simply advocating a central bank of banks. A central bank such as I have described, Mr. Chairman, or a central bank such as Andrew Jackson destroyed, is the very last thing that the great banks of this country would desire to see, for the reason that such an institution would necessarily import for them competition of the very sharpest description. Hence, in the construction of the bill of the Monetary Commission, great pains were observed and much ingenuity exercised to avoid anything of this kind.

VICES AND DANGERS AVOIDED

In the report of the Banking and Currency Committee of the House now before the Members we have in some detail set forth the objections of the committee to this Aldrich scheme, and in the construction of the bill now under consideration the committee very anxiously and carefully sought to avoid the vices and the dangers which are now generally recognized in the Aldrich plan. In that plan there was absolute lack of adequate governmental control; and while there was great pretense of protecting the interests of small banks, the very genius of the scheme and the involved nature of its mechanism made it certain that the practical operation of the system would inure to the advantage of the large financial institutions of the country. Moreover, the possibilities of inflation under this Aldrich scheme were so startling that the banking community of the country itself became alarmed; and the distinguished publicist whose name and fame were chiefly associated with the measure was practically driven from the public platform by the terrific exposure of this defect in the bill by a prominent banker of the West, addressing a society of political economists and showing that it involved expansion to the amount of six thousand millions before the regulating tax applied. Even James B. Forgan, of Chicago, and John Perrine, of California, strong advocates of the scheme, admitted that it provided "such vast credit-extending power as to be almost beyond belief and certainly far beyond requirements in any panic." Aside from its clumsy mechanism, its dangers of inflation, its peril to the independent banking system which the spirit of this Republic and the business habits of the American people have for 50 years sustained, the whole thing was literally saturated with monopolistic tendencies.

In the Federal reserve board, which the bill reported by your committee provides, there will not be discovered any of the defects which were essential features of the Aldrich bill. No capital stock is provided; no semblance of acquisitiveness prompts its operations; no banking incentive is behind, and no financial interest can pervert or control. It is an altruistic institution, a part of the Government itself, representing the American people, with powers such as no man would dare misuse. I do not ignore the fact that the batteries of the big bankers have been directed against this board or that the sharpest criticisms of this bill relate to the powers with which this Federal reserve board is vested; and yet, Mr. Chairman, there is scarcely a power enumerated in section 12 of this bill which has not been exercised by the Government for 50 years or, indeed, which has not been confided to one or two public functionaries.

NO EXTRAORDINARY POWERS

Nearly every power conferred by this bill on the Federal reserve board, composed of seven members, has been for half a century vested by the national bank act in the Secretary of the Treasury and the Comptroller of the Currency, to be exercised in the conduct and control of the national banking system. It does not seem necessary here and now to enumerate these powers; they relate to examination, regulation, publication, and control. Strictly speaking, the Federal reserve board performs no banking function; the banking business of the system is within the exclusive jurisdiction of the regional reserve banks, owned and operated by an aggregation of individual member banks.

But two of the powers conferred by this bill upon the Federal reserve board have been brought in serious question or subjected to pungent criticism. One of these powers is the right of the board to "require, in time of emergency, Federal reserve banks to rediscount the discounted prime paper of other Federal reserve banks." And it is a singular fact that the raging controversy which this provision has aroused was initiated by bankers who contributed thousands of dollars to fasten upon this country the wretched Aldrich scheme, which would have impounded the surplus funds of the entire banking community of America in the vaults of a single central bank, to be by it transferred at any time to any point for any purpose that might appeal to the sweet will or whim of the governing board of that institution. Here we provide, under the severest restrictions, a mobilization of banking strength "in time of emergency," by requiring a strong regional reserve bank to go to the temporary relief of another regional reserve bank in a plain business transaction, without risk, but actually with greater profit to the succoring bank than it might command under ordinary circumstances.

MOBILIZING RESERVES

This power literally correlates the regional reserve bank system ; it is a part of the process of mobilizing reserves. And yet gentlemen of the banking fraternity who have for five years persistently rolled this phrase on their tongues make this provision of the committee's bill an object of bitter attack. They were perfectly willing, under the Aldrich scheme, to confide this power to bankers, operating for gain, but are unwilling to lodge it with the Government of the United States to be used for patriotic purposes under a system devised for the good of the country, including the solvency of the banks themselves. As a matter of fact, Mr. Chairman, strictly safeguarded as we have it here, this power is neither dangerous nor extraordinary. It is essential to the system proposed and somewhat analogous to the power exercised for years by the Secretary of the Treasury alone, when, in time of emergency, he has withdrawn Government deposits at will from banks in one part of the country and transferred them to banks in another part of the country in an effort to cure a desperate situation, the difference being that, whereas the transfers have heretofore been made to the great money centers for the purpose of arresting stock-gambling panics, the transfers under this bill, if ever required at all, will be made to promote legitimate commercial transactions. Such transfers, you will note, are only required by this bill to be made in time of exigency. We believe that the power will not be invoked once in half a century, for the reason that if this bill should be enacted into law it will so withdraw the reserve funds of the country from stock speculative uses and apply them to commercial, industrial, and agricultural transactions, that we shall rarely ever again have bank panics in the United States.

SUSPENDING RESERVES

The other power conferred by this bill upon the Federal reserve board which has been moderately criticised is the right given said board to suspend the reserve requirements against deposit liabilities. Yet, Mr. Chairman, a power akin to this has been exercised by the Comptroller of the Currency with respect to national banks for nearly 50 years. Under section 5191 of the national-bank act, the Comptroller is implicitly authorized to tolerate for a period of 30 days a violation of the reserve requirements of the act without applying any penalty. By this officer the power has sometimes been abused and violations have been tolerated for several years instead of for a single month. The penalty prescribed by the national-bank act for the offense indicated is so radical that it has not been applied in the whole history of the national banking system. But here we have committed the power to a board of seven men charged with the duty of prescribing and enforcing a reasonable penalty for violation of the law. Like the power of enforced rediscounts, this function will rarely, if ever, be exercised by the Federal reserve board. It is, however, important that the Federal reserve board should have this power. It was suggested by the fact that three times within 60 years the British Parliament found it necessary to sanction by law the action of the Bank of England in suspending specie payments in order to arrest panics in Great Britain.

"POLITICAL CONTROL"

But, Mr. Chairman, bitter as has been the criticism leveled at the powers of the Federal reserve board provided by this bill, they have not been comparable to the denunciation by big banking interests of what is termed the "political structure" of this board. It is contended that the banks should have at least a minority representation upon the Federal reserve board; and I frankly admit that the claim upon its face seems both reasonable and expedient. Indeed, the first tentative draft of this bill contained such a provision ; but, after thorough consideration and full discussion, a different conclusion was reached. This Federal reserve board is distinctly a Government institution, and eminent bankers who were here in Washington last winter and spring contending for representation were met with the challenge to cite one instance where private interests were represented on any Government board in this or any other civilized country. They could not answer.

As already pointed out, the associated banks will own and operate the regional reserve banks provided by this bill, which are made after a period of years the exclusive mediums of Government issues and subject to no severer examination nor greater control than national banks of the existing system in their relations to the Government. If it may be said that they have important responsibilities, it may likewise be said that they are given great privileges, holding the reserve funds of the country and the deposits of the Government, amounting in the aggregate to nearly $600,000,000. The Federal reserve board, technically speaking, has no banking function. It is strictly a board of control, properly constituted of high Government officials, doing justice to the banks, but fairly and courageously representing the interests of the people. The danger which the banking community professes to see is not the real danger which I apprehend. The bankers seem to fear that men of their craft will be excluded ; but the real peril of the provision is the possibility of too many bankers being included. Observe what I mean : The Secretary of the Treasury will be a member of this board, and nine times out of ten that functionary is a practical banker. The Comptroller of the Currency will be a member of this board, and nearly always that official is a practical banker. In addition to this, the bill requires that one of the four presidential appointees shall be a person of banking experience ; so that we shall undoubtedly have ample banking representation on the board, and the talk of political control, in the last analysis, is the expression of a groundless conjecture.

A FUTILE OUTCRY

No great reformation in any existing institution was ever accomplished except in the face of severe contention. The clatter which we have heard in certain quarters about the "unconstitutionality" of this proposed system and the "confiscatory" nature of the power conferred upon the Federal reserve board is merely part of a cunningly devised propaganda to force concessions in another direction and to coerce Congress into yielding on certain other points which vitally affect certain big banks with extensive stock exchange connections. We have taken every reasonable precaution against asserting any power here that may be regarded as unconstitutional. We are not proposing to disturb any vested interest. There is nothing of a confiscatory nature in any of the powers to be exercised by the Federal reserve board. This talk takes us back to the predictions of disaster when the Interstate Commerce Commission was established. Then there was an outcry that Congress was about to "disturb the business interests" of the country; then we encountered the frantic contention that the Government was about to "seize private property."

Senator Hoar, of Massachusetts, said:

> Here is a proposition which would be destructive to great business interests of the country, especially to the export business of the principal city of the State which I represent. I hope the public interest affected will have a full opportunity to be heard.

Senator Nelson W. Aldrich, of Rhode Island, said:

> In order to cure evils which are apparent to the farmers of Illinois or Michigan, you propose to demoralize the whole commerce of the country; you propose to establish an arbitrary, unjust, unreasonable, impracticable rule.

Senator Orville H. Platt, of Connecticut, predicted that the passage of the Interstate Commerce bill—

> would result in an immediate rate war by all the railroads of the United States, the evil consequences of which would be greater than any evil now existing under pooling contracts. It would ruthlessly demoralize business and be far-reaching in its injurious results.

Senator Leland Stanford, of California, declared:

> If this bill shall become a law its consequences will be most disastrous to the various business interests of the country.

Senator Joseph E. Brown, of Georgia, said:

> The fact that a few bad men have controlled great lines of railroads is no reason why Congress should seriously cripple the great railroad interests of the country and destroy the property invested in by hundreds of thousands of people. This bill will prevent the rapid and cheap transportation

of commodities, retard the growth of our cities, and do immeasurable damages to our productive resources.

Gen. Charles H. Grosvenor, of Ohio, predicted that:

It will unsettle rates, disorganize the industries of the country, and thus force a reconstruction of systems of production. Meantime labor will suffer, farm products will lack a remunerative market, and uncertainty will discourage industry. It is a dangerous stride toward centralization of power in the hands of the few to the hindrance, vexation, and permanent injury of the many.

William C. Oates, of Alabama, said:

In Holland it is a capital felony to kill a stork, because the stork destroys the eels which bore through the dikes and inundate the country. To my mind this bill is a knot of eels which may bore through the dikes of safety and flood this country with trouble. I view it with grave apprehension.

Charles H. Allen, of Massachusetts, declared:

To pass this bill would be to put us at very great disadvantage, and while I am not prepared to go so far as some and see in imagination the yawning walls marking in desolate ruin the spot where once stood thriving and populous factories, yet I must say * * * that the result of any shrinking of values is quite likely to show itself first upon the poor people. * * * I must protest against the passage of this measure, destined as it is to work an injury against New England and New England interests.

Lewis Hanback, of Kansas, said:

My judgment * * * leads me to believe that the legislation proposed by the bill in question will be fatal to the best interests of my State, as well as to the whole country. I think it is safe to say * * * that these great lines of industry, the product of capital and the employer of labor, ought not to be interfered with, as they will be by the provisions of this bill.

I. Newton Evans, of Pennsylvania, said:

It is also of the utmost importance that we legislate so that the millions and millions of dollars invested and otherwise employed in the internal commerce of this vast country shall not be so deranged as to bring about a crisis in our financial affairs, which not only bankrupt many railroads, but, like the pebble on the smooth waters, its influence would be felt far and wide. Agriculture, commerce, manufactures, and, most of all, labor would suffer greatly by such a result.

The National Republican (Republican), of Washington, commented:

It is fair to suppose that Congress did not intend to wreck railways, to ruin communities, to destroy private property, to impoverish whole sections of the country, to break down manufacturing interests, to give foreign traders the advantage over home ones, to discriminate over one port in favor of another, to advance the interests of the Canadian railways, or to reenact the civil rights bill, yet it did all these things when it passed the bill entitled "A bill to regulate commerce."

The Chicago Journal (Republican) reflected newspaper opinion largely when it said:

> The President should be urged to call Congress together at once that it may rescue the commercial interests of the country from impending disaster. Let the power that enacted the offending statute be given an opportunity to right the great wrong it has done – and the sooner the better.

THE CRITICS CRITICIZED

And now, Mr. Chairman, in connection with this bill, we have the same outcry from interested quarters and through inspired newspaper comment. The critics, whether of one political party or another, accentuate objection to Government control and affect to stand aghast at the tremendous power confided to a political board. This criticism emanates at times from men who should be ashamed to project it; from gentlemen who stood upon this floor and upon the floor of another chamber five years ago and vehemently supported the Vreeland-Aldrich Act. Those who now affect consternation at the powers with which we propose to vest this Federal reserve board should look to their own records in currency legislation. When they complain that we give this Government board of seven public officials the arbitrary right of note issue, for very consistency's sake they should recollect that under the Vreeland-Aldrich Act they voted to confide this power in even more arbitrary degree to the Secretary of the Treasury alone, thus conferring upon a single political appointee of the President the tremendous responsibility, as well as the great power, of dispensing $500,000,000 of currency and, within his sole discretion, determining the validity and sufficiency of $650,000,000 of commercial paper and other securities.

Among other things, the Vreeland-Aldrich bill, section 2, dealing with the application of banks for currency, provides that:

> The Comptroller of the Currency shall immediately transmit such application to the Secretary of the Treasury with such recommendation as he thinks proper, and if, in the judgment of the Secretary of the Treasury, business conditions in the locality demand additional circulation, and if he is satisfied that a lien in favor of the United States on the securities so deposited and on the assets of the banks composing the association will be

amply sufficient for the protection of the United States, he shall direct an issue of additional circulating notes to the association on behalf of such bank, etc.

I beg these critics to note the language of the statute :

If in the judgment of the Secretary of the Treasury business conditions demand additional circulation !

And again :

If the Secretary of the Treasury be satisfied

that the securities deposited are amply sufficient for the protection of the United States. Could anybody conceive of power more arbitrary or of centralization more complete ? There is nothing comparable to it in this bill, for here we commit the power to a board of seven, having a trained and trusted representative at every point of origin, applying every precaution and going through every detail known to prudent banking processes.

When this extraordinary power was conferred by this House five years ago on a single official of the Government and objection was made by Mr. JAMES, now a Senator from Kentucky, the leading Republican member of the Banking and Currency Committee, Mr. BURTON, now a Senator from Ohio, exclaimed with much feeling and effect :

I say that for one I favor lodging authority with the Secretary of the Treasury and allowing him, under the great responsibilities of his position, to determine the amount of issues rather than to leave the decisions to the banks.

With how much more reason, Mr. Chairman, may we who stand for this currency bill insist now that this power shall be lodged with a Government board, composed of high and experienced men, four of them with long tenure of office and all of them, let us hope, keenly appreciating their great responsibilities and courageously determined to do their duty as representatives of the American people. There is no politics in this matter ; there can be none. It is my earnest conviction, based upon long and serious reflection, that no man can conceive, as none has yet pointed out, how any part of this system can be perverted to political uses. In my judgment if the United States has ever had a President ingenious enough to do this evil thing, it has never had one desperate enough, and never will have one shameless enough, to thus betray the confidence of the Nation. I happened to be present when an eminent banker suggested such a possibility to the present occupant of the executive chair, and heard this banker vainly challenged to show how it might be done. I shall not soon forget the emphasis with which the President of the United States declared that no man would ever be found who would be willing to imperil his reputation or tarnish his fame by so flagrant a prostitution of his high office! It brought to mind the splendid declaration made on this floor by Congressman BURTON, of Ohio, five years ago in discussing this very topic, when he compacted the whole thing in a single sentence, exclaiming:

> There are executive acts which are theoretically possible, but which the incumbents, with their weighty responsibilities, would never dare perform, because they would know that if their course was marked by favoritism or injustice they would be discredited while living and dishonored when dead.

The X ray of publicity is turned full upon the operations of this Federal reserve board. There can be nothing sinister about its transactions. Meeting with it at least four times a year, and perhaps oftener, will be a bankers' advisory council representing every regional reserve district in the system. This council will have access to the records of the board and is authorized to give advice and offer suggestions concerning its general policy. How could we have exercised greater caution in safe-guarding the public interest?

BANKING REFORM AND THE FARMER

For a brief period and in certain quarters this bill was assailed by those who professed to believe that it was written in the interest of the creditor class. I suspect, Mr. Chairman, that there are some folks who are incapable of accurately discriminating the real "creditor class" when it comes to the banking business. As a matter of fact, in the great volume of business transactions the "creditor class" is the people who loan money to banks. In this sense the banks themselves are distinctly debtors to their depositors notwithstanding the latter are many times borrowers of money and credit. But, for populistic purposes, the "debtor class" has been craftily turned to mean everybody who borrows or desires to borrow money; and the attempt is made to have it appear that under this bill greater difficulty will be experienced by "the plain people" in negotiating loans than under the existing system.

A persistent and pernicious effort has been made to create the impression that this bill, in some unexplained way, discriminates against the American farmer. To cure these imaginary discriminations there have been suggested financial nostrums that would cause the judicious to grieve and which, if accepted, would involve the whole country in ruin. Presented in the interest of the farmer and in the name of Democracy, they would impoverish the former and eternally discredit the latter. Some of these suggestions have been prompted by an exuberant but utterly misdirected zeal; others by a pitiful ignorance of the subject, and others still have their inspiration in the perennial and ubiquitous demagogy of a certain class of politicians. It would have been sheer foolishness, Mr. Chairman, for the proponents of this bill to have undertaken any discrimination against the American farmer, to whose favor a vast majority of Members here owe their political existence and whose interests they were commissioned to represent. And, sir, it would have been cowardly in the Banking and Currency Committee of the House had it sought to please the agricultural interests by partial legislation, hurtful to the banking and commercial interests of the United States. We have done neither of these things. We have sought to do exact justice to all classes; and any public man who would have us do otherwise affronts the intelligence and disparages the patriotism of the American farmer no less than he outrages the sense of justice of the American merchant and banker. It is gratifying to report to the House that while in some directions there have been manifestations of selfishness and in others amusing rhetorical exhibitions in behalf of the people, the committee has had a clear perception of its duty and has yielded neither to greed nor to declamation. It has steered a straight course, right between Scylla and Charybdis.

The requirements of the American farmer for bank credit are no different from the needs of other members of the community. The farmer requires loanable capital to enable him to extend his agricultural operations as far as there is profit in them, and to take advantage of market conditions which call for the application of more wealth than he actually possesses. However, while thus essentially on the same basis as others in respect to loanable funds and his need of credit, the farmer is peculiar in the respect that he ordinarily requires a longer term of credit than do some other members of the community, and in most countries requires currency in the transaction of his business rather than book credit with the bank.

FARM LOANS

The present bill is intended to render capital available to banks through the rediscount operation, and at this point I desire briefly to call attention to those phases of the bill which bear upon the farmer and his welfare and in regard to which it is probable that the agriculturist will be directly helped.

In section 14 of the bill we have provided for the rediscounting of paper possessing a maturity of not more than 90 days in one case and in another case paper possessing a maturity of not more than 120 days. In the same section we have provided for the making of acceptances by national banks and the rediscounting of those acceptances by Federal reserve banks.

There has been a great deal of misapprehension in many quarters with reference to the meaning of the 90-day provision in this paragraph. The claim has constantly been made that this 90-day provision would be of no service whatever to the farmer, because the farmer never bothers with so short a loan as 90 days. This, of course, is an entire misapprehension of the whole situation. The terms of the bill do not provide that the paper shall not be discounted if it runs more than 90 days, but merely that it shall not be discounted until it is within 90 days of maturity. In other words, the bill enables the banker who holds the farmer's paper to shorten the life of the farmer's paper by 90 days and to that extent get new funds with which to aid the farmer. Now, just what does this mean? Suppose that the loans of a farming community made by national banks will average 90 days, with a renewal for 90 days, or six months in all. It is evident that a bank which had loaned, let us say $25,000, for four months would be able to present this paper at the end of the first 30 days of the life of the loan and to get a rediscount for the remaining 90 days. That is to say, it would be able to draw back the amount of the farmer's credit at the end of the first 30 days and to relend that sum to other people. When the time came for renewal the bank would, of course, have to be in position to pay its loan or rediscount to the Federal reserve bank if it extended the farmer's accommodation for another 90 days out of new funds that have come in meanwhile; but it could again rediscount at the end of another 30-day period. In other words, if the community were doing its banking upon a four months' period of credit the bank would be able to shorten this in practice to a 30-day period of credit. It is entirely conceivable that by this process it should practically treble the amount of banking capital which it could, if necessary, place at the disposal of the community.

Now, let us suppose that the country bank, as is no doubt frequently the case, does not have a steady run of loans such as would justify the use of the method just described. Let us suppose instead of that that the demand for loans is likely to be "bunched" in the late spring and then to slacken so that the funds of the banks are tied up on, let us say, six months' paper. Under the 120-day provision of this bill such banks would be able to take six months' paper as soon as it was two months old to a Federal reserve bank and rediscount it. In other words, funds that would ordinarily have been tied up for four months longer will now be actually available to meet such additional demands as may come to the bank in the course of the summer and early autumn. Here, again, it is evident that the loan period being practically cut down by two-thirds the loaning power of the bank is trebled, assuming that it is able to obtain from the Federal reserve bank the rediscounts for which it has the basis in the shape of paper growing out of agricultural transactions.

HANDLING FARM CROPS

I have been constantly hearing that the proposed bill afforded no basis for accommodating the farmer who had raised his crops and who desired to get means that would enable him to carry them along pending improvement of prices. Nothing could be more unjust or further from the facts of the case than this. As a matter of fact, the bill makes ample provision for the handling of the great export crops of the country, such as cotton, wheat, corn, and the like. Not only does it provide for loans of the kind already referred to, but in the paragraph relating to acceptances it makes ample provision for enabling the owner or raiser of crops to retain the title to them while they are being disposed of abroad. Let us see how this works. If a cotton grower in the South, for example, needs funds he may arrange with a bank near his home to grant him a specified credit of, say

$50,000. In this event he would draw a bill of exchange or draft on the bank in question for, say, six months and would attach to it the documents showing shipment. The bank would accept this paper and he would then be in position to sell the bill practically anywhere. The credit would be based on an actual ownership of cotton protecting the actual amount of the bill and investors practically everywhere would feel entirely at liberty to purchase this paper freely because it had been guaranteed by the bank which accepted it. Everywhere in the country where there were idle funds there would be a demand for these bills. Not only Federal reserve banks, but other banks would constitute a market for such bills. When rediscounted there they would constitute a virtual extension of credit to these banks, enabling them to increase their loaning power tremendously and thereby to give to their customers accommodation which the latter could not otherwise have expected.

LOWER INTEREST TO THE FARMER

The unquestionable effect of this new system would be to draw funds now idle in various parts of the country to those regions where they could be used to best advantage, and as a result to diminish the rate of interest prevailing in the communities which thus receive the additional capital through the use of the acceptance method. There is no reason why at the present time there should be variations in rates of interest from 3 per cent in New York City to 12 or 15 per cent in small towns in the cotton-growing regions. If a standard kind of paper were provided it should command exactly the same confidence and bear exactly the same rate of interest in one part of the country as in another. This would mean that acceptances based upon goods – protected by cotton in this instance – would constitute a standard kind of paper which would be available for rediscount at any Federal reserve bank, as well as purchasable by investors and banks everywhere throughout the country. The consequence would be, as already stated, a very great reduction in the rate of interest to the grower or factor who had produced cotton and merely required loanable funds as a basis for business.

It is true that the use of the acceptance principle is limited in this bill to those commodities and operations that are connected with exportation and importation. This limitation has been complained of by many of those who believe that its extension to domestic operations would be highly advantageous to industry and would be free from the dangers which others have predicted. Whatever opinion may be entertained on this head, however, it is certain that the cotton grower or the wheat shipper can not share it in any such proportion as can other commercial factors. The fact that so much of our cotton goes abroad and that we still ship grain in enormous quantities means that those who are concerned in the exportation of these items have been exceptionally favored through the restriction of the acceptance business to them so that whatever funds are ready to be employed in that line of paper will go directly and without interference into the channels afforded to them by the trade in these commodities.

I want to add an emphatic word upon the other phase of the subject to which I have already referred — the farmer's interest in getting not only accommodation under the terms of this bill, but his interest in getting it in the cheapest possible way. I have already indicated the reasons for thinking that the working of the discount portions of the bill will greatly reduce the farmer's interest burden and supply him with means for marketing his crops to advantage. From the standpoint of the mechanism employed by the farmer there is, however, much to be said in addition to what I have already pointed out. To-day the farmer in many parts of the country wants his accommodation in the form of currency. This he can not get under the existing conditions without involving the bank in heavy expense and consequently necessitating the payment of a materially higher rate of interest by himself. The reason for the conditions to which I have thus referred is this:

Under the national-banking act the bank which wants $100 in notes must buy $100 in bonds and deposit them with the Treasury. Assuming that these bonds were bought at par, it cost $100 in cash to get $100 in notes, and the bank must furthermore place with the Treasury a 5 per cent redemption fund for the purpose of bearing the redemption of the notes when they are brought to the Treasury. I will not go into the details of the cost of issuing notes further at this point than barely to refer to these matters and to the additional outlay involved in getting the plates and paying the charge for transportation of paper necessitated by the present note system. The bank gets 2 per cent interest upon its bonds and whatever interest it can secure from the community by lending the notes. When allowance has been made for the expenses already mentioned and for the due share of administrative outlay involved in the process of conducting the bank, and presumably assigned to the loans made by the issue of notes, in proportion to their amount, as compared with the total loans of the bank, it is clear that the percentage of profit is very small where anything like a reasonable rate of interest to the borrower is charged. The borrower must therefore, and is in practice, required to pay a very high rate of interest to any bank which habitually makes its loans by issuing its own notes. Obviously, therefore, anything that will reduce the cost of this necessary instrument will reduce the charge for loans to the farmer.

Under the proposed bill it is clear that banks may obtain a supply of notes for customers who want their loans in this form by paying to the Federal reserve bank of the district in which they are situated such rate of rediscount as may be necessary to get the reserve bank to take their paper. As the reserve bank can then get the notes by segregating the borrower's paper to protect the accommodation thus secured, it is evident that there is no reason why the notes should cost the farmer anything more than the rate of rediscount fixed by the Federal reserve bank plus such commission as the local bank may charge for indorsing the borrower's paper and passing it on to the reserve bank. This change alone ought to reduce the cost of getting notes for bank loans by a very material proportion of its present amount. While no one can calculate the exact saving which will thus be made with precision, I should be inclined to estimate that through the elimination of bond security and the substitution of the new plan of issue there should be no good reason why the note loans made by banks in agricultural regions should run to a higher figure than perhaps 6 or 7 per cent as against the charge of 12 to 15 per cent that may now be found in many of the small towns of the West and South during the height of the season.

As previously stated, Mr. Chairman, we have not sought in this bill to help the farmer because he is a farmer, but to help the community which resorts to the banks for loans and to help the farmer as a necessary and important figure in that community. We have helped him as we have helped the merchant and manufacturer and other members of the body politic, by enabling him to secure, as we think, better and more abundant bank accommodation. But, in addition to this, we have removed the exceptional burdens which rest upon the rural borrower under the system of national bank-note issue which now prevails, and we have thereby placed him upon a footing of greater equality and of equity of treatment by making his credit instruments as reasonable in their expense to him as are those employed by the merchant and manufacturer. We have not attempted to exalt him and his interests above those of other elements in the community, but we have sought to give him what we believe he wanted — an open and fair share upon equal terms in the commercial credit of the country.

Exactly the same advantage, and in like degree, that will be afforded the farmers of the country under the rediscount provision of this bill will extend to every description of legitimate business and industry ; hence I will not further consider this section of the measure.

BANK RESERVES

Section 20 of the pending bill, Mr. Chairman, constitutes one of its vital features. It is the real point of attack by the big bankers of the central reserve cities. Recently at their Chicago conference and now before a standing committee at the other end of the Capitol these gentlemen enumerate various alterations which they would have made in this bill. But in real truth their fundamental and insuperable objection is to the reserve requirement. All other fault finding is simply strategic. This is no conjecture of my own ; I assert it as a fact which has been borne in upon me time and time again since the first print of this bill came from the press. I assert it as a fact and have conclusive proof of its verity. Not one of the bankers who have recently testified before the Senate committee can controvert the statement.

The whole fight of the great bankers is to drive us from our firm resolve to break down the artificial connection between the banking business of this country and the stock speculative operations at the money centers. The Monetary Commission, with more discretion than courage, absolutely evaded the problem ; but the Banking and Currency Committee of the House has gone to the very root of this gigantic evil and in this bill proposes to cut the cancer out. Under existing law we have permitted banks to pyramid credit upon credit and to call these credits reserves. It is a misnomer; they are not reserves. And when financial troubles come and the country banks call for their money with which to pay their creditors they find it all invested in stock-gambling operations. There is suspension of payment and the whole system breaks down under the strain, causing widespread confusion and almost inconceivable damage.

THE REAL FIGHT

The avowed purpose of this bill is to cure this evil; to withdraw the reserve funds of the country from the congested money centers and to make them readily available for business uses in the various sections of the country to which they belong. This we propose to do cautiously, without any shock to the existing arrangement, graduating the operation to prevalent conditions and extending it over a period of 36 months. This affords ample time to the reserve and central reserve city banks to adjust themselves to the reserve requirements of the new system. Out of abundant precaution we have actually given them a longer time than the best practical bankers of the country have said was needed. But, Mr. Chairman, the plaint of these gentlemen is not as to time but as to fact. They do not want existing arrangements disturbed; they desire to perpetuate a fictitious, unscientific system, sanctioned by law, but condemned by experience and bitterly offensive to the American people — a system which everybody knows encourages and promotes the worst description of stock gambling. The real opposition to this bill is not as to Government control, upon which we shall never yield; it is not as to the capital subscription required, which is precisely that of the Aldrich scheme unanimously indorsed by the American Bankers' Association; it is not as to the 5 per cent dividend allowed member banks, the exact limit prescribed in the Aldrich bill; it is not as to compulsory membership, which was provided in another way in the Aldrich scheme; it is not as to the bond-refunding proposition, infinitely simpler and less expensive than the Aldrich device. It is none of these things, Mr. Chairman, that vexes the big bankers. It is a loss of profits derived from a system which makes them the legal custodians of all the reserve funds of the country, $240,000,000 of which funds on the 24th day of November, 1912, they had put into the maelstrom of Wall Street stock operations.

DISAGREEING CRITICS

I distinctly am not appealing to the prejudice against great bankers. No man worthy to be a representative of the American people ought to deal with a problem of such magnitude without feeling profoundly the obligation to be fair and just to every interest involved. But so should the big bankers deal with us. They have assured us that the bill is workable; yet in another place they say it is not. The critics are not agreed among themselves even as to what the bill provides or as to what it means. Mr. James B. Forgan, the Nestor of American bankers, testified before the Senate committee last Friday that this measure would contract credits to the extent of $1,800,000,000, whereas Mr. Chas. G. Dawes, an ex-Comptroller of the Currency, now president of a large bank in Mr. Forgan's own city, publicly asserted a week ago that the bill involves an enormous inflation. So in the East recently an eminent banker of New York City declared that under this bill there would be a frightful contraction of credit, whereas in the same city the foreign exchange expert of one of the biggest banks there figured out for the president of the institution that possible expansion under the bill would reach the aggregate amount of nearly $2,000,000,000.

And thus the conflict of opinion runs. As a matter of fact, Mr. Chairman, neither of these postulates is true. Certainly it is impossible that both of them can be true. It may be confidently asserted that there will not be one dollar of harmful contraction under this bill; and those who undertake to figure otherwise conveniently ignore the fact that we have released a considerable portion of existing bank reserve. Frankly, there can be expansion under the bill; and, according to Mr. Frank Vanderlip, of the National City Bank of New York, the country just now greatly needs credit expansion. He figures that $2,000,000,000 can be used within the next five years in developing a single industry in America. But the committee has carefully provided against dangerous or undue expansion. If the banks of the country will not exercise common prudence in the matter, it is within the power of the Federal reserve board to compel them to do so by laying a firm hand upon the rate of discount. Moreover, the gold-reserve requirement and the redemption facilities afforded by the bill will have a powerful tendency toward checking expansion. But I will not longer claim the attention of the House upon this particular phase of the subject. I desire briefly to demonstrate the entire feasibility of the scheme provided by this bill for shifting the reserves without contracting credit. The matter has been figured out by the best experts in the country. It has been gone over with extreme care and we confidently challenge criticism of the facts and figures presented.

PRESENT RESERVE REQUIREMENTS

Section 22 of the bill provides for a revision of the existing reserves of national banking associations, which, under the present reserve system, are divided into three classes, (a) country banks, (b) reserve city banks, (c) central reserve city banks. Country banks are required to hold 6 per cent of their deposit liabilities in lawful money and 9 per cent in balances with other banks; reserve city banks are required to hold 12½ per cent of their deposits in lawful money and 12½ per cent in balances with other banks in central reserve cities; central reserve city banks are required to hold 25 per cent of their deposits (including those of other banks with them) in lawful money in their own vaults.

The aim of this measure is to transfer these reserves away from banks other than those to which they belong, so that ultimately bank reserves will be held partly in the vaults of the banks to which they belong, and party in the regional reserve banks, the reserve banks taking the place of existing reserve city and central reserve city banks in their relation to member banks.

PROPOSED RESERVE REQUIREMENTS

Carrying out this plan, it is provided (a) that 5 per cent of the outstanding deposits of all banks shall be carried in the new reserve banks; (b) 5 per cent of the deposits of present country banks to be carried in cash in their own vaults; (c) 2 per cent of the deposits of present country banks to be carried either in cash in their own vaults or as a balance with new reserve banks; (d) 9 per cent of the deposits of present reserve city and central reserve city banks to be carried in cash in their own vaults; (e) 4 per cent of the deposits of present reserve city and central reserve city banks to be carried either in cash in their own vaults or as balances with the new reserve banks.

It may be here explained that the "balances" spoken of can be obtained by rediscounting paper with the new reserve banks.

THE DEMONSTRATION

From the foregoing it is clear that as some discretion is left to the banks about their reserves the exact position of those reserves at any given time can not be predicted. Maximum and minimum limits can, however, be fixed. This is done as follows:

At the rate of June 4, 1913 (comptroller's last report), the present bank reserve in central reserve cities was $409,601,424 held in cash.

At the same date, the reserve which would have been required under this bill would have been 9 per cent of net deposits then subject to reserve requirements in cash, and 9 per cent in balances with the new reserve banks, as follows:

To be held in cash	$141,127,835
To be held as balances	141,127,835
Total	282,255,670

From this it is clear that if the balances under the new plan were established by taking actual money and putting it in the reserve banks the actual release of cash as compared with the present plan would be the difference between the total new reserve and the present reserve, while if the reserve balances were created by rediscounting the cash released under the new plan would be the difference between the cash required to be held under the new plan and the cash now actually held. That would signify:

Maximum release of cash	$268,473,589
Minimum release of cash	127,345,754

At the same date mentioned above the banking reserve in reserve cities as held by the banks was:

Held in cash	$250,383,926
Held in balances	232,799,679
Total	483,183,605

Under this bill these banks would have to hold in cash 9 per cent of their net deposits subject to reserve requirements and a like amount in balances which would be for the reserve cities as a group:

Held in cash	$175,128,701
Held in balances	175,128,701
Total	350,257,402

Comparing these figures with the present requirements as already given it is seen that the new plan might mean either a —

Maximum release of cash	$75,255,225
Or a maximum contraction of cash	99,873,476

At the same date mentioned above the banking reserve in country banks was held as follows:

Held in cash	$289,392,177
Held in balances	310,689,129
Total	600,081,306

Under this bill the cash required would be 5 per cent of their net deposits subject to reserve requirements and 7 per cent in balances (2 of this at the bank's discretion). This would mean:

To be held in cash	$180,533,642
To be held in balances	252,747,100
Total	433,280,742

On the same principle as before this would mean a maximum release or contraction as follows:

Maximum release	$108,858,535
Maximum contraction	143,888,565

Thus it appears that there would be a possible maximum contraction as follows:

Reserve city banks	$99,973,476
Country banks	143,888,565
Total	243,862,041
Deduct central reserve city release	127,345,754
Net contraction	116,516,287

It is also evident that the result might work out as follows:

Released by central reserve city banks	$268,473,589
Released by reserve city banks	75,255,225
Released by country banks	108,858,535
Total	452,587,349

It might reasonably be asked which of these results would probably be reached? Assume that the first (contraction) was the net result owing to banks fulfilling their reserve requirements by depositing cash in every instance. The Government balances which are now to be poured into trade channels through the new reserve banks will run from $200,000,000 to $250,000,000. Bearing in mind the fact that the capital of the new banks has to be raised in cash, it will be seen that independent of this capital the monetary situation would be left about the same as it is today, except that the new reserve banks would be in position to add their loaning power to that of the older banks. If we now assume that the transfer of reserves resulted in the extreme limit of expansion already referred to, it would be noted that the cash is released only on the assumption that the reserve requirements are met by rediscounting. If, however, the new reserve banks have to hold one-third in lawful money in order to make these discounts, it is clear that only two-thirds of $452,587,349, or about $300,000,000, will be released. Of this sum a certain part would be needed in bringing the reserves of State banks which may become members of the new associations up to the level which is required of them. How much this would be can not be positively asserted.

If it be asserted that this process will lead to inflation the answer to be made is that whether it will or not is a matter in the hands of the reserve banks, which have it in their power, by fixing their rate of discount suitably, to prevent the banks from creating reserve balances in excess of the required 5 per cent. If the reserve banks should do this, it would be found that the required 5 per cent referred to would be about $356,000,000, while the amount which the banks at their option might or might not obtain in this way would be about $213,000,000, the actual cash required to be held by them under the new plan being as follows:

Central reserve city banks	$141,127,835
Reserve city banks	175,128,701
Country banks	180,533,642
Total	496,790,178

Add to this the amount which the reserve banks can at their option make it worth while for the other banks to hold in cash, or to deposit with them in cash, and we have a total of about $710,000,000. The actual cash held today by the banks at home and in the redemption fund is about $950,000,000. Something like $240,000,000 would thus be released under the probable working out of the system and this would be drawn upon for the other purposes already referred to.

COUNTRY BANKS UNDER THE BILL

There has been a strenuous effort to prejudice the country banks against the bill, inspired, as I believe and have reason to assert, by banking institutions with close and extensive Wall Street affiliations. The propaganda was not prompted by any special solicitude for the country banks, but by chagrin over the prospect of being deprived by this bill of the reserve funds of the country banks. Mr. OWEN, the Senator from Oklahoma, in a letter which has since been made a Senate document, sharply pointed out the fallacy of the contention that country banks are offered no inducements to come into this system; so it would seem superfluous for me to present this aspect of the case here. However, I shall do so very briefly.

Let it be assumed that a bank of $100,000 capital (no surplus) is the owner of $75,000 in United States 2 per cent bonds and has outstanding $75,000 of circulation. Let it also be assumed that this bank has total outstanding deposits of $400,000. The bank is a country bank.

How will the new plan affect this institution? In the first place, the bank in question, if it has $400,000 of deposits, must have on hand in its own vaults 6 per cent of that amount in cash, or $24,000, and must have 9 per cent of that amount, or $36,000, as a balance with the reserve city bank.

Under this bill this bank must have a reserve of 12 per cent instead of 15, of which 5 per cent, or $20,000, must be in cash in the vaults, while $20,000 must ultimately be placed with the reserve bank and $8,000 may be kept either in the one place or in the other, when the whole measure has become operative at the end of three years.

As the bank has $24,000 cash when it enters the system, it is $4,000 ahead of the amount required to be held in its own vaults. It can draw for the remaining $28,000 required of it upon its present reserve city correspondent, with which it holds $36,000, sending the $28,000 check to the new Federal reserve bank. After the transaction is over its reserves will be complete, and it will have $4,000 in cash and $8,000 in balances over and above what it needs to meet its reserve requirements.

The bank, however, must contribute $10,000 to the capital stock of the Federal reserve bank which it has joined. If it pays this amount out of the $12,000 surplus it will become the owner of $10,000 stock in the new reserve bank and will still have $2,000 surplus out of its former balances.

This bank was receiving probably 2 per cent upon the $36,000 balances it carried, making in all $720 a year. Assuming that the stock in the new reserve bank pays 5 per cent, it will yield an income of $500 a year. The bank, moreover, has $2,000 of free cash still remaining which it can loan after withdrawing it from its present correspondents – say, at 5 per cent, bringing in $100 annually. Or if it were to use this $2,000 as a reserve upon which to build up new loans it could lend about $16,000 thereon, which at 5 per cent would yield it $800. On this basis the changed situation of the bank might result in a loss of about $120 a year or in a gain of $580 or in anything between those two sums. The reasonable expectation would be that the bank would get a material increase in its revenue. Just how much would depend upon the extent of the loans it could make in response to demand in the community.

The bank would be able to exchange each year 5 per cent of its present $75,000 of 2 per cent bonds, or $3,750. If we assume that the bank sells the 3 per cent bonds it receives through this exchange at par, and with the proceeds pays off the notes now outstanding against them, the effect is simply to reduce its assets and liabilities by equal amounts, at the same time releasing it from the necessity of retaining the 5 per cent redemption fund in Washington which at once becomes available as a basis for reserve loans at home. This 5 per cent redemption fund would be on $3,750 equivalent to about $185. If this were loaned directly at 5 per cent it would yield an income of $9.25. If the $185 were used as a 12 per cent reserve against loans, about $1,500 of loans could be made which at 5 per cent would yield $75. This if taken in connection with the showing made above would reduce the loss to $45 a year or would increase the gain to $655, with corresponding changes in intermediate points between these two extremes. If the banks had no notes outstanding against the bonds which it converted and sold, it would get fluid funds equal to the amount of the bonds thus sold which could be loaned at 5 per cent instead of the 2 per cent now paid by the bonds. This would be a difference of 3 per cent per year in favor of the new plan on a principal of $3,750. On the other hand, if the bank simply paid off its outstanding notes out of nonreserve money on hand (as in many cases it might) and held the new 3 per cent bonds as an investment it would profit to the extent of 1 per cent over the existing situation on a principal of $3,750 a year or $37.50 the first year, $75 the second year, and so on. At the end of 20 years it would be 1 per cent ahead on its whole $75,000 bonds, or $750 annually. In this event it is clear that within three years the increased revenue from its bonds would offset any possible loss due to the sacrifice on the 2 per cent interest on reserves. Against this might fairly be set off the income, if any, that it might have made by loaning the cash used to cancel its outstanding bank notes.

Summarizing, it is safe to say that upon the narrowest possible basis likely to present itself in the case of this bank the institution would, if it paid up its whole reserves under the new plan in cash, fully clear itself and make an additional revenue of from $200 to $500. If instead of paying up its reserves in cash it got the reserve credit by rediscounting, it might profit to a very much greater degree ; how much greater can not be estimated without knowing the rate of interest in the community and the extent to which it could obtain paper eligible for rediscount.

REFUNDING BONDS

Retirement of the national-bank circulation, frequently redundant and never elastic, is regarded as one of the essentials of currency reform. During the 12 years that I have served as a member of the Banking and Currency Committee the universal testimony of banker and business man, text writer and political economist has favored this alteration in the existing system. All political parties are pledged to this reform, notably the Democratic Party, which has repeatedly declared for it. In its platform of 1896 it declared :

> Congress alone has the power to coin and issue money, and President Jackson declared that this power could not be delegated to corporations or individuals. We therefore denounce the issuance of notes intended to circulate as money by national banks as in derogation of the Constitution, and we demand that all paper which is made a legal tender for public and private debts, or which is receivable for dues to the United States, shall be issued by the Government of the United States and shall be redeemable in coin.

Again, in 1900, the Democratic platform on the same subject declared that —

> A permanent national-bank currency, secured by Government bonds, must have a permanent debt to rest upon, and if the bank currency is to increase

the debt must also increase. The Republican currency scheme is therefore a scheme for fastening upon the taxpayers a perpetual and growing debt. We are opposed to this private corporation paper circulated as money but without legal-tender qualities and demand the retirement of the national-bank notes as fast as Government paper or silver certificates can be substituted for them.

This measure provides for the gradual retirement of national-bank circulation over a period of 20 years and the reversion of the right of note issue to the Government of the United States. Such an alteration in the existing system necessitates the refunding of United States 2 per cent bonds, which afford the basis of bank-note circulation. To my mind it needs no argument to determine that both the honor and the credit of the Government are involved in the proposition that whenever the Government withdraws the circulation privilege from its 2 per cent bonds it should reimburse the holders of its securities for the inevitable depreciation which will ensue. The refunding scheme which we have here provided contemplates this; and while it involves the assumption by the Government of a slightly increased interest charge, it is perfectly manifest that the Government has long ago received its compensation in the abnormally low rate at which it has been enabled for years to float its indebtedness under the existing system.

But aside from this, Mr. Chairman, the bill provides other compensations. It enables the Government to resume and exercise a function which for 50 years has been confided to private corporations, the value of which has been variously computed to be between 1½ to 2¼ per centum on the amount of circulation outstanding. In addition to this the Government shares in the excess earnings of the regional reserve banks; and finally, but most important of all, this new system will provide a rediscount scheme so much less expensive than the existing bond-secured currency plan as to make certain a reduction in the interest charge upon commercial transactions with the banks; so that, from every practical point of view, as well as upon considerations of public honor, the 2 per cent Government bonds should be refunded into 3 percents or paid by the Government at par with accrued interest. I am well aware that there are critics of this plan who are not mere cavilers; but we do not fear to subject our attitude on this question to the dispassionate judgment of the American people.

DIVISION OF EARNINGS

The division of earnings provided by this bill for the Federal reserve banks will stand the test of fair disputation, albeit many of the bankers are insisting that the cumulative dividend provided should be increased from 5 to 6 per cent. The rate fixed by this bill is exactly the rate fixed by the Aldrich bill, which the bankers unanimously indorsed. But the contention is that the Aldrich bill did not shift reserves and thus deprive the country banks of the 2 per cent interest which they have received upon their balances with correspondent banks. That is true. Neither did the Aldrich bill reduce country reserves from 15 to 12 per cent and other reserves from 25 to 18 per cent, nor did the Aldrich bill provide, in addition to a cumulative dividend, that the stockholding banks might receive 40 per cent of the excess earnings of the system. I have already pointed out that the interest to be derived by country banks from credit extensions based on the reserve-release clause of this bill will greatly more than compensate them for the loss of interest on their balances, to say nothing of the vastly superior advantages of a banking system which will never break down over a banking system which has repeatedly involved all the banks and the whole country in disaster.

NOTE ISSUES

In this country there is sharp division of opinion upon the question of note issues, one school of thought contending that it is strictly a banking function and another that it is an essential function of government. In this bill we have provided that the Government shall issue the notes, but only upon application by the banks and through the banks. The controversy over this provision is entirely sentimental. The section as it stands constitutes a compromise; but there is not a single element of unsoundness in the provision. Behind the notes is a gold reserve of 33⅓ per cent, commercial security amounting to dollar for dollar, a first and paramount lien on all the assets of the reserve banks and, superimposed, the obligation of the United States. To those who advocate Government issue, it may be said that they have it here in terms, with discretion in the Federal reserve board to issue upon application or to withhold. To those who contend for bank issues, we may say that, in the practical operation of the system, you have it here; because only upon application of the bank can the Government issue. To those who affect, or sincerely entertain, solicitude for the Government's credit, it may be pointed out, as a practical fact, that the security behind the notes here provided is many times more than sufficient to protect the Government before the note holder would reach the Treasury counter. Whatever other objections may be urged to the system, not a critic of this bill — banker, business man, or specialist — has ever suggested that the note here provided is not as sound as gold itself. [Applause.]

CONCLUSION

I will not, Mr. Chairman, weary Members with an explanation now of the minor details of this measure; these are fully set out in the printed report which accompanies the bill. We have made provision for foreign banking, designed to extend our foreign trade by furnishing quicker exchanges and affording infinitely better banking facilities in that field of enterprise. We have incorporated in the bill a savings-department clause, which will enable the national banks of the country to do business of this nature under authority of the statute rather than in disregard of the law. We have provided a more effective and less expensive method of domestic exchange and collection and also a system of examination and publicity which better safeguard the banking operations of the country.

The work of the Banking and Currency Committee has been tedious and laborious, dealing with a subject exceedingly complex and upon the details of which, if not upon the general principles involved, there are wide divergencies of opinion and varying degrees of antagonism. We have done the best we could. Without practical banking experience, disclaiming expert knowledge of the subject, I have tried as chairman of the committee to reconcile conflicting views, to compose all friction from whatever source arising, to embody in the bill the technical knowledge of the banker, the wisdom of the philosophers, and the rights of the people. We have not desired to approach or consider the question from the standpoint of party politics. It is too universal a problem for that. It is not a matter for party advantage. I have kept in constant contact and pleasant intercourse with the ranking minority member of the committee, giving him every successive reprint of the bill, affording all the information that he might desire, and inviting in good faith such suggestions as he might care to make. And now, Mr. Chairman, sure of our ground, yet conscious of human limitations, we submit this bill to the judgment of the House, challenging a fair consideration of its provisions and devoutly invoking the patriotic cooperation of our colleagues in what should be a great service to the country and a memorable achievement of the Sixty-third Congress. [Loud applause.]

ANNUAL REPORT

OF THE HON. CARTER GLASS, SECRETARY OF THE TREASURY

November 20, 1919

Discussed America's strong economic, financial and political position in the world-wide unrest and anxiety created in the readjustment and reconstruction period immediately following the World War.

Paid tribute to not only the actual combatants in the war but those who showed their patriotism by helping make successful the various Liberty and Victory Loans. Also lauded the efficient work of the Treasury, Federal Reserve and Liberty Loan Committees.

Explained plan of issuing loan certificates of five months maturity.

Discussed international financial situation, post-armistice loans to Allies and America's plans to aid in rehabilitation of war-torn Europe by means of Federal assistance and American private investments on a sound investment basis.

Discussed problem of whether progressive rise in commodity prices and wages had led to currency inflation, concluding that currency expansion was an effect and not a cause of advancing prices. Concurred in Federal Reserve Governor Harding's recommendation to Congress that any currency legislation at that time was unnecessary and undesirable.

Gave warning that extraordinary success of the Treasury in financing stupendous war expenditures might lead to a riot of public expenditure after the war, with consequential disastrous results. Discussed various forms of taxation and their relative merits and effects on all classes of American life. Urged denial of Government expenditures unless they represented imperative and unquestioned need.

Recommended necessity for revision of the revenue law, expressing Treasury's objections to excess-profits tax even as a war measure. Stated that such tax became in peace times a material factor in increased cost of living. Strongly urged Congress to determine in advance of the year's business the basis upon which taxes are to be imposed.

Discussed cost of the War. $32,830,000,000 gross cost from

April 6, 1917 to October 31, 1919, or $23,424,000,000 exclusive of loans to foreign Governments.

Gross public debt amounted to $26,210,530,000 on October 31, 1919. An increase of $24,928,561,000 since April 6, 1917.

Fourth Liberty Loan — greatest issue of bonds in history — amounting to $6,964,524,650. Subscribed for by 22,777,680 persons. 84% of that number subscribed in amounts of $50 and $100. More than 99% subscribed in amounts ranging from $50 to $10,000.

Victory Liberty Loan — discussed necessity for — outlined plans for — set forth sentiment for and against — intensive campaign necessary to bring needs of government before people. Secretary's tour of the nation on behalf of the Loan. Gratifying patriotic response. Success of the Loan by oversubscription.

Treasury Certificates of Indebtedness as a means of temporary financing of the government. Activities of nation's banks in distributing these securities to their customers. Value of tax certificates to taxpayers enabling them to not only assist government but serve their own convenience by saving in anticipation of their taxes by means of wise investment assuring liberal return.

Described sale and distribution of war-savings stamps and certificates.

Discussed loans to foreign governments — the need for these and the great results accomplished by these advances.

Paid tribute to the great work done by the volunteers in the War Loan Organization, numbering well over 2,000,000 persons.

Discussed War Loan Publicity in all its ramifications.

Outlined efforts of the Treasury in purchasing liberty bonds in order to stabilize the market prices whenever heavy sales were pressing upon the market.

Discussed uses of liberty bonds as security for sureties on penal bonds, acceptances in payment of estate or inheritance taxes.

Discussed illegitimate traffic in liberty bonds and war-savings stamps and certificates. Outlined efforts of Treasury to frustrate operations of swindlers in fleecing owners of these securities by purchase for less than market value.

Invited attention of Congress to necessity of enacting legislation to protect the people from losses growing out of the issue of fraudulent and worthless securities. Unscrupulous promoters tempted patriotic liberty loan subscribers to part with their bonds in exchange for these worthless stocks.

Federal Reserve System.

Paid tribute to the Federal Reserve System for its service in assisting Government in its war finance operations and by enabling the banks to support the efforts of the Treasury without neglecting the interests of commerce and industry.

Discussed post-war amendment to War Finance Corporation Act and the service rendered by that Corporation in sudden emergencies.

Lauded work done by Capital Issues Committee in passing upon issues of securities entirely from national standpoint, thereby conserving investment capital, labor and material for the use of the Government and essential industries.

Bond Secured Circulation of the National Banks.

Amount of bonds available for securing circulation was reduced by reason of maturity of the Spanish-American war 3 per cent bonds on August 1, 1918. Amount of national bank circulation secured by U. S. Bonds on October 31, 1919, was $722,-394,325, as compared with $721,471,138 on October 31, 1918. Applications from member banks for sale of bonds securing circulation were negligible during year.

Strongly urged the creation of a Budget System in order to eliminate duplicated effort, waste and inefficiency. Outlined proposed set-up for a budgetary system.

Called attention of Congress to grave menace to the control of appropriations and to the finances of the Government involved in the so-called "revolving funds" during peace times.

Discussed subject of incorporated government agencies. Stated that there can be no longer any justification for the creation of new Government-owned corporations or continuance of those in existence now that the national emergency has passed.

Urged Congress to give careful consideration to question of salaries in public service. Pointed out necessity of paying suitable compensation in order to retain in the public service a group of highly trained, well paid and permanent officials. Recommended prompt action by Congress in building up a permanent and dignified civil service which will include men of great ability and assuring a living wage to all employees commensurate with their relative value to the Government.

Stressed imperative need of an equitable retirement law for civil service employees.

Successful operation of the Federal farm-loan system.

Discussed the Internal Revenue Bureau, the important changes in the Bureau's organization at Washington and establishment of new collection districts throughout the country.

Discussed formation and evolution of the Bureau of War Risk Insurance.

Discussed the Public Health Service, laying particular stress on the records of the draft registration boards which showed that over 34% of all draft registrants were rejected on account of physical defects and diseases, which in a large measure could have been prevented by previous proper attention especially in childhood.

Called Congress' attention to great and urgent need of providing funds for construction of proposed National Archives Building.

Service performed by Coast Guard, particularly during the War.

All previous records broken by Bureau of Engraving and Printing in the work incidental to engraving, printing, and delivery of Liberty bonds, Victory notes, war-savings stamps, thrift stamps, certificates of indebtedness, farm-loan bonds, stamps and currency.

The work of the International High Commission.

Suggested desirability of plan whereby the Government would bond its own employees who would pay premiums into a mutual fidelity fund to be used for the payment of losses arising under the bonds.

[*The Report ran to* 180 *pages*]

THE FACTS ABOUT THE FISCAL POLICY OF OUR GOVERNMENT DURING THE PAST FEW YEARS

By SENATOR CARTER GLASS

Radio Speech by Former Secretary of the Treasury, Delivered November 1, 1932

No person of sensibility could welcome the task of directly assaulting the record of persons in high places with whom he has associated in the business of government at Washington. Especially is it repugnant to an accepted sense of propriety, except in imperative circumstances, to contravene statements made by the President of the United States or his more responsible cabinet ministers. It is because these imperative circumstances have arisen that I am venturing now to examine certain assertions made from public rostrums by President Hoover and disseminated throughout the country on the eve of a vitally important national election.

I do this with less hesitation because the action of the President in making these statements involves an amazing degree of rank ingratitude toward those in the legislative branch of the government at Washington whose non-partisan cooperation he constantly implored during the entire last session of Congress and even for weeks before the Congress convened. Moreover, the statements made, as well as the conclusions deduced, are flagrantly contrary to the facts, thus presenting a picture to the American people which is far away from the truth and which, in a vital sense, exaggerates conditions only that the President might magnify his own alleged achievements in correcting situations and saving the country.

To speak with suitable restraint, I may say that neither Hans Christian Andersen nor Karl Grimm, in appealing to the fancies of children, ever overtaxed his imagination as President Hoover repeatedly has done in his endeavor to regain the lost favor of the American people. Contrasted with his speech of acceptance and his addresses at Des Moines, Cleveland and elsewhere, Aesop's Fables deserve to rank as an accurate history of things that actually occurred.

That I have delayed, to this late moment, drawing these fabulous statements into question, is due only to the fact that I have been precluded from platform participation in the pending political campaign by reason of illness due to excessive physical and mental strain at the past session of Congress, for which reason I have lain on my bed racked with resentment at shocking perversions of fact concerning problems with which I have some degree of intimate knowledge, and amazed at *a priori* conclusions based on these false statements.

It is not too late to make a searching review of economic events with a view of determining the predominant causes of the prevailing depression, nor to examine the nature of the legislative and administrative expedients which were devised for recovery. Bad as were the expedients adopted, they are not as vicious as originally proposed by the Administration. Nevertheless, at the expense of the taxpayers, President Hoover has converted the Treasury at Washington into a national pawn-shop and infected the central government with the fatal germ of financial socialism. All semblance of state initiative and community pride has been extinguished, and the minions of Federal bureaucracy are given full sway to distribute huge sums of money picked from the pockets of the American People. Instead of being the servant and instrument of the people, with certain delegated powers, the Washington government has been made the creditor and overlord of the States, with power to coerce and subjugate these sub-divisions of the nation at the will of the party in power whenever pay-day approaches or an election needs to be won.

The President and his cabinet ministers insist that the collapse in the United States "was superinduced by economic convulsions abroad," and that this country was the unavoidable victim of European disturbances. This is a strange doctrine from those who have persisted in a policy of isolation of the United States so severe as that we must not participate with all other nations in promoting the peace of the world; but must pursue a detached and independent course in all things.

I insist that the very reverse of the President's contention is largely true. I assert that the improvidence, if not the direct profligacy, of incompetent Republican administrations at Washington is measurably, if not predominantly, responsible for the deplorable situation in which we find ourselves today.

With the advent of the Harding administration in 1921 (not to speak of its shameless disorder and corruption, which every sensitive citizen would like to forget), we were started forth on a prolonged era of cheap money and unrestrained speculation in every conceivable pursuit of business. President Coolidge actually boasted of the cheap credit policy of the Republican party at a time when caution was essential. Those in authority manifested their impatience and discontent with existing institutions by setting up bureau upon bureau to expand expensive federal activities and agency after agency to enable groups of people readily to increase the measure of their indebtedness; and, not satisfied with the almost incredible domestic expansion, they induced our people to engage in an orgy of foreign speculation.

I judge from one of President Hoover's speeches that he himself made a considerable purchase of the utterly debased currency of Germany, and exhibited at Cleveland his holding of depreciated German marks as a warning against the monetary "printing press." Thousands of others were induced to speculate in the depraved currencies of foreign nations. With insatiable avarice, great banking institutions in the United States, through their lawless affiliates with their high-pressure salesmanship, brought over and unloaded on the investing public of America billions of dollars of foreign securities, now practically worthless. The total amount has been computed as high as sixteen billions of dollars, equal to the total national indebtedness of the United States up to 1929, and twice as great as the credit facilities of our Federal Reserve Banking system. Witnesses before the Senate Finance Committee estimated the volume of these foreign securities at a minimum of ten billions of dollars, equal to two-thirds of the entire bonded indebtedness of the United States. The record warrants the assertion that the Republican administration at Washington, through its Department of State, was consequentially responsible for the flotation of these worthless foreign securities.

The State Department, without sanction of law constitutional or statutory, and in utter disregard of all precedent, assumed the function of passing on these loans. It required the great international bankers and their affiliates to submit to the government every one of these projected foreign flotations for objection or approval. The State Department, when called to task for this usurpation of authority, set up the childish, technical distinction between the term "approval" and the term "unobjected." The Administration's ablest spokesman on the floor of the United States Senate frankly admitted that, in the circumstances, the State Department's failure to object to these foreign loans was tantamount to approval. Individual investors and bankers imputed moral responsibility to the government; and expert salesmen, not too scrupulous to invoke the moral obligation thus incurred by the State Department, were enabled to sell these high-interest-bearing, but now worthless, foreign securities in competition with our own state, municipal, industrial and commercial securities. Undeniably, they filled the portfolios of interior banks, sometimes by coercion, with this immobile junk, so that when the crash came these banks were in a state of paralysis, utterly unable to respond to the legitimate requirements of their respective communities. There resulted an era of bank failures unprecedented since the foundation of the Republic, unapproached by financial collapse in any other nation on the globe. The State Department at Washington may deny its culpability until its spokesmen are black in the face, but the record explicitly condemns them.

The official explanation given to the Senate of the United States was so manifestly puerile and untrue that by unanimous vote regardless of party division, that body rejected it and warned the State Department to desist from this dangerous and ruinous usurpation of authority. Secretary Stimson treated the unanimously expressed sense of the United States Senate with a contempt that entitled him to impeachment. He persisted in his denial that the State Department was doing the very things which the record shows it was doing.

As I speak, I have before me a written communication from the late J. P. Cotton, transmitting a list of foreign loans passed on by the State Department within fourteen months theretofore, aggregating $1,193,000,000. More than a year previously I had, as a responsible member of the Banking and Currency Committee of the United States Senate, textually warned the State Department that —

> The supply of American funds for investment purposes is not inexhaustible ; and when the overload of those prodigious foreign flotations begins to sour or default in the hands of those attracted by the will-of-the-wisp of Government approval the authorities at Washington may then realize that my criticism is neither partisan nor unfriendly, but is a reasonable protest against transferring financial transactions from the realm of sound economy to the bogs and pitfalls of evil politics.

This and similar protests and warnings were contemptuously treated by President Coolidge and the Secretary of State. They evidently expected the Congress and the public to accept the silly and insufficient excuses offered by them.

In the earliest centuries, when that Florentine spendthrift called Lorenzo the Magnificent held sway over continental Europe, the average diplomat thought there was nothing better in life than a successful lie. The State Department at Washington had not yet learned that there are few things worse in life than a stupid lie.

Aside from the prodigious amount of these foreign securities crowded in our bank portfolios and exhausting the investment capabilities of the people, our Federal Reserve Banking System for five years or more gave more attention to stabilizing the finances of Europe than it gave to the requirements of American commerce and industry. Under the chairmanship and dominance of "the greatest Secretary of the Treasury since Alexander Hamilton," the twelve great Federal Reserve banks themselves loaned hundreds of millions of dollars abroad. It is asserted upon reliable authority that our Reserve Banks endorsed millions of dollars of acceptances for foreign banks – a thing unprecedented, I am advised, in the whole history of central banking.

The very spirit and text of the Federal Reserve Act indicate that the system was set up solely for the purpose of rendering assistance to our own commerce and industry. Its credits and currency were intended to rest upon business transactions in the United States; but under the chairmanship and predominant influence of "the greatest Secretary of the Treasury since Alexander Hamilton" the rediscount operations of the system were submerged in the open-market transactions in an unwise, if not actually lawless, attempt to cure the financial maladies of European nations. Our Reserve Banks dealt in alleged "trade" to the extent of millions of dollars that represented no more of a domestic business transaction than stored goods abroad shipped from one foreign country to another.

Worse than these things, in utter defiance to the text and shameless disregard of the spirit of the Federal Reserve Act, the facilities of the Federal Reserve banks were further misused. With Mr. Andrew W. Mellon as Chairman of the Board and the predominant figure, in a single six-month period in 1929 ten of the largest banks in New York alone were given access to seven hundred and fifty millions of dollars of Federal Reserve credits under the fifteen-day provision of the Act. Plainly interpreted, this means that a large, if not a greater, part of this sum, was being loaned to brokers for stock-gambling purposes.

An official communication inserted recently in the Congressional Record by the Republican chairman of the House Banking and Currency Committee showed that, in two recent years, the enormous sum of one hundred and eighteen billions of dollars was loaned to member banks of the Federal Reserve System under the fifteen-day provision of the Act, which means that, at the very peak of speculative orgies, when stocks were quoted at seventy-five times their earning capacity, incredible reserve sums were utilized for stock-gambling purposes. The open-market provision of the Act was put in for emergency purposes, with no particle of expectation that it would ever be put to stock-gambling uses; but under the benign chairmanship and influential administration of Secretary Mellon the System was largely driven away from its commercial and industrial purposes and made a medium for speculative investment activities.

Protest after protest was uttered by those who had vital responsibility in the enactment of Federal Reserve legislation. Warning after warning was given that the foreign security loans floated with the assistance of the State Department at Washington and the speculative use of the Federal Reserve facilities and the riot of gambling in real estate mortgages and commodities of all kinds, especially in stocks and bonds on the exchanges, were heading this country toward the brink of ruin. President Hoover in his Cleveland address contemptuously asserted that he "did not notice any Democratic Jeremiahs" during this period. It was not certain that he or his predecessor wanted to be bothered with the warnings of prophets.

We have seen that Mr. Coolidge approved the lawless foreign activities of his State Department. The country was literally shocked when this President of the United States figuratively jumped into the stockpit and cheered on the gamblers when brokers' loans had reached the stupendous figure of $3,810,023,-000.00! He said there was no cause for concern; and that these loans were far from excessive. He said this when Paul M. Warburg, among the foremost international bankers in the world, was earnestly warning the country against the inevitable consequences of this insane riot of speculation. Said Mr. Warburg:

> If a stock exchange debauch is quickly arrested by prompt and determined actions, it is not too much to hope that a shrinkage of inflated stock prices may be brought about without seriously affecting the wider circles of general business. If orgies of unrestrained speculation are permitted to spread too far, however, the ultimate collapse is certain not only to affect the speculators themselves, but also to bring about a general depression involving the whole country.

There was a Jeremiah for Mr. Coolidge and Mr. Hoover to heed. But they heeded not. Mr. Coolidge's response to the warning was to declare that he could see nothing except "a natural expansion of business in the securities market, and nothing unfavorable in it." And the wildest of the gamblers agreed with him. One of them told Federal Reserve authorities to go to hell, and another immediately sought to have me disciplined in Virginia for seeking to curb wicked speculation with the trust funds of the Federal Reserve system.

Dr. Ralph W. Robey, lecturer in banking at Columbia University and a financial writer of distinction, ascribed to President Coolidge tremendous responsibility for the continued upswing of the market; and so the "debauch" spoken of by Mr. Warburg continued at a rapid pace. A little later, President Hoover and Secretary Mellon followed Mr. Coolidge into the stockpit as cheer-leaders for the speculators, until these brokers' loans reached the stupendous total of eight billions of dollars! Thus, credits and currency were sucked into this financial maelstrom from every hamlet between the two oceans and drawn from foreign nations.

Yet in the face of this ineradicable record the President and his Secretary of the Treasury now talk about our troubles having originated in Europe. The fact is that our excesses contributed to European distress. Sir Philip Snowden, Chancellor of the British Exchequer, as well as other foreign ministers of finance, complained bitterly of the draughts on their resources to feed the flames of stock-gambling in this country. In a budgetary talk, exactly twenty days before the October break, Sir Philip warned the British public against being drawn into these transactions to the serious embarrassment of their own country.

Long after his inauguration as President, Mr. Hoover, the superman, could see nothing alarming in this situation. Ten days before the crash of October 24, 1929, his Secretary of Commerce petulantly "denied rumors that a severe depression in business and industrial activity was impending." The day after the crash President Hoover was quoted as saying: "The fundamental business of the country is on a sound and prosperous basis." Six months after the crash President Hoover said: "I am confident we have now passed the worst. We have succeeded in maintaining confidence and courage. We have avoided monetary panic and credit stringency. These dangers are behind us." And Dr. Klein, that ever convenient and accommodating statistician of the Administration, ten days after the crash said: "We have come to see more clearly that the stock-market is not the principal barometer of business, and that our American prosperity is deeply and firmly rooted."

Secretary Mills insists that our troubles started in Europe. Here was a financial crash right under his nose in New York City, involving a loss of $82,423,000,000 in security values alone, to say nothing of its blighting effects on general business. In its pitiful consequences the disaster reached into the remotest recesses of our business and social fabric, ruining as well the fortunes of thousands of adventurous people in foreign lands! Yet Mr. Mills says our "panic" originated in Europe with the failure of a great bank in Austria eighteen months after the "panic" started in New York. Mr. Mills ascribes our financial troubles over here to England's abandonment of the gold standard, which took place exactly two years, lacking one month, after the enveloping crash here described on the New York Stock Exchange. Thus, according to the President and his chief Cabinet minister, our depression and consequent consternation originated in Austria, was communicated to Germany, and found its last expression in England's temporary relinquishment of the gold standard.

Ten million idle men were tramping the streets and countrysides of the United States before the bank failure in Austria and before the abandonment of the gold standard by England. Miles of breadlines ranged along the streets of our towns and cities, and free-soup kitchens were as numerous as the leaves in Vallombrosa before anybody could know of the financial difficulties in Austria or of the temporary expedient at the Bank of England.

I do not exactly comprehend Mr. Mills' meaning of "panic." If we had no "panic" in this country that paralyzed banking and business long before the events described by Mr. Mills, what did we have? We had "panic" that had no relation to foreign financial transactions; panic that produced cessation of business and frightful decrease in industry of all kinds; panic that threatened starvation and created humiliation and made unwilling beggars of people who were proud to work; and the only thing that Europe had to do with the situation was to stand by in consternation while we erected a tariff wall which literally wrecked our trade with that continent and with the nations of every other continent, causing these nations in a spirit of retaliation to place tariffs and embargoes against the products of our fields and factories, so that our foreign trade in two years dropped from $9,640,356,268 to $4,513,561,337; exports being reduced by $2,817,235,963 and imports by $2,309,558,968. So eager were Mr.

Hoover and his Republican legislators for this tariff wreckage that he called Congress in extraordinary session for the avowed purpose of equalizing agricultural privileges with the benefits of protected industry, only to wind up the session by multiplying the inequalities and exacting further enormous tribute from agriculture.

The Smoot-Hawley-Grundy tariff act constitutes moral insensibility as well as economic insanity. It will take its place in history as a legislative and administrative enormity, purchased from the Government at Washington by the contributors to Mr. Hoover's campaign fund. Equally with the frightful financial debacle, this measure is responsible for unemployment. Along with that intolerable legislative bastard, known as the Farm Board Act, these measures have reduced the American farmer to the point of penury.

Thus, I have traced, with unerring accuracy I think, the causes of the panic and the inevitable consequences. These were not caused by the World War or by European disturbances, as alleged by Mr. Hoover. We had in 1922 largely gone through the processes of liquidation and of deflation in financial, commercial and industrial enterprise. The country was prepared to go forward in an orderly fashion, when the speculators seized the reins and, under the stimulating influence and applause of Republican administrations at Washington, embarked us on a career of adventure and inordinate inflation that carried us over the precipice. The World War had no more to do with this, nor Europe either, than the wars of the Phoenicians or the conquest of Gaul by Caesar. It was caused by the combination of factors which I have recited in the course of this address.

Now, what were the remedies proposed and applied; where rests the responsibility or credit for them, and in what degree have they been or are they likely to be effective?

The President of the United States was pathetic and importunate in his plea for "non-partisan cooperation" in the effort to rescue business after he could no longer escape the conclusion that something needed to be done. For months and months Mr. Hoover seemed utterly ignorant of the stupendous disaster which had overtaken the country. From time to time he persisted in telling us that prosperity was just around the corner, and his Department of Commerce statistician figured it out on paper accordingly.

However, when the President was actually brought to his senses and made to see that men and women were shivering in the cold; that unemployment and actual distress had reached alarming proportions, he resorted to the use of psychological poultices. He summoned railroad executives and captains of industry to a mass-meeting at the White House, and seemed to think he had exacted from these gentlemen an explicit agreement not to curtail employment or to reduce wages. In the existing situation the very suggestion betokened an utter misunderstanding of economics, if not mental aberration. The simplest person on earth should have known that men would not be employed if their services were not needed, and that wages would not remain unmolested if there was no market for the products of fields and factories.

It was predicted at the time of the White House announcement that if these railroad executives and captains of industry made the promise imputed to them by the President they had exposed themselves to the bitter charge of bad faith whenever curtailment and reduction should occur. And so it happened. Responsible officials of the American Federation of Labor made exactly this complaint because there occurred curtailment of employment of 6,230,000 laborers with an annual wage or cash earning power of $7,507,155,000, together with a loss of work for 2,670,000 trained persons with a cash earning power of $5,564,280,000. This made a total of 8,900,000 persons out of employment, with a loss of $13,071,435,000 in earning power, since that famous White House conference. Thus this psychological device proved futile; and only ten days ago the country witnessed the humiliating spectacle of the President of the United States begging railroad executives not to reduce wages further until after the Presidential election.

Then we had the moratorium on foreign debts, which was supposed to prove a psychological blessing. Those having intimate knowledge of the situation knew perfectly well that a moratorium or repudiation was inevitable and that if this country should not grant it some of our foreign debtors would be compelled to take it; and so the psychological effect of that device soon faded away, and confidence was not yet restored.

Next we had the pitifully amusing expedient of organizing mass-meetings to persuade against runs on banks and hoarding. Since this silly movement was more calculated to disturb confidence than to assuage fear, it was soon laughed out of existence. They tell us now, nearly a year after this absurd psychological attempt, that hoarding, computed to amount to a billion and a half dollars, has ceased to the extent of $250,000,000. This is a mere pre-election conjecture, based upon attenuated inferences and in no wise substantiated by substantive bank figures, which show that deposits in member banks of the Reserve System alone have fallen off $2,882,000,000 since January 1, 1932. Mere reduction in circulation is by no means an exact index to hoarding. Any patriotic citizen could cheerfully wish that a more encouraging picture might truthfully be drawn ; but nobody should have one particle of tolerance for partisan pre-election assertions designed only to magnify the alleged achievements of a candidate for the Presidency.

The next expedient in order was the White House announcement that certain Eastern bankers in the money centers had been induced by the President generously to promote a National Credit Corporation, making itself responsible for the use of five hundred millions of dollars to acquire the frozen assets of threatened banks to prevent continued failures. It was suspected at the time that this corporation would be permitted, as was subsequently proposed, to dump its frozen assets in the lap of the Federal Reserve banking system. Those of us responsible for legislation in Congress set our faces severely against anything of the kind ; but it is now disclosed that before taking a step in the premises these Eastern bankers, at a secret meeting with the President of the United States and his Secretary of the Treasury, at Mr. Mellon's apartment in Washington, were definitely promised that a Government agency would take over the acquired assets of the Corporation. This meant, in plain terms, that this "burden" of these generous Eastern bankers was to be unloaded on the shoulders of the taxpayers of the United States ! And, in a round-about way, this has been done ; because the Reconstruction Finance Corporation, using exclusively the public funds, has already taken in excess of one hundred millions of dollars of the assets of the National Credit Corporation by extending loans to individual banks throughout the country to enable them to repay the loans made by the National Credit Corporation under the secret promise of the President and his Secretary of the Treasury to take over these loans. I assume that nobody will deny the accuracy of this statement ; if any one does, I refer him to the statement of Percy H. Johnston, President of the Chemical Bank and Trust Company of New York City, before the Senate Banking and Currency Committee on March 25, 1932, as recorded on page

147, Part I, of the Hearings. There Mr. Johnston definitely asserts that he was present when the President of the United States and Secretary Mellon made this agreement.

This National Credit Corporation did practically nothing for months until prodded into action by a threatened Congressional inquiry. The Senate Committee could not even persuade the chairman of the corporation to come to Washington and tell us what they were doing. Great banks were failing at its very doorsteps in the East; eight hundred and twenty-five were tottering in three months throughout the country. Hence, the President was compelled by this inaction to suggest a revival of the old War Finance Corporation, organized under the Wilson Administration to assist industries that were contributing to the conduct of the war. The Hoover idolaters acclaim his great genius for devising this instrument of relief. He had not one thing on earth to do with it. The act is almost a complete paraphrase of the act drawn by the Treasury Department under Mr. Wilson. Coincidentally, the very man appointed by me as director of the War Finance Corporation, with the approval of Mr. Wilson, was picked to run this revised edition of this resurrected corporation, and was worked to the point of death. While the legislation was pending, it was a profusely and repeatedly avowed fact that but for the unstinted cooperation of Democratic leaders in the House and Senate nothing whatsoever could have been done. Now all this is forgotten in order to magnify the alleged achievements of the man who besought this aid.

Even at that, the bill as sent up from the Treasury was saturated with unsound and dangerous provisions, amounting to an assault upon the very integrity of our banking system. Under its terms two billions of dollars of hazardous loans were made eligible for purchase and rediscount at the Federal Reserve banks. One can reasonably conjecture that this proposal was in pursuance of the secret agreement made by the President and Mr. Mellon with the National Credit Corporation. Those of us who adhered to safe and sound banking principles were compelled, up to the last moment, to resist this and other questionable suggestions.

I assert that there is not a safeguard in the Reconstruction Finance Corporation Act, few as they are, that was not written into it by a Democrat or Progressive-Republican after the bill came from the Treasury Department. I assert that but for the constant vigilance and active cooperation of the Democratic leaders in House and Senate this revived War Finance Corporation could not have gotten on the calendar of either branch of Congress. This was repeatedly asserted by Administration spokesmen in terms of grateful appreciation at the time ; and we are now justified in resenting the attempt of President Hoover, in sheer campaign desperation, to appropriate to himself and his party whatever credit may attach to this irregular and unorthodox method of relief, the permanent effectiveness of which is far away from being established. In my thirty years of public life I have never witnessed such an exhibition of political ingratitude.

I shall not attempt here to discuss the seemingly profligate waste of the taxpayers' money in fabulous schemes, few of which would be dreamed of in the ordinary course of business. I will say, however, that the President will never be able to justify this waste of public funds by craftily imputing responsibility to an alleged "Democratic majority" on the spending Board. We are told that the astounding loans of this Board, apparently reeking with political significance, will not cost the American taxpayers a dollar ; but few people should be simple enough to credit this preposterous assertion. The very fact that not one dollar of the Corporation's debentures has been offered to private investors, but every dollar of them unloaded on the Federal Treasury, is a clear portent of the burden which the taxpayers of the country will be compelled to endure. Some of its loans have been so opportunely timed and so geographically distributed as to make some people wonder why the Republican party should trouble itself to raise a campaign fund when the Reconstruction Finance Corporation, as in the case of California and other debatable states, is acting with such singular promptitude and precision. The country must wait until pay-day shall have come to contrast the profligacy and the wisdom of this corporation. Only in the final reckoning may the country know whether it has definitely helped or largely disorganized and cripped legitimate business – whether indignant denial of partisan political influence is pardonable sham or upon a frank basis. At all events, there was neither genius nor statesmanship nor engineering skill in the resurrection of Mr. Wilson's war device with which to cure the timidity and culpabilities of Mr. Hoover's administration. We shall later, perhaps too late, determine whether there has not been extraordinary political guile in its administration.

The next legislative contrivance was the Glass-Steagall bill, made desirable by Presidential representations to the country that we needed to "broaden the base" of Federal Reserve credit facilities. This Executive misrepresentation of the credit situation persisted in the face of the fact that the Federal Reserve Board, justified by authentic reports from every member bank of the system, officially declared that three billions of dollars of commercial paper in excess of outstanding discount was available for loans, together with five billions of dollars of Federal securities held by the member banks. Back of this eligible paper was a supply of gold sufficient to expand bank loans by four billions of dollars! It was in proof, by authentic statistics, that the distribution over the country of this excess in eligible commercial paper and in bonds was almost ideal. While I supported the bill to please the President's fancy, I nevertheless stated the facts to the Congress and the country. The ensuing results justify every prediction we made. Not a dollar has been loaned to a single bank under the first provision of the act, relating to associations of banks; and but thirty-nine limping banks out of a membership of 7,600 were aided in the comparatively inconsequential sum of twenty-seven million dollars under section 2 of the Act. When it is considered that the total loans of member banks at the time amounted to nearly thirty-one billions of dollars, the insignificance of this transaction is apparent, and the utter vice of Mr. Hoover having created alarm over our credit structure is mathematically demonstrated.

Even this Glass-Steagall bill, when brought to us by spokesmen for the President, was saturated with hazardous provisions. It would have permitted member banks to unload their frozen assets on the Federal Reserve banks while retaining their liquid assets in their own possession. It would have made eligible for rediscount at the Federal Reserve banks as many billions of foreign securities as the banks might be willing to receive. It would have permitted the big banks to absorb the credits of the Reserve banks to the practical exclusion of the smaller banks. As in the case of the Reconstruction Finance Corporation bill, every safeguard in the Glass-Steagall bill was written after the measure had left the Treasury building.

In Republican official quarters it has been proclaimed that this Glass-Steagall bill kept the United States on the gold standard. I assert that this is false in fact and implication. I assert that those of us responsible for legislation never had the remotest intimation from the Administration that the gold standard was in danger. I assert that the President and accredited spokesmen bitterly denounced the mischievous talk. I repeat the assertion that anybody who now says anything to the contrary of what is alleged here is either ignorant of the facts or indifferent to the truth.

Anybody who says this country was within two weeks of being "driven off the gold standard" actually impeaches the official integrity of the President of the United States and of the Secretary of the Treasury. The latter official, from January 1, 1932, to June 30, 1932, with the approval of the President, sold to the banks and private investors in the United States $3,709,213,450 of Treasury notes and certificates of indebtedness, redeemable in gold at the Treasury. Of this amount $2,014,224,050 represented one-year certificates, and $1,034,152,000 were redeemable in ninety days from issue. If the President and the Secretary of the Treasury had knowledge of the fact that this country was faced with imminent disaster by being "driven off the gold standard in two weeks," and failed to so advise the banks and private investors who purchased nearly four billions of dollars of these federal securities, they were guilty of amazing dishonesty ; they were cheating the investing public ; and could not even appropriate to themselves the solace of future oblivion, because their names would have been remembered in terms of anathema for a century to come.

Despite this suggested infamy, the authentic figures and facts show that no such situation existed as that which politicians have conjured up for discreditable campaign purposes in order to exaggerate the executive prowess of a candidate for the Presidency. The figures are conclusive ; and persons who repeat this campaign hoax do not seem to realize that they are impeaching the common honesty of the President of the United States and the Secretary of the Treasury.

The third section of the Glass-Steagall bill was not even used until nearly three months after the time now fixed by Administration spokesmen for this imaginary disaster ; and shocking maladministration of the Act, in direct conflict with repeated promises to the contrary, came nearer inciting both foreign and domestic raids upon our gold supply than anything that happened before the enactment of the law.

Mr. Hoover insists that the very essence of prosperity for the nation is public confidence ; and, that being so, just behold the plight of this country when the foremost publicist of continental Europe felt justified in cabling to the metropolitan press of America that Mr. Hoover's gold-standard assertion at Des Moines, repeated at Indianapolis, was in such direct conflict with assurances given last winter and spring as that the banks and responsible officials of France were finding it impossible to attach importance to any statement from the President of the United States.

In this connection, the newspapers report that Secretary Hurley, of the War Department, has openly proclaimed from the public rostrum that should the Democratic party succeed at the November election "the United States will be driven off the gold standard." For the sake of decency, it must be hoped that Mr. Hurley did not say that. If he did say it, he was guilty of a dangerous calumny. If he said it, he is totally unfit for official responsibility, and the President should have booted him out of office before breakfast time of the following day. Indecency, even in a political campaign, has its limitations. This alleged declaration, if made by this strutting trumpeter of the President, was not far short of treason to the country.

I come now to the last so-called relief measure. It bears the name of Wagner, the Democratic Senator from New York, who spent days and nights and weeks and months in reviewing the problems involved. Other members of the Senate of both parties contributed thought and effort to the measure. It was a composite bill, reflecting the varying judgment of many minds. It provided for huge expenditures of public funds for special purposes. Vicious proposals by the Administration were rejected ; others of a different nature were accepted by the Senate. Inadvisable proposals by the House of Representatives were cast aside and others of a different nature were embodied in the bill. Personally, I regard the measure as utterly extraordinary and unorthodox ; but I and others agreeing with me, not caring to appear as obstructionists, went along with this mammoth measure for relief.

No one man, be he the President of the United States or a legislative leader, can truthfully appropriate all the credit attaching to this relief act. No group of men of either party can with good grace make any such claim ; and it is amazing to those who would prefer to respect the President of the United States that he should parade over this country and pretend that he and his party only are entitled to praise for this yet undemonstrated relief act.

If I were asked to pick out the three men in Washington most responsible for legislative relief to the unemployed and to the destitute of the country, I should never name President Hoover. I'd name Robert Wagner, Democratic member of the Banking and Currency Committee of the Senate ; Bob La Follette, Republican chairman of the Senate Committee on Manufactures, and Bob

Bulkley, junior Senator from Ohio. This does not mean that there were not many Senators and Representatives in Congress, Republicans and Democrats, who devoted their very souls to the problem.

I have given you briefly a recital of the causes of panic and depression in the United States, and have told you of the expedients employed in Washington to arrest the ravages. Nowhere in this picture can you discern the martial figure of Herbert Hoover in death-grapple with the panoplied forces of financial, commercial and industrial disaster! Naturally, the President's eyes were too intently gazing on foreign convulsions to permit him clearly to see the wreckage at his feet. With great agitation he noted the failure of the Bank of Austria and ignored the 6,208 banks which toppled in this country before the Austrian debacle. He saw a temporary renunciation of the gold standard in England on September 21, 1931, and imagined that it caused the failure of over five thousand banks in the United States before September 21, 1931.

Secretary Mills tells us that there was no "panic" in this country before the bank failure in Austria and the momentary abandonment of the gold standard in Great Britain. He thinks the greatest era of bank failures and of losses to depositors since the foundation of the government came about in a quiet way without business agitation or loss of confidence until a bank failed in Austria and until England went off the gold standard! And Ogden Mills has a brilliant mind!

But now let me turn to the flagrant charges made by the President and Secretary Mills against the Democratic party.

They say the Administration was obstructed in its efforts to reduce Federal expenses by the resistance of Democratic leaders in Congress. I assert that, on the contrary, every effort made by the two houses of Congress to reduce expenses of government was resisted by the President's own cabinet ministers. No attempt was made in this direction until nearly three years after Mr. Hoover was inaugurated. Meanwhile rank government extravagance was reflected in enormously increased expenditures. Mr. Hoover seemed to think the nation could squander itself into prosperity. His slogan for the government and the populace was "Spend! Spend! Buy! Buy!" Budgetary disaster should have been foreseen in swiftly mounting costs and frightfully declining revenues. Taxes had been abolished which should have been retained. Four million taxpayers, at one swipe, had been released from all obligation to their government. President Hoover, like Mr. Coolidge, permitted things to drift. The great engineering instinct seemed to have dried up. Although terrifying deficits threatened, Mr. Hoover played the part of a Presidential Micawber, "waiting for something to turn up." Not until last December was there one particle of interest manifested in these budgetary disarrangements. Then the President frantically began to urge economy on Congress, and the next day after, Cabinet ministers would troop to the Capitol, not only to resist, but to denounce Congressional efforts at economy. Notwithstanding this, the official records, as attested by the Republican Chairman of the Senate Committee on Appropriations, show that Congress reduced appropriations $334,294,094.18 under the approved budget estimates of the President himself!

I assert from actual knowledge of the facts that at the very moment the President was lustily preaching economy his Cabinet ministers were appearing before the Appropriations Committee of the Senate and offensively characterizing efforts at economy. His suave Postmaster General was disseminating throughout postal officialdom, from one end of the country to the other, a classified statement of thirty thousand postal employees that he claimed he would be compelled to discharge should he carry out a Senate order to reduce expenses in his department by ten per cent. This document was sent out obviously to incite all these employees to deluge Congress with protests against discharges that were never contemplated. We had hoped to make the ten per cent reduction without discharging anybody, but by reducing salaries, cutting expenses and revoking, if possible, improvident and shameless subsidies for which the Post Office Department had contracted, paying in a single instance $820,000 for carrying seventeen hundred dollars worth of mail to South America! Scores of such items appear in the list of expenditures. The Secretary of the Treasury appeared before the Senate Appropriations Committee and was so denunciatory of the attempt of the Senate to bring about economy as to create intense resentment among the committee members. He characterized the Senate resolution as "brutal" and "inhuman."

These are but passing examples of the difficulties encountered by Congress in getting cooperation from the Administration to effect economy. I am not seeking to minimize the gravity of President Hoover's difficulties; but he shall not be permitted, without protest, to lay them on the Congress. Our adversaries started this debate ; I am simply giving them "a Roland for their Oliver."

The President and Mr. Mills charged Congress with obstructing the efforts of the Administration to balance the budget. I shall not waste your time and mine with a repetition here of the diverse views and contrasting figures submitted by each side to the controversy. Congressional disputants allege with apparent reason that it was never possible to get anything like an accurate estimate from the Administration of the amounts required to balance the budget. This I do know and assert : the pretense on the eve of adjournment that the budget was balanced was pure political subterfuge and as far from the truth as any other pre-election claim. Members of the Appropriations Committees of both Houses openly charged that the budget was not balanced and that the Administration, in a Presidential election year, had not courage enough to reduce expenses sufficiently or to propose a tax levy high enough to effectively balance the budget. It was charged upon the expert computations of competent actuaries, that the measure finally passed would not come within a billion dollars of balancing the budget. Treasury receipts and disbursements to date, after all mitigating factors are considered, would seem to indicate that we did not come within one and one-half billion dollars of balancing the budget. Hence, additional taxes must be levied unless extraordinary expenditures are discontinued.

It is an indisputable fact that beyond sending messages to Congress in general terms the President gave no particle of help. At the very last moment of the session, after Democratic leaders had agreed with him at the White House on the final abortive attempt to balance the budget and when Senate action was imminent, the President breathlessly rushed to the Capitol and publicly addressed the Senate in order to get publicity for himself. In the newspapers he was figured as "forcing the Senate" to do something that had been agreed on the night before and the consummation of which by the Senate was delayed for the exact time required for Mr. Hoover to thus uselessly pose in public on the stage. The camera men were at hand to snap the super-man and exhibit him on the screen. The self-advertising machine was in full swing ; but the President seemed not to know that the budget was not balanced. It was a billion dollars out of gear. The only thing he had done was to fool himself and get in the pictures.

The President and his Secretary of the Treasury put responsibility on the Democratic party in general for the so-called Patman bonus bill, merely because the Democrats have a slender margin of five votes in the House of Representatives, where the bill was projected by intra-party revolts. They make this charge in spite of the recorded fact that sixty Republicans in the House voted for this bill, which would have been defeated but for Republican support; and in spite of the much more pregnant fact that an overwhelming majority of Democratic Senators defeated the bill in the Senate. The only body authorized to speak for the Democratic party of the country was its national convention. The platform committee of that convention had the courage to vote down every importunate plea for immediate payment of bonus certificates. The Republican convention was too cowardly to even intimate opposition to a legislative measure which the Republican President had said would debase our currency and wreck the Federal Treasury!

In the last analysis this bonus problem is a legacy of sordid Republican politics. This government obligation was incurred by a Congress overwhelmingly Republican in both branches, with the almost fatal and predicted result of burdening the American taxpayers in behalf of more than two millions of able-bodied men who never got within three thousand miles of the European battlefront, thus rendering impossible more generous treatment of the men actually disabled in war and the widows and orphans of men who were killed. The President suggests that, when paid, the bonus should be paid with "a sound dollar." Given four years more of President Hoover and there will not be left a sound dollar in the Federal Treasury to pay anybody for anything.

Moreover, in response to the President's charge that the legislation proposed in the House and adopted with Republican aid involved "fiat money," I assert that we had from the Administration at the last session of Congress inflationary proposals that would have rocked the foundations of our banking system. The adoption of them would not only have tempted foreign raids on our gold reserves, but would have incited a dangerous domestic demand for redemption. Had these proposals been adopted, they would have made millions of dollars of foreign securities with which this country was deluged by Administration connivance a basis for tremendous credit expansion; and, while I voted against the bonus to able-bodied men and against the House bill for immediate payment, I assert that the government certificates of indebtedness to the World War veterans are sounder security for credit or currency expansion than the securities of tottering South American republics and other foreign nations. Both are dangerous and unorthodox.

Finally, under this head, I direct your attention to the fact that the Democratic national platform declares for "a sound currency, to be maintained at all hazards." But, if the Republican party captures the next Congress, the chairman of the Banking and Currency Committee of the House of Representatives will be the Honorable Louis T. McFadden, until last December chairman of that committee. Mr. McFadden voted for the Patman "fiat money" bill, which the President charges threatened to wreck the Treasury and "debase our currency." McFadden will be the Republican pilot in banking and under a Republican majority! Mr. Hoover expatiates on certain dangerous provisions of a House bill, involving individual loans; but he very carefully withholds the fact that he and Secretary Mills urged a measure on the Banking and Currency Committee of the Senate authorizing loans of public monies to private business concerns. He fails to disclose the fact that, when asked by a foremost Republican Senator to give an example of the type of concerns he had in mind, the President "happened" to designate an automobile corporation, the head of which is asserted to have contributed twenty-five thousand dollars to Mr. Hoover's campaign fund and to have been given an ambassadorship in requital. But for Democratic and Progressive-Republican vigilance, this sort of appalling abuse of public funds would now prevail.

President Hoover and Secretary Mills charge the Democratic party with responsibility for the proposal to guarantee bank deposits; but they refrain from telling the country that such an overwhelming number of House Republicans voted for this untried experiment as that it was impossible to get one-fifth of the membership to order a recorded vote. Mr. Hoover and Mr. Mills fail to reveal that this proposition sought the approval of the Democratic National Convention and was so overwhelmingly defeated as that it would not get the one-fifth parliamentary requirement to call the roll of States. Must the country infer that there is no longer any frankness left in Republican campaign speakers, who seek thus to deceive the people? The primary cause for the revival of this deposit-guarantee question is the four billion dollar potential loss of deposits under the incompetent administration of

Mr. Hoover. The overwhelming vote of Republican members for this "guarantee" scheme may be regarded as their contribution to the conscience fund for the benefit of pillaged depositors.

Three times President Hoover has denounced a Democratic House of Representatives for passing the so-called Goldsborough stabilization bill, tauntingly characterizing the measure as "the rubber dollar bill." He charges it was a Democratic scheme, ignorant of the fact that it was a mere revival of a measure drafted by a New England Republican and urged for adoption in the House for five years successively by Mr. Strong, of Kansas, ranking Republican member of the House Committee on Banking and Currency. Infinitely worse than this, the President studiously concealed the fact that 117 Republican members of the House, constituting two-thirds of the entire Republican force, voted for this eccentric bill! Will the President dare go into the states of these one hundred and seventeen Republican Congressmen and advise their rejection at the polls because they voted for this "rubber dollar bill"? The President also failed to state that the passage of this bill, so ridiculous in its terms, was arrested by a Democratic Senator, on whose motion every word after the enacting clause was stricken out and a substitute adopted over Presidential protest, under which one hundred and twenty million dollars of sound national bank currency has been issued to 450 banks suffering from lack of expansive resources. Have frankness and honesty ceased to be a desirable element in political campaigns?

In order to frighten business Mr. Hoover makes scare-crows of alleged Democratic measures that were not enacted into law even with overwhelming Republican support; he appropriates exclusive credit to himself for Democratic measures that were enacted into law. This vice permeates every speech the President has delivered. The other day he avowed that the United States had saved the railroads from bankruptcy. The country wants to know what is to save the United States from bankruptcy with four years more of Hoover.

The President and his Secretary of the Treasury warn the country that the selection of a Democratic Congress and a Democratic administration would retard the business of recovery. And this coming from an administration that has increased the debt liability of the United States four billion dollars in three years! In face of the facts here cited that warning amounts to positive audacity; and in face of facts and figures that I shall now give it amounts to amazing effrontery. Every effort of relief by this Republican administration at Washington last winter and spring constituted a shuffling appeal to measures devised by a Democratic administration. The Reconstruction Finance Corporation Act is a resurrection in exaggerated form of Wilson's War Finance Corporation Act; and the chief reliance of this country, great as have been some of the mistakes made, was and is the Federal Reserve banking system, devised and adopted under the administration of Woodrow Wilson. This act was voted against by an overwhelming majority of the Republicans in the House and voted for by only three Republicans in the Senate, and denounced by Republican politicians throughout the nation. This is the Democratic measure that has saved this country from total wreck and that now, under wise administration, will make recovery possible.

Listen to this amazing recital in response to the amazing declaration of President Hoover and Mr. Mills that a Democratic administration cannot be trusted to conduct the government.

1. There have been more bank failures in the United States nearly every month under the Hoover administration than there were in the entire eight years of Woodrow Wilson's administration, although four years of the Wilson regime had to contend with the convulsions of a World War.

2. There were almost as many business failures in the past three and a half years under Hoover as there were in the entire eight-year period of the Wilson administration.

3. The amount of business losses in the past three and a half years under Hoover was approximately a billion dollars more than the business losses in the entire eight years of the Wilson administration — an excess greater than the entire bonded indebtedness of the United States before the World War.

4. To be exact, in the eight years under Wilson there were 112,635 business failures, involving a loss of $1,882,953,000; whereas, from January 1, 1929, to October 1, 1932, there were 102,556 business failures under Hoover, involving a loss of $2,645,476,000. The losses averaged nineteen million dollars per month under Wilson, including four years of World War, and fifty-eight million dollars per month under Hoover in three years of profound peace.

5. But sixty-nine national banks failed during the whole eight years under Wilson, whereas eight hundred national banks have failed in three years and two months under Hoover.

6. The last three years of the Wilson administration witnessed

the failure of eight national banks, whereas the past month witnessed the failure of twelve national banks under Hoover.

7. In the last three years of Wilson's administration 201 State banks failed, whereas in the last three years and two months under Hoover 4,061 State banks failed! Bank failures during three years under Hoover caused the jeopardy or actual loss of $4,198,358,000 to depositors!

Undertaking to minimize the horrible consequences of the nearly seven thousand bank failures in the United States, Secretary Stimson, lawlessly responsible for many of them, made the astounding assertion in New York some nights ago that our bank failures were consequent upon "the failure of banks in countries all about us." Never was there a more shameless falsification of fact indulged in by a responsible public official. England has not had a bank failure in ten years. Her Dominion of Canada, across the St. Lawrence River, has not had a bank failure since 1925. France, during this financial convulsion, had not a single bank failure, nor had Italy. Even German and Austrian banks stood up until thousands in the United States had failed. Where are the bank failures "in the countries all about us," of which Mr. Stimson spoke? They were in his imagination and brought out solely for political effect in the desperation of a losing campaign.

Secretary Mills at Baltimore asserted that things were improving for banks, attributing the improvement to the Reconstruction Finance Corporation; but Mr. Mills failed to tell his audience and the country that, with all the desperate and doubtful expenditures of the taxpayers' money to help decrepit banks, 1,096 banks have failed since the Reconstruction Finance Corporation began its work of salvage last January. These failures involved the jeopardy or actual loss to depositors of $603,757,000. Mr. Mills proudly tells us that stock prices and bond values have recently "moved up." If they moved at all they had to move up, because under this Republican administration they were, like McGinty, at the bottom of the well. Mr. Mills failed to tell the country that while there was a slight increase in the value of stock exchange securities, there was a pitiful actual decrease in all commodity prices and that the products of field and factories are at the lowest ebb in the entire economic life of the nation.

After this history of fright and helplessness and humiliation, Mr. Hoover and his really lovable Secretary of the Treasury have the assurance to warn the American people that a return of Democratic administration would menace the business interests of the United States. The Democrats couldn't do worse were they to try ; and, unless the signs of the times are completely out of joint, after the 8th day of November, the Democrats are going to be given a chance to rescue the country.

Franklin D. Roosevelt as Governor of one of the largest states of the Union, clean of body and clear of mind, dealing promptly with almost insuperable difficulties, is amply prepared for the tremendous task of reconstruction which will face the next Federal administration. He will not go to sleep at his post. The Congressional contacts and understanding and plain common sense of John Garner preeminently equip him for helpful service in promoting the legislative program of a Democratic administration.

We shall not make impossible promises and then proceed to break them. We shall not employ Lydia Pinkham political pills nor psychological poultices as a cure for the maladies of the country. We shall not rely upon transient devices and mere temporary remedies for serious situations ; but, holding fast to sound Jeffersonian principles and applying tested orthodox processes, we shall hope to rescue the government and the country from the unendurable confusion and distress into which Republican maladministration has thrust us. So serious is the situation that only by the help of Almighty God can this be done.

CONSTITUTIONAL IMMORALITY

Radio Address by

Hon. Carter Glass, of Virginia

On March 29, 1937

The speaker this evening is Carter Glass, senior Senator of Virginia in the Congress of the United States.

Never in my career until now have I ventured to debate before the public a measure pending in the Senate and awaiting decision there ; but the proponents of the problem to which I shall address myself tonight have seemed fearful of a deliberate consideration of the proposal to pack the Supreme Court of the United States ; they have defiantly avowed their purpose to take the discussion into every forum, with the unconcealed intention of bringing pressure to bear on Members of Congress to submit obediently to the frightful suggestion which has come to them from the White House. The challenge has been accepted by those who oppose the repugnant scheme to disrupt representative government in the Nation ; and the battle is on to the end.

Confessedly, I am speaking tonight from the depths of a soul filled with bitterness against a proposition which appears to me utterly destitute of moral sensibility and without parallel since the foundation of the Republic. However, I am not speaking my own mind alone ; the character and intelligence of the Nation are aroused, and I am reflecting as best I can the indignant protests of thousands upon thousands of individual citizens whose telegrams and letters to me as a single Senator are on the desk before me as an inspiration against any faltering in this time of extreme peril to that charter of our liberties which Gladstone pronounced "the most wonderful work ever struck off at a given time by the brain and purpose of man."

There has been some talk about "organized propaganda" against this unabashed proposition to pack the Supreme Court for a specified purpose ! Propaganda was first organized in behalf of the scheme right here in Washington and has proceeded with unabated fury from the White House fireside to nearly every rostrum in the country.

POLITICAL JANIZARIES PARADING THE STATES

Political janizaries, paid by the Federal Treasury to perform services here and charged with no official responsibility for determining questions affecting the Nation's judiciary, are parading the States in a desperate effort to influence the public against the Supreme Court of the United States. One of these visionary incendiaries spoke recently in a Southern State and exceeded all bounds of rational criticism in his vituperation of the eminent men who have served with great distinction on the Supreme Bench. He is said to have been applauded by the audience of his partisans, which caused me to wonder if they could have known the type of person to whose unrestrained abuse of the Supreme Court and the great jurists who constitute its membership they approvingly listened. Did they know that he recently reproached the South for providing separate public schools for the races; that he urged repeal of every statute and ordinance of segregation; that he practically committed the administration at Washington to a new force bill for the South, declaring that not since Lincoln's day has it better been realized than now the necessity of laws to strictly enforce the three post-Civil War amendments to the Constitution which kept the South in agony for years and retarded its progress for well-nigh half a century? This infuriated propagandist for degrading the Supreme Court practically proposes another tragic era of reconstruction for the South. Should men of his mind have part in picking the six proposed judicial sycophants very likely they would be glad to see reversed those decisions of the Court that saved the civilization of the South and in spite of the menace of passionate partisans, with their violent threats to "reorganize" the Court, prohibited the seizure and confiscation, without pay, of the estates of private citizens. It was the Supreme Court of the United States that validated the suffrage laws of the South which saved the section from anarchy and ruin in a period the unspeakable outrages of which nearly all the Nation recalls with shame.

This, however, is merely an incidental aspect of the case, reflecting my intense personal resentment and sharply revealing the sectional animosity of some of the fierce defamers of the Supreme Court. Infinitely graver questions are presented. This entire Nation is aroused over the many definite proposals to reverse the deliberate judgments of an independent Court and to substitute for them the previously pledged opinions of judicial subalterns. With men of this undisguised radical type campaigning the country, and freely applying their wretched opprobriums to the Supreme Court, those who resist the shocking movement are impertinently reproached with "organizing propaganda." I challenge any proponent of this packing contrivance to examine the thousands upon thousands of personal letters and telegrams sent to me and find in them anything but individual indignation at the proposal to make an Executive puppet of our supreme judicial tribunal. For myself, I think we should right now have "organized propaganda" in the sense that the men and women of America who value the liberties they have enjoyed for 150 years should, with unexampled spontaneity, exercise their constitutional right of petition, and with all the earnestness of their souls protest to Congress against this attempt to replace representative government with an autocracy.

AN INDEFENSIBLE LIBEL ON THE FAME OF GREAT MEN

Aside from these observations, let us consider the glaring proposal of the White House to pack the Supreme Court immediately with the President's own legal adherents for a specified purpose, and to enable him during his present term, even should there be not another, to entirely reconstitute the Court with persons entertaining his extraordinary views of government. The Attorney General in inaugurating "organized propaganda" in behalf of the project undertook to identify the names of Washington, Jefferson, and other eminent Americans with expedients akin to the unprecedented proposal of the President. Already I have publicly pronounced the assertion an indefensible libel on the fame of these great men, and was glad to note that the Attorney General omitted in his statement before the Senate Judiciary Committee to repeat the aspersion. The White House proposal is without precedent in the history of American jurisprudence. Its consequences portend evils beyond the anxiety of any person concerned for a decent administration of justice in this country. There is a precedent, dating back to the infamous Star Chamber processes of Great Britain, to which I shall presently refer.

George Washington, of course, was compelled to nominate a full Supreme Court at the very beginning of our national life, but no reputable person charged then or has ever believed since that Washington "packed" the Court with men pledged to any certain line of conduct beyond faithful compliance with the required oath to uphold the Constitution in the sight of God, uninfluenced by the machinations of politicians or the self-interests of any group of men intent on draining the Federal Treasury. The men he selected for Chief Justice and associates were not only persons of eminence in the profession of the law but in character literally incapable of going on the bench to submit obediently to Executive decrees.

I here and now challenge the proponents of this startling scheme to pack the Supreme Court for the avowed purpose of validating acts of Congress already decided to be unconstitutional to produce one word written or spoken by Thomas Jefferson in advocacy of such a thing. If there ever was a public man who, aside from an unimpeachable character, could have been suspected of a desire to do such a frightful thing, it was Thomas Jefferson. He hated John Marshall, Chief Justice of the Court, who was his kinsman, and Marshall hated Jefferson. The latter bitterly condemned Marshall's opinions. Recently emerged from under the tyranny of a mad King, Jeffersonians of the period dreaded the transformation of this Republic into a monarchy. They suspected Marshall of a desire, if not the purpose, to do this "step by step, insidiously," through judicial interpretations. They knew Alexander Hamilton, who was Marshall's powerful political associate, could well wish it to be done. Jefferson was incensed at the obiter dicta in Marshall's famous opinion in the case of Marbury against Madison and other notable causes. Perpetually afterward he bitterly censured this and other opinions of Marshall. However, for six years after the delivery of Marshall's celebrated federalistic opinion, concurred in by the Court, Thomas Jefferson was President of the United States, with full opportunity to propose reorganization of the Supreme Court to compel obedience to his views ; but, with overwhelmingly supporting Congresses, he never then or at any time in all his life would have done such an abominable thing.

STANDING READY TO CURSE THEM

Aside from his clear discernment of the vital importance of the checks and balances incorporated in the Constitution and his conception of judicial propriety, Jefferson would never have suggested such a thing for the reason subsequently stated with characteristic clarity and force by Woodrow Wilson when he said :

"It is within the undoubted constitutional power of Congress to overwhelm the opposition of the Supreme Court on any question by increasing the number of Justices and refusing to confirm any appointments to the new places which do not promise to change the opinion of the Court. But we do not think such a violation of the spirit of the Constitution is possible, simply because we share and contribute to that public opinion which makes such outrages upon constitutional morality impossible by standing ready to curse them."

"Standing ready to curse them!" That vividly describes the attitude of thinking men and women everywhere in America today toward this hateful attempt to drive eminent jurists from the bench in order to crowd into the Court a lot of judicial marionettes to speak the ventriloquisms of the White House. What Woodrow Wilson pungently described as an expedient to "overwhelm the Supreme Court" by "an outrage upon constitutional morality" is, in my view, the exact thing now proposed; and it requires little astuteness to predict with confidence that the prophecy of Wilson would come true and the curses of the American people, in the end, would be visited upon those responsible for this device to deprave the Supreme Court and to make a political plaything of the Constitution of the United States.

In like tenor with views entertained and frequently expressed by Woodrow Wilson were the profound convictions of another illustrious Democrat of the modern era. A practical student of government, a lover of his country, preeminent for courage and common sense, Grover Cleveland had a reverential regard for the Constitution and the courts. Nothing on the earth could have induced this stern patriot to lay impious hands upon either or to say or do anything designed to inflame uninstructed public opinion against them. Just prior to his second election to the Presidency, Cleveland made a notable address at a centennial celebration of the Supreme Court, reciting the sacrifices of the American people to be free and admonishing his hearers that the writers of the Constitution knew from bitter experience how readily instrumentalities of government were prone to trespass upon the liberties of the governed.

Cleveland pointed out that, nevertheless, the founders of the Republic "calmly and deliberately established as a function of their Government a check upon unauthorized freedom and a restraint upon dangerous liberty." Said he, "The attachment and allegiance of the founders to the sovereignty of their States were warm and unfaltering; but that did not prevent them from contributing a fraction of that sovereignty to the creation of a court which should guard and protect their new Nation, and save and perpetuate a government which should, in all time to come, bless an independent people. Let us be glad in the possession of this rich heritage of American citizenship, and gratefully appreciate the wisdom and patriotism of those who gave to us the Supreme Court of the United States."

THE PLAYTHINGS OF POLITICIANS

Telegram after telegram, letter after letter, sent me by the thousands, have said, "God bless the Supreme Court." But who wants God to bless a packed Supreme Court? Who wants to invoke divine blessing on a Court not constituted to put "a check upon unauthorized freedom and restraint upon dangerous liberty," but reorganized to validate acts of Congress in contravention of the Constitution as now interpreted and to expound the Constitution in subservient obedience to the whims or obsessions or misguided judgment of a President of the United States? Woodrow Wilson said such a Court and those responsible for it would receive the curses of the American people. Grover Cleveland said the Supreme Court was created for no such sinister purpose. Our God still being in the heavens, it is my belief He would regard as unhallowed any invocation of His blessing on a Court like that. We would better abolish the Supreme Court and, by the required process, do away outright with the Constitution if they are to be made the playthings of politicians.

What did Cleveland mean by checks and balances against "unauthorized freedom and dangerous liberty"? He was uttering a monition against legislative or Executive invasion of the rights of the States, reserved to them under the Constitution, and to be "guarded and protected" by the Supreme Court. He meant what a Governor of a great State, afterward President of the United States, meant when seven years ago he made a vehement plea for respecting State rights and unsparingly denounced government by "commissions and regulatory bodies and special legislation." The Governor warned that:

"To bring about government by oligarchy – masquerading as democracy – it is fundamentally essential that all authority and control be centralized in our National Government. We are safe from the danger of any such departure from the principles on which this country was founded just so long as the individual home rule of the States is scrupulously preserved and fought for whenever they seem in danger."

This was Franklin D. Roosevelt in March 1930. When before, may I venture to ask, in the history of the country has this Nation more nearly approached the situation thus deplored? With Federal regulatory bodies in every community of the States and Federal bureaus in Washington bursting the bounds of marble palaces and overflowing into business houses and private homes, and with the States required supinely to submit their legislative statutes to the approval of bureaucratic boards here before they can get back a pittance of the prodigious sums picked from the pockets of their people in the form of taxes, State rights, as well as the security and independence of private enterprise, are fast disappearing.

With private property seized at will; the courts openly reviled; rebellion rampant against good order and peace of communities; with governments pleading with mobocracy instead of mastering it, we seem to have reached that period of peril which Governor Roosevelt visioned 7 years ago. This, with other dangerous evils, contrived or connived at, by governments, is the real crisis which faces the Nation and cannot be cured by degrading the Supreme Court of the United States.

SIX JUDICIAL WET NURSES

What does this Court-packing scheme signify if it does not reflect the fury of its proponents against the Supreme Court of the United States for certain of its recent decisions asserting the rights of the States and individuals and private business under the law and prohibiting the proposed invasion of these by ill-digested congressional legislation, largely devised by inexperienced and incompetent academicians? That is precisely what it is all about. Had the judicial decisions sanctioned these rankly unconstitutional measures, who believes there would have been this unrestrained abuse of the Court and this unprecedented attempt to flank the Constitution by putting on the bench six judicial wet nurses to suckle the substance out of the opinions of jurists whose spirit of independence keeps pace with their profound knowledge of the law?

That the purpose of the Court project has accurately been stated by me is no longer in serious question. The President in his message to Congress implicitly conceded the proposition when he said if given legislative sanction for this irregular scheme there would be no necessity of appealing to the people to so amend their Constitution as to authorize the things for which the Supreme Court had said there is now no authority, as well, perhaps, as unmentioned schemes of "unfettered" delegation of legislative power. That can mean nothing else than that it was then the Executive determination to select six new judges who would validate acts of Congress already pronounced unconstitutional and contemplated acts of a similar kind. Every speech made since, whether at the fireside or elsewhere, has confirmed this interpretation of the President's message to Congress. If that, in plain terms, is not "packing the Supreme Court" for well-defined purposes, I confess my inability to supply a better definition.

REVIVED FOR REVERSAL

Moreover, the advocates of the scheme themselves reveal this purpose — some of them warily enough to have produced merriment in the committee room, while others have bluntly, and with evident lack of shame, said outright that this is the ghastly object of the proceeding. Still others specify some of the voided acts they propose to revive and render valid by the votes of the six new Justices whom the country is assured will be selected for their "bias." One of these acts, which lost American farmers their export markets and necessitated the importation of foreign foodstuffs to feed our own people, was nullified by two-thirds of the Supreme Court; but by adding to the minority the six "biased" votes to be packed onto the Court, this decision may be overridden.

Another of the acts, voided by a unanimous vote of the Supreme Court and proposed to be revived for reversal, would severely test the persuasive powers and great legal attainments of the six "biased" Justices, since it is difficult for six votes to subvert nine, no matter what the disparity of ages. All nine Supreme Court Justices threw out the so-called N. R. A. as an "unfettered" delegation of power, as it was an amazing thrust of Federal jurisdiction into every conceivable private business of the country.

Among its other vices it actually suspended for a period the laws of the Nation against the depredations of monopoly and confided to Executive discretion, under a hateful species of coercion, involving fines and imprisonment, the fate of every business interest in the United States. Its administration was confided to a man, long a respected friend of mine, of unsurpassed accomplishments, with no selfish interest whatsoever to subserve; but in these circumstances he was as ruthless and harsh as human nature ever gets. The act and its administration created a reign of terror in the country; and everybody except the large industries, which profited by the enforced failure of the smaller, hailed the decision of the Court with satisfaction.

We are told this is to be revived, along with the Guffey coal bill of somewhat a like nature, also declared unconstitutional by the Supreme Court ; and I am wondering if we are to witness the same sort of organized propaganda in their behalf as distinguished one oracle of the N. R. A., now prominently mentioned as one of the "biased" wet nurses of the Supreme Bench. In his first speech this man impudently denounced every American citizen as a "slacker" who should not volunteer obedience to the N. R. A. He urged the women of the country to pin white feathers on every person who would not willingly cooperate with enforcement ; thus he would have put a badge of disgrace on all men and women who would not submit to the atrocious exactions of an act of Congress which all nine judges of the Supreme Court, young and old alike, pronounced unconstitutional. The effrontery of this attempt to terrorize the people was in no degree abated by the fact that this valiant propagandist, now conspicuously pictured as one of the probable selections for the Supreme Court Bench, sat in a swivel chair during the whole period of the World War, never hearing a percussion cap pop or sensing the smell of gunpowder or getting near enough to a training camp to learn the difference between "Order, arms" and "Forward, march." With Jacobins of this type constituting the wet-nurse section of the Supreme Court, what an era of peace and contentment could the American people confidently anticipate with the revival of the N. R. A. and kindred vagaries of the brain-truster variety !

NO MANDATE TO RAPE THE SUPREME COURT

What other and how many peculiar schemes of government are to be presented for submissive legislative action in confident expectation that they will meet with the favor of the "biased" half dozen who are to adorn the bench is left to our imagination because not exactly specified in the proclaimed program. We are simply given to understand that the President has a "mandate from the people" to so reconstitute the Supreme Court as to have it sanction whatever the White House proposes to an agreeing Congress, particularly if it involves no "check upon unauthorized freedom," to quote Grover Cleveland again, or "restraint on dangerous liberty."

But we know there has been no such mandate from the people to rape the Supreme Court or to tamper with the Constitution. The Constitution belongs to the people. It was written by great representatives of the people, chosen for the purpose, and was ratified by the people as the Supreme Charter of their Government, to be respected and maintained with the help of God. With the consent and by mandate of the people their Constitution provides how it may be amended to meet the requirements of the ages. It has always been so, and no administration in the history of the Republic has attempted to flank the Constitution by a legislative short-cut so vividly denounced by Woodrow Wilson as "an outrage upon constitutional morality."

The people were not asked for any such mandate. They were kept in ignorance of any such purpose. They were told that the liberal aims of the President could very likely be achieved within the limitations of the Constitution ; and if not, we would suggest to the people amendments that would authorize such certain things to be done. When once it was intimated by political adversaries that the Supreme Court might be tampered with, the insinuation was branded as a splenetic libel. No word in the platform of the prevailing party could be interpreted into advocacy of any such abnormality as that now in issue. Quite the contrary, every platform declaration on the subject gave promise of the customary constitutional procedure. But somebody badly advising the President was evidently afraid of the people. The Attorney General apparently feared to "ask a mandate from the people" for his wretched scheme, defended so weakly in reason as to invite expressions of contempt. Convicted by his own official reports of inaccurate assertions about congestion of the Supreme Court calendar, and now flatly contradicted on this and other points by the Chief Justice and associates, there is nothing left of his bitter assault on the Court more notable than the brutal contention that six eminent members "get out" and give place to six others of a compliant type, in the selection of whom the Department of Justice would probably have a cunning hand. Of course, the proposal being discussed will not contribute to the efficiency of the Court. It will do in this case particularly what Thomas Jefferson pungently deplored when he declared "the multiplication of judges only enables the weak to outvote the wise." The fact is their proposed bill will cure none of the alleged evils which offend their ideas of judicial reform.

LET US MEET THE ISSUE

Why should we not proceed, as in honor we are bound to do, by first contriving legislation for social and economic security, painstakingly drafted by competent lawyers with a clear conception of the constitutional prohibitions against invading the rights of business and individuals by a species of confiscation and by utter indifference for reserved powers of the States? Why should we not quit legislating by pious preambles and conform our enactments to the requirements of the Constitution and thus put upon notice the cabal of amateur experimenters that we will have no more of their trash? Let us have no more bills for "unfettered" delegation of authority, so obviously unconstitutional as to have prompted the President to make an unhappy appeal for disregarding all "reasonable doubts." Let us meet the issue confidently but with a determination to promote the general welfare of the Nation and not merely to surrender control of the Government to special groups.

If it then be found that we were mistaken in the expressed belief that the Constitution is ample to our purposes, let us do what we promised to do and appeal to the people to amend their supreme law. Let the impatient proponents of the pending scheme turn to the advice of George Washington in his famous Farewell Address, in which he admonished against disregarding "reciprocal checks in the exercise of political power," saying: "If, in the opinion of the people, the distribution or modification of the constitutional powers be in any particular wrong, let it be corrected by an amendment in the way in which the Constitution designates. But let there be no change by usurpation; for, though this in one instance may be the instrument of good, it is the customary weapon by which free governments are destroyed."

Let those who would confide to the President complete control over the Supreme Court by sanction of an obedient Congress reread the farewell address of Andrew Jackson in which he cautioned the country against the jeopardy to their liberties of a consolidated Government and the evil consequences of "permitting temporary circumstances, or the hope of better promoting the public welfare, to influence, in any degree, our decisions upon the extent of the authority of the General Government. Let us abide by the Constitution as it is written," he urged, "or amend it in the constitutional mode if it be found defective."

And in this connection it might be well for the proponents of this court-packing scheme, who started their campaign by taking the name of Thomas Jefferson in vain, to remember that Jefferson's bitterness against the Supreme Court was provoked by the very thing they now advocate. Jefferson condemned the Court for its failure to void the unbridled actions of Congress in invading the rights of the States, whereas the Court packers are incensed against the Court for restraining the unconstitutional actions of Congress in disregarding individual and community rights. Their position is in sharp antagonism to that of Jefferson, who never dreamed of packing the Supreme Court to compel obedience to his views. Evidently Jefferson thought, as Woodrow Wilson afterward proclaimed, that such a thing involved "constitutional immorality."

I venture to beg the public not to be diverted from the real issue involved in this controversy. Contesting the Court's constitutional authority to void acts of Congress is idle surplusage. The Court has exercised this implied power for 130 years. It has been regarded as an indispensable power in government under a written Constitution. There must be a supreme tribunal to which every citizen, high or humble, rich or poor, may appeal for the vindication of his rights and the preservation of life, liberty, and property. Long before the Supreme Court was established this principle was presented by Chancellor Wythe, Jefferson's law teacher, with respect to acts of Parliament and decrees of the crown. It is a waste of time to discuss now this and other moot questions not touched in the remotest sense by the pending proposition. Under the bill sent up to Congress, prepared by God knows whom, the six substitute Justices would exercise the established power to rule finally on the acts of Congress ; and the dangerous circumstance faces the Nation that we know pretty well in advance what their rulings would be. The question of majority or other numerical decisions is not comprehended in the White House proposal, nor the right of Congress to review and reverse the Court's decisions.

SHEER POPPYCOCK

The predominant question is whether the practice of a century under an independent judiciary is to be abruptly terminated by authorizing the President to seize the Court by the process of packing in order to compel agreement with the Executive views. Should this be done without "a mandate from the people" ? Should the people be ignored and, without asking their consent in the usual way, submit helplessly to having their Constitution tortured into meanings which have been declared in contravention of the fundamental law ? If Andrew Jackson was right in asserting that "Eternal vigilance by the people is the price of liberty," God knows that never before since the establishment of the Republic could the people better be warned to preserve their priceless heritage. The talk about "party loyalty" being involved in the opposition to this extraordinary scheme is a familiar species of coercion. It is sheer poppycock. No political party since the establishment of the Government ever dared to make an issue of packing the Supreme Court. But a single one of the Presidents of the United States was ever accused of doing such a thing, and the mere suspicion, however ill founded in truth, has proved a taint upon his reputation which his memorable military achievements have not been able entirely to wipe away. Moreover, his alleged offense was inconsequential in contrast with that which now threatens the Nation. As Warren says in his history of the Supreme Court: "To the proposal advanced at various times of intense party passion, that the Court be increased in number to overcome a temporary majority for or against some particular piece of legislation, the good sense of the American people has always given a decided disapproval." And as James Bryce, in his American Commonwealth, says, whenever such a thing should occur "the security provided for the protection of the Constitution is gone like a morning mist." Thomas Jefferson in a single sentence comprised the unalterable detestation of honest men for the packing of the Court when he said, "It is better to toss up cross and pile in a cause than to refer to a judge whose mind is warped by any motive whatever in that particular case." Later he wrote: "An officer who selects judges for principles which necessarily lead to condemnation, might as well take his culprits to the scaffold without the mockery of trial." This Jefferson said of packed juries. How infinitely worse would be a packed Supreme Court, albeit in one case the penalty is imprisonment and in the other the universal abhorrence of mankind.

A SERVILE COURT

I have said this proposal to pack the Supreme Court is without precedent in American jurisprudence and that we must go back for a corresponding scheme to the infamous processes of the British Star Chamber. Macaulay gives us the incident. When the King wanted a servile court to sanction his purposes contrary to decisions rendered, he summoned the Chief Justice to the palace and told him peremptorily that he would be dismissed unless he changed his opinions. "Sire," said the courageous Chief Justice, "my position is of little concern to me, since I have not many years to live; but my convictions are of vital importance, and I am humiliated to find that Your Majesty could think me capable of altering my mind merely to retain my place." The Chief Justice then bravely admonished his kingly master : "Your Majesty may find twelve judges of your mind, but hardly twelve honest lawyers." Needless to say the Chief Justice was dismissed, just as the offending members of the Supreme Court have been rudely told to "begone" if they do not relish the proposed mortification of being supplied with six judicial wet nurses ; and well might any one or all of these eminent jurists, in imitation of that fearless Englishman, say to the appointing power : "You may find six judges of your mind, but not six constitutional lawyers." Should the iniquitous scheme go through, the intelligence and character of the Nation will be interested to know what lawyer of notable attainments or independent spirit would be willing to go on the Supreme Court bench in such circumstances or could regard such an appointment as an honor. Doubtless there are practitioners eager for such recognition ; but are they men whom the Nation would prefer or who could feel comfortable in association with those now constituting the Court ? I am but an unlearned layman, untrained in the ethics of the legal profession ; nevertheless, I cannot escape the conclusion that any man of approved sensibility who should accept such a distinction would experience trouble in outliving the mistake. Moreover, I have a distinct premonition that the people of America would not confidently trust to the supreme decision of such a Court the life, liberty, and pursuit of happiness guaranteed by the Constitution.

THE REAL FRIEND

I am far from intimating that the President of the United States is incapable of selecting suitable men for the Supreme Court. I am simply accepting his own word and that of his spokesmen to the effect that he wants men "biased" in behalf of his legislative and administrative projects, who may be counted on to reverse the Supreme Court decisions already rendered and give such other decisions of policy as may be desired. This is not my view alone ; it is the conclusion of millions of alarmed citizens throughout the Nation.

The assumption of the proponents of this scheme to tamper with the Court and the Constitution that only they are the President's real friends has no justification in fact. He is not a friend of the President who would subject him to the biting indictment which Rudyard Kipling applied to a famous autocrat who answered a petition from his people with the imperious assertion that, "This is my country. These are my laws. Those who do not like to obey my laws can leave my country." Wrote Kipling :

He shall break his judges if they cross his word ;
He shall rule above the law, calling on the Lord.
Strangers of his counsel, hirelings of his pay,
These shall deal out justice ; sell – deny – delay.
We shall take our station, dirt beneath his feet,
While his hired captains jeer us in the street.

Rather is he the real friend of the President who will command to his serious attention the ringing words of Thomas Jefferson when he proclaimed himself "against writing letters to judiciary officers" because he "thought them independent of the Executive, not subject to its coercion, and therefore not obliged to attend to its admonitions."

THE SOLEMN WARNING

In conclusion, my friends, let me press upon you the solemn warning of a world-renowned student of representative government, John Stuart Mill, when he said :

"A people may prefer a free government ; but if from indolence, or carelessness, or cowardice, or want of public spirit, they are unequal to the exertions necessary for preserving it ; if they will not fight for it when directly attacked ; if they can be deluded by the artifices used to cheat them out of it ; if by momentary discouragement, or temporary panic or a fit of enthusiasm for an individual, they can be induced to lay their liberties at the feet of even a great man, or trust him with powers which enable him to subvert their institutions – in all these cases they are more or less unfit for liberty."

Abraham Lincoln at Gettysburg thought the Civil War was a test of whether a "government of the people, by the people, for the people" should perish from the face of the earth. Just as profoundly are some of us convinced that no threat to representative democracy since the foundation of the Republic has exceeded in its evil portents this attempt to pack the Supreme Court of the United States and thus destroy the purity and independence of this tribunal of last resort.

INDEX

Date Due

MAR 20			
MAY 28			
FEB 25			
MAR 26			
DEC 10			
[illegible]			
Oct. 9, 63			
APR 25 '56			
NOV 13 1960			
NOV 6 1968			

Library Bureau Cat. no. 1137